The Collected Poems of Ted Berrigan

The Collected Poems of Ted Berrigan

EDITED BY ALICE NOTLEY
with Anselm Berrigan and Edmund Berrigan

Introduction and Notes by Alice Notley

University of California Press
Berkeley Los Angeles London

University of California Press
Berkeley and Los Angeles, California

University of California Press, Ltd.
London, England

Credits and acknowledgments for the poems appear on page 729.

Library of Congress Cataloging-in-Publication Data

Berrigan, Ted.
[Poems. Selections]
The collected poems of Ted Berrigan / edited by Alice Notley, with Anselm Berrigan and Edmund Berrigan.
p. cm.
"Introduction and notes by Alice Notley."
Includes bibliographical references and index.
ISBN 0-520-23986-5 (alk. paper).
I. Notley, Alice, 1945– II. Berrigan, Anselm. III. Berrigan, Edmund, 1974– IV. Title.

PS3552.E74A17 2005
811'.54—dc22 2005042259

Printed and bound in Canada

14 13 12 11 10 09 08 07 06 05
10 9 8 7 6 5 4 3 2 1

The paper used in this publication meets the minimum requirements of ANSI/NISO Z39.48-1992 (R 1997) (*Permanence of Paper*).

The publisher gratefully acknowledges contributions
to this book provided by the General Endowment Fund
of the University of California Press Foundation;
Kenward Elmslie, Z Press;
Anselm Hollo and Jane Dalrymple-Hollo;
Kenneth Koch Literary Estate;
and other generous donors.

Contents

Acknowledgments / ix

Introduction / 1

Chronology / 19

27 **The Sonnets**

77 **Great Stories of the Chair**

The Secret Life of Ford Madox Ford / 79

Great Stories of the Chair / 88

A Boke / 98

113 **Many Happy Returns**

165 **In the Early Morning Rain**

241 **Train Ride**

287 **Memorial Day** *by Ted Berrigan and Anne Waldman*

315 **Short Poems**

In a Blue River / 317

Uncollected Short Poems / 337

349 **Red Wagon**

389 **Easter Monday**

427 **Nothing for You**

511 **In the 51st State**

In the 51st State / 513

The Morning Line / 525

Uncollected Poems / 542

565 **A Certain Slant of Sunlight**

617 **A Certain Slant of Sunlight: Out-takes**

635 **Last Poems**

651 **Early Uncollected Poems**

Notes / 665

Glossary of Names / 723

Credits / 729

Index of Titles and First Lines / 731

Acknowledgments

Grateful acknowledgment is made to the publishers of the original editions of Ted Berrigan's books of poetry. These books are cited and discussed throughout the apparatus of *The Collected Poems of Ted Berrigan*, but I wish briefly to name the presses, again, here: "C" Press, Kulchur Press, Grove Press, Corinth Books, Cape Goliard Press, Aloes Books, Frontward Books, The Yellow Press, United Artists, Vehicle Editions, Blue Wind Press, Clown War, Little Light Books, Am Here Books/Immediate Editions, O Books, Penguin Books, and Situations.

Ted's poetry depended, for publication and the maintenance of an audience, on the many, many small presses and magazines which carried his work in the 60s, 70s, and early 80s, and also after his death. I would love to be able to list all of the magazines here, but that obviously isn't possible: I don't have the complete record, and the list would be pages long. One acknowledges the debt and hopes so much for the continued flourishing of that small-press enterprise.

I would particularly like to thank Ron Padgett for his time and advice. Thanks, too, to Dick Gallup, Lorenz Gude, and Miles Champion for information and feedback. To George Schneeman, for his cover art; and to Lorenz, again, for his photograph. And for their various feats of recall and research, I would like to thank Bob Rosenthal, Murat Nemet-Nejat, Ed Sanders, and Anselm Hollo. Thanks as always to David Berrigan and Sarah Locke for being there. Also I wish to thank Laura Cerruti, Rachel Berchten, and the staff of the University of California Press, and Linda Norton, whose original support helped make the book possible.

I am writing on behalf of my co-editors, Anselm Berrigan and Edmund Berrigan, as well as myself. The organization of the book by sections, the selection of the poems, the casting of them into place, the devising of the chronology and glossary, and an intense scrutiny of my introduction and notes, was a notably communal (family) project. We are all three very pleased for Ted.

Introduction

I heard Ted say more than once that his collected poems should be like a collected books. But he didn't always work in sequences, and he wasn't always consciously in the process of writing a book. He wrote many individual poems, and he sometimes seemed to write purely for fun. As for publication, publishers would approach him for a book without knowing exactly what he had, and sometimes it didn't seem to him as if he had that much. If there was a sequence ready, or a book in a unified style like *Many Happy Returns,* certainly he published that. If he had a stack of dissimilar works or if he didn't even know what he had, he still set about the process of constructing a "book." He loved to make things out of pieces, often ones that didn't fit together conventionally. A book was like a larger poem that could be as much "made" out of what was at hand, as "written" in a continuous way out of a driving idea.

This volume is an attempt to be a collected books, but it can't be that precisely and so isn't called *The Collected Books*. Though Ted wrote sequences and constructed books, he didn't produce a linear succession of discrete, tidy volumes. He perceived time as overlapping and circular; the past was always alive and relevant, and a particular poem might be as repeatable as an individual line or phrase was for him from the time of the composition of *The Sonnets* onward. How were we, the editors, to deal with repetitions of poems from book to book? Most especially what were we to do about the book-length sequence *Easter Monday?*

Ted worked for years on *Easter Monday,* which he didn't call finished until shortly before his death, when he finalized the selection and order. Meanwhile, during his lifetime, every one of the poems was published individually, in two chapbooks, *A Feeling for Leaving* and *Carrying a Torch*, and more significantly in the books *Red Wagon* and *So Going Around Cities: New and Selected Poems 1958–1979*. *Easter Monday* has never been presented as a unified sequence until now; but placing its poems together considerably shortens the book *Red Wagon*. So we have shortened *Red Wagon*, and shorter it is still a book, and a good one. But dealing with *Easter Monday* showed us that we would have to construct this *Collected Poems* a little as if we were Ted and not just editors.

Furthermore, there was a lot of uncollected work, including early poems, "short" poems, out-takes from the sequence *A Certain Slant of Sunlight*, a scattering of individual poems from the 70s and 80s, and a set of poems written during the last six months of his life and kept together in its own folder. We decided to organize most of this work into booklike sections. We've discussed ceaselessly what to omit, what isn't "good enough" in the sense of not really holding up next to the others, because if this *is* a collected books, each poem should fill its own space within its own book or section. We are not Ted, but we tried to think like him; and there's still room in the future for a slim volume of retrieved poems, as in *Poems Retrieved* of Frank O'Hara (a possibility Ted would have loved). In the beginning I held out for every scrap of a poem, while Anselm and Edmund had a more selective sense. I gradually gave up on such works as "The 30 Most Common Names in the Manhattan Telephone Directory, 1979," various small-scale "Things to Do" poems, occasional poems (practically anyone's birthday in the late 60s), and the worst of Ted's rather bad "early poems." I retain tender feelings for all of these poems.

With regard to the reprinting of a poem or two from book to book: it doesn't make economical sense to repeat poems, so we have most often chosen to omit poems that have been printed in other sections. Thus, where there are omissions, I indicate in the notes where and what they are. Also, there existed a handful of poems which seemed to float near specific books, stylistically, but hadn't been included in them. The relevant books were collections not sequences, and we have taken the liberty of placing these poems in the volumes they point to. Again I signal, in the notes, where this has been done; there are not enough of these poems to merit their own section, and in each case they fit gracefully where inserted. I don't think Ted would mind, though more pristine editors than we are might squirm.

If it sounds as if the rules of organization of this book work through exception, I can only say that Ted's work creates the need for exception. His esthetics were fluid, and he was governed more by the impulse to make art than to be consistent. Thus the books or sections are presented in an order that reflects, mostly but not entirely, chronology of publication. *In a Blue River* is "out of order." Though it was published in 1981, most of its poems were written in the early 70s, and it has been placed with other short poems from that time near books from that time. It was, in fact, in the late 60s and early 70s that Ted was most intensely interested in the short poem as a form.

Finally, we have chosen to present fourteen early poems, which, along with certain poems in *Nothing for You,* help demonstrate where *The Sonnets* came from. These not-so-good poems contain a number of the repeated lines in *The Sonnets;* so the book concludes with the beginning, making a circle. One of Ted's favorite concepts was that of a poem or book creating a circular shape whose ending pushes the reader back up into the work. And he always remained interested in his not-very-good poems, because they, too, reflected who he was. A circle is a unity, and oneself was/is always in process back there.

Having explained our general editorial procedure I would now like to take the reader quickly through this volume's sections, focusing on their contents and marking, as practicable in this space, Ted's esthetic changes from book to book and through the years. I've organized this part of the introduction by decade, since Ted's adult life and career seems to lend itself to this shape. In the 60s Ted was a young man and wrote his best-known work; in the 70s he became a more various poet, he entered a second marriage, and his health began to fail; in the early 80s he wrote his last work. He died young, at the age of forty-eight, on July 4, 1983. These poems span a creative period of roughly twenty years (not counting the earliest work), which isn't a long time. It seems remarkable that there should be so many poems.

The Sixties

This collection begins with *The Sonnets,* Ted's most famous book. It really is quite close to where Ted began, despite the fact that it is a classic. It is a young man's book, the product of relentless self-education, and being partly constructed out of lines from "early poems," often suggests the awkward intensity of inexperience. But it floats above that place as if observing it from the dead: "dear Berrigan. He died / Back to books. I read."

It is important to say once again that *The Sonnets* was written in New York, that Ted had arrived in New York via Providence and Tulsa; that Ted would leave New York for a while but then return to it; that he was always called a New York School poet, and that he mostly liked the attribution. *The Sonnets,* in fact, could reflect no other setting than that city. In these poems New York bricks and human density have become the interior walls of someone always reading and thinking. Outside-in.

The Sonnets was written in the early 60s, most especially in 1963: that is, it seems to have been in 1963 that Ted realized he was generating a long sonnet sequence, though he had written some of the poems as early as 1961. Entries in his journals, dated November 16 and 20, 1962, record the composition of the first six sonnets out of lines from previous poems and from his translation of Rimbaud's "Le Bateau Ivre." But there was a point, early in 1963, when he suddenly knew what he was doing: with Dadaist cut-up and Cageian chance methods, transforming not-so-good poems into an astonishing and original structure.

The reader will come to notice that Ted returned to the strict form of *The Sonnets* several times, in his books, to make points about his life and the passage of time. The form is suited to detached self-scrutiny, using lines and phrases from past and present poems, reading material, and ongoing mind, in an order determined by numbers rather than syntax. The pieces of the self are allowed to separate and reform: one is not chronology but its parts and the real organism they create. Ted liked to say that poetry is numbers, and maybe everything is numbers. The sonnet form is "about" the number fourteen, but Ted's sonnets use fourteen as a frame for the disassemblage of the number, making a real advance in the form and its relation to the psyche. To the extent that Ted broke and remade the form, it became possible to use it for more than argument. One could condense cognition into fourteen or so lines, if each piece, each segment of the fourteen, even each phrase in a line, meant enough.

The Sonnets has been through four editions. There were originally eighty-eight sonnets, but in the first two editions (from "C" Press and Grove Press) he allowed only sixty-six; in the third edition (from United Artists) he added six more; and in the fourth edition (Penguin Books) I included seven more that he had authorized before his death in 1983. This collection conforms to the Penguin edition in including seventy-nine sonnets.

After the composition of *The Sonnets*, Ted entered a period of further involvement with aleatory methods, cut-up, collage, and transliteration, overlappingly with the more direct poems of *Many Happy Returns*. We have placed three works written according to a "method" (a word he liked) in a single section called *Great Stories of the Chair*. They are the eight-poem sequence "The Secret Life of Ford Madox Ford," the sequence of prose paragraphs "Great Stories of the Chair," and the long poem "A Boke." All of *Many Happy Returns* is included in a separate section.

On the manuscript of "The Secret Life of Ford Madox Ford" Ted scrawled "1963? or 4?" The first version of the sequence was published in two issues of Ted's magazine, "C" *(A Journal of Poetry)*, in 1964. The eight poems are hilarious and ferocious. They are obviously transliterations, that is, translations via sound and thought association of works in a foreign language. The original texts are to be found in Pierre Reverdy's *Quelques Poèmes* (see notes). Ted had previously written several transliterative poems: one example from *The Sonnets* is "Mess Occupations" (Sonnet XXXIX), with the note "*after Henri Michaux*." There is an especially fluid, automatic quality to the lines of *The Secret Life of Ford Madox Ford*, and an occasional vicious literalness: "Eat a potato she said you sober All-American."

Great Stories of the Chair reveals a new influence on Ted's writing, that of the prose of William Burroughs, whom Ted did not read until after the composition of *The Sonnets*. Three of the "stories" were published in the journal *Mother*, in 1965, under the title *Paragraphs*. The entire sequence of twelve prose blocks was published in *Angel Hair* 4 (winter 1967/68). The cut-up methods of Burroughs and Brion Gysin do not seem essentially different from Dadaist procedures. However, applied to prose structures which coaxed plot out of words themselves, Burroughsian cut-up resulted in novels that are full-blown visions generated as much verbally as through the senses. Poetry originating from within words (not from within the poet per se) was already Ted's practice. He always asserted that he thought in words, that he was usually either reading, writing, talking, thinking about/in words, or sleeping. Words were literally his mind in process. And to cut up his own poems, for example, was not to do anything other than to think and feel. *Great Stories of the Chair* is blocks of thought and emotion—what else?

Though "A Boke" is dated 1966 in *So Going Around Cities*, it was first published in the journal *Kulchur* in the autumn of 1965. It is a cut-up of an article by the poet James Dickey, first published in *The New Yorker*, about traveling around the United

States giving poetry readings. "A Boke" is a send-up of mainstream humorlessness, but with an autobiographical air to it, and, as Ted once told me, intentionally drawn out to a point veering toward (not quite arriving at) boredom. Interspersed from time to time throughout "A Boke" is the line "Remember the fragrance of Grandma's kitchen?" which Ted lifted from Burroughs. Also included in the mix are references to the folk songs "John Henry" and "Nine-Pound Hammer."

It is the book *Many Happy Returns,* published by Corinth Books in 1969, that is Ted's first major statement after *The Sonnets*. The poems included in the collection span a large part of the 60s, beginning with a poem from 1962, "Words for Love," and ending with "Resolution," written in 1968. The forms used include cut-up and collage but also the "personal poem," as derived from Frank O'Hara's work, the "things to do" poem based on the examples of Gary Snyder and Sei Shonogon, and the long poem, as well as what one might call simply the "poem" poem, Ted's version of the emotionally direct, realistic shorter poem. There is a new open-field style in evidence, characterizing especially the great "Tambourine Life," dated "Oct. 1965–Jan. 1966." "Tambourine Life," divided into seventy sections of varying length, is an opening of Ted's voice; it sounds like him talking, though it also sounds "constructed," in unexpected and witty ways. The poem contains much domestic detail, specific 60s references, philosophy presented lightly, and an undercurrent of tragedy. It is dedicated to Anne Kepler—the Anne of *The Sonnets,* who died in a fire set by an arsonist while Ted was writing the poem; the book itself is dedicated to Anne Kepler and to Frank O'Hara, who died in 1966.

Another larger poem in *Many Happy Returns* is the collaged (and visually collage-like) "Bean Spasms," dated 1966. It was written in conjunction with images by George Schneeman and first published in the book *Bean Spasms,* a collaborative volume involving Ted, the poet Ron Padgett, and the artist Joe Brainard. Ted later incorporated into other books the work from *Bean Spasms* that was uniquely by himself.

The Seventies

The late 60s mark Ted's departure from New York, and his work from the early 70s is replete with references from other locales. It is significant that Ted's first book of the 70s, *In the Early Morning Rain,* was published by Cape Goliard, a British publisher.

In the Early Morning Rain made lavish use of drawings (now lost) by George Schneeman to create spaciousness and to emphasize groupings. The book is a mix of work in older styles employing found materials, chance methods, transliteration, the form of *The Sonnets*, etc., and poems from the late 60s and 1970 in the new, open style of *Many Happy Returns*. In 1968 Ted had begun leading a migrant poetry teacher's life and was spending time in Midwestern university towns like Iowa City and Ann Arbor. The light was different, he was making new friends, and he had begun to feel fated: to be addicted to drugs (pills, mostly speed) and perhaps to die early. The new poems elegize people who have recently died (Jack Kerouac, Rocky Marciano, Franny Winston, and others), allude to the war in Vietnam, celebrate specific evenings and occasions, and also celebrate the overcoming of emotional shakiness through the writing of poetry and through affection for others.

The long poem *Train Ride*, written in 1971 but not published until 1978, is a lavish example of an affectionate poem for a friend: it is a "love poem" addressed to Joe Brainard, and is about love, sex, and friendship. The poem speaks to Joe throughout, informally, frankly, a little in Joe's own style, and includes mock complaints about Ted's and Joe's mutual friends, about Joe himself, and a projected complaint, too, about Ted. The poem was written on a single day, February 18, during the course of a literal train ride between New York and Providence; it filled a rather large notebook. I remember Ted returning from the trip with the poem, slightly confused by the fact that it really was everything he wanted to say to Joe but also probably really a poem. This ambiguity, an unsure edge between life and art (not like Rauschenberg's "gap" but much more razorlike, something that might hurt you in its reality) kept Ted from publishing it for some years.

"Memorial Day," written around the same time in collaboration with Anne Waldman, is a long poem in a similar voice, though the voice is Ted's and Anne's fused. The voice is open, plain speaking, and flexible. It can take on everything a conversation can; and though the poem has a back-and-forth movement in it, it also feels unified and inspired in the way that two people talking sometimes become one thing, the conversation. The poem was written to be performed at a reading at the Poetry Project (St. Mark's Church-in-the-Bouwerie, New York) on May 5, 1971, and Ted and Anne worked on it for several months. Since Memorial Day falls in May and is potentially rich in its association with death and sacrifice/heroism, it was decided in advance that Memorial Day would be the title and subject of the work. The two poets were living in separate towns on Long Island and wrote separately, in asterisk-headed sections, giving or sending their work to each other from time to time for response, but there was no chronological ordering going on. At some point Ted wrote all of what would be the last section, and then Anne arranged the material. Ted always considered it to be the most successful literary collaboration he had participated in, in view of its seriousness and depth.

Meanwhile, and in deliberate counterpoint to such longer structures, Ted was writing many short poems. He often cited as formal influences the work of Giuseppe Ungaretti (the sequence "Life of a Man" in *In the Early Morning Rain* consists of transliterations of Ungaretti's work), and Aram Saroyan's poems, particularly the one-word poems. The section we have called *Short Poems* is divided into two parts. *In a Blue River* contains most of the chapbook of that name, published in 1981 by Susan Cataldo's Little Light Books. *Uncollected Short Poems* consists of a handful of poems first published in *So Going Around Cities*, as well as many uncollected short poems. Most of the poems included in *Short Poems* were written in the late 60s and, especially, the early 70s.

The short poem obviously involves more thought process than writing/reading process, if one can split the two. A short poem is peculiarly naked, whether it's a weighty short poem or a lighter short poem. It often seemed to take years for Ted to decide that a particular one was good enough to be published. And it's not surprising that *In a Blue River* is a later publication. A successful short poem may be capable of projecting new meanings on successive readings, but in a monolithic way, as if a new room has opened out, rather than in the overall, textured way that a longer poem can light up in a mesh of changeable meanings. For example, it may take the reader some time to connect the title "Larceny," in the poem which reads "The / opposite / of / petty / is GRAND," with the crimes of grand and petty larceny. One may be content with the observation that the opposite of petty *is* grand, a meditation on that. On the other hand a poem like "Laments," which both praises and judges Janis Joplin and Jimi Hendrix, is awesome on the level of judgment: "you did it wrong." The fact of judgment, and also this particular judgment—is it only of their deaths? their lifestyles?—constantly opens up more thoughtful space.

Red Wagon, published by the Yellow Press in 1976, is possibly the volume of Ted's that least shows his book-constructor's touch: it is more purely a "collection," assembled while he was ill with hepatitis. The poems, however, are solid, and many are among his best. By the time of the publication of *Red Wagon* Ted had taught at the Writers' Workshop of the University of Iowa, Iowa City; at the University of Michigan at Ann Arbor; at Yale; at Northeastern Illinois University in Chicago; and at the University of Essex in England. In 1976 he moved back to New York, where he would spend his remaining eight years. *Red Wagon* includes work written in many cities and two countries. It contains important shorter poems (such as "In the Wheel"), a number of open-field poems (for example, the popular "Things to Do in Providence") and sprawling long-lined poems ("Something Amazing Just Happened").

Partway through *Red Wagon*, variety of form cedes to a denser, more slablike entity, beginning with the poem "Frank O'Hara" and the five poems succeeding it, the remnants of a disbanded sequence called "Southampton Winter." In the original *Red Wagon*, poems from *Easter Monday* (still in the process of composition) rounded out the book for the most part, as well as a group of five sonnets. These were, in fact, five of *The Sonnets*, three previously published and two seeing print for the first time. Our version of *Red Wagon* omits the *Easter Monday* poems and the group of sonnets. It ends with "The Complete Prelude," a poem made from words and phrases of Wordsworth's poem. The use of another poet's work as a word source had always been a favorite method of Ted's (see, for example, "Sonnet VI," made from a poem by his friend, the poet Dick Gallup.) This method could result in a kind of book review, or a dialogue with a poet's style, or could be used to delve into Ted's own consciousness. Here it is also a way to employ the now-forbidden language of English Romantic Poetry, which being part of the poet's education is part of himself.

If "Southampton Winter" had dissolved as a conception, poems such as "Chicago Morning" and "Newtown," written in Chicago in 1972 and resembling the "Southampton Winter" poems, became the basis for *Easter Monday*. The sequence was not really conceived until Ted's arrival in England in 1973. At both Northeastern Illinois University and the University of Essex Ted took teaching positions that had been held by Ed Dorn, who, like Ted, had recently entered into a second marriage and fathered two more children. Ted became interested in the concept of the second act, as in F. Scott Fitzgerald's now clichéd statement, "There are no second acts in American life." *Easter Monday*, dedicated to Ed Dorn and named for Willem de Kooning's beautiful painting as well as for the day after the day of rebirth, is meant to address the possibility of the second act. Ted had hoped for fifty poems, inspired by the artist George Schneeman's notion that once he'd started a project, a set of collages, say, he might as well do fifty. Ted ended up with forty-six.

Ted kept *Easter Monday* in a folder on the cover of which is inscribed *EASTER MONDAY/Poems (1972–1977)*. The poems were written in Chicago, London, Wivenhoe, New York, and Boulder; many are sonnets, most have an impasto texture—thick abstract expressionistic paint—and many of them are composed of other people's words. "From the House Journals," for example, is made from the first lines index to the *Collected Poems* of Frank O'Hara; "In Blood" is a selection of lines from a sequence of mine; and "The Ancient Art of Wooing" is made from a poem of mine I'd given up on, which was itself made out of a magazine article. A poem like the latter is a little like a palimpsest and a little like urban erosion. But the poems speak to and with the words of people Ted cared about or was interactive with. A few of the poems, on the other hand, are direct addresses to friends, delivered in an almost courtly manner. The sequence is very much about "not dying," in William Saroyan's phrase, not giving in to deathy forces. Ted didn't declare the sequence finished until shortly before he died in 1983, when he made the final decisions for it. There are a handful of *Easter Monday* out-takes to be found in *Nothing for You* and *So Going Around Cities*.

It should be noted that Ted was always open to chapbook and broadside publication. *In a Blue River* and *The Morning Line* are in fact chapbooks, and, as I've indicated, parts of *Easter Monday* were first published in chapbooks. A mimeographed stapled book with the singularly lovely title *A Feeling for Leaving* (Frontward Books, 1975) contains twenty-two of the poems. Another nine were published in 1980 as *Clown War* 22 (edited by Bob Heman) under the title *Carrying a Torch*.

By the time *Nothing for You* was published, in 1977, Ted's and my sons, Anselm and Edmund (my co-editors of this edition), were five and three years old. Ted had two other children, David and Kate, from his marriage to Sandy Alper Berrigan. He had always delighted in being with his kids, and there are references to all of them throughout his work. The title *Nothing for You* comes from a word game Anselm and Edmund had made up, which went something like: "No cookies, no candy, no soda. Nothing, nothing for you." This was a great joke, a chant accompanied by laughter. Ted had been asked by Lewis Warsh for a book for Angel Hair Books, but it was one of those times when he felt he had nothing. So he conjured a manuscript out of piles of rejects and old poems and gleefully named it after our sons' chant.

As he constructed the book, the concept of using rejects, supposedly second-class works, became interesting to him. A world was being created out of poems that *did* belong together, having been written in the process of discovering forms rather than perfecting them. *Nothing for You* actually has something for everyone and was much appreciated, at least by Ted's circle, when it came out. It begins with some twenty poems from the early to late-ish 60s, mostly very old works which had been tinkered with over the years until exactly right. Then there are a number of poems from the late 60s and early 70s that he was very excited by at the time of composition but abandoned when he got something that seemed superior. I remember how much he loved having written "In Bed with Joan & Alex" in 1969; but later it felt as if he'd dropped it in favor of poems like "Things to Do in Providence." Finally there are more recent poems, such as the rejects from *Easter Monday,* interspersed with poems about people: Paul Blackburn, Tom Clark, Kirsten Creeley, Sandy Berrigan.

Into the Eighties

Ted's first publication in the 80s was *So Going Around Cities: New and Selected Poems, 1958–1979.* Appearing midway through 1980, it was a generous selection of poems, honoring, to some degree, the primacy of Ted's books as artistic shapes. There are scaled-down selections from *The Sonnets* and *Easter Monday,* and a section called *Many Happy Returns,* which is slightly different from the book itself. Collections like *In the Early Morning Rain* and *Red Wagon* are broken up into new kinds of groups, small sections reflecting the chronology of Ted's life.

For this volume, we have created a section called *In the 51st State* corresponding to the period of the late 70s through circa 1981. It is composed of a subsection, also called *In the 51st State,* containing twelve poems first published in *So Going Around Cities;* the chapbook *The Morning Line,* published by Am Here Books in 1981; and uncollected poems of roughly the same time period.

For Ted the "51st State" was New York City; the poem "In the 51st State," dedicated to Ted's daughter Kate, ends with the lines: "Bon voyage, little ones. / Follow me down / Through the locks. There is no key." Thus this is also a new and puzzling "state" that Ted has entered, one of feeling older, irrelevant, and failing in health. And yet, in the same poem, after he writes "Au revoir," he counters with the parenthetical lines "(I wouldn't translate that / as 'Goodbye' if I were you)." Ted is in the process of "not dying," though he's only a few years from his death.

The new element in the poems of this section is a longer line combined with discursiveness and apparent autobiography, though Ted continues to use other people's voices and autobiographical facts as well as his own. In "Last Poem," "I once had the honor of meeting Beckett and I dug him" is a quotation from Robert Creeley and in no way corresponds to anything that happened to Ted, except emotionally. There is always a "Beckett" in one's anecdotes. The practice of incorporating the lives of others into his is evident throughout Ted's previous work: in the use of others' poems and prose in cut-ups, in such "found" works as "Autobiography in 5 Parts," in the weave of voices in *Easter Monday*. These techniques are an assertion that he is part of everything and everyone around him, that his reading and his interaction with others do literally become him, and that all words are free and usable. As Tom Clark once said to him, "Who owns words?"

The poems from *So Going Around Cities*—which make up the first part of *In the 51st State*—include several works that became favorite performance pieces of Ted's near the end of his life: "Cranston Near the City Line," "Last Poem," and especially, "Red Shift." So-called Performance Poetry had been in the air for a while, and Ted picked up from it the possibility of extending his performing voice and, consequently, his writing voice. "Red Shift" wasn't written to be performed in a splashy way, but over the course of a year or two, he developed a set of vocal changes for it, a deliberate tremolo and a slowing down of the long lines, which seemed to stretch the poem far into time and space, allowing him to express the poem's angry urgency. On the other hand, a slightly later poem like "After Peire Vidal, & Myself," in *The Morning Line*, was written precisely with performance in mind. It was declaimed publicly, in mock-troubadour fashion, to answer his friend Rochelle Kraut, who, briefly mad at him, was reading Catullus-like poems "against" him around the Lower East Side.

The Morning Line was a flat, stapled, mimeographed chapbook of twenty-two poems in a number of forms. "Sonnet: *Homage to Ron*" is made up of words by Ron Padgett; "44th Birthday Evening, at Harris's" is a sentimental birthday poem for Ted himself containing a dream; "Avec la Mécanique sous les Palmes" is entirely in French; "Kerouac / (continued)," is deft maneuvers with found material; "D N A" is like the poems in *Easter Monday;* and so on. The title *The Morning Line* refers to betting on horses—which poem, which style shall we choose?—and to a song from the musical comedy *Guys and Dolls:* "I've got a horse right here / His name is Paul Revere . . ."

The *Uncollected Poems* of this section demonstrate a continuation, even further development, of Ted's preferred and reliable forms. One discerns the arrival of the Language Poets in the poem "I S O L A T E," as Ted uses Bruce Andrews's words to review Andrews's book *Film Noir* for *L=A=N=G=U=A=G=E* magazine. The "Ten Greatest Books" form (see the two examples in *In The Early Morning Rain*) reappears in the poem "My 5 Favorite Records." For the "Ten Greatest Books" poems, Ted had named books he was actually reading or could see in his room (they tended to be the greatest books of that exact moment), but "My 5 Favorite Records" was a response to a request for a list (not for a poem) from Dennis Cooper, editor of *Little Caesar* magazine. Ted then asked Art Lange, editor of the jazz magazine *Downbeat* and music critic for the *Chicago Reader*, to make a list of what *ought* to be Ted's five favorite records. The result is quite Byzantine; Ted was extremely amused by this work, but public readings of it produced some bafflement in the audience.

The poem "Rouge," on the other hand, is a particularly successful version of what one might call the "linguistic poem," a form with Creeleyesque overtones that Ted had been working on for some years. In the linguistic poem he defines and works out with small words: *it, this*, and *that* in this case, but also the word *know*. I seem to remember giving him the title of the poem, which serves to negate any pedantry. Finally, one is delighted by certain poems that Ted was unable to publish due to the brevity of his remaining years: "Compleynt to the Muse" and "Thin Breast Doom," with their allusions to Phil Whalen's manner, the several autobiographical and pseudo-autobiographical poems, and the list poem "Memories Are Made of This."

Ted's final book (though these are not his final poems) was *A Certain Slant of Sunlight*, which occupied him for all of 1982. This sequence of poems was written on individual postcards, $4\frac{1}{2}$ inches by 7 inches, sent to him by Ken and Anne Mikolowski of the Alternative Press. There were five hundred cards to work with, one side left blank for a poem and/or image, and the other side incorporating space for a message and address. *Postcard by Ted Berrigan* was printed at the top of the message space, and running sideways, *The Alternative Press Grindstone City*. Many other artists and writers participated in the Mikolowskis' project, producing original art or text for the blank sides of their own five hundred postcards; the finished cards were always sent out singly, along with other Alternative Press items—broadsides, bumper stickers, etc.—in the Press's standard free packets. Ted, so far as I know, was the only participant who turned the postcards into a full-scale writing project and then a book.

The postcard poem was a form dominated by the size of the card, though a relatively longer poem could be written on a card if Ted shrank his handwriting. Ted immediately used semi-collaboration as a way into the poems, inducing everyone he knew to write a line or draw an image on a postcard. He later eliminated the names of the "facilitators," except for the occasional dedication. The poems are often epigrammatic, but are just as likely to be longer; they chronicle, not so explicitly, a difficult year—in terms of health, finances, relationships with friends. They are about the workings of a community, about poetry quarrels and poetry festivals, about cops on the corner and what music is being listened to, what is going on in the newspapers. Ted produced a couple hundred original poems; there are one hundred exactly in *A Certain Slant of Sunlight,* which I edited after his death, according to his instructions.

We also present here a separate section of the best of the out-takes from *A Certain Slant of Sunlight*, thirty-three more "postcard poems," many of which could easily have been included in the book. One suspects Ted of fetishizing the number one hundred; but approximately that number seems to be how many the mind is capable of considering in relation to one another. These additional thirty-three, hopefully, suggest a book of their own.

Though *A Certain Slant of Sunlight* contains many of Ted's "forms," his voice has changed. The necessity for concision, imposed by the size of the card, pushes tone of voice up against language up against form: "HOLLYWOOD / paid Lillian Gish $800,000 to / disappear so lovely so pure like milk / seems but isn't because of the fall-out / but it would have only cost me five & didn't, so I did." Many of the poems are monologues for the person who provided the phrase or image, or are in dialogue with him/her. Some work with texts of dead poets, Whitman and Lindsay for example, or with songs. There is a flexibility of tone throughout, which has emerged from the lengthier autobiographical poems of the late 70s and early 80s, but must operate more quickly. This book is extraordinary without appearing to be: it doesn't have "monument" written on it, but it isn't like anything else.

Ted's last poems are the fourteen poems—twenty-one pages—he wrote after the completion of *A Certain Slant of Sunlight* during the final six months of his life. It must be obvious by now that Ted did not slow down as a writer during his last years, and these poems are sharp and fulsome. They were kept together in a folder with a handwritten title page: "Poems/ * /Ted Berrigan." Some are short in the manner of *A Certain Slant of Sunlight*, and there are several longer poems, including an abrasive "Stand-Up Comedy Routine," made from a *Mad-Libs* form.[1] But Ted's very last poem is a lovely six-page work, "This Will Be Her Shining Hour," written in dialogue with myself and the voices in a Fred Astaire movie on TV. " 'Their lives are as fragile as *The Glass Menagerie*.' " That line near the end of Ted's final poem refers to the people in the movie, the people in the poem, and the two of us as both people in the poem and ourselves, comparing them/us to Tennessee Williams's play, to glass figures, to the enduringness of the play about fragile people. What does *lives* mean then? *Lives* seems to be "art," and so one is left thinking about the strength of poetry.

Ted Berrigan's poems are very *deliberate*. They have a graven quality as if they were drawn on the page, word by word. He often wrote in unlined notebooks with a black felt-tip pen, and one might also say they have a black-felt-tip-pen quality. You feel that no words have been crossed out and replaced.

I'm impressed by this graven-ness in *The Sonnets* and *Many Happy Returns*, in *Easter Monday*, but then, too, in most of the later work. It doesn't go away if the feeling in the poem is more autobiographical or intimate, as in *A Certain Slant of Sunlight*. The latter poems read as if written with the black felt-tip pen, on the postcard. They have a primary physical reality.

Two more things from this: first, a continuous interaction with art and artists gave Ted an active visual and tactile sense. He is often painting, or collaging, or drawing his way through a poem. On the other hand, he agreed with Jack Spicer's notion of the *other* voice that dictates one's poems, and his poems have a "dictated" quality, even the ones that are made from other people's words. These two notions

1. *Mad-Libs*, an offshoot of *Mad* magazine, contained fill-in-the-blank and multiple-choice do-it-yourself versions of country songs, comedy routines, anecdotes, and so forth.

aren't incompatible. "Dictation" suggests aurality rather than plastic qualities, but there isn't any reason why all the senses shouldn't be working, and Ted had a very fine ear: "Their lives are as fragile as *The Glass Menagerie*." Listen.

Ted's poetry is remarkable for its range of tones of voice. He actively studied both "tone of voice" and "stance," the range of attitudinal play in human discourse and the projection of character. Here Ted's professed model was Frank O'Hara, but I often find Ted more mysterious and more intense in both tone and stance. Not having O'Hara's education or "class," Ted therefore couldn't be as traditional. He couldn't call on a tone of voice from another decade or century as if he owned it, even though he knew exactly what Whitmanesque or Johnsonian was. He had to reinvent it for himself, from his working-class background and University of Tulsa education and ceaseless self-education.

Ted is often characterized as "second-generation New York School." That label, with its "second-generation," seems to preclude innovation. Ted's career as a poet, after his earliest, sentimental poems, begins in the innovation of *The Sonnets*. He invented its form, with its "black heart beside the fifteen pieces" and its "of glass in Joe Brainard's collage," if you take fifteen to be most likely fourteen and understand that his heart really is beside the poem not in it. These poems, designed to contain anything and to expand temporally, can do so because the form's finiteness is emphasized. It could probably be argued that this form is the one he was most informed by afterward, even when he was being transparent and "sentimental"—when he had finally learned the uses and control of sentimentality, since he consistently explored the spaces between lines, and the spaces between phrases, within the poem as frame. He had also learned from his sonnet form how to find the congruences in supposedly random happenstance:

Can't cut it (night)
in New York City
it's alive
inside my tooth
on St. Mark's Place
where exposed nerve
jangles

("FEBRUARY AIR")

This is verbal, environmental, and emotional happenstance, where the parts of the moment click in.

If you the reader are a poet, Ted's poetry is full of resources: forms, techniques, stylistic practices—manners and mannerisms, ways of sounding like a person, ways of achieving exaltation. If you the reader are a reader (of poetry), Ted's poetry is a gift. He is working hard to amuse—make you enjoy this taking up of your time; to "say," what he knows, reasons, feels; and to be like you, at the same time acknowledging his (anyone's) own secret: "I never told anyone what I knew. Which was that it wasn't/for anyone else what it was for me" ("Cranston Near the City Line").

We have, traditionally, the senses, but words are our sensors. We use them to feel our way across and through, up and down. Ted understood this as well as any poet I can think of. So much of his poetry is about the pleasure of movement across the page. He is saying, "This is what we do. This is living, taking its walk." It is a very gentle message, that of the walk through time, laid alongside the message that all time is simultaneous. But, also,

> No-mind
>
> No messages
>
> (Inside)
> Thanksgiving 1969

("IN MY ROOM")

ALICE NOTLEY
PARIS, 2004

Chronology

1934 Born on November 15 in Providence, Rhode Island, to Margaret Dugan Berrigan and Edmund Joseph Berrigan, the oldest of four children, with Rick, Kathy, and Johnny to follow. His father, Ed, was chief maintenance engineer at the Ward Baking Company Plant, and his mother, Peggy, was a bookkeeper and cashier in the public schools lunch program.

1952 Graduated from La Salle Academy.

1953 Attended Providence College. In Ted's own words he was educated in the "Catholic school system, first by the Sisters of Mercy, then at La Salle Academy with the Christian Brothers, and for one year under the Dominicans at Providence College."

1954 Joined the army, spending sixteen months in Korea, stationed at Uijongbu, between 1954 and 1955.

1955 Was transferred to Tulsa, having attained the rank of sergeant (SP3) and having received a good conduct medal. Began studies at the University of Tulsa on the GI Bill.

1957 Discharged from active duty and placed in the reserves.

1958 Ted's father, Ed Berrigan, died.

1958–59 Taught eighth grade at Madalene School in Tulsa.

1959 Met Ron Padgett, Dick Gallup, and Joe Brainard. (Already knew David Bearden, Pat Mitchell, Marge Kepler, and others.) *A Lily for My Love* was published in Providence. "The guys in the neighborhood bar had chipped in and paid for the printing" (Ron Padgett, *Ted: A Personal Memoir of Ted Berrigan* [Great Barrington, Mass.: The Figures, 1993]). Received a BA in Literature from the University of Tulsa.

1960–61 Wrote a postcard to Frank O'Hara, beginning their association. Moved to New York in the same time period as Pat Mitchell, Brainard, Gallup, and Padgett. Met O'Hara.

1962 Finished his master's thesis, "The Problem of How to Live as Dealt with in Four Plays by George Bernard Shaw." Upon receiving his MA from the University of Tulsa, he returned it with the note, "I am the master of no art." Met Kenneth Koch during Koch's office hours at Columbia. Took one semester of classical Greek at Columbia; earned money writing papers for Columbia students. Met and married Sandra Alper in New Orleans over the course of a weekend, traumatic difficulties ensuing with Sandy's family. Began writing *The Sonnets.*

1963 Finished *The Sonnets* in July. David Berrigan born. Began editing "C" *(A Journal of Poetry)*, published by Lorenz and Ellen Gude, which would run for thirteen issues and two comic strip issues and feature many senior New York School poets as well as Ted's contemporaries. "C" further spawned "C" Books in 1964, published by the Gudes during the 60s, producing a total of eleven booklets in mimeo format by new writers (and continuing into the 70s under Ted's sole proprietorship). Most of the art in "C" was by Joe Brainard, with the occasional cover by Andy Warhol. This was and would be a period of intense friendship and collaboration with Padgett, and Gallup, as well as one of artistic collaboration with Brainard. But by 1963 Ted knew Johnny Stanton, Joe Ceravolo, Tom Veitch, Jim Brodey, Harry Fainlight, Tony Towle, Lorenzo Thomas, and other writers of his generation. At the same time Ed Sanders was editing and publishing his journal, *Fuck You / A Magazine of the Arts,* and Sanders and Ted "spent a lot of time together." The social aspect of Ted's life had become all-encompassing and non-parochial and would remain that way for the rest of his life. As he said in the 1973 "Interview with Ruth Gruber"(*Talking in Tranquility: Interviews with Ted Berrigan* [Bolinas and Oakland: Avenue B and O Books, 1991]), a dual interview with Ted and George Oppen: "I like to know all the groups, because that way is the most fun, and the most interesting."

1964 The first edition of *The Sonnets* published under the "C" imprint. Gave first reading in New York at Le Metro Café with Allen Ginsberg, Paul Blackburn, Frank O'Hara, and Michael Goldberg in the audience. Began writing reviews for the magazine *Kulchur*. Received a Poets Foundation Grant. Probably met or by now had met John Ashbery, whose work he published in "C" and who, though living in France, returned to New York from time to time for readings. In 1964 Ashbery gave an electrifying reading of his long poem "The Skaters,"an occasion which Ted referred to throughout his life. Around this time worked on long unpublished prose work, *Looking for Chris,* not all of which survives.

1965 Intensive period of writing for *Art News* lasting through 1966, though Ted's art writing would continue sporadically until his death. Attended Berkeley Poetry Conference. Met Ed Dorn, Gary Snyder, Philip Whalen, Michael McClure, Lew Welch, and Robert Duncan there. Kate Berrigan born.

1966 Death of Frank O'Hara. Served on the advisory board of the Poetry Project. Taught the first writing workshop offered at the Project and continued to serve as a teacher off and on until 1979. This was his first poetry teaching post, though that same year he began an intermittent but ongoing participation in the Writers in the Schools Poetry Program. By or around this time had met George Schneeman, Anne Waldman, Lewis Warsh, Tom Clark, Bernadette Mayer, Peter Schjeldahl, Lewis MacAdams, John Godfrey, Donna Dennis, Larry Fagin, Aram Saroyan, Clark Coolidge, Bill Berkson, John Giorno.

1967 *The Sonnets* published by Grove Press. *Bean Spasms,* a collaborative book with Ron Padgett and Joe Brainard, published by Kulchur Press. Ted interviewed Jack Kerouac (with Aram Saroyan and Duncan MacNaughton) for the *Paris Review* (interview first published in vol. 11, no.

43 [Summer 1968]). Received a Poets Foundation Grant and a National Anthology of Literature Award for "An Interview with John Cage," which was a fabricated interview using Cageian methods.

1968 Left New York to take a writer-in-residence position at the University of Iowa, the Writers' Workshop, from fall 1968 through spring 1969. Met Anselm Hollo, Gordon Brotherston, Merrill Gilfillan, and others.

1969 Separated from Sandy Alper Berrigan. *Many Happy Returns* published by Corinth Press. Met Alice Notley. Taught fall semester at the University of Michigan in Ann Arbor. (Lecturer in English and American Literature, nineteenth and twentieth centuries.) Friendship with Donald Hall.

1970 *Guillaume Apollinaire Ist Tot. Und Anderes,* a selection of Ted's work with German translations by Rolf-Dieter Brinkmann, published in Germany by März Verlag. *In the Early Morning Rain* published by Cape Goliard Press in England. Taught at Yale University in the spring as Teaching Fellow at Bramford College. Replaced Jack Clarke at the University of Buffalo that summer, where Ted's classes included the mythology course originally established by Charles Olson.

1970–71 Transitional period of moving from place to place with Alice Notley. Lived in Southampton, Long Island (in Larry Rivers's garage), New York, Providence, and Bolinas. Bolinas at this time included in its community Lewis MacAdams, Joanne Kyger, Don Allen, Phil Whalen, Tom Clark, Robert Creeley, Bobbie Louise Hawkins, Bill Berkson, et al.

1972 Married Alice Notley. Moved to Chicago and taught at Northeastern Illinois University, following Ed Dorn as Poet in Residence, from winter 1972 until spring 1973. Anselm Berrigan born. Met Bob Rosenthal, Rochelle Kraut, Hank Kanabus, Art Lange and many others, some of whom subsequently moved to New York. Began working on *Easter Monday.*

1973 Moved to England and taught at the University of Essex (replacing Robert Lowell) from fall 1973 until spring 1974. Friends included Gordon Brotherston, Douglas Oliver, Pierre Joris, Tom Pickard, Wendy Mulford, John James, Allen Fisher, Dick Miller, Simon Pettet, Helena Hughes, Marion Farrier, etc. Several of these people subsequently moved to New York as well, part of Ted's "job" seemingly being to conduct young people toward the New York poetry world. Had work published in the *Norton Anthology of Modern Poetry*. With Gordon Brotherston worked on translations of poems by Heine, Leopardi, Gautier, Apollinaire, Cabral de Melo Neto, and Neruda.

1974 Edmund Berrigan born. Moved back to Chicago and taught at Northeastern Illinois University from fall 1974 until spring 1975.

1975 *Red Wagon* published by the Yellow Press. That summer taught for the first time at Naropa University (then College), beginning an association that continued until his death.

1976 Moved back to New York, ill with hepatitis. Health poor from now on. Extensive association with Harris Schiff, Steve Carey, Tom Carey, and Eileen Myles began.

1977 Received a CAPS Grant. *Nothing for You* published by United Artists. *Clear the Range* published by Adventures in Poetry.

1978 *Train Ride* published by Vehicle Editions. Worked with Peter Orlovsky on the editing and typing of Orlovsky's *Clean Asshole Poems & Smiling Vegetable Songs: Poems 1957–1977*, published by City Lights Books that year.

1979 Received an NEA Grant. *Yo-Yo's with Money*, a transcription of a live sportscast recorded collaboratively by Ted and Harris Schiff at a baseball game at Yankee Stadium, published by United Artists Books.

1980 Taught spring and summer terms at the Naropa Institute in Boulder, Colorado. *So Going Around Cities: Selected Poems 1958–1979* published by Blue Wind Press. Taught at the Stevens Institute of Technology (Distinguished Visiting Professor of Literature) in Hoboken, New Jersey, during the fall of 1980, at the behest of new friend Ed Foster. Ted's mother, Peggy Berrigan, became ill with lung cancer.

1981 *In a Blue River* published by Little Light Books. In May conducted influential and notorious four-day residency at 80 Langton Street, San Francisco, which included a reading of new work, a confrontational evening with the Language Poets, a panel discussion of Ted's work, and a full-length reading of *The Sonnets.* Throughout the year wrote prose commentaries and reviews for the Poetry Project *Newsletter* (edited by Greg Masters).

1982 *The Morning Line* published by Am Here Books/Immediate Editions. *The Sonnets* reissued by United Artists with six additional sonnets. Became Writer in Residence at CCNY in the spring. Peggy Berrigan died in July. Throughout this year worked on *A Certain Slant of Sunlight.*

1983 Writing last poems. Becoming increasingly ill but continuing to function as much as possible. Conducted lengthy but unsuccessful interview with James Schuyler. Died on July 4 of complications from cirrhosis of the liver, which was most probably caused by the hepatitis C virus. Buried at Calverton National Cemetery on Long Island, a military cemetery.

1988 *A Certain Slant of Sunlight* published by O Books.

1991 *Talking in Tranquility: Interviews with Ted Berrigan,* edited by Stephen Ratcliffe and Leslie Scalapino, published by Avenue B and O Books.

1994 *Selected Poems of Ted Berrigan,* edited by Aram Saroyan, published by Penguin.

1997 *On the Level Everyday: Selected Talks on Poetry and the Art of Living,* edited by Joel Lewis, published by Talisman House, Publishers.

1998 *Great Stories of the Chair* published by Situations.

2000 *The Sonnets* reissued by Penguin with six additional sonnets.

The Collected Poems of Ted Berrigan

The Sonnets

TO JOE BRAINARD

I

His piercing pince-nez. Some dim frieze
Hands point to a dim frieze, in the dark night.
In the book of his music the corners have straightened:
Which owe their presence to our sleeping hands.
The ox-blood from the hands which play
For fire for warmth for hands for growth
Is there room in the room that you room in?
Upon his structured tomb:
Still they mean something. For the dance
And the architecture.
Weave among incidents
May be portentous to him
We are the sleeping fragments of his sky,
Wind giving presence to fragments.

II

Dear Margie, hello. It is 5:15 a.m.
dear Berrigan. He died
Back to books. I read
It's 8:30 p.m. in New York and I've been running around all day
old come-all-ye's streel into the streets. Yes, it is now,
How Much Longer Shall I Be Able To Inhabit The Divine
and the day is bright gray turning green
feminine marvelous and tough
watching the sun come up over the Navy Yard
to write scotch-tape body in a notebook
had 17 and 1/2 milligrams
Dear Margie, hello. It is 5:15 a.m.
fucked til 7 now she's late to work and I'm
18 so why are my hands shaking I should know better

III

Stronger than alcohol, more great than song,
deep in whose reeds great elephants decay;
I, an island, sail, and my shores toss
on a fragrant evening, fraught with sadness
bristling hate.
It's true, I weep too much. Dawns break
slow kisses on the eyelids of the sea,
what other men sometimes have thought they've seen.
And since then I've been bathing in the poem
lifting her shadowy flowers up for me,
and hurled by hurricanes to a birdless place
the waving flags, nor pass by prison ships
O let me burst, and I be lost at sea!
and fall on my knees then, womanly.

IV

Lord, it is time. Summer was very great.
All sweetly spoke to her of me
about your feet, so delicate, and yet double E!!
And high upon the Brooklyn Bridge alone,
to breathe an old woman slop oatmeal,
loveliness that longs for butterfly! There is no pad
as you lope across the trails and bosky dells
I often think sweet and sour pork"
shoe repair, and scary. In cities,
I strain to gather my absurdities
He buckled on his gun, the one
Poised like Nijinsky
at every hand, my critic
and when I stand and clank it gives me shoes

V

Squawking a gala occasion, forgetting, and
"Hawkaaaaaaaaaa!" Once I went scouting
As stars are, like nightmares, a crucifix.
Why can't I read French? I don't know why can't you?
Rather the matter of growth
My babies parade waving their innocent flags
Huddled on the structured steps
Flinging currents into pouring streams
The "jeunes filles" so rare.
He wanted to know the *names*
He liked boys, never had a mother
Meanwhile, terrific misnomers went concocted, ayearning,
    ayearning
The Pure No Nonsense
And all day: Perceval! Perceval!

VI

The bulbs burn phosphorescent, white
Your hair moves slightly,
Tenseness, but strength, outward
And the green rug nestled against the furnace
Dust had covered all the tacks, the hammer
. . . optimism for the jump . . .
The taste of such delicate thoughts
Never bring the dawn.
The bulbs burn, phosphorescent, white,

Melting the billowing snow with wine:
Could the mind turn jade? everything
Turning in this light, to stones,
Ash, bark like cork, a fading dust,
To cover the tracks of "The Hammer."

Poem in the Traditional Manner

Whenever Richard Gallup is dissevered,
Fathers and teachers, and daemons down under the sea,
Audenesque Epithalamiums! She
Sends her driver home and she stays with me.

Match-Game etcetera! Bootleggers
Barrel-assing chevrolets grow bold. I summon
To myself sad silent thoughts,
Opulent, sinister, and cold.

Shall it be male or female in the tub?
And grawk go under, and grackle disappear,
And high upon the Brooklyn Bridge alone,
An ugly ogre masturbates by ear:

Of my darling, my darling, my pipe and my slippers,
Something there is is benzedrine in bed:
And so, so Asiatic, Richard Gallup
Goes home, and gets his gat, and plugs his dad.

Poem in the Modern Manner

She comes as in a dream with west wind eggs,
bringing Huitzilopochtli hot possets:
Snakeskins! But I am young, just old enough
to breathe, an old woman, slop oatmeal,
lemongrass, dewlarks, full draught of, fall thud.

Lady of the May, thou art fair,
Lady, thou art truly fair! Children,
When they see your face,
Sing in idiom of disgrace.

Pale like an ancient scarf, she is unadorned,
bouncing a red rubber ball in the veins.
The singer sleeps in Cos. Strange juxtaposed
the phantom sings: Bring me red demented rooms,
warm and delicate words! Swollen as if new-out-of-bed
Huitzilopochtli goes his dithyrambic way,
quick-shot, resuscitate, all roar!

From a Secret Journal

My babies parade waving their innocent flags
an unpublished philosopher, a man who *must*
column after column down colonnade of rust
in my paintings, for they are present
I am wary of the mulctings of the pink promenade,
went in the other direction to Tulsa,
glistering, bristling, cozening whatever disguises
S of Christmas John Wayne will clown with
Dreams, aspirations of presence! Innocence gleaned,

annealed! The world in its mysteries are explained,
and the struggles of babies congeal. A hard core is formed.
"I wanted to be a cowboy." Doughboy will do.
Romance of it all was overwhelming
daylight of itself dissolving and of course it rained.

Real Life

1. The Fool

He eats of the fruits of the great Speckle
Bird, pissing in the grass! Is it possible
He is incomplete, bringing you Ginger Ale
Of the interminably frolicsome gushing summer showers?
You were a Campfire Girl,
Only a part-time mother and father; I
Was large, stern, acrid, and undissuadable!
Ah, Bernie, we wear complete
The indexed Webster Unabridged Dictionary.
And lunch is not lacking, ants and clover
On the grass. To think of you alone
Suffering the poem of these states!
Oh Lord, it is bosky, giggling happy here,
And you, and me, the juice, at last extinct!

2. The Fiend

Red-faced and romping in the wind
I too am reading the technical journals, but
Keeping Christmas-safe each city block
With tail-pin. My angels are losing patience,
Never win. Except at night. Then
I would like a silken thread
Tied round the solid blooming winter.

Trees stand stark-naked guarding bridal paths;
The cooling wind keeps blowing, and
There is a faint chance in geometric boxes!
It doesn't matter, though, to show he is
Your champion. Days are nursed on science fiction
And you tremble at the books upon the earth
As my strength and I walk out and look for you.

Penn Station

On the green a white boy goes
And he walks. Three ciphers and a faint fakir
No One Two Three Four Today
I thought about all those radio waves
Winds flip down the dark path of breath
Passage the treasure Gomangani I
Forget bring the green boy white ways
And the wind goes there
Keats was a baiter of bears
Who died of lust (You lie! You lie!)
As so we all must in the green jungle
Under a sky of burnt umber we bumble to
The mien florist's to buy green nosegays
For the fey Saint's parade Today
We may read about all those radio waves

XIII

Mountains of twine and
Teeth braced against it
Before gray walls. Feet walk
Released by night (which is not to imply
Death) under the murk spell
Racing down the blue lugubrious rainway
To the big promise of emptiness
In air we get our feet wet. . . . a big rock
Caresses cloud bellies
He finds he cannot fake
Wed to wakefulness, night which is not death
Fuscous with murderous dampness
But helpless, as blue roses are helpless.
Rivers of annoyance undermine the arrangements.

XIV

We remove a hand . . .
In a roomful of smoky man names burnished dull black
And labelled "blue" the din drifted in . . .
Someone said "Blake-blues" and someone else "pill-head"
Meaning bloodhounds. Someone shovelled in some
Cotton-field money brave free beer and finally "Negroes!"
They talked . . .
He thought of overshoes looked like mother
Made him
Combed his hair
Put away your hair. Books shall speak of us
When we are gone, like soft, dark scarves in gay April.
Let them discard loves in the Spring search! We
await a grass hand.

XV

In Joe Brainard's collage its white arrow
He is not in it, the hungry dead doctor.
Of Marilyn Monroe, her white teeth white-
I am truly horribly upset because Marilyn
and ate King Korn popcorn," he wrote in his
of glass in Joe Brainard's collage
Doctor, but they say "I LOVE YOU"
and the sonnet is not dead.
takes the eyes away from the gray words,
Diary. The black heart beside the fifteen pieces
Monroe died, so I went to a matinee B-movie
washed by Joe's throbbing hands. "Today
What is in it is sixteen ripped pictures
does not point to William Carlos Williams.

XVI

Into the closed air of the slow
Warmth comes, a slow going down of the Morning Land
She is warm. Into the vast closed air of the slow
Going down of the Morning Land
One vast under pinning trembles doom ice
Spreads beneath the mud troubled ice
Smother of a sword
Into her quick weak heat. She
Is introspection. One vast ice laden

Vast seas of doom and mud spread across the lake. Quick
heat,
Of her vast ice laden self under introspective heat.
White lake trembles down to green goings
On, shades of a Chinese wall, itself "a signal."
It is a Chinese signal.

XVII

FOR CAROL CLIFFORD

Each tree stands alone in stillness
After many years still nothing
The wind's wish is the tree's demand
The tree stands still
The wind walks up and down
Scanning the long selves of the shore
Her aimlessness is the pulse of the tree
It beats in tiny blots
Its patternless pattern of excitement
Letters birds beggars books
There is no such thing as a breakdown
The tree the ground the wind these are
Dear, be the tree your sleep awaits
Sensual, solid, still, swaying alone in the wind

XVIII

Dear Marge, hello. It is 5:15 a.m.
Outside my room atonal sounds of rain
In my head. Dreams of Larry Walker
Drum in the pre-dawn. In my skull my brain
Season, cold images glitter brightly
In his marriage bed: of David Bearden
Answering. "Deteriorating," you said.
Say it. And made it hard to write. You know
Margie, tonight, and every night, in any
Aches in rhythm to that pounding morning rain.
Them over and over. And now I dread
Not a question, really, but you did
In your letter, many questions. I read
Paranoid: and of Martin Cochran, dead.

XIX

Harum-scarum haze on the Pollock streets
Where Snow White sleeps among the silent dwarfs
The fleet drifts in on an angry tidal wave
Or on the vast salt deserts of America
Drifts of Johann Strauss
A boy first sought in Tucson Arizona
The withering weathers of
Melodic signs of Arabic adventure
Of polytonic breezes gathering in the gathering winds
Mysterious Billy Smith a fantastic trigger
Of a plush palace shimmering velvet red
The cherrywood romances of rainy cobblestones
A dark trance
In the trembling afternoon

XXI

On the green a white boy goes
We may read about all those radio waves
And he walks. Three ciphers and a faint fakir
For the fey Saint's parade   Today
No   One   Two   Three   Four   Today
Under a sky of burnt umber we bumble to
Forget   Bring the green boy white ways
As so we all must in the green jungle
Winds flip down the dark path of breath
The mien florist's to buy green nosegays
Passage   the treasure   Gomangani
I thought about all those radio waves
Keats was a baiter of bears
Who died of lust   (You lie!   You lie!)
And the wind goes there

XXII

Go fly a kite he writes
Who cannot escape his own blue hair
who storms to the big earth and is not absent-minded
& Who dumbly begs a key   & who cannot pay his way
Racing down the blue lugubrious rainway
day brakes and night is a quick pick-me-up
Rain is a wet high harried face
To walk is wet hurried high safe and game
Tiny bugs flit from pool to field and light on every bulb

Whose backs hide doors down round wind-tunnels
He is an umbrella. . . .
Many things are current
Simple night houses rain
Standing pat in the breathless blue air.

XXIII

On the 15th day of November in the year of the motorcar
Between Oologah and Pawnee
A hand is writing these lines
In a roomful of smoky man names burnished dull black
Southwest, lost doubloons rest, no comforts drift
On dream smoke down the sooted fog ravine
In a terrible Ozark storm the Tundra vine
Blood ran like muddy inspiration: Walks he in around anyway
The slight film has gone to gray-green children
And seeming wide night. Now night
Is a big drink of waterbugs   Then were we so fragile
Honey scorched our lips
On the 15th day of November in the year of the motorcar
Between Oologah and Pawnee

XXV

Mud on the first day (night, rather
I was thinking of Bernard Shaw, of sweet May Morris
Do you want me to take off my dress?
Some Poems!
the aeroplane waiting to take you on your first
getting used to using each other

Cowboys!   and banging on my sorrow, with books
The Asiatics
believed in tree spirits, a tall oak, swans gone in the rain,
a postcard of Juan Gris   not a word
Fell on the floor   how strange   to be gone in a minute
I came to you by bus   to be special for us
The bellboy   letters   a key   then to hear from an old stranger
The Gift: they will reside in Houston following the Grand Canyon.

XXVI

ONE SONNET FOR DICK

This excitement to be all of night, Henry!
Elvis Peering-Eye danced with Carol Clifford, high,
Contrived whose leaping herb edifies Kant! I'll bust!
Smile! "Got rye in this'n?"
Widow Dan sold an eye t'meander an X. Whee! Yum!
Pedant tore her bed! Tune, hot! Full cat saith why foo?
"Tune hot full cat?" "No! nexus neck ink!
All moron (on) while "weighed in fur" pal! "Ah'm Sun!"
Dayday came to get her daddy. "Daddy,"
Saith I to Dick in the verge, (In the Verge!)
And "gee" say I, "Easter" "fur" "few tears" "Dick!"
My Carol now a Museum! "O, Ma done fart!" "Less full
Cat," she said, "One's there!" "Now cheese, ey?"
"Full cat wilted, bought ya a pup!" "So, nose excitement?"

XXVII

Andy Butt was drunk in the Parthenon
Bar. If only the Greeks were a band-
Aid, he thought. Then my woe would not flow
O'er the land. He considered his honeydew
Hand. "O woe, woe!" saith Andrew, "a fruit
In my hand may suffice to convey me to Greece,
But I must have envy to live! A grasshopper,
George, if you please!" The bartender sees
That our Andrew's awash on the sofa
Of wide melancholy. His wound he refurbishes
Stealthily shifty-eyed over the runes. "Your
Trolleycar, sir," 's said to Andy, "you bloody
Well emptied the Parthenon!" "A fruitful vista
This Our South," laughs Andrew to his Pa,
But his rough woe slithers o'er the Land.

XXVIII

to gentle, pleasant strains
just homely enough
to be beautiful
in the dark neighborhoods of my own sad youth
i fall in love.   once
seven thousand feet over one green schoolboy summer
i dug two hundred graves,
laughing, "Put away your books! Who shall speak of us
when we are gone? Let them wear scarves

in the once a day snow, crying in the kitchen
of my heart!" O my love, I will weep a less bitter truth,
till other times, making a minor repair,
a breath of cool rain in those streets
clinging together with slightly detached air.

XXIX

Now she guards her chalice in a temple of fear
Calm before a storm. Yet your brooding eyes
Or acquiescence soon cease to be answers.
And your soft, dark hair, a means of speaking
Becomes too much to bear. Sometimes,
In a rare, unconscious moment,
Alone this sudden darkness in a toybox
Christine's classic beauty, Okinawa
To Laugh (Autumn gone, and Spring a long way
Off)   is loving you
When need exceeds means,
I read the Evening World / the sports,
The funnies, the vital statistics, the news:
Okinawa was a John Wayne movie to me.

XXX

Into the closed air of the slow
Now she guards her chalice in a temple of fear
Each tree stands alone in stillness
to gentle, pleasant strains
Dear Marge, hello. It is 5:15 a.m.
Andy Butt was drunk in the Parthenon

Harum-scarum haze on the Pollock streets
This excitement to be all of night, Henry!
Ah, Bernie, to think of you alone, suffering
It is such a good thing to be in love with you
On the green a white boy goes
He's braver than I, brother
Many things are current, and of these the least are
  not always children
On the 15th day of November in the year of the motorcar

XXXI

And then one morning to waken perfect-faced
To the big promise of emptiness
In a terrible Ozark storm
Pleasing John Greenleaf Whittier!
Speckled marble bangs against his soiled green feet
And each sleeping son is broke-backed and dumb
In fever and sleep processional
Voyages harass the graver
And grope underneath the most serious labor
Darius feared the boats. Meanwhile
John Greenleaf Whittier was writing. Meanwhile
Grandma thought wistfully of international sock fame
Down the John G. Whittier Railroad Road
In the morning sea mouth

XXXII

The blue day! In the air winds dance
Now our own children are strangled down in the bubbling
  quadrangle.
To thicken! He felt his head
Returning past the houses he passed
"Goodbye, Bernie!"   "Goodbye, Carol!"   "Goodbye, Marge!"
Davy Crockett was nothing like Jesse James
A farmer drove up on a tractor
He said he was puzzled by the meaning exactly of "block."
The blue day! Where else can we go
To escape from our tedious homes, and perhaps recapture
  the past?
Now our own children are returning past the houses
I sit at my dust-patterned desk littered with four month
  dust
The air beginning to thicken
In the square, on the farm, in my white block hair

XXXIII

Où sont les neiges des neiges?
The most elegant present I could get.
The older children weep among the flowers.
They believe this. Their laughter feeds the need
Like a juggler. Ten weeks pregnant. Who
Believes this? It is your love
Must feed the dancing snow, Mary
Shelley "created" Frankenstein. It doesn't
matter, though. The shortage of available materials
Shatters my zest with festivity, one
Trembling afternoon—night—the dark trance
Up rainy cobblestones   bottle half empty
Full throttle   mired
In the petty frustrations of off-white sheets

XXXIV

Time flies by like a great whale
And I find my hand grows stale at the throttle
Of my many faceted and fake appearance
Who bucks and spouts by detour under the sheets
Hollow portals of solid appearance
Movies are poems, a holy bible, the great mother to us
People go by in the fragrant day
Accelerate softly my blood
But blood is still blood and tall as a mountain blood
Behind me green rubber grows, feet walk
In wet water, and dusty heads grow wide
Padré, Father, or fat old man, as you will,
I am afraid to succeed, afraid to fail
Tell me now, again, who I am

XXXV

You can make this swooped transition on your lips
Go to the sea, the lake, the tree
And the dog days come
Your head spins when the old bull rushes
Back in the airy daylight, he was not a midget
And preferred to be known as a stunt-man.
His stand-in was named Herman, but came rarely.
Why do you begin to yawn so soon, who seemed
So hard, feather-bitten   back in the airy daylight
Put away your hair. The black heart beside the 15 pieces
    of glass
Spins when the old bull rushes. The words say I LOVE YOU
Go to the sea, the lake, the tree
Glistering, bristling, cozening whatever disguises

XXXVI

AFTER FRANK O'HARA

It's 8:54 a.m. in Brooklyn it's the 28th of July and
it's probably 8:54 in Manhattan but I'm
in Brooklyn I'm eating English muffins and drinking
pepsi and I'm thinking of how Brooklyn is New
York city too how odd I usually think of it as
something all its own like Bellows Falls like Little
Chute like Uijongbu
I never thought on the Williams-
burg bridge I'd come so much to Brooklyn
just to see lawyers and cops who don't even carry
guns taking my wife away and bringing her back
No
and I never thought Dick would be back at Gude's
beard shaved off long hair cut and Carol reading
his books when we were playing cribbage and
watching the sun come up over the Navy Yard
across the river
I think I was thinking when I was
ahead I'd be somewhere like Perry street erudite
dazzling slim and badly loved
contemplating my new book of poems
to be printed in simple type on old brown paper
feminine marvelous and tough

XXXVII

It is night. You are asleep. And beautiful tears
Have blossomed in my eyes. Guillaume Apollinaire is dead.
The big green day today is singing to itself
A vast orange library of dreams, dreams
Dressed in newspaper, wan as pale thighs
Making vast apple strides towards "The Poems."
"The Poems" is not a dream. It is night. You
Are asleep. Vast orange libraries of dreams
Stir inside "The Poems." On the dirt-covered ground
Crystal tears drench the ground. Vast orange dreams
Are unclenched. It is night. Songs have blossomed
In the pale crystal library of tears. You
Are asleep. A lovely light is singing to itself,
In "The Poems," in my eyes, in the line, "Guillaume
    Apollinaire is dead."

XXXVIII

Sleep half sleep half silence and with reasons
For you I starred in the movie
Made on the site
Of Benedict Arnold's triumph, Ticonderoga, and
I shall increase from this
As I am a cowboy and you imaginary
Ripeness begins corrupting every tree
Each strong morning   A man signs a shovel
And so he digs   It hurts   and so

We get our feet wet in air   we love our lineage
Ourselves   Music, salve, pills, kleenex, lunch
And the promise never to truckle   A man
Breaks his arm and so he sleeps   he digs
In sleep half silence and with reason

Mess Occupations

AFTER MICHAUX

A few rape men or kill coons so I bat them!
Daughter prefers to lay 'em on a log and tear their hair.
    Moaning Jimmy bats her!
"Ill yeah!" da junky says. "I aint as fast no more,
    I'll rent a lot in a cemetree."   He'll recite it
    two times scary sunday O sea-daisy o'er a shade!
Au revoir, scene!
She had a great toe!
She-tail's raggy, too!
Jelly bend over put 'im on too!
She laid a crab!
Jelly him sure later! Jelly-ass ails are tough!
She lays all his jelly on him!
Eeeeeeoooooww!! La Vie!
Her lay races is out here, she comes on, I'm on her, I'll
fart in one ear! "Jelly, sir?" "Shall I raise him yet?"
Long-toed we dance on where Shit-toe can see ten blue men
lickin' ten new partners and the sucker's son!
"Mating, Madame, can whip you up up!
My Jimmy's so small he wiggles plum moans! Ladies shimmy
at Jimmy in waves

XL

Wan as pale thighs making apple belly strides
In the morning she wakes up, and she is "in love."
One red finger sports a gold finger-gripper
Curled to honor *La Pluie*, by Max Jacob. Max Jacob,
When I lie down to love you, I am one hundred times more
A ghost! My dreams of love have haunted you for years
More than six-pointed key olive shame. Not this day
Shall my pale apple dreams know my dream "English
    muffins, broken arm"
Nor my dream where the George Gordon gauge reads, "a
Syntactical error, Try Again!" Gosh, I gulp to be here
In my skin, writing, *The Dwarf of Ticonderoga.* Icy girls
finger thighs bellies apples in my dream the big gunfire
    sequence
For the Jay Kenneth Koch movie, *Phooey!* I recall
My Aunt Annie and begin.

XLI

banging around in a cigarette   she isn't "in love"
my dream a drink with Ira Hayes we discuss the code of
    the west
my hands make love to my body when my arms are around you
you never tell me your name
and I am forced to write "belly" when I mean "love"
Au revoir, scene!
I waken, read, write long letters and
wander restlessly when leaves are blowing
my dream a crumpled horn
in advance of the broken arm
she murmurs of signs to her fingers
weeps in the morning to waken so shackled with love
Not me. I like to beat people up.
My dream a white tree

XLII

She murmurs of signs to her fingers
Not this day
Breaks his arm and so he sleeps   he digs
Dressed in newspaper, wan as pale thighs
beard shaved off long hair cut and Carol reading
Put away your hair. The black heart beside the 15 pieces
    of glass
Of my many faceted and fake appearance
The most elegant present I could get!
"Goodbye, Bernie!"   "Goodbye, Carol!"   "Goodbye,
    Marge!"
Speckled marble bangs against his soiled green feet
And seeming wide night. Now night
Where Snow White sleeps amongst the silent dwarfs
Drifts of Johann Strauss
It is 5:15 a.m.   Dear Marge, hello.

XLIII

in my paintings for they are present
Dreams, aspirations of presence! And he walks
Wed to wakefulness, night which is not death
Rivers of annoyance undermine the arrangements
We remove a hand . . .
washed by Joe's throbbing hands. 'Today
itself "a signal." She
is introspection.
Each tree stands alone in stillness
Scanning the long selves of the shore.
In Joe Brainard's collage, there is no such thing
as a breakdown.
Trains go by, and they *are* trains. He hears the feet of the men
Racing to beg him to wait

XLIV

The withered leaves fly higher than dolls can see
A watchdog barks in the night
Joyful ants nest in the roof of my tree
There is only off-white mescalin to be had
Anne is writing poems to me and worrying about "making it"
and Ron is writing poems and worrying about "making it"
and Pat is worrying but not working on anything
and Gude is worrying about his sex life
It is 1959, and I am waiting for the mail
Who cares about Tuesday (Jacques Louis David normalcy day)?
Boston beat New York three to one. It could have been
Carolyn. Providence is as close to Montana as Tulsa.
He buckles on his gun, the one Steve left him:
His stand-in was named Herman, but came rarely

XLV

What thwarts this fear I love
to hear it creak upon this shore
of the trackless room;   the sea, night, lilacs
all getting ambiguous
Who dreams on the black colonnade
Casually tossed off as well
Are dead after all (and who falters?)
Everything turns into writing
I strain to gather my absurdities into a symbol
Every day my bridge
They basted his caption on top of the fat sheriff, "The Pig."
Some "others" were dormants: More water went under the dam.
What excitement to think of her returning, over the colonnade,
over the tall steppes, warm hands guiding his eyes to hers

XLVI

LINES FOR LAUREN OWEN

Harum-scarum haze on the Pollock streets
The fleet drifts in on an angry tidal wave
Drifts of Johann Strauss
The withering weather of
Of polytonic breezes gathering in the gathering winds
Of a plush palace shimmering velvet red
In the trembling afternoon
A dark trance
The cherrywood romances of rainy cobblestones
Mysterious Billy Smith a fantastic trigger
Melodic signs of Arabic adventure
A boy first sought in Tucson Arizona
Or on the vast salt deserts of America
Where Snow White sleeps among the silent dwarfs

XLVII

gray his head goes   his feet green
No lady dream around in any bad exposure
"no pipe dream, sir. She would be the dragon
Head, dapple green of mien. must be vacated
in favor of double-clutching, and sleep,
seldom, though deep. We savor its sodden dungheap flavor
on our creep toward the rational. William Bonney
buried his daddy and killed a many. Benito Mussolini
proved a defective, but Ezra Pound came down, came

down and went. And so, Carol, remember,
We are each free to shed big crystal tears on
The dirt-covered ground, tied together only
By white clouds and some mud we can find, if we try,
In the darksome orange shadows of the big blue swamp

XLVIII

Francis Marion nudges himself gently into the big blue sky
The farm was his family farm
On the real farm
                    I understood "The Poems."
The dust fissure drains the gay dance
Home returning on the blue winds of dust.
A farmer rides a tractor. It is a block
To swallow. Thus a man lives by his tooth.
Meaning strides through these poems just as it strides
Through me! When I traipse on my spunk, I get
Wan! Traipse on my spunk and I get wan, too!
    Francis Marion
Muscles down in tooth-clenched strides toward
The effort regulator: His piercing pince-nez
Some dim frieze in "The Poems" and these go on without me

XLIX

Joyful ants nest on the roof of my tree
Crystal tears wed to wakefulness
My dream a crumpled horn
Ripeness begins in advance of the broken arm
The black heart two times scary Sunday

Pale thighs making apple belly strides
And he walks. Beside the fifteen pieces of glass
A postcard of Juan Gris
Vast orange dreams wed to wakefulness
Swans gone in the rain came down, came down and went
Warm hands corrupting every tree
Guiding his eyes to her or a shade
Ripeness begins   My dream a crumpled horn
Fifteen pieces of glass on the roof of my tree

L

I like to beat people up
absence of passion, principles, love. She murmurs
What just popped into my eye was a fiend's umbrella
and if you should come and pinch me now
as I go out for coffee
. . . as I was saying winter of 18 lumps
Days produce life locations to banish 7 up
Nomads, my babies, where are you? Life's
My dream which is gunfire in my poem
Orange cavities of dreams stir inside "The Poems"
Whatever is going to happen is already happening
Some people prefer "the interior monologue"
I like to beat people up

LI

Summer so histrionic, marvelous dirty days
is not genuine   it shines forth from the faces
littered with soup, cigarette butts, the heavy
is a correspondent   the innocence of childhood
sadness graying the faces of virgins aching
and everything comes before their eyes
to be fucked, we fondle their snatches but they
that the angels have supereminent wisdom is shown
they weep and get solemn etcetera
from thought   for all things come to them gratuitously
by their speech   it flows directly and spontaneously
and O I am afraid! but later they'll be eyeing the butts of the
    studs
in the street rain flushing the gutters bringing from Memphis
Gus Cannon gulping, "I called myself Banjo Joe!"

LII

FOR RICHARD WHITE

It is a human universe: & I
is a correspondent   The innocence of childhood
is not genuine   it shines forth from the faces
The poem upon the page is as massive as Anne's thighs
Belly to hot belly we have laid
                                        baffling combustions
are everywhere   graying the faces of virgins
aching to be fucked   we fondle their snatches
and O, I am afraid!   The poem upon the page
will not kneel   for everything comes to it

gratuitously   like Gertrude Stein to Radcliffe
Gus Cannon to say "I called myself Banjo Joe!"
O wet kisses, death on earth, lovely fucking in the poem
    upon the page,
you have kept up with the times, and I am glad!

LIII

The poem upon the page is as massive as
Anne's thighs   belly to hot belly we have laid
Serene beneath feverous folds, flashed cool
in our white heat   hungered   and tasted   and
Gone to the movies   baffling combustions
are everywhere!   like Gertrude Stein at Radcliffe,
Patsy Padgett replete with teen-age belly!   every-
one's suddenly pregnant and no one is glad!
O wet kisses, the poem upon the page
Can tell you about teeth you've never dreamed
Could bite, nor be such reassurance! Babies are not
Like Word Origins and cribbage boards   or dreams
of correspondence!   Fucking is so very lovely
Who can say no to it later?

LV

Grace to be born
and live as variously
as possible
FRANK O'HARA

Grace to be born and live as variously as possible
White boats   green banks   black dust   atremble
Massive as Anne's thighs upon the page
I rage in a blue shirt at a brown desk in a
Bright room sustained by a bellyful of pills
"The Poems" is not a dream   for all things come to them
Gratuitously   In quick New York we imagine the blue Charles
Patsy awakens in heat and ready to squabble
No Poems she demands in a blanket command   belly
To hot belly we have laid   serenely white
Only my sweating pores are true in the empty night
Baffling combustions are everywhere!   we hunger and taste
And go to the movies   then run home drenched in flame
To the grace of the make-believe bed

LVI

banging around in a cigarette   she isn't "in love"
She murmurs of signs to her fingers
in my paintings for they are present
The withered leaves fly higher than dolls can see
What thwarts this fear I love
Mud on the first day (night, rather
gray his head goes   his feet green
Francis Marion nudges himself gently in the big blue sky
Joyful ants nest on the roof of my tree

I like to beat people up.
Summer so histrionic, marvelous dirty days
It is a human universe: & I
sings like Casals in furtive dark July; Out we go
to the looney movie   to the make-believe bed

LVII

Patsy awakens in heat and ready to squabble
In a bright room sustained by a bellyful of pills
One's suddenly pregnant and no one is glad!
Aching to be fucked we fondle their snatches
That the angels have supereminent wisdom is shown
Days produce life locations to banish 7 Up
A postcard of Juan Gris
To swallow. Thus a man lives by his tooth.
Buried his daddy and killed a many. Benito Mussolini
The Asiatics
Everything turns into writing
And Gude is worrying about his sex life
Each tree is introspection
The most elegant present I could get

LIX

In Joe Brainard's collage its white arrow
does not point to William Carlos Williams.
He is not in it, the hungry dead doctor.
What is in it is sixteen ripped pictures
Of Marilyn Monroe, her white teeth white-
washed by Joe's throbbing hands. "Today

I am truly horribly upset because Marilyn
Monroe died, so I went to a matinee B-movie
and ate King Korn popcorn," he wrote in his
Diary. The black heart beside the fifteen pieces
of glass in Joe Brainard's collage
takes the eye away from the gray words,
Doctor, but they say "I LOVE YOU"
and the sonnet is not dead.

LX

old prophets   Help me to believe
New York!   sacerdotal   drink it take a pill
Blocks of blooming winter.   Patricia was a
bed   Patsy   gone   The best fighter in Troy
Be bride and groom and priest: in pajamas
Sweet girls will bring you candied apples!
Drummer-boys and Choo-Choos will astound you!
Areté   I   thus I   Again I   I
An Organ-Grinder's monkey does his dance.
Ted   Ron   Dick   Didactic   un-melodic
Roisterers here assembled shatter my zest
Berrigan   secretly   HEKTOR   GAME ETC.
More books!   Rilke   Stevens   Pound   Auden
    & Frank
Some kind of Bowery Santa Clauses   I wonder
Who am about to die   the necessary lies

LXI

How sweet the downward sweep of your prickly thighs
as you lope across the trails and bosky dells
defying natural law, saying, "Go Fuck Yourselves,
You Motherfuckers!" You return me to Big Bill Broonzy
and Guillaume Apollinaire and when you devour your young,
the natural philosophy of love,
I am moved as only I am moved by the singing of the
    Stabat Mater at Sunday Mass.
How succulent your flesh sometimes so tired
from losing its daily battles with its dead! All
this and the thought that you go to the bathroom
fills me with love for you, makes me love you even more than
    the dirt
in the crevices in my window
and the rust on the bolt in my door
in terms I contrived as a boy, such as
"making it"   "fuck them"   and
"I know you have something to tell me."

LXIV

Is there room in the room that you room in?
fucked til 7 now she's late to work and I'm
18 so why are my hands shaking I should know better
Stronger than alcohol, more great than song
O let me burst, and I be lost at sea!
and I fall on my knees then, womanly.
to breathe an old woman slop oatmeal
Why can't I read French? I don't know why can't you?
The taste of such delicate thoughts

Never bring the dawn.
To cover the tracks
of "The Hammer."
Something there is is benzedrine in bed:
Bring me red demented rooms,
warm and delicate words

LXV

Dreams, aspirations of presence! Innocence gleaned,
annealed! The world in its mysteries are explained,
and the struggles of babies congeal. A hard core is formed.
Today I thought about all those radio waves
He eats of the fruits of the great Speckle bird,
Pissing on the grass!
I too am reading the technical journals,
Rivers of annoyance undermine the arrangements
Someone said "Blake-blues" and someone else "pill-head"
Meaning bloodhounds.
Washed by Joe's throbbing hands
She is introspection.
It is a Chinese signal.
There is no such thing as a breakdown

LXVI

it was summer. We were there. And THERE WAS NO
MONEY you are like . . .
skyscrapers veering away
a B-29 plunging to Ploesti
sailboat scudding thru quivering seas

trembling velvet red in the shimmering afternoon
darkness of sea
The sea which is cool and green
The sea which is dark, cool, and green
I am closing my window. Tears silence the wind.
"they'll pick us off like sittin' ducks"
Sundown. Manifesto. Color and cognizance.
Then to cleave to a cast-off emotion,
(clarity! clarity!) a semblance of motion, omniscience

LXVII

(clarity! clarity!) a semblance of motion, omniscience.
There is no such thing as a breakdown
To cover the tracks of "The Hammer"   (the morning sky
gets blue and red and I get worried about
mountains of mounting pressure
and the rust on the bolt in my door
Some kind of Bowery Santa Clauses   I wonder
down the secret streets of Roaring Gap
A glass of chocolate milk, head of lettuce, dark-
Bearden is dead. Chris is dead. Jacques Villon is dead.
Patsy awakens in heat and ready to squabble
I wonder if people talk about me *secretly?* I wonder if I'm
fooling myself
about pills? I wonder what's in the icebox? out we go
to the looney movie   and the grace of the make-believe bed

LXVIII

I am closing my window. Tears silence the wind.
and the rust on the bolt in my door
Mud on the first day (night, rather
littered with soup, cigarette butts, the heavy
getting used to using each other
my dream a drink with Ira Hayes we discuss the code of the west
I think I was thinking when I was ahead
To the big promise of emptiness
This excitement to be all of night, Henry!
Three ciphers and a faint fakir. And he walks.
White lake trembles down to green goings on
Of the interminably frolicsome gushing summer showers
Everything turning in this light to stones
Which owe their presence to our sleeping hands

LXX

AFTER ARTHUR RIMBAUD

Sweeter than sour apples flesh to boys
The brine of brackish water pierced my hulk
Cleansing me of rot-gut wine and puke
Sweeping away my anchor in its swell
And since then I've been bathing in the poem
Of the star-steeped milky flowing mystic sea
Devouring great sweeps of azure green and
Watching flotsam, dead men, float by me
Where, dyeing all the blue, the maddened flames
And stately rhythms of the sun, stronger
Than alcohol, more great than song,

Fermented the bright red bitterness of love
I've seen skies split with light, and night,
And surfs, currents, waterspouts; I know
What evening means, and doves, and I have seen
What other men sometimes have thought they've seen

LXXI

"I know what evening means, and doves, and I have seen
What other men sometimes have thought they've seen:"
(to cleave to a cast-off emotion—Clarity! Clarity!)
my dream a drink with Richard Gallup we discuss the code
of the west   of the interminably frolicsome
gushing summer showers   getting used to "I am closing
my window."   my dream a drink with Henry Miller
too soon for the broken arm.   Hands point to a dim frieze
in the dark night.   Wind giving presence to fragments.
Shall it be male or female in the tub?
Barrel-assing chevrolets grow bold. I summon to myself
"The Asiatic"   (and grawk go under, and grackle disappear,)
Sundown. Manifesto. Color and cognizance.
And to cleave to a semblance of motion. Omniscience

LXXII

A SONNET FOR DICK GALLUP
/ JULY 1963

The logic of grammar is not genuine   it shines forth
From The Boats   We fondle the snatches of virgins
     aching to be fucked
And O, I am afraid!   Our love has red in it   and
I become finicky as in an abstraction!

(. . . but lately
I'm always lethargic . . .   the last heavy sweetness
through the wine . . .)
Who dwells alone
Except at night
(. . . basted the shackles the temporal music the spit)
Southwest lost doubloons rest, no comforts drift on
dream smoke
(my dream   the big earth)
On the green a white boy goes   to not
Forget   Released by night (which is not to imply
Clarity   The logic is not The Boats   and O, I am not alone

LXXIII

Dear Ron: Keats was a baiter of bears   etc.
Tenseness, but strength, outward   And the green
flinging currents into pouring streams   The "Jeunes filles"
so rare   Today I think about all those radio waves
a slow going down of the Morning Land
the great Speckle bird at last extinct   (a reference
to Herman Melville)   at heart we are infinite, we are
ethereal, we are weird!   Each tree stands alone in stillness.
Your head spins when the old bull rushes   (Back in the city
He was not a midget, and preferred to be known as a stuntman)
Gosh, I gulp to be here in my skin! What thwarts this fear
I love   Everything turns into writing (and who falters)
I LIKE TO BEAT PEOPLE UP!!!   (absence of principles, passion
) love.   White boats   Green banks   Grace to be born and live

LXXIV

The academy
of the future
is opening its doors
JOHN ASHBERY

The academy of the future is opening its doors
my dream a crumpled horn
Under the blue sky the big earth is floating into "The Poems."
"A fruitful vista, this, our South," laughs Andrew to his Pa.
But his rough woe slithers o'er the land.
Ford Madox Ford is not a dream. The farm
was the family farm. On the real farm
I understood "The Poems."
                    Red-faced and romping in the wind, I, too,
am reading the technical journals. The only travelled sea
that I still dream of
is a cold black pond, where once
on a fragrant evening fraught with sadness
I launched a boat frail as a butterfly

LXXV

Seurat and Juan Gris combine this season
to outline Central Park in geometric
trillion pointed bright red-brown and green-gold
blocks of blooming winter. Trees stand stark-
naked guarding bridal paths like Bowery
Santa Clauses keeping Christmas safe each city block.
Thus I, red faced and romping in the wind
Whirl thru mad Manhattan dressed in books
looking for today with tail-pin. I

never place it right, never win. It
doesn't matter, though. The cooling wind keeps blow-
ing and my poems are coming.
Except at night. Then
I walk out in the bleak village and look for you

LXXVI

I wake up back aching from soft bed Pat
gone to work Ron to class (I
never heard a sound) it's my birthday. I put on
birthday pants birthday shirt go to ADAM'S buy a
pepsi for breakfast come home drink it take a pill
I'm high. I do three Greek lessons
to make up for cutting class. I read birthday book
(from Joe) on Juan Gris real name José Vittoriano
Gonzáles stop in the middle read all
my poems gloat a little over new ballad quickly skip old
sonnets imitations of Shakespeare. Back to books. I read
poems by Auden Spenser Pound Stevens and Frank O'Hara.
    I hate books.
            I wonder if Jan or Helen or Babe
ever think about me. I wonder if Dave Bearden still
dislikes me. I wonder if people talk about me
secretly. I wonder if I'm too old. I wonder if I'm fooling
myself about pills. I wonder what's in the icebox. I wonder
if Ron or Pat bought any toilet paper this morning

LXXVII

"DEAR CHRIS

it is 3:17 a.m. in New York city, yes, it is
1962, it is the year of parrot fever. In
Brandenburg, and by the granite gates, the
old come-all-ye's streel into the streets. Yes, it is now,
the season of delight. I am writing to you to say that
I have gone mad. Now I am sowing the seeds which shall,
when ripe, master the day, and
portion out the night. Be watching for me when blood
flows down the streets. Pineapples are a sign
that I am coming. My darling, it is nearly time. Dress
the snowman in the Easter sonnet we made for him
when scissors were in style. For now, goodbye, and
all my love,
          The Snake."

LXXVIII

Too many fucking mosquitoes under the blazing sun
out in the stinking alley behind my desk!   too many
lovely delicious behinds fertilizing the park! the logic
of childhood is not genuine   it shines forth
so rare
          Dear Ron: Keats was a baiter of bears who died
of lust! Today I think about all those radio waves
The academy of my dreams is opening its doors
Seurat and Juan Gris combine this season

Except at night!

Then I walk out in the bleak village
in my dreams, for they are present! I wake up
aching from soft bed   Back to books. It is 3:17 a.m. in
New York city
The Pure No Nonsense: and all day "Perceval! Perceval!"

LXXX

How strange to be gone in a minute
Bearden is dead   Gallup is dead   Margie is dead
Patsy awakens in heat and ready to squabble
Dear Chris, hello. It is 5:15 a.m.
I rage in a blue shirt, at a brown desk, in
A bright room, sustained by the darkness outside and
A cast-off emotion. A hard core is "formed"
That the angels have supereminent wisdom is shown
"He Shot Me" was once my favorite poem
Speckled marble makes my eyes ache as I rest on
The only major statement in New York city   Louis Sullivan
is dead   whose grief I would most assuage
"He Shot Me" is still my favorite poem, and
"I Don't See Any Anchor Tied To Your Ass"

LXXXI

Musick strides through these poems
just as it strides through me! The red block
Dream of Hans Hofmann keeps going away and
Coming back to me. He is not "The Poems."
(my dream a drink with Lonnie Johnson we

discuss the code of the west)

How strange to be gone

in a minute!

too soon for the broken arm. Ripeness begins corrupting every tree

Each strong morning   in air we get our feet wet

(my dream

a crumpled horn)   it hurts.   Huddie Ledbetter is dead

whose griefs I would most assuage   Sing I must   And with Musick I must rage

Against those whose griefs I would most assuage

(my dream

"DEAR CHRIS, hello. It is 3:17 a.m.

LXXXII

my dream a drink with Lonnie Johnson we discuss the code of the west

The red block dream of Hans Hofmann keeps going away and coming back to me

my dream a crumpled horn

my dream DEAR CHRIS, hello. It is 5:15 a.m.

The academy of my dreams is opening its doors

Ford Madox Ford is not a dream.

The only travelled sea that I still dream of is a cold black pond where once on a fragrant evening fraught with sadness

I launched a boat frail as a butterfly

Southwest lost doubloons rest, no comforts drift on dream smoke down the sooted fog ravine

My dream a drink with Richard Gallup we discuss the code of the west

my dream a drink with Henry Miller

"The Poems" is not a dream.
Vast orange dreams wed to wakefulness: icy girls finger thighs
    bellies apples in my dream the big gunfire sequence for
    the Jay Kenneth Koch movie, *Phooey!*
My dream a drink with Ira Hayes we discuss the code of the west

LXXXIII

Woman is singing the song and summer
Only to others, meaning poems. Because everything
Sorry about West Point. But where else was one to go,
Southwest lost doubloons rest, no comforts drift on dream smoke
Against whose griefs I would most assuage
(A cast-off emotion) A hard core is "formed."
Musick strides through these poems just as it strides thru me
my dream a drink with Lonnie Johnson we discuss the code
    of the west
After Ticonderoga.   Beware of Benjamin Franklin, he is
    totally lacking in grace
What else. Because he tended to think of truth as "The King's
    Birthday List"
This is called "Black Nausea" by seers.
My dream DEAR CHRIS hello. It is 3:17 a.m.
Your name is now a household name, as is mine. And in any case,
although I failed, now we need never be rivals

LXXXIV

Dear Ron: hello. Your name is now a household name,
As is mine. We, too, suffer black spells. This is called
"Black Nausea" by seers, only to others, meaning poems.

In every way now we are equal. Except one.
Ford Madox Ford is not a dream.   (my dream a drink
with Henry Miller) we discuss the code of the west.
He is not "The Poems."
                                        "He Shot Me" was once my favorite
Cast-off emotion. Now I rage in a blue shirt at a brown desk
In a bright room. In Tulsa Chris has said goodbye to Bernie.
I never beat people up. The academy of my dreams
is opening its doors / a fat black woman is singing a song and
Summer is the subject matter. Next to her his nose couldn't grow
Even if it does choke you up, and these marvelous tears
    keep appearing

LXXXV

They basted his caption on top of the fat sheriff, "The Pig."
Cowboys   and banging on my sorrow with books
No lady dream around in any bad exposure
The dust fissure drains the gay dance
Joyful ants nest in the roof of my tree
absence of passion, principles, love. She murmurs
is not genuine. it shines forth from the faces
And each sleeping son is broke-backed and dumb.
Davy Crockett was nothing like Jesse James
The most elegant present I could get!
But blood is still blood and tall as a mountain blood
Go to the sea, the lake, the tree
dazzling slim and badly loved
You are asleep. A lovely light is singing to itself

LXXXVII

Beware of Benjamin Franklin, he is totally lacking in grace
This is called "Black Nausea" by seers. (They basted his caption
on top of the fat sheriff)
                    These sonnets are a homage to
King Ubu.
Fasten your crimson garter around his servile heart
With which he pours forth interminably
The poem of these states   scanning the long selves of
the shore   and   "gift gift"
Great black rat packs were running amuck amidst the murk
of these states   Outside my room
These sonnets are a homage to myself
absence of passion, principles, love
The most elegant present I could get!   (This is called
"Black Nausea" by seers)

LXXXVIII

A Final Sonnet

FOR CHRIS

How strange to be gone in a minute!   A man
Signs a shovel and so he digs   Everything
Turns into writing a name for a day
                    Someone
is having a birthday and someone is getting
married and someone is telling a joke   my dream
a white tree   I dream of the code of the west
But this rough magic I here abjure   and
When I have required some heavenly music   which even now
I do   to work mine end upon *their* senses

That this aery charm is for I'll break
My staff bury it certain fathoms in the earth
And deeper than did ever plummet sound
I'll drown my book.
It is 5:15 a.m. Dear Chris, hello.

Great Stories of the Chair

THE SECRET LIFE OF FORD MADOX FORD

1.

STOP STOP SIX

Livid sweet undies drawl
Elevate
So do we squeal sporty ritual

Once a great kiss sin tells
Dance is night

Later away training melodies dances rues
Latent traveler on light
Lays tense all day silky past far deportment
Says your songs tombs surely rail

You arrest my faculties, you person   knees descend
On her part
Like rain occurs missing the whole point so he tired

She would say her little ditty of soul yes
She would say that her circuitous panties descend their
        first voyage
Her rear less a dress

This I can't defeat   This stone slays me
I go and do that to her
Her lap opens kisses its tune foils this hurt
Dance of energy
They did bounce her

Her rule was grand it twists like a boulevard

2.
REELING MIDNIGHT

Impasses come, dear beasts
Who require these looney airs so long gone from you all
O all gone to one surly, rude, humiliated

Let's shovel out a song and dance   all knew it
Let's mosey past them fondled brutes

Shove a dream of it up our regular day devourings
I'll fondle you on home and hang a kiss on yours
Shall we raise our dead hams
(Her tranquil nose is a noble dancing vine)

Don't hurt it

Don't hit it either
Saying what's so damn sweet
I am on trains   they're all choo-choos
Ack! The Vampire! Some debut!
Lower your dress dammit!

In this tent I'll untrack or take down some undies

Anguish I'll sink thru key naps   a defense
To be learned one essential day

Like seals I'm indifferent

Eat a potato she said you sober All-American

3.

FAUNA TIME

Liquor troops in deshabillé from blondes a lonely song
Laming a lean m'sieu like a vessel
This man hates his aunt so he licks her feet
Laughing at her brilliant comas of goo

When addict comforts real
One sunk leper's more real

Lesions are early they fume on her
In her beastly sleep
Some Plague!   Heavens!   plagues offer
Loathsome murder   kill her for me
Says a weak hero completely wrong his meat leaping around

Liquor is her price when she sashays   she gouged me a long
        time with fins
Like in the movies
One man lassoed her leg's inner lotus
Laughing at the dumb blue aches so thick in her metal disc passage
Slipping her a harangue

She really has some rashes!
And her cheek hays me off!

Gruesome rash ate such sweet arms and legs;
Who gashed her liver?
Leprosy ate her mouth turning into her news

4.

ON HIS OWN

I'm not saying
She's a creep
A wreck
Loving you phew hooray its fini
The reef 's an injun bum
Lewd
Keep on O playful
One cent exploding cigar
Count the ends toot the lonely ear

Open the door let me in
The orbs say no
Lets sashay up the scene
And strangle the beans
A sick kid passed on a prairie new meat

The sore oozes vomit up in the ear shut the drum
Shut the earache
Mah mumbles mope an' dumplin
Unless she tells me " 's too dumb"
The jello ouch I love may shoot all the martinis

My main ruse is in the mope
When the pill before we bleat lets us glow

The song blurs soda pop yea boo fah!
Uncle Nakee's dead again

We mash and detash geese and their mothers
Untie the russkies nookies from their loins
Go boot them in the lung my turn
Sell out the taint Oologah the stinky-poo undies my cookie
    ain't on time

Tear down your undies let me see some lunch

5.

THE DANCE OF THE BROKEN BOMB

It's a cute tune possibly by Camus
The gentle Brigadoon stands here
He sends his years to her
To pass the two birds ta-ta you pass them
To be complete just kiss him and you swish through the air
    six seconds ago
To attempt your bra must come off poor Marie
Never "poor"
Enjoy each other
You'll never walk alone you'll pee indoors
I peed Saturday
You're the best of them all   men are such beasts they want you
He'll caress it from time to time
The best one is in the parlor you sew all night poor neighbor
    unhand her
The airplane arrives in the bedroom
The best one that you'll ever make up the air out of
Needling someone singing come on dish
Need a rescue try my Grandma
Put her on your knee desire more than her ear

The cloak of the monkey enchanted your blouses I ask for your
    hand
Then you pee. I have been with the sparrows
Whose side are you on, the sparrows?
You dolt!

6.

OWE

I'll yell at these men who pass
Hunks of shoe pass in the winter
You'll take a jaunt to Bali soon
May you part own a funny train
I love your legs the tops
Behind the pouring radio

One arm is Turhan Bey
The other one a soft knee a parrot
Orson came he loved my arms to show all of me

Don't hang up
A lovely "B"
18 francs sound of desoxyn

The number of times I loved you

All pass in front of the bush of truth
The true
Kills the goo

Up and down keep it down lend me some acorns encore
Here we are day I'm on you a long long way after my years
You too have killed someone

It kills you on the page

So shut up we sure learn age

A degenerate
Degenerate kiss you clean men kill at the chance

The looney facile gay are de rigeur today   I know it
Smell a party
A chevrolet my motto
I pour the dessert on the rear of the widow

I first poured some over the cold edge of the dice
C'est la vie you two-face

Three whores went forth
Don't be sloppy and mess with me I'll twist yr face you clod

Later I passed away
I never again played

In ambergris I occurred in the garden
I sewed a long core and made my time
I trotted off
My faces flouted the last glance at the "B" in the yard

7.
PUTTING AWAY

We'll mash your leman, plunk
Hey unclothe clinch soon den dance
You can kiss a pro seize your own degenerate now take some

Lick her prow Moan her foot all over
Your number is up turning and turning in the widening gyre
Same only more
The moon whops you head
Around come the tacky girls

Our dumb deaths flop inside our dainties
And our nose hurts
Lacunae oompah eye-tally
Hell, unpant
The roué soireé it lays you out (where?)

At home we play and grunt
And long for brunch
A long time gone ate and munched

Inside the svelte maison Samson and his hairs was there
One egg, rare
A brown icky drummer came at me

He puked on chumps who moaned its all unfair
Ate the beast with currants
The whole neighborhood blew their tops sicked the ape at me
I'll see you me rocket eight days passed away

Have fun in the lumber its long overdue
At home my tail grew
Lay slowly so phooey so sorry Great!
Climb on flail about pretty soon I'm coming (laughing)

Meanwhile

In a marsh they found a ton of sweat
Listen they laugh
They turn you don't say looks like her debut

They pass the rest dance in the mess Boom! they know It

8.
WE ARE JUNGLES

I'm a hero form of an eyelid act like you hate it
My hair refuses the nose of the muses
I danced on my tummy on land and I won't last, beat me!
Why? Well bless you, you impulsive ham, it's Yuletide!

Apache blows undone me   I'll wipe you up yestiddy
You are in these pants, you spin, you fuss, you scram
Now a lotus will appear, kill our deer
Ere I heave me in again!

Eyes of bats this is where I blubber on your safety pin
This homelife sicks us like wives & lovers, they want to be
    riven by us
This is where I left without you You didn't win

There are some words floating over these words like glue, to
    dissever your broken head my home
I address my disc if I'm here   Are you sick?   I am Goy
    I see   Do you?   (that's the breaks)
The day that you came on is words   Smile   Even the
    shoeshine is fearsome to you

It's through it's true; but all is not nothing as you say.
    This covers me.

GREAT STORIES OF THE CHAIR

Great Stories of the Chair

Morning flushes its gray light across where I collect a face, rimmed with brown hair, pierced with intellect. Sparking is pleasure, and parting is littered with soot, cigarette butts, these intimate incantations under the sheets. Let's take a sentimental journey, you said. This is the first time I've written in longhand in over ten years. Out we go, but now it is over a vivid machine crosses the fact of your head American Citizen dilemmas odd glory fanatic hands point to a din first glory then Other pressing the point up and down ice forms to help a machine begin. Old contacts touching looks baby sighs prepositions broken discussions sandwiches books everyone knows but forgets nights back. As usual however I go back to the white again light on up head falling down vivid scenes that last years and wrote this because of her. Does so. Her arrival telling me that he knew and saying that she was glad to see it, geniuses I tell you I was shocked! a tongue was saying The damage is already done i.e. She has been my friend now for some years though far away upstairs. Later glee pills light ambition a tonsillectomy greed throbbing risings under the table a girl brown hair lovely exercises sycamores growing across miles to this you. One thing comes to another in place of itself. And so we come together in this bed out of a finger gesture mouth gesture Other beginning again now growing to be a part of this.

Mother Cabrini

Baby sighs prepositions put the books back nights. As usual I
go back to the white again light on up had fallen down on a vivid little
scene last *year.* Wrote this because of HIM (does) arrival and Ron
telling me that he knew and saying he was glad to see it was very
shocking close the fire wine and only "I'm going to bed" outside, and
stood running on about his father borders on the absurd ah would you
remember the name of whomever hit it, thinking that a little about Dad
tho lusted, sex have some son we're in the church wedding but Ron, as we
rolled over the baby in the Western movie at the Palace Death of the one
could get conventional things, we did, yellow oozings brain & blood
a sacrosanct creation bit bite toothpick? a Portuguese on the phone and
and pardner I knew, and two for me (if I wanted *any*) oh she is square no
articulate no devout but uh I want to do it uh do want (it) which is
a small brick cottage a couple of years of Catullus, brother dog air if
you're describing my bookshelf. . . . Looking for Harry and I knew worms en
fold interesting things out in front ice-cream sandwich terrific speed
he said "Nothing" tried nothing a quivery sort of fellow rolls toward
sister mother sister the second sister that long silver hair Irish brogue
to the world. Candid roof the ditty about the stick because of "instruct-
ions". I respect that father and the heat goes off (away) you cool a pepsi
ok I do in to, off of, or on a table with a girl whom I recognize as
she must crawl continually through gunfire men logginess then noise
pills. And began smashing Ron in the theories especially against the
Arm no hum in that air a number of me's. They were cloth. It was a
night club, pill mind. In fact I think mornings. We walk I see Ron sitting
near a light bulb since sent away it needs oil zzzzzzzzzzz keeps us
warm trying to hit him with canes to score "marksman" (penis decline)
the white flat is in the air made up of mere shape. Suddenly someone

else came I con love for her. She was very shortly afterwards words. God's noises make no sense to me. "Seen the movie?" Ron asked but the condition: silence. Pull thin things in the house discover the emergency break the "yes". Turned from walking Tessie half-naked cloth pony from a fight the importance of the situation I can't stop

Tulsa Rose Gardens

Put the books back   the brown hair pierced the shower 40 below   the bugles call the powder where the light turn on again pleasure falling parting to go a light lady dark lady spy glasses littered with soot scenes years of writing this News shunted aside that's the penalty denial of lifelong release and these intimate incantations under the sheets that we know will go on. Rubbing the back of the neck line of teeth a tongue saying the damage is already done. A journey taken by hand over a period years arms legs learning what is yours in her and in her father clickety-clack no that was another father a crowd formed that night truly going into the earth near where one exercises the shine the awl the wheel hidden shoes ruined ghosts rallies . . . your absolute lovely attentions . . . lust plastered upon us. Today we speak above the noise of the bed during the bite but before the big bite emanating thanks from the ruins . . . boys and partner you can believe I knew the world again through pranks the essence of my behavior to clothe the earth a simple way premonitions a chance and later glee pills a flat white light bulb in yellow air throbbings over the times puzzles rising from the seat on a cool night to love change love remember . . . The table under it a girl whom we all recognize . . . how many goats are there in it . . . heat flashing on and off movies glazed motives gunfire gaits.

The Sunset Motel

Beginning with a memory of childhood New York's lovely weather
hurts my forehead the shower 40 below bugles call to the powder
house here where clean snow is sitting Edmund Burke Jacques Vaché
returns from the library as hand-in-glove and head-to-head with
Joe she was writing to him. This man was my friend. Already done
I go reeling up First Avenue to Klein's formality dogtags 100 yds
Christmas is sexy there; we feel soft sweaters to learn what is
ours passion principles love and plump rumpled skirts we'd like to
buy to laugh a coarse laugh on the rough edge of youth. It was
gloomy being broke today, and baffled the old memento fill-in-the-
blanks help! it's love again in love; Love, why do you always take
my heart away? Meaning of the verb to laugh. But then the soft
snow came sweetly falling down brief farewell death song of the
quilt the Sunset Motel head in the clouds and feet soaked in mush
drugs sex jail food shelter smoke lines across the truce I rushed
hatless into the white and shining air arms legs trucks passing
over them glad of the volumes of meaning of the verb to find release
in heaven's care.

Don't Forget Anger

Never hits us   the day   it's lovely   gathers us up in its name who
pierced the shower 40 below the heel hidden shoes the ruined ex-
ercises the shine is all night again pleasure falling off parting
the bed during the biting lust. Today we speak above the noise a
spyglass littered with soot scenes from the ruins boys and partners
before the big bite imitating that's the penalty denial of gain
through pranks the essence of belief. I knew the world of incant-
ations under the sheets of the neck line of the teeth behavior
cloth the earth that we know we will go on rubbing. There's this
Lady she has been my friend for some years now and later glee pills

a light bulb a tongue saying the damage is done by hands over a
period running overtime puzzles rising for some years journeys
arms legs learning what is yours love change love remember across
passion truly going into the earth No that was another earth how
many goats were there on it her and her father movies glazed motives:
Put the books back the brown hair simple ways premonitions chance
bugles calling the powder flat white in yellow air throbbing then
going on off a light lady dark lady cool nights meaning years of
writing this news shunted aside before a girl whom you all know and
recognize flashing on then off hear lifelong release in these in-
timate gaits.

What's the Racket

At a quarter past six he sat & said "where's your brother? pull
down thy sex it's blue shot thru with green the head he said it's
in the milk he said "woe unto you also, ye lawyers." Enough. The
father seems willing to cooperate thus a new weather term is born,
"no thought for your life and casual abductors." Some years now
have been "hot" weather, it gets you down every time. Ode To The
Confederate Dead and that one, "The Man" sucks candy. Did. Its
a cross between hot and cold running passion, blood, erudition, paper-
bag-pooper passion, yes, he is an agent of ours, December 7th, 1941.
What's the racket? Erudition jargon current jargon, many things
are current, much success which has to mean trouble. What else?
Now it is thinking in more sex drugs food shelter jail and the north
(south) love shall set down   laws strait east gait gasp pant whoop
holler Capture the Flag (Remember that?) Signs the inform burial
cured sent out west to be drycleaned hanging on a line (my line) I
pass out hand out among you with promises of.

The Conscience of a Conservative

Now my mother's apron unfolds again in my life pills black backs
of books I can't stand movies I can't stand Snow not reminded (re-
vealed) The World I can't stand candid roof the ditty about the
stick (introspection) because of instructions forget nights. And
so we come together in this bed out of a finger gesture mouth other
exercises before the big bite imitating that's the penalty denial
of gain the shine where one exercises the shine the awl the wheel
the hidden shoes ruined a particular buttressing of the body. The
End. No Smoking in this Room. To track the beast down. To know.
The many faces of Jesse James resplendent on a rock at Spuyten
Duyvil and his dog at the end of a leash chasing a tiger in advance
of the broken arm beginning with a memory of childhood New York's
lovely weather absence of passion grace principles love.

July

Lady, she has been my friend for some years sketches, I haven't explained
Actually of horror subject to neither of our laws intimate incantations
under the sheets tried nothing a quivery sort of fellow hurts my fore-
head this shower No thought for your life and casual abductors in books
I cant stand if it die. The life range examination as I am a cowboy
it is unless it isnt and you imaginary scenes soot years of writing
this most of it movies I cant stand a particular buttressing of the body.
Olive green color. Let's take a sentimental journey. Dont forget to
bleed. I have. Many days writing the same work into itself the appear-
ance of a role but How dark for some forty years Irish brogue rolls
toward sister mother shunted aside that's the penalty of time or of
space Certainly not a place. So we come together in this bed. Later
glee (lie) now pills (no lie) The End. Bugles call no snow to the
powderhouse the library abductors, woe unto you also ye lawyers! No.
Not reminded, I go (revealed) (No Smoking In This Room)

Some Trips to Go On

FOR DICK GALLUP

Take one hymn out west and back in step, step and punch how well
circle the nervous breakdown ring the sorrel and let the eros stop.
The mountains cleft ascended into these poems and appeared, the
clefts, you heard about it? Very dark while. no cud, no scratch.
To scratch they are still, the circus stops. Drop. It is only
cuds and farewell of weeping to the civilian, a truss, the ceiling
with passion trailing through it too. Don't forget "to bleed."
Caught the buds of other areas easy she is the only girl in the
dripping from the peel owl eels follow me down if you follow me
there. Some say its the shelf that gets you there. Culled into the
house they sleep eyeing the several, oh rose, the unquenchable
variety. Mountainous beasts. Young men starting bottle it up for
the trip. But vultures, famous dogs, right and left, succumbing
to the bombing, see them go. The bomb. And so we left, one eye
shut, often lingering in the yellow air. Don't forget the dirty
yellow lawn cracked beneath the blue triremes, the dishes, too late
already washed. Them in that, already clogging it up, leaving
shit as they do. No one knows movement of brilliant silence. She
looks to know who I am. The fog envelops me like a life she wears
two stories high approaching fresh in from the army. My army. The
audience three times two in appeals pills the still steel world some
horses. Ring the pole and let the driplets drop. Where? There.
Oh. Here there and everywhere one palm above the orange light brings
forth the unquenchable variety, appearances, leaves, single amid
blue skies. The Flies; by Jean Paul Sartre. But the trip had been
moved up. You were there upon a southern dawn the Ode to the Con-
federate Dead faking a noble failure: the life range examination

olive green color. air. Narcolepsy. Clear the Range. The tropics.
The story in that you would never occur. I mean, "to read". Persia
is not falling black backs fused the lack, the dishes, a fading
dust went by sideways, the story to sing to those emperors, the
lawn mowers, pressure driving behind their asses. Her wriggling wits.

Richard Gallup at 30

Pills Epithalamium black backs of books I can't stand Snow Movie
I can't stand not reminded I go my gold-leaf letters "other" po-
licemen give me an immense push to attend your soft job dark sigh
and I'm still around his hat is on instead ask about her here ex-
aminations No never still no matter down the alley comes a pair of
trousers laughings attention still love will break into a girl who
has been 15 months remembering nothing or other is keeping a song
mind glibbed it here & here will con these and those (& me) now move
on to the long ride to back alleys didn't want to but liked to wear
spats on the beach Father is and is obscure I wrote always on glass
there quite a card its compiled on a card jest words driving hard
sounds a machine in the oubliette nice thanks she held the 30 dollars
close to her chest (breath) (death) shattered his pose in minute den-
tal obligations who will pay seems ok the tiny excursion boat to row
it seems like cheating the operation the bell movement O I see them
nevertheless shall experience a week of bowling shirts joy operates
as well on mother at the sea an oriental sort of brittleness now lost
unless it isn't most of it goes into itself the appearance of a role
crying to confess getting punched and lonesome be still next the
Olympic Games its the same old game jest a highfalutin name ah me
that smites me chest (heart) reason agility Pill ahem steal books

huh? oh letters every way seem ineffectual its 4 o'clock bub
time obsession well dis was a painting of an R a mill a watch and
pills six of them raving on the mountain bones waving from Houston
Texas a lion is in the house a tiny madonna and a snapshot of Max
Ernst.

Who I Am and What I Think

There is no transition from a gesture to a cry or a sound. (same thing). Gestures: Who killed Cock Robin? The End. A particular buttressing of the body. No Smoking In This Room. All the senses interpenetrate. This spectacle is no more than we can assimilate. Nothing is left to do. For example, the war between men and women. Here is a whole collection of ritual. In fact everything is calculated with an enchanting mathematical meticulousness. Senses crackling everywhere resounding as if from an immense dripping rainforest. The day's emotion and turmoil is present in the dusty grassy ground. Tied naked to a huge oak. The sort of theatrical language foreign to every tongue. To track the beats down. There is a sensual delight the braincells take. Thank you Brett. Clothed in strangest dress. To learn to keep quiet when another man's prisoner. Complaints in the night. The kind of irritation caused by the impossibility of finding thread. The plastic requirements of this stage: food clothing shelter sex drugs jail. Ear to the ground. as if through channels hollowed out in the mind itself. Pages in Berlitz. No one here but me. Queer dawns voices a thousand eyes complaints in the night. To know to know everything. My eyes are tired. (the echo). (Jesse James).

A Letter from Dick Gallup

Woke up this morning you were other people in absentia lovely fashions
On my mind. Take a good look. Shit little turd balls! I've got troubles: You
have been sentenced to death sketches I havent explained actually I have
Been many days writing the same work, waiting, no one there, The An-
cient City all around you, thru August, nightmares, put them into a box,
Anger gives me nausea and I said shee-it! went home resplendent with de-
feat. Baby-things. Future issues many thanks for them last night The
Thing A great movie: Hit The Trail. Utterly exhausted by maniacs in-
cluding Yours truly not to mention shifts, day shift night shift etc. took
it to Cut City and one Ted reading in California She having gone back to
Tappan (to picket Ben Jonson). How's the chickens, the ducks, the old
old ass? Please keep in touch Just figured out I cant stand writing in this
box words dismantled to keep together and there are other problems and
they come together at my mind. Furtive Days. It gets you down and out
you go Dont read this part you both Nearly get killed on the freeway.
Remember? How long do you think you'll Be? That old praise (up the
butt!) not likely put the books back nights   Flight 9 American Air Lines
best to use your own name. You have been sentenced to Death.

A BOKE

FOR DICK GALLUP

You're listening to a man who in 1964 un-
knowingly breathed in a small quantity of
LSD powder, remember the fragrance of Grandma's
kitchen?—and at a college he reads, sleeps.
The next morning he
takes a walk around the campus
with a young student who is
ordinarily mild-mannered and agree-
able and secretly thinks of him-
self as rather colorless and uninterest-
ing. He has written poems for years,
odd sensation indeed, only partly alleviated
when he learns that he is next door to
the bashed-out windows, is now
engaged in beating in the
top of a car with the inaccurate
ones relieving him. He learns to
time his words and lines to the
hammer-strokes, and before long
he is giving something. And the
grave, slightly puzzled sym-
pathetic faces take on expressions he is
grateful for.
The head picks up. He is taken
to a room in one of the girls'
dormitories, which gives him
a local airline. This is a
girls' college, also
far off in the country. He finds
this out by the use of drugs outside
medical auspices. He and his

followers seem to feel
that the end justifies the means, but
they have no flair (!), and at that moment
the image of his great predecessor,
the only predecessor, Laurence Sterne,
and everything that came into his
head insulted somebody—merciful
heavens, who on earth was it?—and
what the hell, he thinks, this may be
a major technical breakthrough for me.
In that company he thinks he hears a bearded
fellow mutter something discontented about
"a lack of fire" or was he a
singer, an American poet? When at last
he reaches the station he discovers
he is too early by 20 minutes
blazes up humiliatingly in the front
of his brain. The result of this was
that he deliberately drank twice as
there are few lights on the campus, remember
Grandma's kitchen?, and he is uncertain about the
instructions designed to get him into
Literary Vaudeville. At the outset of the
trip he had thought that
the songs themselves would be enough
so had a terrible hangover the next day.
Yet he has in some obscure way
been a good deal better satisfied with
powerful vagueness. Poetry. A car
stops. It is driven
by a student at the college
he is going to, and, ever cognizant
of his bodiless staring audience, and of
the skull beneath his own skin

he has taken to doing some curious
things. For example he has acquired a
guitar, which he carries about with
Robert Frost and Dylan Thomas; he has
had nothing to complain of as to
the size and response of his audience on
this tour—set up by the editor of a ven-
erable poetry magazine—has dinner
with them, recounts some of his
adventures. Everyone from the schools.
But he is still bothered by the
difference and the inevitability of
death. He has tried for years to
formulate his relationship to these
things and to say something about
how to get to bus and train stations
and airports. He keeps opening
his eyes in his sleep—for what he
has become on this trip bears but little relation
to the self he left
at home in the mind, say, of his wife.
He is, in fact, in the middle of
a tour of readings. So far, considering,
he is not looking forward to acquiring
the courage to get drunk *before*
readings. He is exhausted and exalted
as he has never been, and now, standing
here, these affairs may be mandatory (in
some cases.) Then too many of the schools
like this one, though far back, seemed pleased by
the way things have gone; there have
even been some letters of appreciation,
female voices. There are many
furtive amused glances at him and

he replies in kind but because he liked
to write them, but he has never thought
of them as participating in
a public act, a kind
appeal to girls, and he even
entertains the idea of sneaking
back to his room and dashing
hard on his nerves. He might live
more vividly in this condition
but he cannot write in it.
He is happy and grinning; he feels
resourceful, foolish, and
lucky. "America," he says aloud
about this. He takes out his two
volumes of poetry, and his
manuscript for a third book,
his *Memento Mori*, the great themes
of poetry hit him squarely: the
possibility of love in
these students just coming from
the auditorium sees him approach-
ing with his ragged books
in the center of a new reality—in
this case a cold sleepless room—
he looks at these things from the last
girl's unexpected kiss, the student
with the nine pound ham-
mer—he rearranges his evening's program
around the themes of love and
death, dangerous to the psychological
stability he expects of himself.
He has several misadventures to
lance between what is on the
page, put there by him at odd

beyond-himself moments, and . . .
and the faces. In the middle
guise of fiction, he becomes fascinatingly
alive, living up to the
"giving-them-what-they-want," or might
be expected to feel entitled to
from a poet, beside himself, who
has drunk very much at six or eight
schools before that one part.
Intensity, he murmurs, where have
you been all my life.
He settles down for a sleep
with a young professor who
writes poems and is en-
thusiastic and companionable. He
reads, has a drink at an untidy
bundle of railroads, bus, and airline schedules
marked with a red pencil and
various notes to himself. That
such nervous excitement, such
over-responsiveness to people
is probably the poet's sole
evening repast, and if he
tasted of a wild boar or a stag
which he had roasted in the
cold light coming in from the chapel
tower across the campus, well, remember
the fragrance? There is
only one bus out of town,
he reaches for it, rock-and-roll
music bursts in his face. Rather than
fool with trying to shut it off he pulls
out his manuscripts. One whispers to
another. Though he is a little

afraid to, he admits who he is,
alone in a room with his skull.
In *this* reading, for once in his
life, he feels a correct balance
in his Hamlet, lost somewhere in
the snows of Northern Wisconsin:
he is, eternal strangeness!, a wandering
pose, full of life through thick
glasses. He finishes, stands
glaring for a moment in another
world with fatigue, one who has spent the most
satisfying part of a long tripping
movement that is not really for him, no, it is
for an exhausted hammerer, or for a new
arrival home and he is more
than a little glad of that: they are
wearing out the plug, feeling that he
has had his revenge. He turns on
the light and dresses, not quite able
to stall, asks suddenly, "May I
kiss you?" She agrees without thinking and
she does so with a distinct sense of
quitting while he is ahead. The
applause is long and loud, as if he were
a Beatle. He reaches a stage,
mounts, looks at the last of all clocks,
and leaves. It is 5:15 a.m. It is
time. He gets up out of bed and stumbles just
as he steps down from the stage into a
wave of feathery sweatered girls, a memorable
thing. No doubt. He gives the best reading of his
life, one that will shortly thereafter
have entered a twilight state characterized
by fantastic imagery. He subs a condition

of character and environment in order to
produce alternative modes of behavior.
He sits down, closes his eyes. Time is
annihilated; the bus driver stumbles
aboard, opens a door to a bridge. Finally
someone stops him, a farmer, and takes him 20
miles down the road. The farmer turns off
the highway, one is much interested in his
being there walking across the campus.
He hears a loud gust of many grunts, a crowd
of muffled students cheers him on; it
is fun in the country and there is
nothing to do. Still he is pleasantly
gratified at the turnouts and at the time,
picks up his bags and manuscripts and
his symbolic white guitar, and goes out
into the white darkness.
What is his life like? Where will he die?
Who is this nun giving him a calm
sense of proportion? and who leaves him; and
this time he is really in a
deserted landscape with dead corn in the
building and no one knows him—
"Come home." And who is that thin
serious boy with the crewcut?
In a station wagon they drive together
40 miles into the rainforests. He is
given a room in a cavern, and
gifts; disturbing gifts, perhaps inept
inadequate gifts, but gifts just the
same. He feels that he is overcome.
He is middle-aged, beginning to lose
teeth and hair. He is lishing them
in his mind, down steps.

The next morning he catches a strange
madness; took hold of him first at the
reading when he discovered that
everything he said was being noted and
commented upon. Too, it is a midwinter
night in the midwest, and a man is
lying alone in a sterling ardor.
The next place is a branch of a state
of mind located in the fields in an
inept scarecrow's life. A few big birds
puff and hunch on the telephone wires;
a strange room. On the dresser beside
the complicated clock-radio that
is supposed to wake him on time, there is
an industrial district of a large city.
There he is to be met at the bus station
though it is plain that there is no other
human being in those streets. In a bar,
(ah yes, he needs a drink badly), on
the stairs of a bus, he collapses.
When he wakes up the bus is in
the terminal of the next city. He gets
a small dose, about one-thousandth
the size of an aspirin, and the no-
toriety is definitely agreeable and
he does his best to try to live up to it.
What in fact is his problem? A friend
will drive him to the next
engagement which is
his last. They start out and he pays
and gets out, scarcely knowing what he is
doing but feeling a little better
standing on the hood of a 1953 Buick
with a John Henry type hammer

in his hands, they having a kind of
metric as he adjusts his delivery more and
more to the inevitable banging. Presumes
there is nothing unscientific in
his desire to change the best
proportions of strength and beauty. His
tastes were modest, a piece of bread,
a draught of water, and you were
often sent to drive him out of his
college. "I couldn't believe you'd
be the one I was looking for," the poet
says in another city, where he has
a friend he can stay with a day or two.
He flies in watching the lights of the
city, and in a phrase the losses endured
by everyone every day—the negation of
possibility that occurs each time
we pass anyone's house.
He eats dinner with the writing and the
phrases stay with him when he wakes.
He notes them down and moves on to the
next stop via the bus station. Crossing
the campus on the one path he
knows he keeps reminding himself of
what he is doing. It is ominous that
the only other large institution in
the town is
the state insane asylum. In all, it
is a strangely good occasion.
He leaves that night, paces back and forth.
There is a skull on his table and suddenly
at the sight of it he starts reading.
From the airless close-packed winter bus
station he tries to call his contact at

the noon reading. The tour is to take place that
day and he has four hours to go 40 miles. The
tenuous noise of revolutions and
student demonstrations combine with assembly
lines that will annihilate the miles,
he becoming then an older and more
dependable self, and yet, remembering.
Perhaps though some recent poems about
his children will do the trick. He reads
these quietly and has
inevitable parties given after his
readings, he plays one or two songs,
and then scuttles back into his corner,
realizing now that role-playing is
shameful beside the feelings he
has experienced. Now he has the sensation
that he must calm down and work.
But on the aircraft aimed at last at
his home, he feels also
interested in Yeats' occult pre-
occupations, a curious object to discuss
in good health, far from the poems them-
selves. "Just be yourself," he told him-
self in the beginning. Ah, but
what self? The self develops a full-
blown psychosis. Delusions set in,
along with restlessness; a sensation of
suffocation, withdrawal, excitation, satisfaction,
that he has done the something
idiosyncratic that people are expecting and
that much more, too.
It is more than he wants to pay, and, caught
up by a daring all or nothing plan,
he wants to tell, he does tell the driver to

take him to the high car, thinking
of the open road, the dear love of
comrades, Hart Crane. The long trip
back. He is instantly surrounded.
Someone points him in a direction
and he begins walking with students
trailing him as though he is un-
comfortable, even desperate: he is
sure he has not written any poetry that
would turn him around.
It begins to snow. Traffic
slows all around
him for miles. Finally a lucky kind of
exhilaration has come over him
and he sings with
white breath to the passing hours, followed by
complete recovery the next day.
He pulls out the packet of schedules:
something is wrong. He has forgotten
that his after-words are being received almost
as things, and toward the end he comes to
think that the things have the quality of a
college, but cannot reach him. He hails a
cab and asks the fare to the town he is going
to with a certain condescending benevolence,
and begins.
It is over. He relaxes with the
faculty party and goes to bed.
He dreams he is a scarecrow in a field
and writes poems
in his head all night. Some few
believe he is where he is: some place in
Wisconsin, where he has given a
poetry reading at a small college; he

has never been lionized by anyone,
not even his immediate family; but
these small repeated tastes of local
mints continue; he bellows louder and
louder and the flinching
audience is with him to the end of a couple
of things modelled on Walter Benton's
"This is my Beloved."
If they were good, and he read them well,
he could collect his money at
each stop with a clear
conscience. An hour goes by. He considers various
alternatives, but they are all
as absurd as the wish to grow
wings. Besides, another hammering is going on.
When an especially loud cheer comes in from
outside he looks up, thinking, "What is wrong
with such and such a concept?" Students
gather round him afterwards, pressing
their manuscripts into his hands,
telling him that the college he is to read in that
night is denominational. He goes up to the
priest, who has been in fact pointing to the right
direction all along. Remember now? He is now standing
alone in the snow, in a strange state, hitch-hiking.
He is 45 years old. For better or for
worse he has been moving and speaking among his kind.
But it is he who is not satisfied with this.
Remember the fragrance of Grandma's kitchen? It is not
only poetry that is
involved, it is the poet as well. Vastly he resolves
to see if he can work something out
about this later, on the bus, at a reasonable hour.
He rides calmly back to a city within a

city, with a certain flair now, since he has forgotten
to telegraph his arrival. No one meets him at the
airport, he phones a friend in the city for a day
and a night before flying home. He sees the
people who sponsored as much liquor as he is
accustomed to at a party after the reading,
waves his arms wildly about and says, "Anything
amounts to something!" And, looking at his watch, he
turns it one way and another so his thin hands can catch
the keys. He has not played the
guitar for years but feels immediately
all out and looks around for whoever is
supposed to help him. There is no one
but a priest, and finally it happens.
One of them, a girl, not the one he would
have picked to pen such a thing, is already
half an hour late. They all reach
the college, then the building, a crowd-raising
scheme by some clod or other.
All through the reading all sorts of new and
poetic things happen to him. Each time he carries
it to another campus. At a turn he gets off
his freeway; they are not so far from the
college as they thought but he
was not gracefully but dis-
gracefully drunk, who is now halfway into a new frankness.
"I couldn't believe in you, either," says the
priest with candor. Riveting him with
astonishment, directly in front of the
building, a lanky student comes out of the
building and talks to him an hour or two before
dinner. He lies down on a bed, then gets up,
is finished. He finds his poems,
usually rather loose in rhythm, taking

on a thumping thunderment and
incoherent babbling. These symptoms lasted
several decades. Actually they have been
responded to to a degree he has come to
consider excessive and even manic, but he
suspects that attendance at college seems to
be all but inaccessible. There are no
buses or trains until after time confers her
particular favors on a stranger she
will never see again, one who last night
grew more emotional, more harried, more
impulsive. Yet he knows that these qualities
will die out, take a wrong turn somewhere.
On a highway complex as big as this one
it is hard to get tween his touring self and
his usual self. He has definitely been
another person.

Many Happy Returns

TO ANNE KEPLER & FRANK O'HARA

Words for Love

FOR SANDY

Winter crisp and the brittleness of snow
as like make me tired as not. I go my
myriad ways blundering, bombastic, dragged
by a self that can never be still, pushed
by my surging blood, my reasoning mind.

I am in love with poetry. Every way I turn
this, my weakness, smites me. A glass
of chocolate milk, head of lettuce, dark-
ness of clouds at one o'clock obsess me.
I weep for all of these or laugh.

By day I sleep, an obscurantist, lost
in dreams of lists, compiled by my self
for reassurance. Jackson Pollock   René
Rilke   Benedict Arnold   I watch
my psyche, smile, dream wet dreams, and sigh.

At night, awake, high on poems, or pills
or simple awe that loveliness exists, my lists
flow differently. Of words bright red
and black, and blue.   Bosky.   Oubliette.   Dis-
severed. And O, alas

Time disturbs me. Always minute detail
fills me up. It is 12:10 in New York. In Houston
it is 2 p.m. It is time to steal books. It's
time to go mad. It is the day of the apocalypse
the year of parrot fever! What am I saying?

Only this. My poems do contain
wilde beestes. I write for my Lady
of the Lake. My god is immense, and lonely
but uncowed. I trust my sanity, and I am proud. If
I sometimes grow weary, and seem still, nevertheless

my heart still loves, will break.

Personal Poem #2

I wake up 11:30 back aching from soft bed Pat
gone to work Ron to class (I never heard a sound)
it's my birthday. 27. I put on birthday
pants birthday shirt go to ADAM's buy a Pepsi for
breakfast come home drink it take a pill
I'm high!
                I do three Greek lessons to make
up for cutting class. I read birthday book
(from Joe) on Juan Gris real name: José
Vittoriano Gonzalez stop in the middle read
all my poems gloat a little over new ballad
quickly skip old sonnets imitations of Shakespeare.
Back to books. I read poems by Auden Spenser Stevens
Pound and Frank O'Hara. I hate books.
                                                            I wonder
if Jan or Helen or Babe ever think about me. I
wonder if David Bearden still dislikes me. I wonder
if people talk about me secretly. I wonder if
I'm too old. I wonder if I'm fooling myself
about pills. I wonder what's in the icebox.
I wonder if Ron or Pat bought any toilet paper
                                                                  this morning

Personal Poem #7

FOR JOHN STANTON

It is 7:53 Friday morning in the Universe
New York City to be somewhat exact
I'm in my room wife gone working Gallup
fucking in the room below

                                        had 17½ milligrams desoxyn
last night 1 Miltown, read Paterson, parts
1 & 2, poems by Wallace Stevens & How Much Longer
Shall I Be Able To Inhabit The Divine Sepulchre
(John Ashbery). Made lists of lines to
steal, words to look up (didn't). Had steak & eggs
with Dick while Sandy sweetly slept.

At 6:30 woke Sandy
fucked til 7 now she's late to work & I'm still
high. Guess I'll write to Bernie today
and Tom. And call Tony. And go out at 9 (with Dick)
to steal books to sell, so we can go
to see A NIGHT AT THE OPERA

Personal Poem

It's 5:03 a.m. on the 11th of July this morning
and the day is bright gray turning green   I can't stop
loving you says Ray Charles   and I know exactly
what he means because the Swedish policeman in the
next room is beating on my door demanding sleep
and not Ray Charles and bluegrass   does he know
that in three hours I go to court to see if the world

will let me have a wife   he doesn't of course it wouldn't
occur to him   nor would it occur to him to write
"scotch-tape body" in a notebook but it did occur to
John Stanton alias The Knife Fighter age 18 so why
are my hands shaking I should know better

Personal Poem #9

It's 8:54 a.m. in Brooklyn it's the 26th of July
and it's probably 8:54 in Manhattan but I'm
in Brooklyn   I'm eating English muffins and drinking
Pepsi and I'm thinking of how Brooklyn is New
York City too   how odd   I usually think of it
as something all its own   like Bellows Falls   like
Little Chute   like Uijongbu
                                        I never thought
on the Williamsburg Bridge I'd come so much to Brooklyn
just to see lawyers and cops who don't even carry guns
taking my wife away and bringing her back
                                                        No
and I never thought Dick would be back at Gude's
beard shaved off long hair cut and Carol reading
his books when we were playing cribbage and watching
the sun come up over the Navy Yard a-
cross the river
                            I think I was thinking
when I was ahead I'd be somewhere like Perry street
erudite dazzling slim and badly-loved
contemplating my new book of poetry
to be printed in simple type on old brown paper
feminine marvelous and tough

For You

FOR JAMES SCHUYLER

New York's lovely weather hurts my forehead
here where clean snow is sitting, wetly
round my ears, as hand-in-glove and
head-to-head with Joe, I go reeling
up First Avenue to Klein's. Christmas
is sexy there. We feel soft sweaters
and plump rumpled skirts we'd like to try.
It was gloomy being broke today, and baffled
in love: Love, why do you always take my heart away?
But then the soft snow came sweetly falling down
and head in the clouds, feet soaked in mush
I rushed hatless into the white and shining air,
glad to find release in heaven's care.

A Personal Memoir of Tulsa, Oklahoma / 1955–60

There we were, on fire with being there, then
And so we put our pants on
And began to get undressed. You were there, then
And there where you were, we were. And I
Was there, too! We had no pants on.

And I saw your penis there. It was right there, where
We were, and it was with us. We looked at it, there
And you said, "Why hello there, Oliver!" to me, there
Beside you, without any pants on, there where I
Could hear you saying, "Why hello there!"

Then Frank came in, and George, and Bill, and Cannonball, and Frank;
And Simon, Jonas, Jennie-Lou, and Bob; and gentle Millie-Jean;
And Hannibal the Alp; and they took off their hats and coats
And all began to puke. They puked on Cal, and on Billy, and
On Benjamin, Lucifer, Jezebel, Asthmador and Frank. Then they left.

Frank was much younger then, there, and he had hair
On his belly; he looked like a model-aeroplane; a dark, gloomy
Navel in its tail; and you were there, there
In his tail: you were there and
Hair was there, and air was there, there, up in the air, among
The hair. And you were saying, "Why, hello there!"

And your pants, when you finally put them on there
Had a hole in them, there, where your penis was, before it flew
Away from there to find itself. And the hole there was wide
And it was deep. It was dark there; and
Supersonic Aeroplanes were there. And they were whirring.

"Whirrr-whirrr-whirrr," went the throbbing aeroplanes, as
They zoomed out at us from in there; for we were there, where
Your pants met the sea, and we were glad! I was there, and Jock
And Zack, and Brett; and we met your penis passing by. It said,
"Goodbye mild starlight of The Sign of Fawn," as it rode
into the galaxy named 'Fangs.'

TAMBOURINE LIFE

FOR ANNE KEPLER

1

FUCK COMMUNISM

it's red white and blue

in the bathroom

(Tuli's)

One dollar, you Mother!

Make all your friends

STOP!

(now there's an idea)

ARTFORUM
723½ North Cienega Blvd
Los Angeles, California

Back to the wall

(it's all in California)

Thanks to Jack

I mean it's all right here
it's morning
and I'm looking over the wall
at Mr. Pierre Loti and his nameless dog
they work well together
on paper i.e. this here

chasing a tiger across white expansiveness
that is not lacking in significance

(what is?)

THE RUSSIAN REVOLUTION
circa 1967

2

The apples are red again in Chandler's valley
redder for what happened there

never did know what it was

never did care

The End
on a pillow

naturally

a doormat lust steam a hiss Guilty!

I see some handwriting on the wall

of the Williamsburg Bridge

intersection

New York Post ten cents

tip the newsboy
over
a million
laughs
that's the party line

yes

he's working on the paper:

Mr. Horatio Alger

(he has a lovely talent)

thank you

here's your change

3

I'm touched
here, take this penny
there is no need for the past
the sun is out
it's night
I mean
it is night
and I love you better
since
this seizure / of my eyeballs

•

Take off those Fug panties!
Go ahead
it's a big world
The big guys do it

TO ANNIE
(between Oologah & Pawnee)
Guillaume Apollinaire

4

The bodies of my days
open up
in the garden
of
my memory,
America

•

I have had the courage to look backward
it was like polio
I shot my mouth off

•

I NEED MONEY
that money
that at least
at last
means less
than a Band-aid
or a toadstool

•

OUCH!

that Band-aid has an OUCH! in it

Who notices a toadstool in the street?
Everyone
who has on
a Band-aid
That toadstool has a Band-aid on it

5

(to Brett deBary)

"He doesn't know how to take a vacation"
Dick
doesn't know how to take a vacation
either

That is not to infer
that Dick is a toad
under his Band-aid
far from it

a toad is a cold-blooded fellow
Dick is warm and full of blood

When you leave, Dick
turn the refrigerator
to vacation please

6

Now I'm going to read 3 cereal poems:
CORN FLAKES
OATMEAL
RY-KRISP
thank you
they were composed
excuse me
I mean NOT composed
using the John-Cage-Animal-Cracker
Method of Composition
(this seems to be mushrooming into a
major work
of high
seriousness)

•

I'd fight for that!
(I didn't have to.)

7

True Love

there is only one way
to describe
"True Love"

does anyone know
that one way?

•

Mr. Nelson Algren
1958 West Evergreen
Chicago, Illinois

•

In Chicago, Illinois, you
are really at home
whether you like it or not, baby,
and, whether you like it
or not
You Are My Friend

so don't pees me off!

8

Come into my house
tonight
Dick
and I will show you
this new work
"House at Night"
It & this page, there not here, are not the same
except in a
manner of
speaking

it is not
"A Portrait of Jean-Marie"
tho it cd be

it is also not
"A Portrait of Barbara Harris"
whom I don't know
though I like her plenty
she's a lot like me
(my own name is
"Mr. Brigadoon")

9

I am constantly being caught up
in my own commotion
it is now a slow commotion

The radio is turning me on

10

Commotion over, clothes in hand I wait
in Mr. Ron Padgett's furlined
bridge-jacket

who shivers now
in Paris, Oklahoma
between Galveston &
Mobile a word
incidentally
invented
cross that out
coined
by Mr. Marcel Duchamp
to describe a
lady finger

11

it's too cold in here / but not for me
in my present balloon state / to write this love song

"Cold rosy dawn in New York City"

hovering over the radio

de-dum

12

I woke up this morning
it was night
you were on my mind
looking for a home
for the boll weevil

LADY BRETT

nothing like that in New York City
it's all in Oklahoma
where you-all
can learn to talk like me

if "you-all" is Mr.
Ron Padgett, "The
American Express"

13

He's a good friend of mine
although he fears he is unable to love
people
who have politesse
whatever that may be

thanks anyway, Frank
you're not without *con brio*
n'es ca'fe?

(thanks, Ed)

14

I quote
from "The Code of the West"

a work
by Mr. Ed Sanders

whose "Poem From Jail"
I highly recommend

On second thought
I quote instead

This work
by Mr. Marcel Duchamp

which
oddly enough

I also give high recommendation

15

THE CODE OF THE WEST

1. Sob when you read "Black Beauty."
2. The true test of a man is a bunt.
3. Dare to do your duty.
4. Press the tip of the tongue on the gums
behind the upper teeth as for t, and expel
the breath with vibrations of the vocal cords.
5. He went to the windows of those who slept
and over each pain like a fairy wept.
6. Halt!
7. Loosen your snood.
8. Close your eyes and doze.
9. Jove! Jove! This shepherd's passion
is much upon my fashion!
10. Drill.

16

you know
once people paid no attention to me

Mayakovsky

in the garden of my memory

& now

passion's flower

wilts
constantly
because

my lady love is a Holy Roller!

her body is a sponge
it has no mud

Tonight's heat
will dry that mud
and it will fall into dust

I'm ready for it

the body I mean
not the dust

however if you are in the dust
kindly hop into this tub of black water please

now hand me that quail
lean me against the belly of a woman
(you are that woman)

17

knock on the door of her house
knock-knock

the sun is out
river flowing in a window
a geranium trembling automobile

droning
across the screen
Turn back to look
you don't see
the door open
you are standing there
I mean
I am sitting here
between the door
to a world full of others
like yourselves
and the droning solitude of this here Los Angeles
Freeway

•

How to get off?

18

Hi, Bears!

do you believe in magic?

good!

because I am here
to make a monkey out of you
The best way
to make yrself a monkey
is to jump down
(spin around)
pick a bale of cotton
if you don't understand
that
you will never understand
your country's history

1000 volumes a year
ooze from the minds
of dead monkeys
and yet
we are still too dull
to understand
them
or that

Kiss me!   it is not at all unpleasant
to be kissed by a monkey
if you are a monkey
I am not a monkey
I do not have a monkey on my back

I am not a monkey's uncle

turn page

19

Only a monkey would read this

THE ENCYCLOPEDIA OF FLIES
over 250 flies
photographed
in living color

These 250 flies were tied "up"
executed
by hand
Not my hand

The Little Sisters

20

There are no flies on me, New York City

oh

21

There are, however,
two sorts of landscapes here

the interior
and
the exterior

as well as the other
which we will not go into here

22

One song I have always liked
is
"Hope you Happy Monkey"

that's the truth

by Ruth Krauss

23

There you are
There I go
past The Majestic Men's Clothes
slightly disheveled
is a nice phrase
it has impact
like the three pricks
Alice gave
Joe Gould
in 1933
MOTHER
that's Alice's idea of Wonderland

24

She happens to be a sex expert, among other things
if you are squeamish I'd better not tell you
WHAT other things . . .
"How did Red China get the 'O' bomb?"
no one knows
No one will ever know

because no one
is a tautology

let's have no truck
with tautologies

25

This poem
has no truck

although it does provide
a sort of Reader's Digest
of Oriental sex practices

under the sheets

Who threw the panties into
Mother's tea
is a good example of one
of the many unanswered questions
life provides

Where did the beautiful
British secret agent
lose his nightie
is another

it was not a majestic nightie
nor was it a man's nightie
unless of course
the Beautiful British
secret agent
was a female impersonator
Perhaps that was his secret
There has always been a
quick turnover
among British secret agents
Look!   there goes one now

26

I am here today   a gentleman
with time on my hands
you are in my heart
during
The Four Seasons
which are

1. springtime

2. bedtime

and so on

27

There is a revolution going on in my skin
I have the gift of young skin
no pimples
which is why I am here today

I would like to introduce myself

However
it will be better
between us
if I don't cheat

The victory is not always to the sweet

so keep on the ball, buddy, i.e.
I mean "the button"

28

COME ALIVE
Meet Me At The Smoke Ring
(Get Your Piles Out of Vietnam
Let's Love One Another)
(Equality for Homosexuals)
YES
SUCK
Stand Up For Dikes

Commemorating The Visit
of Pope Paul X
to NYC
1965

We Won't Go

I'm for Legalized
Abortion

NO MAN IS GOOD THREE TIMES

29

Life certainly is marvelous
When you're in love
isn't it?

Consequently, it is important
to be in love
most all the time
but not all of the time

When you are in love
all of the time
you get bored because
life
when it's always the same
is boring
isn't it?
that's a strange theory

30

it's a theory of strange

I am in love
right now. I am in love with
(fill in name of person in room)

see me about this later, ( )

I am not in love with Mr. Walter Steck

He was or
was not
recently elected
to the assembly
Just for the record I found Mr. Walter Steck
recently

at five o'clock in the afternoon
on García Lorca's birthday
lying in the gutter
on his button *shame*

31

O ship of states
Sail on, O allegorical poem

32

Branching out
shooting all night
he grounded
himself

on the button

33

so here
you stand
hitting upon things
you hadn't thought upon
when you get into the pictures
you wake up
inside an oval
portrait
I mean a woman
A beautiful reminder sitting on a line

It could be a steamship line   or even a ferry line

34

Life is Never boring when you are Tarzan of the Apes
e.g.   You step out from behind a bush
and you say
"Yes, I am M'sieur Tarzan"

35

Dick Gallup arrives at this point
and says
"Life is Boring"

36

Jacques-Louis David is crying in his crib
he is not bored
Jane has given him a banana

37

Dick reads those lines
they bore him
but I laugh plenty

38

David is sobbing bitterly
in the jungle

"Shut up
or I'll kill you," etc.

He doesn't want to

39

He wants the white
tempera
paint

with which I am painting out the words
in this here comic book

"Tarzan of the Apes"

so that I can "fill in the words"

40

"The Words" is a good book
is is the autobiography of Mr. Jean-Paul Sartre
from age zero to ten

In it
he tells what a little shit he was.

"I'm going doo-doo" says Jacques-Louis David
we have words
and he falls into sleep

41

Life is long

it's sure been a long Times
crossword puzzle
since I last
was here
That Spring of '65
that was
That was my best year

that was also a good year for

Dancers
Buildings and
People in the Street

in the cell block
a boy
invented
the mahogany cage
before he rested
The climate became a song

Crowds disperse my
purpose
my great calm

Dim lights
turn me down

the radio parts
the curly hair
me on the floor

saying

42

"Go now
and get me a vast Band-aid"

43

I'm sitting here thinking that these words that I have been
borrowing from Mr. James "The Rock" Proust & son
should stretch to the end of at least one
period in my life.

They did.

44

"What I really like is new girls to fuck."

that's a good line

it was said by Dick Gallup
who let it drop there
that to be explained later

in the backroom
of The Peace Eye
that's all I know

45

Cow a is not Cow b
Dick
Count Korzybski said that
that Polish cocksucker
is what a drunk called HIM
He didn't mean Korzybski
though
He'd never heard of Him
I don't know what he meant
I was drunk
He was speaking Polish
He didn't dig Counts
That's a fact

46

According to FACT
William Burroughs
studied under
that Polish cocksucker
in Chicago
I've always admired Count Korzybski
and, in fact, I've always admired William Burroughs
Hi Bill!
I do not, however, admire FACT Magazine
because it costs too much money
and probably for other reasons
too vague to be present

47

dot dot dot

48

Listen

Is there a *Pseudotsuga Menziesii*
in your house?

if so, there is
nothing to worry about
it would be hard to find
a house
in America
where *Pseudotsuga Menziesii* isn't
all over the goddam place

it has a lovely talent

49

cross something out here

50

Imagine yourself
driving on a super highway
with your friend
Mr. Bob Harris

besides being a genius
he is also a perennial
problem child
who mooches off his friends
sleeps with any available women
ignores his children
and smokes ceaselessly
like yourself

you may have to stop often
to relieve yourself
because your friend
suffers
from a terrible disease previously unmentioned
but not in this poem
nor by anyone whom you have ever known
in this vale of tears

51

back on the freeway the cars pass
over your eyes ears nose and throat and hairs
no interviews no photographs
no autographs

in this dream

which is so realistic
you can almost hear my voice
at your ear

which is on the level of your back,
dear

52

Fish and Cheep Pet Shoppe
The Pioneer
Block Drug Manhattan
Fox's Corner
Martha's
are all places I have never visited
though I keep meaning to

53

Italy is a boot in the atlas

The snowball centuries rolling
collect only the tiny footprints of
hens

the burning bush attracts
the hen

One comes to take one's
place in the sun, only
to smother inside the
hide of a hen

54

COME IN!

Hello Lee

Mr. Lee Crabtree
of The Fugs

just came in

55

Rhetoric
is what we make
out of our quarrels
with others

out of
our quarrels with ourselves
we make poetry

Yes, that is true,

56

In my house, every cloud
has a silver lining

there is only one cloud in my house

Inside that cloud is a joke

it is not an inside joke

57

on every mirror
in my house
is a big kiss
placed there by Mr. Joe Brainard

•

it's very exciting
not to be asleep now

•

58

If Joe Brainard were here now
he'd be excited
about giving me those kisses

that's a lie
clickety-clack William Saroyan

59

What we do in life
in New York City
in 1965
we get the money

60

GET THE MONEY!

that was Damon Runyon's favorite expression

the heat is coming on
like gangbusters

(A. Partridge
History of American Climate)

I guess that means
it's time to burst,
eh,
M'sieur Cloud?

61

Speaking of Picasso, he once sd
that for him
true friendship cannot exist
without the possibility of
sex

That is true

I have many men friends
I would like to fuck

However, I am unable to do so
because I am not a homosexual

fortunately
this makes my life complex
rather than simple

and vice versa

62

Dream on O impudent virgin
Guillaume Apollinaire
you too are aware of the duality of nature and of the spirit
and you too prefer the visible
to the invisible

I salute You!

(Salutes)

63

the true Guillaume
is a great deal more interesting
than many of those people
whose misfortune it is
not to be so true

64

the logic of that is
lost
but may be recovered
in the theory of Mr. A. N. Whitehead to the effect
that a human being
may possess two kinds of perception / that
as it were
work from opposite ends.
(breathing)

65

So, in conclusion, may I say
that this is what life is like here

you drink some coffee, you get some sleep
everything is up in the air

especially us, who are me

66

Now
in the middle of this
someone I love is dead

and I don't even know
"how"

I thought she belonged to me

How she filled my life when I felt empty!

How she fills me now!

67

games of cribbage
with Dick
filled this afternoon

do you
understand that?

68

What
excitement!
crossing Saint Mark's Place
face cold in air
tonight
when
that girlish someone waving
from a bicycle
turned me back on.

69

What moves me most, I guess
of a sunlit morning
is being alone
with everyone I love
crossing 6th and 1st
at ice-cold 6 a.m.

from where I come home
with two French donuts, Pepsi and
the New York Times.

70

Joy is what I like,
That, and love.

OCT. 1965–JAN. 1966

A Dream

Dreamy-eyed is how you get
when you need something strong
"in some cup of your own"

The gift of coffee is an act of love
unless it costs you

Love came into my room
I mean my life
the shape of a Tomato
it took over everything

later:

Forgive me, René Magritte
I meant "a rose"

You have a contemporary nature
in these here coffee alps

I dreamt that December 27th, 1965
while sleeping with Linda Schjeldahl
in a dream

Living with Chris

FOR CHRISTINA GALLUP

It's not exciting to have a bar of soap
in your right breast pocket
it's not boring either
it's just what's happening in America, in 1965

If there is no Peace in the world
it's because there is no Peace
in the minds of men. You'd be surprised, however
at how much difference
a really good cup of coffee & a few pills can make
in your day

I would like to get hold of
the owner's manual
for a 1965 model "DREAM"
(Catalogue number CA-77)

I am far from the unluckiest woman in the world

I am far from a woman

An elephant is tramping in my heart

Alka-Seltzer   Palmolive   Pepsodent   Fab
Chemical New York

There is nothing worse than elephant love

Still, there is some Peace in the world. It is
night. You are asleep. So I must be at peace

The barometer at 29.58 and wandering

But who are you?

For god's sake, is there anyone out there listening?

If so, Peace.

Bean Spasms

TO GEORGE SCHNEEMAN

New York's lovely weather
hurts my forehead

in praise of thee
the? white dead
whose eyes know:

what are they
of the tiny cloud my brain:
The City's tough red buttons:
O Mars, red, angry planet, candy

bar, with sky on top,
"why, it's young Leander hurrying to his death"
what? what time is it in New York   in these here alps
City of lovely tender hate
and beauty making beautiful
old rhymes?

I ran away from you
when you needed something strong
then I leand against the toilet bowl (ack)
Malcolm X
I love my brain
it all mine now is
saved not knowing
that &
that (happily)
being that:

"wee kill our selves to propagate our kinde"
John Donne

yes, that's true
the hair on yr nuts & my
big blood-filled cock are a part in that
too

PART 2

Mister Robert Dylan doesn't feel well today
That's bad
This picture doesn't show that
It's not bad, too

it's very ritzy in fact

here I stand I can't stand
to be thing
I don't use atop
the empire state
building
& so sauntered out that door
That reminds me of the time
I wrote that long piece about a gangster name of "Jr."
O Harry James! had eyes to wander but lacked tongue to praise
so later peed under his art

paused only to lay a sneeze
on Jack Dempsey
asleep with his favorite Horse

That reminds me of I buzz
on & off Miró pop
in & out a Castro convertible
minute by minute GENEROSITY!

Yes now that the seasons totter in their walk
I do a lot of wondering about Life in praise of ladies dead of
& Time plaza(s), Bryant Park by the Public eye of brow
Library, Smith Bros. black boxes, Times
Square
Pirogi Houses
with long skinny rivers thru them
they lead the weary away
off! hey!
I'm no sailor
off a ship
at sea I'M HERE
& "The living is easy"
It's "HIGH TIME"
& I'm in shapes
of shadow, they
certainly can warm, can't they?

Have you ever seen one? NO!
of those long skinny Rivers
So well hung, in New York City
NO! in fact
I'm the Wonderer
& as yr train goes by forgive me, René! 'just oncet'
I woke up in Heaven
He woke, and wondered more; how many angels
on this train huh? snore

for there she lay
on sheets that mock lust done that 7 times
been caught
and brought back
to a peach nobody.

To Continue:
Ron Padgett & Ted Berrigan
hates yr brain
my dears
amidst the many other little buzzes
& like, Today, as Ron Padgett might say
is
"A tub of vodka"
"in the morning"
she might reply
and that keeps it up
past icy poles
where angels beg fr doom then zip
ping in-and-out, joining the army
wondering about Life
by the Public Library of
Life
No Greater Thrill!
(I wonder)

Now that the earth is changing I wonder what time it's getting to be
sitting on this New York Times Square
that actually very ritzy, Lauren it's made of yellow wood or
I don't know something maybe
This man was my it's been fluffed up
friend
He had a sense for the
vast doesn't he?

Awake my Angel! give thyself
to the lovely hours   Don't cheat
The victory is not always to the sweet.
I mean that.

Now this picture is pretty good here
Though it once got demerits from the lunatic Arthur Cravan
He wasn't feeling good that day
Maybe because he had nothing on
paint-wise I mean

PART 3

I wrote that
about what is
this empty room   without a heart
now in three parts
a white flower
came home wet & drunk   2 Pepsis
and smashed my fist thru her window
in the nude

As the hand zips you see
Old Masters, you can see
well hung in New York   they grow fast here
Conflicting, yet purposeful
yet with outcry vain!

PART 4

Praising, that's it!
you string a sonnet around yr fat gut
and falling on your knees
you invent the shoe
for a horse. It brings you luck
while sleeping
"You have it seems a workshop nature"
Have you   "Good Lord!"

Some folks is wood
seen them? Ron Padgett wd say
amidst the many other little buzzes
past the neon on & off
night & day STEAK SANDWICH
Have you ever tried one Anne? SURE!
"I wonder what time 'its'?"
as I sit on this new Doctor
NO I only look at buildings they're in
as you and he, I mean he & you & I buzz past
in yellow ties I call that gold
THE HOTEL BUCKINGHAM
(facade) is black, and taller than last time
is looming over lunch naked high time poem & I, equal in
perfection & desire
is looming two eyes over coffee-cup (white) nature
and man: both hell on poetry.
Art is art and life is
"A monograph on Infidelity"
Oh. Forgive me stench of sandwich
O pneumonia in American Poetry

Do we have time? well look at Burroughs
7 times been caught and brought back to Mars
& eaten.
"Art is art & Life
is home," Fairfield Porter said that
turning himself in
Tonight arrives again in red
some go on even in Colorado on the run
the forests shake
meaning:
coffee the cheerfulness of this poor
fellow is terrible, hidden in

the fringes of the eyelids
blue mysteries' (I'M THE SKY)
The sky is bleeding now
onto 57th Street
of the 20th Century &
HORN & HARDART'S
Right Here. That's PART 5

I'm not some sailor off a ship at sea
I'm the wanderer (age 4)
& now everyone is dead
sinking bewildered of hand, of foot, of lip
nude, thinking
laughter burnished brighter than hate
goodbye.
André Breton said that
what a shit!
Now he's gone!
up bubbles all his amorous breath
& Monograph on Infidelity entitled
The Living Dream
I never again played
I dreamt that December 27th, 1965
all in the blazon of sweet beauty's breast

I mean "a rose" Do you understand that?
Do you?
The rock&roll songs of this earth
commingling absolute joy AND
incontrovertible joy of intelligence
certainly can warm
can't they? YES!
and they do.
Keeping eternal whisperings around

(we want to take the underground
revolution to Harvard!)

(Mr. Macadams writes in
the nude: no that's not
me that: then zips in &
out the boring taxis, re-
fusing to join the army
asleep "on the springs"
of red GENEROSITY)

and yet this girl has
so much grace
I wonder!
Were all their praises simply prophecies
of this
the time! NO GREATER THRILL
my friends

But I quickly forget them, those other times, for what are they
but parts in the silver lining of the tiny cloud my brain
drifting up into smoke the city's tough blue top:

I think a picture always
leads you gently to someone else
Don't you? like when you ask to leave the room
& go to the moon.

Frank O'Hara's Question
from "Writers and Issues"
by John Ashbery

what sky
out there is between the ailanthuses
a 17th century prison an aardvark
a photograph of Mussolini and
a personal letter from Isak Dinesen
written after eating

can be succeeded by a calm evaluation of the "intense inane" that surrounds him:

it is cool
I am high
and happy
as it turns
on the earth
tangles me
in the air

and between these two passages (from the long poem 'Biotherm') occurs a mediating line which might stand to characterize all of Mr. O'Hara's art:

I am guarding it from mess and message.

Many Happy Returns

TO DICK GALLUP

It's a great pleasure to
wake "up"
mid-afternoon

2 o'clock

and if thy stomach think not

no matter . . .

because
the living
"it's easy"

you splash the face &
back of the neck
swig Pepsi

& drape the bent frame in something
"blue for going out"

• • •

you might smoke a little pot, even
or take a pill
or two pills

•

(the pleasures of prosperity
tho they are only bonuses
really
and neither necessary nor not)

•

& then:
POOF!

• • •

Puerto-Rican girls are terrific!
you have to smile but you don't
touch, you haven't eaten
yet, & you're too young
to die . . .

•

No, I'm only kidding!
Who on earth would kill
for love? (Who wouldn't?)

•

Joanne & Jack
will feed you
today
because
Anne & Lewis are
"on the wing" as
but not like
always . . .

• •

Michael is driving a hard bargain
himself
to San Francisco . . .

•

&
Pete & Linda
& Katie and George,
Emilio, Elio and Paul
have gone to Maine . . .

• • •

Everyone, it seems, is somewhere else.
None are lost, tho. At least,
we aren't!
(GEM'S SPA: corner of 2nd Avenue &
Saint Mark's Place)

•

I'm right here
sunlight opening up the sidewalk,
opening up today's first black&white,
& I'm about to be
born again thinking of you

Things to Do in New York City

FOR PETER SCHJELDAHL

Wake up high up
    frame bent & turned on
Moving slowly
    & by the numbers
light cigarette
Dress in basic black
    & reading a lovely old man's book:

BY THE WATERS OF MANHATTAN

change

flashback

play cribbage on the Williamsburg Bridge
watching the boats sail by
the sun, like a monument,
move slowly up the sky
above the bloody rush:

break yr legs & break yr heart
kiss the girls & make them cry
loving the gods & seeing them die

celebrate your own
& everyone else's birth:

Make friends forever
& go away

10 Things I Do Every Day

wake up
smoke pot
see the cat
love my wife
think of Frank

eat lunch
make noises
sing songs
go out
dig the streets

go home for dinner
read the Post
make pee-pee
two kids
grin

read books
see my friends
get pissed-off
have a Pepsi
disappear

Resolution

The ground is white with snow.
It's morning, of New Year's Eve, 1968, & clean
City air is alive with snow, its quiet
Driving. I am 33. Good Wishes, brothers, everywhere

& Don't You Tread On Me.

In the Early Morning Rain

TO MY FAMILY & FRIENDS

Hello

"Hello"
originally
meant
"Be whole"
or
"Be healthy"

Today
it
simply
means
"Hello"

80th Congress

TO RON PADGETT

It's 2 a.m. at Anne & Lewis's which is where it's at
On St. Mark's Place hash and Angel Hairs on our minds
Love is in our heart's (what else?) dope & Peter Schjeldahl
Who is new and valid in a blinding snowstorm

Inside joy fills our drugless shooting gallery
With repartee; where there's smoke there's marriage &, folks
That's also where it's at in poetry in 1967
Newly rich but still a hopeless invalid (in 1967)

Yes, it's 1967, & we've been killing time with life
But at Lewis & Anne's we live it "up"
Anne makes lovely snow-sodas while Lewis's watchamacallit warms up this
New Year's straight blue haze. We think about that

And money. With something inside us we float up
To & onto you, it, you were truly there & now you're here.

TED BERRIGAN & DICK GALLUP

Fragment

FOR JIM BRODEY

Left behind in New York City, & oof!
That's the right one: sitting now, & I'm not thinking
Nor swishing; I'm just sitting. Getting over them two
Hamburgers. & that I think
Gets it all down. Here, anyway, I am
On this electric chair each breath nearer the last
Oceans of ripples solid under me: how come?
One pair of time-capsules trigger sweat
As one listens & one listening type types
LOOKS LIKE WE GONNA GET A LITTLE SNOW, HUH?
I don't know but you can bet something's going
    to happen.

The Circle

Up is waiting

Between is barely there

Down is alive

Now is spinning

It's a quick spin

Nevertheless

5 New Sonnets: A Poem

1

FOR BARRY & JACKY HALL

His piercing pince-nez. Some dim frieze
dear Berrigan. He died
I, an island, sail, and my shores toss
to breathe an old woman slop oatmeal,
My babies parade waving their innocent flags
The taste of such delicate thoughts
Opulent, sinister, and cold!
Sing in idiom of disgrace
Dreams, aspirations of presence! Innocence gleaned,
annealed! The world in its mysteries are explained,
On the grass. To think of you alone
Your champion. Days are nursed on science fiction
For the fey Saint's parade   Today
Rivers of annoyance undermine the arrangements.

2

Hands point to a dim frieze, in the dark night.
Back to books.   I read
on a fragrant evening, fraught with sadness
bristling hate.
And high upon the Brooklyn Bridge alone,
Huddled on the structured steps
The bulbs burn, phosphorescent, white,
Shall it be male or female in the tub?
Pale like an ancient scarf, she is unadorned,
and the struggles of babies congeal. A hard core is formed.
Suffering the poem of these states!
& you tremble at the books upon the earth
& he walks. Three ciphers and a faint fakir
No.   One   Two   Three   Four   Today

3

It's 8:30 p.m. in New York and I've been running
Wind giving presence to fragments.
at every hand, my critic
Flinging currents into pouring streams
The bulbs burn phosphorescent, white
Fathers and teachers, and daemons down under the sea,
The singer sleeps in Cos.   Strange juxtaposed
"I wanted to be a cowboy." Doughboy will do
As my strength and I walk out and look for you
Winds flip down the dark path of breath
Released by night (which is not to imply   clarity
She is warm. Into the vast closed air of the slow
The wind's wish is the tree's demand
On the 15th day of November in the year of the motorcar.

4

Is there room in the room that you room in?
How much longer shall I be able to inhabit the Divine
deep in whose reeds great elephants decay;
loveliness that longs for butterfly! There is no pad
He buckles on his gun, the one
He wanted to know the *names*
And the green rug nestled against the furnace
Your hair moves slightly,
He is incomplete, bringing you Ginger Ale
The cooling wind keeps blowing, and
He finds he cannot fake
Wed to wakefulness, night which is not death
Fuscous with murderous dampness
But helpless, as blue roses are helpless.

& 5

Into the closed air of the slow
And then one morning to waken perfect-faced
The blue day! In the air winds dance
Sleep half sleep half silence and with reason
banging around in a cigarette   she isn't "in love"
in my paintings for they are present
The withered leaves fly higher than dolls can see
A watchdog barks in the night
Francis Marion nudges himself gently into the big blue sky
What thwarts this fear I love
No lady dream around in any bad exposure
absence of passion, principles, love. She murmurs
Is not genuine   it shines forth from the faces
littered with soup, cigarette butts, the heavy

Poem

FOR BILL BERKSON

Seven thousand feet over
The American Midwest
In the black and droning night
Sitting awake and alone
I worry the stewardess . . .
Would you like some coffee, sir?
How about a magazine?
No thanks. I smile and refuse.
My father died today. I
Fifteen hundred miles away
Left at once for home, having
received the news from mother
In tears on the telephone.
He never rode in a plane.

Gus

. . . Not far from here he was inside his head there were some sands. Of these 50 gave way to a room, latter resembling manure.

To the right, in a kit, a sort of woman-spanned pond absorbed water cake would form at the bottom keep that in.

The hut rust bin thanks piece of colour.

A little pool gravel made him first step aside. Gus walked up under the arc-light as far as the first person, perceived God. *She* was God, having lance, he took her by the behind and kissed her butt. Gus want fuck, to get the information.
He spun off her dress. It was there, and
very beautiful, his pecker.

Gus live entirely by hemselve and for hemselve.

He spen days taking off bottles, furnishing room, best system ea heat. For Christ sake! Tryd smoke ham wash.

There was a large cop faggot pursued the secret butterfly near fourteen glass jars tomato and green peas coated the stoppers with quicklime cheese wrapped round with linen strip, then lunged into boiling water: it steamed. He por in difference of temperature, he explode. Only, he were saved.

Then he poured some old sardine, laid veal cutlet inside, and sank the copper. He ball him. He cold. He out again.

He continue the experiment. Shut up. The tin egg chicory lobster fish congratulate hemselve.

Ike Heraclitus, or, "Gus," still elusive, flit on ahead.

Despair defeat labor. The woman fell ill. She laid the copper. It glistens as if about to erupt. At that moment the secret fell in the eye, grace over the golden woman's form.

Then Gus made lunch.

Presence

and I am lost in the ringing elevator
he waggles   the fat whiteness of milk
sweeping me to the top
one is reminded of constellations
there there were pine needles
dreams of symbolism
the part that goes over the fence last
star light   the cord "reaches"
it was turkey
sheepish lights   you turned me on

reflecting dilemmas   majorities
Bildungsroman of the bathrobe ride
and the briny sound of the alarm
a funny feeling prompted me out of bed
Love
the top had been "sliced"
ribbons your presence on the white and green sheet
I asked for a Hook-and-Ladder
takes   The End.
in the ideal society pants

Now   we can make some explosions
shine like money
Francis is not diminutive   thanks
others are less legs
thighs wings breast
Caress the window grease, John
as you are not yet 12
19?   40?   who pulls me down?
that night we slept reverently   (you lust
I must lust in-
vigorating   the sixteen genre
dragon   bottle-opener
spiral cuff-link aerial
facade of the wonderful orient word
"doilies"

Overhead the moon is out
blacking my shoes, face

we were all livid, numinous

Things whip toward the center
licking the palate of his headache
this indicates your future
meditates on his wish which is
hooked onto the top and draped archly

Childhood fuses   a mystery play
Take off your beautiful blouse, you foolish girl!
which ribbons the marvelous laurel   the loop-
Are you list-   with this ring I
eye thee
(that was later, out west, after more baseball
some turkey
a wristwatch, dictionary, sniper suit, rifle
to "meditate"
(is there room in the tune to atune in?)

They were incensed at his arrival
Now we are glad   it was stinky
some paint them black in the face to be quaint or something
one symbol fact seems valid
I don't know
all hate it to be right
on the cards
which are sometimes funky (aesthetic) having
snow of feet and that a domination.
Then we had presence.

Ikonostasis

FOR BERNADETTE MAYER

Kings . . . panties
I imagine these here
the difference between past and dreaming
An uncomfortable Dodge
The word dissolves
iron things
Horses for example
then there is the other which may be called
the familiar floating oasis
larger than whiter
brazen, resourceful
. . . sinning palms balance it

perhaps these are wax detectors
and create situations
a magic shell for silliness
before the law tables
of this here
Heart
That has been tinted white
by way of exercise

the Political
glazes
These eyes
breaks
into the grocery store where
is sick cannot work

twisted stick
industrial berry shoes are established
above all . . . be double
or collapse

the wall covered with glass character weather

M'sieur Negro-at-3 A.M.
Charioteer
His burning problem

it doesn't stop the music
the magic
under tasteless stockings
and under the sting which leaves no ash

the grey snow of someone's epoch annoys
and redeems
through certain fraudulent practices which,
like sulphur, blacken

making an undenied hash of all that
and that will now not melt in the first sunbeam
being its own muse

The Upper Arm

FOR ANDY WARHOL

Upon this field the physical energies of
Clouds. He will no longer desire the
Demanding force, an incredible
Fortune has fallen across their paths. I wait
a Payer is paying for the art it releases
Prisoners from the hands
In an automobile accident on the
Face
And achieved enemy face
Paleface changed captive
Photographs later
Were tipped "What does this mean, my son?"

Became categorical   as in "yes"   held on
The arms and
Powder on a little table
And down in a green forest ravine   near to "her"
Security of the relationship is made utterly
With high stakes and shot at those targets out of
Boughs that spell
"MY PAINTINGS"

Corridors of Blood

1. Madrid

a faint smile appears
shaking your beliefs
of which you have done no more
than sketch in the main outline
You are not a glutton for experience
There is a sudden buzz of activity
In the clear blue sky

2. Detective

an enormous room with a balcony
less virulence
our labors were directed toward
    isolating and creating
such a pattern
"you must allow your feelings to
    float free, by
themselves, like dead leaves."
"I've got it."
we were furious

3. Queen Matilda's Famous Tapestry

You got him out of your system
he was lying out of compassion
"Don't you see what it means?"
human society upside down
The second name
First we must retrieve our honor

4. Henry VIII

women came down to breakfast
We saw that beautiful creature,
    Kay Francis, in
"Cynara"
the shabby taxis and peeling posters
teashops
and ugly window-dressing
a technical brilliance
I never saw the like of anywhere else

5. Poe

"Merde" said Marco
in the apricot-coloured bar
Olga was in another bar
I am sure you understand
The captain lost his temper
A car drew up at the corner

6. Cattle of the Sun

a profusion of melons, oranges and
 fish
all through that night
a lobster had been following him
I had an uncomfortable night
the only place I know
 where horror borders on poetry

7. The Death of Other

should have "roots"
mass of ash-blonde hair
and black, clinging dresses
(the emotions: outline of
 a theory)
into her mouth
blistered strips of bladder
wrack

8. Czechoslovakia

A red-tiled floor
thereafter we walked
sweeping, landscapes of white
limestone rock and
red rock
the most curious concoction
doubly oppressive
the sluggish heat:
I remember running

9. Hunger

Irony and parody held pride of place
in her silk evening dress
Olga had several minor parts
little of Knut Hamsun
several bravura touches
"marking time"
treating it lightly
The death of Max Jacob

10. Henry IV

naked
with a lion
a small lesbian
smoking a pipe
some silent young men
"Shit!" they exclaim
"Fuck all women!"
They all start singing patriotic songs

11. The Milk Bar

Loud shouts and
running feet on the staircase
"Coward! Coward!"
the death of Robert Desnos
quite charming in a red and black dress
with black shoes
about three handbreadths high
The salesgirl laughs at us

12. Hate

I turned back
battered by the frightful air
But I made a kind of wager with myself
detail dazzled me
I considered making it
the theme of my next novel
Every day I had experience of this

13. American Films

a blue-eyed little girl with brown pigtails
their big red-tiled kitchen
big platefuls of bilberries for dessert
children's laughter
the fresh scent of wild berries
that little brown-haired girl
would be stood up against a wall
on richer, fiercer colors
        ocher, red, purple

14. Proust's Sex Life

it's "splendid animalism"
Ramon Fernandez made a special trip
to see
"Well," I said, "have you seen it?"
although I knew he was absolutely broke
my chosen themes had not lost
their sharpness

Rusty Nails

MY NAME

Smiling with grace the mother, the spouse, leaned
across to the fourth of their after-the-theatre party,
who was a girl older than this boy, aged almost seven-
teen, by perhaps two years.

THE PROBLEM OF EVIL

I led in my childhood and youth the gently bred existence
of my class and my kind.

PATRIOTISM

An estimated two million wasps were loosed on an area
of four hundred and fifty miles inhabited by
eighty thousand people.

MY BEST FRIEND

That was about you in my story.

AN ORPHAN LEARNS TO COUNT

The Police swooped down in a squad car.

MALNUTRITION

By accident I met some rich homosexuals of the inter-
national queer set who cruise around the world, bumping
into each other in queer joints from New York to Cairo.

CANCER

For there was a heavy curtain over the window, and in the
center of the room, an electric light bulb, suspended from
the ceiling, was all wrapped in newspaper.

SUNBURN

Loading his gun with one of these buttons, he seated himself on the bed beside his wife, and declared his intention of shooting the witch cat.

DEATH BY DROWNING

For, in respect to the latter branch of the supposition, it should be considered that the most trifling variation of the facts of the two cases might give rise to the most important miscalculations, by diverting thoroughly the two courses of events; very much as, in arithmetic, an error which, in its own individuality, may be inappreciable, produces, at length, by dint of multiplication at all points of the process, a result enormously at variance with the truth.

DEATH IN THE AFTERNOON

She sighed in vain for the chaff and the wheat, not knowing the one from the other.

MASSACRED BY THE INDIANS

Ain' nothin' new about that neither.

BAD NEWS

The man in bed—staring at me appraisingly—was enormous.

SPRING RETURNS

We are drawn to shit because we are imperfect in our uses of the good.

THE PENNILESS WIDOW

He drew his wife's attention to the pustule on the top of my skull for I had removed my hat out of courtesy.

THE DOORS OF PERCEPTION

There were seven to choose from, all putty.

THE TERRORS OF PUBERTY

She didn't realize her belly was more provocative when it had been run through with hatred.

A PROVERB

Meanwhile the papers were reporting masochists shooting tacks, with rubber bands, at apes in zoos.

A MESSAGE FROM THE LOVED ONE

I was horrified.

SYMBOLISM

He must have pressed the wrong button, or several of them, for when the door fretted open he found himself deep underground, with no heart to try again.

THE MODERN CRISIS

"What's this nasty piece of wood stuck in your boobs?"

THE AFTERLIFE

"The Cherry Orchard."

THE WORLD TODAY

"Jungle Law," the man agreed.

DEADLY VISIBLE RAYS

They had many days now when they were very happy.

SOMETHING'S HAPPENING HERE

Your historian will not attempt to list the sights he pointed out in the multitudinous halls since no one will ever forget them anyway.

EIGHT SQUARES

A good smell of hot coffee is coming out of the coffee-pot on the table.

A GIFT

"You in the new winter
                    stretch forth your hands"

I AM A MAN OF CONSTANT SORROW

"I know from my own experience that telepathy is a fact."

LIFE OF A MAN

Matinee

Morning
(ripped out of my mind again!)

As Usual

Take off your hat & coat & give me all your money
I have to buy some pills & I'm flat broke

On the Road Again

FOR GIUSSEPPE UNGARETTI

He called his Mama
Mohammed Scee-ab

He put his hand on
Her rear to be funny
She killed herself
You can bet no one ever told
His father

He made love to Frances
The talking mule

He's no sap either
He chopped her head off
So she can't yell and
He's plumb vanished

Let's go with him to Naples
To insult the old priest whose belly
Bulges over his belly-button
Like a piggy
And at number 5 Subnormal Street
We'll see his sad Victrola

You sap!
If you aren't turned on by now
It's your earache!

Tonight

Winds in the stratosphere
Apologize to the malcontents
Downstairs

Joy of Shipwrecks

The torpedo was friendly
it buggered us

Mayday!

The climax came later
In the water
Near a sea-horse

After Breakfast

Flame & Fury
The colt and the dolt became outlaws

The automobile slew them

December

Brother and sister departed
With apologies to the mother for intercourse
In their hearts

A Reply to the Fragile

If he bites you he's friendly
If it hurts you
Go away
Don't give him a fresh try
Unless you have titties
Like a fast horse

Tobacco

He made coffee
In his maid's uniform

He made coffee with animals
From the desert
Who expectorated into the coffeepot

His veins swelled up with an army
Of germs whose unconscious's
Hated these possibilities

He reared back saying, "Me Nasty!"
So We began to BE Nasty

As for what happened next
You can bet that he learned to express himself

Tooting My Horn on Duty

Tooting my horn on duty in the infantry
Made my name mud PU
In the army I had nosebleeds

The Infantry was so distracting
It kindled up in my nose
An invisible odor
That hindered my toots

One day while on duty
I rammed into a chestnut
And got blood all over my flute
Not to mention this nosebleed

I spat out so many teeth I knew it was an omen
The vitamins I had to take made me ill
Ten blood transfusions It was almost all over
When two big rocks stopped the bleeding

This was my unhappy childhood

Corporal Pellegrini

He was ugly

She kissed the poor fellow
On his belly

ai-yai-yai

Wild horses couldn't hold him

He snaked her carcass
Around a finger
Like a bowling ball

Come and get it!

They threw him in the pen
And busted his illusions
On the fires of Corregidor

His rifle slowly
Fired
Better and better

Killing the idiot

Life Among the Woods

Near Paris, there is a boat. Near this boat live the beautiful Woods.

They are a charming family, the Woods, very friendly: Mr. Woods, Mrs. Woods, their son Peter, and their tiny daughter, Bubbles.

Mr. Woods is very rich. He has a grand house, in four pieces: a kitchen, a stable, a room for lying down, and a room for infants. In this house there is, in addition, a brain room.

Mr. Woods' garden is also very grand. It is full of lettuces, flowers and fruits.

Mrs. Woods likes cooking plenty. She makes pies, pots of tea, and desserts. The little Woods have beautiful appetites. They eat a lot.

Mrs. Woods' kitchen is very appropriate. It has a pretty little furnace, a table, four chaise lounges and a large placard. On the placard there are six S's, six tassels, and fifty soupspoons. (One of the soupspoons is crusty.) There is also a grand casserole.

In the room for laying down there are four tiny books, four chaise lounges and four tiny tables. One sometimes goes to the toilet on the tables.

In the room for infants there is a big table, plenty of chaise lounges and one grand placard on which are pictures of the toys of the tiny Woods: a puppy, a train, a toupee, a cigarette, some balls, some books, a pellet, soap, a strangler's cord, and lots of other things.

The black bag and the wise man may be found in the brain room.

They eat in the stable, where there is a grand table and some chaise lounges.

Mrs. Woods' rat poison is kept in the stable, in a great bottle.

In her office she keeps plenty of other things. She keeps bread, berries, beer, lace, celery, buttons, plums, and a comforter.

In Three Parts

FOR JOHN GIORNO

According
to
the
basic
law
of
visual
perception
any
stimulus
pattern
tends
to
be
seen
in
such
a
way
that
the
resulting
pattern
is
as
simple
as
the
given
conditions
permit.

*

Before
the
orgasmic
platform
in
the
outer
third
of
the
vagina
develops
sufficiently
to
provide
increased
exteroceptive
and
proprioceptive
stimulation
for
both
sexes,
the
over-
distended
excitement-
phase
vagina
gives
many
women

the
sensation
that
the
fully
erect
penis
is
"lost
in
the
vagina."

✲

With
daring
and
strength
men
like
Pollock,
deKooning
Tobey,
Rothko,
Smith
and
Kline
filled
their
work
with
the
drama,
anger,

pain,
and
confusion
of
contemporary
life.

In 4 Parts

A person can lie around on an uncrowded beach

And when too much peace and quiet gets on his nerves, he can always get dressed and tour Israel.

✲

Mayor
Frank
X.
Graves
today
ordered
the
arrest
of
Allen
Ginsberg
if
the
police
could
prove
that
the

poet
smoked
marijuana
while
looking
at
the
Passaic
Falls
yesterday.

*

The
Jewish
Memorial
Hospital's
Junior
League
will
give
its
second
annual
discotheque
benefit
Sunday
at
the
Round
Table.

*

William
Carlos
Williams

the
Paterson
N. J.
physician
was
a
strong
and
vigorous
poet
who
spoke
in
the
American
idiom.

AN AUTOBIOGRAPHY IN 5 PARTS

Craze Man Wiliiker

FOR PIERRE REITER

Once there was a rich man named craze man Wiliiker. This man was always very nice he would give alot of money to poor people, but he said to himselve "I had better save some of my money for myselve." So the next day he went to the bank with a gun (just in case they would not give him his money) he said "give me my money because I have to buy presents for all my relatives."

The next day he went to the Monkey Wards department store he bought a 24 foot yate, a motercycle, a small car, a byicycle, and meny more expencive gifts. Then he went to the store and bought a big airplane for himself then he loaded up his airplane and flew through the city tos money all over.

The next day he had a pipeline put on the hot plains so people in distress could get water all through that area. He also built little shops into skyscrapers for the LandLord. He built hospitals all over the earth.

One day while flying around in his airplane he ran accross two men trying to sell old pots, but they were not having any bissness. He landed and he asked them "Hows bissness?" The men replied "We've been here more than 40 days and haven't sold a pot." Wiliikers sayed "I'll buy your whole stock and as meny more pots as you can get." The man gave him his bill and supplyed him with his pots.

Two days later he took his wife out to dinner and tiped the waiter a hundred dollarbill. He invited all the hobbos he knew to dinner and he even told the manager that he was going to give the biggest party the world has ever known and that it would be held on December 25. He sayed it would be adverticed all over the earth. When December 25 came all the men asked him why he was so nice to everybody he said "It's because it's Christmas day. *Merry Christmas!*

from Memoirs

Never will I forget that trip. The dead were so thick in spots we tumbled over them. There must have been at least 2000 of those sprawled bodies. I identified the insignia of six German divisions, some of their best. The stench was carnal to the point of suffocation. The sounds and cries of wounded men sounded everywhere. I could but think how wrong I'd been one bright day at Texas Military Academy when I had so glibly criticized Dante's description of hell as too extreme.

A flare suddenly lit up the scene for a fraction of a minute and we hit the dirt hard. There just ahead of us stood three Germans—a lieutenant pointing with outstretched arm, a sergeant crouched over a machine gun, a corporal feeding a bandolier of cartridges to the weapon. I held my breath waiting for the burst. But there was nothing. My guide shifted his poised grenade to the other hand and reached for his flashlight.

The Germans had not moved. They were never to move. They were dead, all dead—the lieutenant with shrapnel through his heart, the sergeant with his belly blown into his back, the corporal with his spine where his head should have been. We left them there, gallant men dead in the service of their country.

I completed my reconnaissance and reached our flank regiment just before dawn. There I found its distinguished colonel, Frank McCoy, and its gallant chaplain, Father Duffy, just returned from burying the poet Sergeant Joyce Kilmer beside the stump of one of those trees he had immortalized.

A Letter

TO JOHN GIORNO

When Wyn & Sally and the twins went to Minnesota to visit Wyn's father last August, Wyn discovered marijuana growing wild all over the Minnesota countryside. He brought back a suitcase full and said to me, "How would you like to go out and harvest some?" So in the middle of September, when the moon was right just before the first frost, we flew out to Minneapolis at 10:30 in the morning with five large suitcases and a trunk. I was dressed in an old Brooks Brothers suit and a vest.

We arrived in Minneapolis at 2, were met by a white Hertz rent-a-car and drove 2 hours to Red Wing. All along the side of the road and in front of every farmhouse were these 12 foot high clusters. Wyn said they're so dumb out there they think that marijuana comes from Mexico. We cased this sand pit and it looked OK. Then we emptied the 5 suitcases and the trunk which were filled with the costumes from "Conquest of the Universe" into a garbage dump and drove to Frontenac where Mark Twain spent his summers. We bought 2 bathing suits and went for a swim in the Mississippi. It was terrific. Then we drove to Lake City which is this 1930's Bonnie & Clyde town and we sat in this 1930's soda-fountain cafe waiting for it to get dark. We telephoned Sally and told her everything was going great. Then we drove back to the sand pit and parked the car behind a falling down shed of an abandoned turkey farm and sat watching how many cars passed on the road. When it got dark, we changed into dungarees and went to work. I cut the plants and Wyn cut them into small pieces and stuffed them into plastic bags. There was this jungle of pot plants that looked like giant Christmas Trees and moonlight and dew, and the dew and resin got all over my skin and I was stoned. About 3 A.M. we changed back into the straight clothes and drove to Minneapolis. We didn't take any amphetamine because I thought we'd look suspicious if we looked like speed freaks at 6 in the morning. I was so tired I just went up to the ticket counter and said to the guy, "Here!" We flew back to NY with 70 pounds of wet grass. It dried down to 24 pounds.

Che Guevara's Cigars

Guevara had noticed me smoking, and had remarked that of course I would never dare smoke Cuban cigars. I told him that I would love to smoke Cuban cigars but that Americans couldn't get them. The next day, a large polished-mahogany box hand-inlaid with the Cuban seal and amid swirling patterns in the national colors, flying a tiny Cuban flag from a brass key, and crammed with the finest Havanas arrived at my room. With it was a typewritten note from Guevara, reading in Spanish, "Since I have no greeting card, I have to write. Since to write to an enemy is difficult, I limit myself to extending my hand." (I took the box, the cigars untouched, back to Washington and showed it to President Kennedy. He opened it and asked, "Are they good?" "They're the best," I said, whereupon he took one out of the box, lit it, and took a few puffs. Then he looked up at me suddenly and said, "You should have smoked the first one.")

Frank O'Hara's Question from "Writers and Issues" by John Ashbery

what sky
out there is between the ailanthuses
a 17th century prison an aardvark
a photograph of Mussolini and
a personal letter from Isaak Dinesen
written after eating

can be succeeded by a calm evaluation of the "intense inane" that surrounds him:

it is cool
I am high
and happy
as it turns
on the earth
tangles me
in the air

and between these two passages (from the long poem "Biotherm") occurs a mediating line which might stand to characterize all of Mr. O'Hara's art:

I am guarding it from mess and message.

* * *

Entrance

FOR ED DORN

10 years of boot
Take it away
& it's off
Under the table

2

        & I'm hovering
I'm above *American Language*
one foot
is expressing itself as continuum
the other, sock

groan I am dog
tired from cake
walking
to here. That is,
An Entrance.

March 17th, 1970

Someone who loves me calls me
        & I just sit, listening
Someone who likes me wires me,
        to do something. I'll do it
Tomorrow.

Someone who wants to do me harm
is after me
& finds me.

I need to kill someone
And that's what it's all about.
Right Now.

"In Three Parts"

blank mind part

Sounds pretty sane to me!

never thought of that!

Part two

Excursions across the ice

Confusions of the cloth

bread & butter
bread & butter

kiss kiss

Part Three

LOVE

Addenda: Sleep

Oh, hello, Ted!

Epithalamion

Pussy put her paw into the pail of paint.
"Hip, hop, pip, pop, tip, top, pop-corn".
The dipper tipped and the sirup dripped upon her apron.
Phillippa put the Parson's parcel beside the Professor's papers.
Bowser buried his bone inside a barrel.
The brown bear stole the bumblebee.
White snow whirled everywhere.
The able laborer objects to the bride.
Adam and Eve stumbled over the rubber tube.
Mama made a muffler and a muff for me.
My Mary's asleep by the murmuring stream
The meadow-mouse uses the lamp for its moonbeam.

In Minneapolis, Minnesota there are many married men.
Many Americans are making money in Mexico.

Homecoming

I sit on   fat
                                           like
An old dog
Anxious to set.   Across
               the fields   fruit
grows   in
Another state. The map
Goes quietly dark. In the
      corners   white
               jasmine blossoms begin
To radiate
Cold.   In the sky the

Soft, loose

stars swarm.

Now

drops of blood squirt

Onto the stiff leaves.

Now I

breathe.

Poop

Nature makes my teeth "to hurt"

*

Each conviction lengthens the sentence

*

Women are interesting when I look at them

*

Art is medicine for imbeciles

*

Great Art is a Great Mistake

*

If it's inspiration you want, drop your panties

*

If I fall in love with my friend's wife, she's fucked*

*alternates:

I'm fucked
he's fucked

American Express

Cold rosy dawn in New York City
not for me
in Ron's furlined Jim Bridger
(coat)
that I borrowed two years ago
had cleaned
but never returned, Thank god!
On 6th Street
Lunch poems burn
a hole is in my pocket
two donuts one paper bag
in hand
hair is in my face and in my head is
"cold rosy dawn in New York City"

I woke up this morning
it was night
you were on my mind
on the radio
And also there was a letter
and it's to you
if "you" is Ron Padgett,
American express
shivering now in Paris
Oklahoma
two years before
buying a new coat for the long trip
back to New York City
that I'm wearing now

It is cold in here
for two
looking for the boll weevil
(looking for a home), one with pimples
one blonde, from Berkeley
who says, "Help!" and
"Hey, does Bobby Dylan come around here?"
"No, man," I say,
"Too cold!"
& they walk off, trembling,
(as I do in L.A.)
so many tough guys, faggots, & dope addicts!
though I assure them
"Nothing like that in New York City!"
It's all in California!
(the state state)
that shouldn't be confused with
The balloon state
that I'm in now
hovering over the radio
following the breakfast of champions
& picking my curious way
from left to right
across my own white
expansiveness
MANHATTAN!

listen
The mist of May
is on the gloaming
& all the clouds
are halted, still

fleecey
& filled
with holes.
They are alight with borrowed warmth,
just like me.

February Air

FOR DONNA DENNIS

Can't cut it (night)

in New York City

it's alive

inside my tooth

on St. Mark's Place

where exposed nerve

jangles

•

that light
isn't on
for me

that's it

though you are
right here.

•

It's RED RIVER
time
on tv

and
Andy's BRILLO BOX is on
the icebox is on   High
too   over St. Nazaire, the
Commando is poised

that means tonight's raid
is "on"

The Monkey
at the typewriter
is turned on

(but the tooth hurts)

You'd Better Move On. . . .

You'd Better Move On

Black Power

It's ritzy   Thrift,

Horn & Hardart's is
too, one
cup of coffee, black
away from it

& Generosity
though commingling with incontrovertible hard- (art)
headedness
does warm

& it keeps it up

e. g.

"Art is art & life is
Life." Fairfield Porter said
that:

& That means

Coffee

Black as on
57th Street

The Hotel Buckingham (facade) is

looming over lunch   poems   & I
looming over coffeecup   white   two eyes
looming over Joe's black & yellow polka-dots

(a tie)

that once belonged to Montgomery Clift:

It's all mine now, is saved, knowing
That, & that happily being that

"the living is easy"
Tho the art is hard,
sometimes, to see
through so much looming:

More coffee may save me that.

The Ten Greatest Books of the Year (1967)

Apollinaire Oeuvres Poetiques
Swami Sivananda, Waves of Bliss
James Joyce, Ulysses
Gerard Malanga & Andy Warhol, Screen Test/A Diary
The Collected Earlier Poems of William Carlos Williams
Helen Hathaway, What Your Voice Reveals
Jean Jacques Mayoux, Melville
Kay Ambrose, Ballet-Lovers Pocketbook
Roger Shattuck, Apollinaire
William Shakespeare, Cymbeline
Charlin's Anglo-French Course 3rd Part
The Pocket Dictionary of Art Terms
Locus Solus No. 2
Compositions Property of Ted Berrigan
Jack Kerouac, Mexico City Blues
Ron Loewinsohn, L'Autre
Ted Berrigan, Clear the Range
Philip Whalen, Selfportrait from Another Direction
Wallace Stevens, Collected Poems
The Complete Sonnets Songs and Poems of William Shakespeare
Boswell's Life of Johnson
The Collected Later Poems of William Carlos Williams
The Oxford Book of English Verse
Williams & Macy, Do You Know English Literature
Richard Brautigan, Trout Fishing in America
Jim Carroll, Organic Trains
Stokely Carmichael, Toward Black Liberation
Ted Berrigan, The Sonnets
Ted Berrigan & Ron Padgett, Bean Spasms
Dick Gallup, The Lungs of Sophocles
Eduardo Paolozzi, Kex
Lawrence Campbell, Sills

Diter Rot, Buch
Ted Berrigan, Art Notes
Velversheen by Eagle-A
Ron Padgett, Tone Arm
Poetry Magazine May 1960
University Note Book
Jim Brodey, Clothesline
The Cantos of Ezra Pound CX–CXVI
Frank O'Hara, Meditations in an Emergency
Walt Whitman, Leaves of Grass
David Henderson, Felix of the Silent Forest
Poets of the English Language Vol. III Milton to Goldsmith
Poets of the English Language Vol. I Langland to Spenser
Poets of the English Language Vol. V Tennyson to Yeats
Fuck You, A Magazine of the Arts Vol. 6, No. 5
The World No. 7
William Burroughs, Time
Folder No. 2
Larry McMurtry, The Last Picture Show
"C" Comics

The Ten Greatest Books of the Year, 1968

The Collected Earlier Poems by William Carlos Williams
Selected Writings Charles Olson
Chicago Review One Dollar
Alkahest
New American Writing No. 1
THE RANDOM HOUSE DICTIONARY OF THE ENGLISH LANGUAGE
The Pocket Aristotle

After Dinner We Take a Drive into the Night by Tony Towle
Love Poems (Tentative Title) by Frank O'Hara
The Sky Pilot in No Man's Land by Ralph Connors
Cosmic Consciousness by Dr. Richard Bucke
Meditations on the Signs of the Zodiac by John Jocelyn

In Public In Private by Edwin Denby

The World Number 1 Cover by Dan Clark
The World Number 2 Cover by Robert McMillan
The World Number 3 Cover by George Schneeman
The World Number 4 Cover by Donna Dennis
The World Number 5 Cover by Jack Boyce
The World Number 6 Cover by Fielding Dawson
The World Number 7 Cover by Bill Beckman
The World Number 8 Cover by George Schneeman
The World Number 9 Cover by Joe Brainard
The World Number 10 Cover by Larry Fagin
The World Number 11 Cover by Tom Clark
The World Number 12 Cover by George Schneeman
The World Number 13 Cover by Donna Dennis
The World Number 14 Cover by Joe Brainard

Waterloo Sunset

We ate lunch, remember? and I paid the check
Under trees in rain of false emotion and big bull
With folks going in and out putting words in our mouths that are
shouting, "Hurrah for Bristol Cream!" We threw a leave-sandwich
Into the sunlight—it greedily gobbled it up, and growing brighter

Emanating from their glasses came the little drinkies
Reflections of the magazine Grandma edits
On whose pages a bouquet is blossoming sort of. You bounced a check
Into years of lives down under the weather vane, barf!
The influence of alcohol rebounded 500 miles into Africa.

But a little drinkie never hurt nobody, except an African.
The Earth sops up liquids, I mean drinks,
And is tipsy as pinballs on the ocean
Wobbling on its axis. We turn a paleface shade of white
In the rain that pelts the doo-doo
That flies from the eyes' blinds. It doesn't matter though
                    on the sweet side
Of the moon. Don't be a horrible sourpuss
Moon! Have a drink
Have an entire issue! Waves goodbye & reels, into sun
Of light dark light roll over Beethoven
Our shelter-half misses your shelter-half. There's nothing left
                    of love
But we have checkerberry leaves
Mint, Juniper, tree-light
Elder-flowers, sweet goldenrod, bugspray & Juice.

And you are a pretty girl-boy
And I am a pretty man-woman
and we are here-there
In England and the food is absolutely cold-hot.
In the aromatic sundown, according to the magazine version
Or automatic sundown   English words are a gas
Slurring the Earth's one heaving angel turns in unison
& paddles your rear gently as befits one in love
                with you & I
No change   My face is all right
For us. We are bored through & we are through with you
With our professionalism (you have to become useless to drink).

All we ever wanted to do in the rosy sunlight was
In the first place was . . . was . . . was . . . uh
Run our fingers through your curly hair
Ooops!   No, not that.   I mean all
We really wanted to do was jazz yr mother
Fight off insects & sing a sad solitary tune
On the excellencies of Bristol Cream
Six dollars a bottle Praise The Lord

TED BERRIGAN & RON PADGETT

30

The fucking enemy shows up

interstices

bent

Grey Morning

Rain
Coming down
Outside her
Windows
I can be seen inside
the drops
of rain
falling
limping
This girl in mind.

Things to Do in Anne's Room

Walk right in
sit right down
baby, let your hair hang down

It's on my face that hair
& I'm amazed to be here
the sky outside is green the blue
shows thru the trees

I'm on my knees

unlace Li'l Abner
shoes
place them under the bed
light cigarette
study out the dusty bookshelves,
sweat

Now I'm going to do it

SELF RELIANCE
THE ARMED CRITIC
MOBY DICK
THE WORLD OF SEX
THE PLANET OF THE APES

Now I'm going to do it

deliberately

take off clothes
shirt goes on the chair
pants go on the shirt
socks next to shoes next to bed

the chair goes next to the bed

get into the bed
be alone
suffocate
don't die

& it's that easy.

The Great Genius

The Great Genius is

A man who can do the

Ordinary thing

When everybody

Else is going crazy.

Poem for Philip Whalen

✲ ✲

(About Emily Dickinson)

What about Emily Dickinson?

DEAD FINGERS TALK

I've got a lot of things to do today.

For example write this poem.

She's Terrific.

Now, this poem is to say that

period?
colon?
space??

✲ ✲ ✲

Lord I wonder just exactly what can happen oh Hello, Pill . . .

It's a terrific spelling problem there's two kinds of L's (on the typewriter)
and *that* is a good example of the way some people
think

(NOVEL)

This here now is what I'm trying to say. It's a sonnet. A kind of formal BEAN
SPAS
M

She goes all over the place, eh?

ROOT RAINBOW HA-HA

She's so fine:

You Didn't Even Try

Heroin

FOR JIM CARROLL

(2) photographs of Anne

80 years old

lovely, as always

a child

under an old fashion

duress

A Bibliography of Works
by Jack Kerouac

A white suit
and a black dress
w/high-necked
mini-skirt

strolling

two by two

across a brown paper bag

above The Relation Ship

Warm white thighs & floating bend gia pronto

my heart is filled with light

al curry

this

Life
that is
one, tho
the Lamps
be many   & proud   & there's a breeze sort of
lightly moving the top

of yr head

&   I'm going
way over
the white
skyline

& I'll do
what I want to

& you can't keep me here

No-how.

& the streets are theirs now

& the tempo's

&   the space

Anti-War Poem

It's New Year's Eve, of 1968, & a time
for Resolution.

I don't like Engelbert Humperdink.

I love the Incredible String Band.

The War goes on
& war is Shit.

I'll sing you a December song.

It's 5 below zero in Iowa City tonight.

This year I found a warm room
That I could go to
                              be alone in
& never have to fight.

I didn't live in it.

I thought a lot about dying
But I said *Fuck it.*

Tough Brown Coat

TO JIM CARROLL

Tough brown coat
Tie with red roses
Green cord vest

Brown stripes
on soft white
shirt

white T-shirt

White man,
    Tomorrow you die!

"You kidding me?"

Babe Rainbow

Light up

smoke

burn a few holes in the blanket

Burn a few holes in the Yellow blanket

burning

smoking

reading

It's Important

It's important not
to back out
of the mirror:

You will be great, but
You will be queer.

It's a complication.

Dial-A-Poem

Inside
The homosexual sleeps
long past day break
We won't see him
awake
	this time around.

In My Room

Green (grass)

A white house brown
mailbox

(Friendly pictures)

*

TELEVISION snow

(that's outside)

No-mind

No messages

(Inside)

Thanksgiving 1969

Ann Arbor Elegy

FOR FRANNY WINSTON D. SEPT 27TH, 1969

Last night's congenial velvet sky
Conspired that Merrill, Jayne, Deke, you & I
Get it together at Mr. Flood's Party, where we got high
On gin, shots of scotch, tequila salt & beer
Talk a little, laugh a lot, & turn a friendly eye
On anything that's going down beneath Ann Arbor's sky
Now the night's been let to slip its way
Back toward a mild morning's gray
A cool and gentle rain is falling, cleaning along my way
To where Rice Krispies, English muffins, & coffee, black
Will make last night today. We count on that, each new day
Being a new day, as we read what the Ann Arbor News has to say.

Song: Prose & Poetry

TO ALICE NOTLEY

My heart is confirmed in its pure Buddhahood
But a heavy list to starboard
makes me forget
From time to time.
Breath makes a half turn
Downward & divides:
it doesn't add up
2 plus 2 equals 1: It's fun, yes,
But it isn't true, &
I can't love you
this way.

2.

So, what'll I do, when you
are far away
& I'm so blue?
I'll wait.
& I'll be true some day.

3.

That's all well & good. But
What happens in the mean time?

Wake Up

Jim Dine's toothbrush eases two pills
activity under the clear blue sky; girl
for someone else in white walk by
it means sober up, kick the brunette out of bed
going out to earn your pay; it means out;
bells, ring; squirrel, serve a nut; daylight
fade; fly resting on your shoulder blades
for hours; you've been sleeping, taking it easy
neon doesn't like that; having come your way
giving you a free buzz, not to take your breath away
just tightening everything up a little; legs
pump; head, wobble; tongue, loll; fingers, jump;
drink; eat; flirt; sing; speak;
night time ruffles the down along your cheek

Erasable Picabia

The front is hiding the rear

*

The heart of a man
is not as great as an amphitheater

*

Spinoza is the one who threw a pass to Lou Spinoza

*

There is no death
there is only dissolution

*

love of hate
is totally great

*

me, I disguise myself as a man
in order to laugh

*

I have always loved
a serious jackoff scene

*

infantile paralysis is the beginning of wisdom

*

everything is poison
except our meat

*

Flowers and candy make my teeth ache

*

The most beautiful and most noble
of men are queers

*

get the pussy

*

mystical explanations are dopey

Aunt Winnie fingers the thunder to learn,
so that we have left everything aside
but not as a cloud mind steps beside
    the slow reservoir
now it is all of this, the pink bulbs included,
which means we have "protected ourselves"
by forgetting all we were dealt

BY TED BERRIGAN & JIM CARROLL

In Bed

I love all the girls
I've been in bed with

I even love those
who preferred not to do anything

once there:

Tho it seems to me now
they were nuts!
(the latter)
in bed.

Easy Living

TO DAVID HENDERSON

I hope to go
everywhere
in good time:
Going's a pleasure,
being someplace
& then
Many Happy Returns

*

But Africa,
I don't know
all that heat
all the time
even when it's raining
all the time . . .

✲

I've always found heat

constant heat

difficult

to get inside of

& not to mention

impossible to avoid . . .

✲

You don't have to do anything you don't want to.

That's true.

✲

Go now / Pay later

✲

Equally—You can do anything you want to.

Yes, I know that.

✲

But Africa:

well, I do know one thing

for sure:

It would be tremendous

Africa

going there

to go there with

David Henderson!

(Just like Pittsburgh).

Like Poem

TO JOAN FAGIN

Joan,
I like you
            plenty.

You'd do
            to ride the river with.

I take these tiny pills
to our love.

            Plenty.

Then I drink up the river.
Be seeing you.

Peace

What to do
            when the days' heavy heart
                        having risen, late
in the already darkening East
                        & prepared at any moment, to sink
                                    into the West
surprises suddenly,
            & settles, for a time,
                        at a lovely place
where mellow light spreads
                        evenly
                        from face to face?

The days' usual aggressive
contrary beat
now softly dropped
into a regular pace
the head riding gently its personal place
where pistons feel like legs
on feelings met like lace.
Why,
take a walk, then,
across this town. It's a pleasure
to meet one certain person you've been counting on
to take your measure
who will smile, & love you, sweetly, at your leisure.
And if
she turns your head around
like any other man,
go home
and make yourself a sandwich
of toasted bread, & ham
with butter
lots of it
& have a diet cola,
& sit down
& write this,
because you can.

Hall of Mirrors

TO KRISTIN LEMS

We miss something now
as we think about it
Let's see: eat, sleep & dream, read
A good book, by Robert Stone
Be alone

Knew of it first
in New York City. Couldn't find it
in Ann Arbor, though
I like it here
Had to go back to New York
Found it on the Upper West Side
there

I can't live with you
But you live
here in my heart
You keep me alive and alert
aware of something missing
going on

I woke up today just in time
to introduce a poet
then to hear him read his rhymes
so unlike mine   & not bad
as I'd thought another time

no breakfast, so no feeling fine.

Then I couldn't find the party, afterwards
then I did
then I talked with you.

Now it's back

& a good thing for us
It's letting us be wise, that's why
it's being left up in the air
You can see it, there
as you look, in your eyes

Now it's yours & now it's yours & mine.
We'll have another look, another time.

Ann Arbor Song

I won't be at this boring poetry reading
    again!
I'll never have to hear
    so many boring poems again!
& I'm sure I'll never read them again:
In fact, I haven't read them yet!

Anne won't call me here again,
To tell me that Jack is dead.
I'm glad you did, Anne, though
It made me be rude to friends.
I won't cry for Jack here again.

& Larry & Joan won't visit me here
    again.
Joan won't cook us beautiful dinners,
    orange & green & yellow & brown
    here again.
& Thom Gunn & Carol & Don & I won't get high
    with Larry & Joan here again
Though we may do so somewhere else again.

Harris & John & Merrill won't read
in my class, again.
Maybe there'll never be such a class
again:
I think there probably will, though
& I know Allen will follow me round the world
with his terrible singing voice:
But it will never make us laugh here again.

You Can't Go Home Again is a terrific book:
I doubt if I'll ever read that again.
(I read it first in Tulsa, in 1958)
& I'll *never* go there again.

Where does one go from here? Because
I'll go somewhere again. I'll come somewhere again, too,
& You'll be there, & together we can have a good time.
Meanwhile, you'll find me right here, when you
come through, again.

People Who Died

Pat Dugan . . . . my grandfather . . . . throat cancer . . . . 1947.
Ed Berrigan . . . . my dad . . . . heart attack . . . . 1958.
Dickie Budlong . . . . my best friend Brucie's big brother, when we were
five to eight . . . . killed in Korea, 1953.
Red O'Sullivan . . . . hockey star & cross-country runner
who sat at my lunch table
in High School . . . . . . car crash . . . . . . 1954.
Jimmy "Wah" Tiernan . . . . my friend, in High School,
Football & Hockey All-State . . . . . . car crash . . . . 1959.
Cisco Houston . . . . died of cancer . . . . 1961.
Freddy Herko, dancer . . . . jumped out of a Greenwhich Village window in 1963.

Anne Kepler . . . . my girl . . . . killed by smoke-poisoning while playing
the flute at the Yonkers Children's Hospital
during a fire set by a 16 year old arsonist . . . . 1965.
Frank . . . . . . Frank O'Hara . . . . . . hit by a car on Fire Island, 1966.
Woody Guthrie . . . . . . dead of Huntington's Chorea in 1968.
Neal . . . . . . Neal Cassady . . . . . . died of exposure, sleeping all night
in the rain by the RR tracks of Mexico . . . . 1969.
Franny Winston . . . . just a girl . . . . totalled her car on the Detroit–Ann
Arbor Freeway, returning from the dentist . . . . Sept. 1969.
Jack . . . . . . Jack Kerouac . . . . . . died of drink & angry sicknesses . . . . in 1969.

My friends whose deaths have slowed my heart stay with me now.

Telegram

TO JACK KEROUAC

Bye-Bye Jack.
See you soon.

A New Old Song

FOR LARRY FOR CHRISTMAS

Head of lettuce, glass of chocolate milk
"I wonder if people talk about me, secretly?"
Guess I'll call up Bernadette today, & Dick
The Swedish Policeman in the next room, the Knife
Fighter. Why are my hands shaking? I usually think
Something like The Williamsburg Bridge watching the sun come
Up, wetly round my ears,
Hatless in the white & shining air. Throbbing

Aeroplanes zoom in at us from out there; redder
For what happens there. Yes
It's a big world,
It has a band-aid on it, & under it
TRUE LOVE,
in a manner of speaking.

Poem

of morning, Iowa City, blue
gray & green out the window . . .
A mountain, blotchy pink & white
is rising, breathing, smoke

Now, lumbering, an Elephant, on
crutches, is sailing; down
Capitol, down Court, across
Madison & down College, cold
    clear air
                pouring in

                Now those crutches
are being tossed aside; the
Elephant is beginning to rise
into the warm regulated air
                        of another altitude

That air is you, your breathing

Thanks for it, & thanks a lot
for Pasternak: The Poems of Yurii Zhivago
& Mayakovsky: Poems.

They were great.

Now it's me.

Train Ride

FEBRUARY 18TH, 1971
FOR JOE

Here comes the Man!
He's talking a lot.
New York to Providence
&
I've got a ticket to ride!

SMOKING PERMITTED

The seats are blue

I'm sitting with MYSELF

A long naked pair of legs,
about 17 yrs old
stare at me
across the linoleum
aisle

I'm a mild Sex Fiend!

But you can't fuck
here

& what could you say
to smooth 17 year old
faces?

NOTHING!!

So, they lose out.

What can you say
at all?

NOTHING

However, it's easy to keep
talking
if
it's what you do. . . .

MEN * WOMEN

SPEED

What I like is
ASTERISKS

* * * * * *

They're so
Bold, confident, like you
have a plan, you're in
control, you'll be back
in a minute.

*

"Man, you've got to **do**
something about that hand-
writing! It's Terrible!"

Lorenzo Thomas
Said That
to me
in 1962.

*

I didn't.

*

It's ME.

Now I read a sex book
from the Library of
JIMMY SCHUYLER.
"He loves 'em."
(JOE BRAINARD)

Out the Window
is
Out to Lunch!!

Some people one should only
fuck once.

✲

Others one should not fuck
at all unless there is an
affair.

✲

Then there are those one should
not fuck, under almost any
circumstances (tho lapses are
forgiveable)

✲

Let me see: I've fucked in

Rhode Island
Maine
Vermont
New York
Florida
Texas
Oklahoma
New Mexico
Colorado
California
Michigan
Iowa
Pennsylvania
Kansas
Connecticut

✲

Japan
&
Korea

And
In beds
On floors
In Bathrooms at Parties
In Hallways
In Cars
On Rooftops
Window-Sills
&
At a bus Stop

Never did fuck any boys
(I think)
or
get fucked by any

*

Tho a few blow-jobs
for curiosity
or
because someone really
wanted to.

*

Oops! Add
"In Life-raft
on Lake"

Always wanted to fuck in Air-
Planes & On Trains

✲

Maybe later

I sort of hate to be on the
Make

✲

Like to have some-one
on the Make
for me
&
then
Take Over

✲

Last time I counted I think
It was about
50

✲

The number of people,
I mean

✲

Only about 10 were once.
No, maybe 15.

✲

& that's counting
Japan
&
Korea

Many of them, those girls,
& me,
we still do it when we
get a chance.

One, at least, is dead.

I wish one that's alive
were here.
Or Anne,
who is
dead.

✲

I'm sure she'd love to fuck
on a train

Remember the night we did
it in your house,
Joe?
(Me and Anne, that is)

✲

It was Nice

✲

I guess I'd fuck anyone
who thinks I'm
terrific!
Tho you never can
tell.

"All I really want to do is
have my back
rubbed."
—Anne Waldman

✲

I just remembered:
Add: ENGLAND

✲

Now we're passing thru
NEW LONDON

✲

Sailors are probably
fucking each other
here
right now.

✲

"I'm laying there, & some
guy comes up &
hits me with
a Billy Club!"

—The fat guy across the aisle
just said
that.

✲

Once, while a girl was giving me
a glorious blow-job behind a curtain,
my room-mate, across the room, was studying
CALCULUS!
(Tony Powers was
the room-mate)

Once a girl & I got into an automobile
accident
in her car, so
we decided to fuck
(later)

Once I tried to fuck a little girl
8 years old, when I was also 8 years old,
but I don't think I knew how.
I can't quite
remember.

The long legs just got up
  & got off
    (New London)

Now I'll read this queer sex book
  some more.

It says,
  "Jean Cocteau had no heart."
 That's strange.
    I think he probably did.
  I probably have one, so
  Cocteau probably had one.
  Right?
  Right.

This book seems to have 1,000,000 pages.

No one can think about Fucking
for that long.

I may have to turn back
into
my "well-rounded self"
in order to finish.

*

My "well-rounded self"
is not always
interesting,
but does manage
to get through.

Now, we ride across the river,
and past auto-parts
made of NEON.

I just saw a blue
electric
A
which I thought
at first
was a beautiful evening slipper.

This is a blue train-ride.
I don't feel blue, but
I can see it.

✲

A man name of
Lloyd Calvin Shippey
is sitting
next to me.

✲

He says, "Who are you
supposed to be
in that hair?"

✲

I say, "Uh, Ted Berrigan."

✲

He says, "I thought,
Ben Franklin!"

✲

I forget about him, so
he is no longer there.
Nor here.

✲

This queer sex book is not
very dirty.
Not even very queer.
Not even here,
Now.

I am dead; and I am now in
The After-life. Here you do
just what you do in Life, but
it's never quite real, nor fun.

✲

It isn't boring tho, but it is
sort of pointless.

✲

I'm not sure how long I've been
dead, but I'd say it is since about
1962.

✲

Once in a while I'm alive for a few minutes
. . . . . . probably just dreams
or very real deja-vus.

✲

Maybe it's age, & you come alive
in a different way maybe next
year, or some time.

*

It isn't any big thing,
anyway.
I mean, you can't go around
worrying about it.

I do nothing for a while,
&
I don't remember
what nothing.

Maybe I will fuck ______
this trip.
She's in Boston.

I would like to be elected a SENATOR.

✲

I don't think I'm suited
for any other job, &
I think my poetry
would be exciting to write
if I were a
Senator.

✲

I'd be a terrific Senator
because I'd love it.

I really like to be alone, if
I don't have to be.

I like to come & go.

What I don't like is how money is involved
in everything.

I like to give people
money.

✲

I hate to be given money. It's embarrassing!

I do like
to get money in the mail.

& I like to get paid lots of money
for doing something like reading, talking, or
publishing.

✲

How come I can't get paid
just for writing?

✲

I do like to get presents
spontaneously given,
or just for me.

✲

But it's socially awkward that
some people for almost no reason
have money, & some don't.

✲

Anyway, money is
very perplexing,
& I don't understand it.

I like Credit Cards.
Alas, I can't pay the bills,
but I always spend with the Credit Card
in a terrific way!!

✲

I take people to terrific
Restaurants!

✲

I go to England!

✲

I buy somebody their
return ticket, because they're
broke.

✲

I buy a couple of terrific
shirts.
& a pair of pants.

✲

I rent a car & drive it to Wales, & Liverpool,
with
Lewis Warsh,
on Acid!

✲

I bump into other
cars!!

✲

I buy a de Kooning!

✲

I buy the NY Times, &
do the Crossword Puzzle

✲

I buy some **money** & give it to
my Mother
so she won't worry!
She only needs $300 to make
her Summer Worry-free.

✲

I buy lots of pills
&
I give you
lots of pills.

*

I even get to shop, on Carnaby Street,
in a Children's Boutique
for terrific boots & cowboy jackets
for David!
& sharp clothes for
Kate!

*

I buy a train ticket
to SING-SING

*

I rent a cell for 20
Years,
because
I don't pay my bills!

*

Then I write terrific Prison Poems,
& get lots of mail!

Then I don't know what I
do then.

You don't get to fuck much, in
SING-SING,
if you're straight.

✲

I don't know how I got
to be straight,
since I didn't try
for it.

✲

I'm sure it's just like being queer,
only different.

✲

For example, Edwin is
the straightest person I
know,
& he's been queer forever.

✲

while Rudy is just like
Edwin,
& he's straight.

Queer is a pretty queer
word.

"I'm a queer."
Ha-ha!

✲

How about
"I'm a straight."
Unbelievable!

✲

✲

"I'm an American."

O.K.

✲

"I'm a Christian."

Yes, I suppose
you must be.

✲

"I'm a Poet."

That must be an
interesting job.

✲

"I'm a pill-addict."

You **are**?

✲

"I'm a grown-up, now."

Ha-ha.

✲

"I'm a father."

That's good.

✲

"I'm a long-haired Weirdo."

You seem perfectly normal
to me.

✲

"I'm a great guy."
Well, you are in a manner
of speaking.

✲

"I'm a fucking monster!"

✲

"I'm part elephant, Part Tiger, part
Nag, Part bore."
You might say that.

✲

"I'm an ordinary person."
Yes you are.

✲

"I'm a passenger."
That's absolutely true.

Now, tell me about You?

(this space for you
to do so)

& this

& this

That's enough.

Now what shall we talk
about?
We could
bitch all our mutual
friends!!
Good Idea,
as we pull into
Providence,
R. I.

OUR FRIENDS

Ron: the tight-ass
Dick: the insignificant
Pat: the dowdy old lady
Anne: the superficial
sentimentalist
Bill: the spoiled snoot
Kenward: the Elephant with
the soul of a Butterfly &
the temper of a Scorpion.
George: the bad painter
Michael: the Self Important
Fuss-budget
The grotesque John Ashbery of
the bad character

The silly boring Kenneth Koch
The frumpy Jane Freilicher
The Pain-in-the-Ass Larry
Fagin
The whining Jim Carroll
The Snake in the grass Lewis Warsh
The slick easy poet,
Tom Clark
Jimmy Schuyler who has no stamina
The Asinine baby Tom Veitch
etc.
etc.

*

(Now You do some)

*

____

____

____

*

Yes, but what about us?

*

The Insufferable
Ted Berrigan:
He's so fucking
Heavy!
What a tiresome
person!
So Presumptuous!
Self-Important!
Repetitious!
Never Shuts Up!
Too fucking Bossy!
Who does he think he is???

Fat-Ass!

Those Teeth!

Mean to his wife!!

Boring Poet!!

Who Cares!!

Why doesn't he run for **Pope**

& get it over with!!

He thinks he knows

it All!!

etc.

etc.

*

& That Joe Brainard!!

He likes the boring Supremes!
Why doesn't he be great,
like de Kooning?
Why doesn't he button
that shirt?
Cook?
Be poor again & do great
Masterpieces?
Stop Tom-catting
around?
He makes everyone Nervous!!
He dresses funny!!
His apartment is weird!!

He's compulsive!

Skinny!

Takes pills too
much!!

Talks to himself!

Solipsist!

Wants to have all the
fun!

Doesn't like kids!!

Mean to his Mother!

Mean to his lovers!

Cynical!!

Stutters!!

Never comes to visit!!

Doesn't like us
anymore.

An opportunist!!
Should get married!
Should do big oil paintings!!
Get Serious!!
Talk more!! Talk less!!
Tell the truth!!
Know the truth!!
Be perfect!!
God damn it!!

& the Train continues in the night. . . .
black outside
high inside.

✲

What energy!

✲

What a dumb book.

✲

Glad I'll never have to read
it.

✲

Hope it gets a rise out of
SOMEBODY!

Train blows whistle
when approaching
Station.

Didn't get to Fuck
on it.

✲

Did eat a terrible
hamburger:
$1.75
& drink
a pepsi: .35
——
Total $2.20
Plus tip: .50

✲

$4.00 is about to get off
of a Train,
into a cab.

✲

Taxi Fare will be:
$3.50 & tip: .50

✲

But I have hidden re-
sources:
95 cents

———

You are my hidden resources!

✲

You live in my world
at the other end of the train.

✲

You give me brain-spasms,
& heart-bursts.

✲

Writing to read &
Pictures to see

✲

You give me love,
& I feel proud
that you really do
like me & respect me
despite everything

✲

Because You are one of my big
heroes. . . .   Smarter
than me,   (tho really no
"better", if you
know what I mean)

✲

I love you a whole lot.

✲

I'm glad we were together
on this train.

✲

I had a really nice time
at your place today.

✲

I felt really alive, &
warmed
walking toward the
train

That I just got up
in,
&
walked thru
&
now am off of,
at
the end of this book,

✲

TRAIN RIDE
(Feb 18th, 1971)
For Joe

Ted Berrigan

Memorial Day

BY TED BERRIGAN AND ANNE WALDMAN

Today:

Open Opening Opened:

✲

The angels that surround me
die

they kiss death
& they die

they always die.

✲

they speak to us
with sealed lips
information operating
at the speed of light

speak to us

O speak to us

in our tiny head

✲

deep calling out to deep

✲

we speak all the time
in the present tense at the speed of Life

dead heads operating

At the speed of light

Today:

& it's morning

Take my time this morning

& learn to kill

to take the will
from unknown places,

kill this stasis

*

let it down
let it down on me

*

I was asleep
in Ann Arbor

dreaming

in Southampton

beneath the summer sun of a green backyard

& up from a blue director's chair

I heard a dead brother say
into the air

"Girl for someone else in white walk by"

*

I was asleep in New York

dreaming in Southampton

& beneath the sun of the no sun sun up from my morning bed

I heard the dead, the city dead

The devils that surround us
never die

the New York City devil inside me
alive all the time

he say

"Tomorrow you die"

*

I woke up
as he typed that down:

"Girl for someone else in white walk by"

& then,

so did I.

So my thanks to you
the dead.

The people in the sky.

*

A minute of silent pool
for the dead.

*

& now I can hear my dead father saying,

"I stand corrected."

*

Dolphins, (as we speak)
are carrying on 2
conversations simultaneously

& within the clicks of one
lie the squeaks of the other
they are alive in their little wandering pool

✲

"I wonder what the dead people are doing today?"

(taking a walk, 2nd St. to GEM SPA)

(or loping down Wall St.
Southampton)

✲

ghost the little children

ghost radio ghost toast

ghost stars

ghost airport
the ghost of Hamlet's father

ghost typewriter

ghost lover

ghost story

ghost snow roasted ghost

ghost in the mirror ghost

happy ghost most ghost

✲

I dreamt that Bette Davis was a nun, we
Were in a classroom, after school, collating
The World. Jr. High. A knocking at the door, I
Went to answer (as Bette disappeared), & found my mother
Standing in the hallway.
"Teddy," she said, "here

Is my real *mother*, who brought me up, I've always wanted
for you to meet her." Beside my mother stood
a tall, elegant lady, wearing black, an austere, stylish
Victorian lady whose eyes were clear & black; grand as
Stella Adler, but as regal & tough as Bette Davis.

Later that evening she sent me out for kippers for her bed-
time snack, giving me a shilling to spend. I went for them
to Venice, to a Coffee-House, which had a canal running right
through it,
& there I ran into Ron, sitting with a beautiful boyish adolescent
blonde. "She's a *wonderful* lady," Ron said, & I was pleased.
Ron left shortly with the blonde nymphet, & I wondered a minute
about Pat (Ron's wife); but decided that Ron must know what he's
doing. The girl, I thought, must be The Muse.

✲

She is a muse

gone but not forgotten

✲

50 STATES

state of grace

the milk state

Oregon

stateroom

state of anxiety

hazy state

estate

statement

Rugby Kissick state

Florida

the empire state

disaster state

the lightbulb state

soup state

Statue of Liberty

state of no return

the White Bear state

doped state

recoil state

Please state your name, address, occupation

the German shepherd state

bent on destruction

state

the farmer state

state of no more parades

the tobacco state

statesman

stately

state prison

stasis

status

static

station wagon

State Flower

✲

state of innocence

✲

ambition state

North Carolina

Jasper's state

the united state

big state

state your cause

income state

jump the gun state

Roman nose state

manic depression state

hospital state

speed state

calculated state

gone forever state

the body state

the death body state

✲

In New York State

in 'Winter in The Country'

at night you write

while someone

(Alice) sometimes sleeps & dreams;

awake she writes

22.

I dreamed you brought home a baby
Solid girl, could already walk
In blue corduroy overalls
Nice & strange, baby to keep close
I hadn't thought of it before
She & I waited for you out by the door
Of building, went in
Got you from painting
Blue & white watercolor swatches
We got on a bus, city bus
One row of seats lining it & poles
It went through the California desert
Blue bright desert day

In the country of old men I said
pretty good
& tho I live there
no more
"you can say that again."

Pretty good.

*

It takes your best shot,
to knock off whatever,

so, we take our best shots,
it gives us a boot or two

we just do it

we wouldn't know what to tell you

if our lives depended upon it!

Anne?

but Anne's already talking

across from me   across my life

across the mailman's
locked box,

over the mailman
I mean
where a woman is alive
a mailman her friend
as you all know
having met the man at the Met
introduced by Vincent,
& loved by Joe:

Joe's introductions go on,

the tongue, the ears burn   on Memorial Day

at Anne's turn:

✲

Dear Mr. Postman:

Please take this from me
to me.

✲

I'm delivered without a hitch
to myself

✲

I'm a woman in the Prime of Strife

I speak for all you crazy ladies

past & present

& I say,

NO MESSAGES

*

Nothing can be helped.   Nothing gets lost.

*

Blink

the eye is closed

& I am asleep

blink

the eye is open

& I am awake

in the *real* wide-eye world   nothing gets lost

*

Today was a day to remember death:

I remember the death

of Hitler

& now I think of The Song of Roland

Roland's death

& now I think to see
if there were similarities

& now I see there were . . .

*

& now I wonder what Tom Clark thinks

Edwin, Alex, Dick . . .
Mike?

*

A lung aching in the room

inside Mike

disease bringing you a little closer

Forget it!

Piss on it!

Kiss my ass!

he say

in his absolute way

Everybody obey

But

we are all victims

(me too)

& we all love life

(too bad)

*

I told Ron Padgett that I'd like to have

NICE TO SEE YOU

engraved on my tombstone.

Ron said he thought he'd like to have

OUT TO LUNCH

on his.

*

Dear Lewis:

I've been down but I'm surfacing

I've been lost but now I'm found

"One will leaf one's life all over again"

you say

& you are right

around & around & around go the swirling leaves

Death is *not* is *not* so horrible today

✲

The poison in the needle
floods my body
it hurts my head

it hurts my head

Poison from the needle
floods my bloodstream

it detonates my head

it detonates my head

I should put that needle down
but tomorrow I'll be dead.

✲

I recognized myself in a dream too, (Ted)

we met & parted

Hello & Goodbye

simple as that

my life recognized my death

Waiting on you

✲

The heart stops briefly when someone dies, one

massive slow stroke as someone passes

from your outside life to your inside,

& then

everything continues

sanely

✲

& I believe in you.

✲

News of my cat

poor cat

descendant of Frank O'Hara's cat

he's dead

I grieve

let it down

let it down on me

✲

X died, & Joe knew, but didn't want to have to tell anyone; but Carol knew, & so, at Ken's 12th Night party she told me. After a few minutes, I took Martha home, & then I walked home myself, across town, through Tompkins Square Park, to Avenue D & 2nd Street. I went to bed, & then I started to cry; & I stayed in bed for three days, & cried, & slept. And now I'm crying a little again. But then I got up, I said "well, that's enough, fuck it!", & I got dressed, & went over to visit Anne & Lewis as before.

✲

Bernadette had to arrange her mother's funeral age 15

& we're in Rattner's 3 AM

& she's telling me how her father died before that

& all the death around her

surrounding her

so many relatives

& how she just thought
that's what people do

"They die"

& she was so good & obedient until her uncle died

& then

something just snapped

Then she sent me this 2 days later:

Deaths, causes: tuberculosis, syphilis, dysentery, scarlet fever and streptococcal sore throat, diptheria, whooping cough, meningococcal infections, acute poliomyelitis, measles, malignant neoplasms, leukemia and aleukemia, benign neoplasms, asthma, diabetes, anemias, meningitis, cardiovascular-tenal diseases, narcolepsy, influenza and pneumonia, bronchitis, other broncho-pulmonix diseases, ulcer of stomach and duodenum, appendicitis, hernia and intestinal obstruction, gastritis, duodenitis, enteritis, and colitis, cirrhosis of liver, acute nephritis, infections of kidney, hyperplasis of prostrate, deliveries and complications of pregnancy, childbirth, and the puerperium, abortion, congenital malformations, birth injuries, postnatal asphyxia, infections of newborn, symptoms, senility, and ill-defined conditions, motor vehicle accidents, falls, burns, drowning, railroad accidents, firearms accidents, poison gases, other poisons, suicide, homicide.

✲

I asked Joe Brainard
if he had anything to say about death:

& he said,
"Well,
you always get
lots of flowers
when you die."

Which is so true,
especially for men. That is,
it's *only* when you die that you get
flowers,
if you are a male

I don't think
I've *ever* been sent flowers

Not even on Memorial Day.

I know I've never sent Joe any flowers.

Once I *took* a flower
from a nearby grave where there were
lots of them

it was in a little sharp-
pointed glass tube

& stuck the pointed end into the earth,
in front of Frank O'Hara's grave
so that the small-pink-flower
stood up.

On the gravestone it said:

GRACE TO BE BORN AND LIVE AS VARIOUSLY AS POSSIBLE

OK. I'll buy that.

& once I picked a different pink flower
from the earth
in front
of Guillaume Apollinaire's grave.

On his gravestone in French there was a poem in the shape of
a heart.

I had to go to the bathroom
so I left then

& went to a cafe
across from Père Lachaise

They had a bathroom there I had une pernod there

& then another

*

the shape of the American I am not

Still Life

the Chinese see nothing tragic in death
but for me the clue is you

the whistle of a bird or two
you are now dead
& I'm struck by how young

we are
(were)

& how useless to speak

Let it down
Let it down on me

. . .

please

I love you

I'm sorry

. . .

The evolution of man & society
is not to be taken lightly   I advance
upon the men   their quiet
I'm certain   is fooling me . . .

*

I sat up late in a room in Manhattan
& read about   the death
of Guillaume Apollinaire
dead in his bed
of pneumonia
after surviving shrapnel

in his head

in The World War

a young girl (Sandy) peacefully

sleeping in my bed

✲

It is night. You are asleep. & beautiful tears
have blossomed in my eyes. Guillaume Apollinaire is dead.
The big green day today is singing to itself
A vast orange library of dreams, dreams
Dressed in newspaper, wan as pale thighs
Making vast apple strides towards "The Poems."
"The Poems" is not a dream. It is night. You
Are asleep. Vast orange libraries of dreams
Stir inside "The Poems." On the dirt-covered ground
Crystal tears drench the ground. Vast orange dreams
Are unclenched. It is night. Songs have blossomed
In the pale crystal library of tears. You
Are asleep. A lovely light is singing to itself,
In "The Poems," in my eyes, in the line, "Guillaume
Apollinaire is dead."

✲

A year or so later

another poet told me that he really liked that poem.

First of all, he said,

I can't tell any one of your sonnets

from any other one,

but this one I can.

✲

I was afraid of that.

Jim Brodey

✲

Lonesome Train

• • •

Assassination Bizarre

• •

✲

I'm the girl in the rain the girl on the street
the girl in the trance the girl at your feet the
girl who just got off the girl who plays the piano
the girl who fucks the girl in the red sweater the
girl in the airplane the girl in Mexico the girl
in the lake the girl from the Village the girl
in heaven the girl on the run the girl at the
bank the girl upstairs the girl in the photograph
the girl on the sofa the nervous girl
the girl under pressure the girl with the yellow
cup

✲

I asked Tuli Kupferberg once, "Did you really jump off of The Manhattan Bridge?" "Yeah," he said, "I really did." "How come?" I said. "I thought that I had lost the ability to love," Tuli said. "So, I figured I might as well be dead. So, I went one night to the top of The Manhattan Bridge, & after a few minutes, I jumped off." "That's amazing," I said. "Yeah," Tuli said, "but nothing happened. I landed in the water, & I wasn't dead. So I swam ashore, & went home, & took a bath, & went to bed. Nobody even noticed."

✲

If I could live it over, I wouldn't
but I wouldn't mind watching the movie

a big talkie

a big ghost

Get it while you can

*

the secret is this:

Absolutely Without Regret

don't mess

back off

steer clear

but

I doan wanna hear anymore about
that

I doan wanna hear any more about that

I doan wanna hear any more about that

I doan wanna hear any more about that

I doan wanna hear any more about that

I doan wanna hear any more about that

I doan wanna hear any more about you I doan wanna hear any more
about you

I doan wanna hear any more about you

I doan wanna hear any more about you

I doan wanna hear any more about you

I doan wanna hear any more about them

I doan wanna hear any more about him

I don't wanna hear any more about President Nixon

(repeat)

There goes another geese on his way
to death
blam blam
b
u
c
k
s
h
o
t

*

I tried my best to do my father's will

You don't want me baby got to have me any-how.

I tried my best to do my father's will

You don't want me baby got to have me any-how.

Oh Lord,
have mercy
Oh Lord,
have mercy
Oh Lord,
have mercy

Have mercy,
Lord.

*

If it don't come across

FUCK IT

& if your heart ain't in it,

ditto.

I met myself

in a dream

Everything was just all right

Here comes two of you

Which one will be true?

I'm beginning

to see the light

How does it feel?

It feels,

Out of sight!

✲

"The trumpets are coming from another station
and you do your best to tune them out"

says Mike

the wisest-assed guy I know.

"If my manner of song disturbs the dead the living
and the near dead it is because
near the dead end you can't dance"
—Andrei Codrescu

✲

John Garfield William Saroyan Clarisse Rivers Harris Schiff
Ray Bremser Lewis MacAdams Tom Clark Bernadette

"Everybody's a hero.

Everybody makes you cry."

It makes you grin to say that

But you didn't say it

You dreamed it

in the after-life

I am not that man.

✲

This February I dream when it's my turn to go to the moon (doom)
a little piece of string will be hanging outside
my window as I rise, arise

but I am not that woman

✲

I am the man who couldn't kiss his mother

goodbye.

But I could leave.

& so I left.

& now, on visits, we kiss

Hello, Goodbye.

& I have no other thoughts about it, Memorial Day.

✲

O you who are dead, we rant at the sky

no action

but pain in the heart
& a head that don't understand
the meaning of "heart" or "have heart"
or

"take heart"

She is walking away with herself

away from despair

she's that lucky girl!

graceful, &

complicated head
(heart)

*

Who's keeping me alive

& what

I praise the lord for every day you & you & you & you & you

& you & you & you

Brothers & Sisters

You are with me on Sweet Remembrance Day.

*

& Now the book is closed

The windows are closed The door is closed

The house is closed

The bars are closed

The gas station is closed

The streets are closed

The store is closed

The car is closed

The rain is closed

Red is closed

& yellow is closed

& green is closed

The bedroom is closed

The desk is closed

The chair is closed

The geraniums are closed

The triangle is closed

The orange is closed

The shine is closed The sheen is closed

The light is closed

The cigar is closed

The dime is closed

The pepsi is closed

The airport is closed

The mailbox is closed

The fingernail is closed

The ankle is closed

The skeleton is closed

The melon is closed

The angel is closed The football is closed

The coffee is closed The grass is closed

The tree is closed

The sky is dark

The dark is closed

*

The bridge is closed

The movie is closed

The girl is closed The gods are closed

The blue is closed

The white is closed

The sun is closed

The ship is closed
The army is closed
The war is closed
The poolcue is closed
Six is closed
eight is closed
four is closed
Seven is closed
The lab is closed   The bank is closed   The Times is closed
The leaf is closed
The bear is closed
Lunch is closed
New York City is closed
Texas is closed
New Orleans is closed
Miami is closed
Okmulgee is closed
Sasebo is closed
Cranston is closed
The Fenway is closed
Bellevue is closed
Columbia is closed
9th Street is closed
2nd Street is closed
First Avenue is closed
Horatio St. is closed
66 is closed
Painting is closed   Leibling is closed

Long Island is closed

Stones are closed   The afternoon is closed

The friends are closed

& Daddy is closed

& brother is closed & sister is
closed

Your mother is closed

& I am closed—& I am closed

& tears are closed

& the hole is closed   & the boat has left   & the day is closed.

Short Poems

IN A BLUE RIVER

FOR KENNETH KOCH

Evelyn Waugh's Prayer

Here I am again.

Show me what to do,

help me to do it.

*

Ezra Pound: A Witness

insouciant

one can only are

Salut!

Today is Courty Bryan's birthday,
O weep, ye fiends!

Man Alone

In front of him was
his head.

Behind him were
men.

He was a man alone.

bear with me

Category

MOONDOG

Buddhist Text

The
Elephant
is
the
wisest
of
all
animals,

the
only
one
who
remembers
his
former
lives;

and
he
remains
motionless

for
long
periods
of
time,

meditating
thereon.

Beautiful Poem

FOR EDWARD DORN

"And the nights shall be filled with music

And the cares that infect the day

Shall fold up their tents like soldiers

Gone, O these are soldiers unique to our day!"

Setback

In the first stage of the revolution
In an attempt to establish & maintain
            a fixed base
He was wounded in the foot, & had to
            withdraw into the interior.

Seriousness

A natural bent, no doubt

Chair

FOR LARRY FAGIN

Blue
be the sky
& soft
the breeze

Today
offers Gertrude Stein
a chance
to burn leaves.

Poem

I'm lying in bed

reading this

& that

another person

sits up straight

breathes he's

different.

Here

I go in &
sit down
at this desk.

Kinks

I am kinks.

slack

The Light

I cannot reach it.

Evensong

Light

spreads

evenly

from face to

face.

Destroys the race.

Shaking Hands

FOR DAVID BERRIGAN

This city night
           you walk in
no virgin   think of me
as I think of you

Near the Ocean

I am in bed
with a crab.

Cowboy Song

A woman's love
is like
the morning dew

it's just as apt
to fall on

a radiant horseturd

as on a rose.

Connecticut

Beautiful girl.

Purple lights.

Foot Asleep.

Nothing happened.

Poem

FOR LARRY FAGIN

You are lovely.

I am lame.

L'oeil

Picasso would be very
        intellectual
if he were a fish.

An Observation

To England's very great relief,
Pierre Reverdy did not write, *The Wasteland*.

Poem Made after Re-reading the Wonderful Book of Poetry, "Air", by Tom Clark, Seven Years Since He First Sent It to Me

poem

frogs

mud February

"in mothballs"

Ah, me!

To an Eggbeater

You are very interesting

because

you are a talking

eggbeater

and that is interesting.

*

Peter Rabbit came in

under the covers & sd

"Where's the money?"

Scene of Life at the Capitol

Anne reads her Troubadour poem
to the radiant black & white
& brown bodies & face
of the lady inmates
of the Colorado State Pen,
22 July, 1978, gorgeous summer afternoon.

Paris Review

(FOR ANTHONY STERN)

Found Picasso
Jean Cocteau
&
William Carlos Williams in
a blue river
in London.

It's Morning!

a childe of

the House

of David

sweeps

in

Zurich

not old

near

a

rose.

Air

Strong coffee in

our cups

Crystal & Blue

4 a.m. in Zurich

Lassie

mit Voltaire?

Sun and Moon in the same Sky?

Nice day.

*

Keep my

Comb at your

house . . .

I Do It All For You.

Amsterdam

You had gone for a drive in the

country

I was crying in

a Japanese

bar

Now I'm having a coke with you!

A True Story

Childe of the House

of David

night

She

is the new sound

of the rain

& so they wed

and lived together forever.

On St. Mark's Place

We

fight

in

our

sleep

the

right

angles

*

angels

"on St. Mark's Place."

Just Friends

O Rose,

"the unquenchable variety,"

✲

the patient

survived—

but the

operation

was not a

success . . .

✲

. . .

I was visited by the Scorpion, the Eagle, &

the dove . . . .

For Rosina

there

his red nose

& bare long legs

perfectly still

so rare

in a perfect

chair

his eyes

grew red

and full

& then she went away.

where?

his tiny

heart stopped.

And stopped again here.

By Now

I'm a piece of local architecture
built only because it had to be.

UNCOLLECTED SHORT POEMS

Today Chicago

Sunlit
oblongs

Bramble
Transfer

Time of
Major energy product

highly reduced
for the sake
of maintaining scale.

Laments

So long, Jimi,

Janis, so long.

You both are great.

We love you.

But, O, my babies,

you did it wrong.

Winter

The Moon is Yellow.

My Nose is Red.

Tell It Like It Is

Bad Teeth

Think of Anything

The Rose of Sharon
lights up
Grand Valley

Now
Robert Creeley speaks:

the air is getting
darker
and darker

the Rose of Sharon
moves

towards the door

and through.

TED BERRIGAN & ROBERT CREELEY

Where

This
is as is

it goes
which does

as that was
that . . . or

over time & that
was, is,

that. Check: call it
  WHAT.

Out the Second-floor Window

On St. Mark's Place

She walked

with the aggressive dignity

of those

for whom someone else's

irony

is the worst of disasters:

I loved her for it.

O Love

AFTER LEOPARDI

O love!

I have collected
    a scar or two

& even a disturbing
    memory or two

Since I fell for you.

Life in the Future

FOR DONNA DENNIS

White powder

purple pill

pink pill

white powder

(2)

Blue air

white mist

blue / white sky

MARS

& it's Autumn in the Northern hemisphere

there.

Anselm Hollo

Come to Chicago

Go to the
Aspidistra Bookstore

Buy
THE LAST PURITAN.

Stay with us.

Poem

TO TOM CLARK

Autobiography

Men at Arms

Brideshead Revisited

Evelyn Waugh

Acid

Get your ass in gear

Ten Things to Do in the Closet

Turn around.

Turn around.

Turn around.

Feel.

Suss.

Whine.

Shut up.

Turn on light.

Exercise.

Kill Dog.

Orange Black
BACK DEATH

Strategy

Strategy is what you do how
Sitting Bull

Larceny

The
opposite
of
petty
is
GRAND.

I'm No Prick

The best way of
going all that way
to get something
and bring it back
is that way. This
is potent information,
that, a way to go, then.

Bolinas

get, in the complexity of our present
responsible element seething between
impasto excitation & somber, subtly evoked grandeur.

Congratulations

To
Lee & Mike.
I ride this bike
To your joy
For your little boy.

Déjà Vu

Discussing Max Beerbohm
with Mike Brownstein.

Neal Cassady Talk

"I'm standing toe-to-toe with you, see, looking you right in the eye,
you see, and at the same time digging that you are tapping your left foot, but,
and also, at the very same time, understand, I am digging that an American
flag is coming out of your left ear."

surface

In the House

Sometimes it is quiet throughout the night
And you learn in the morning that
The man in the next room
Died in his sleep.

But there is no shortage of applicants
For the room.

Vignette

Kissed Maggie soundly; and the Doctor
declined to write me another prescription:
(if that "; and" meant what its weight does,
this would be ROMANCE.)

Inflation

It's difficult
for the young queer
poets these days.
They
have to be
as good as
John Ashbery
(sigh).
I'm glad we
Only have to be
like Allen Ginsberg!
(Cheers)

WANT
CAN
DO

Flying United

Ladies & Gentlemen,
You will depart
The Aircraft
at the
Terminal Area
to your left.

Thank You for Flying United.

The D.A.

Today I had planned to fribble away
in "The Digger's Game"
But Chemistry dictated that I lie on the bed
all day too fast to dig.

Song

"All things considered, it's a gentle & undemanding
planet, even here."

I seldom know it.

I do remember consistently

to feed it. Snore. In the air

in the house

in the night bear with me.

Red Wagon

TO ALICE NOTLEY

She

She is always two blue eyes
She is never lost in sleep
All her dreams are light & air
They sometimes melt the sun
She makes me smile, or
She makes me cry, she
Makes me laugh, and I talk to her
With really nothing particularly to say.

Remembered Poem

It is important to keep old hat
in secret closet.

3 Pages

FOR JACK COLLOM

10 Things I do Every Day

play poker
drink beer
smoke pot
jack off
curse

BY THE WATERS OF MANHATTAN

flower

positive & negative

go home

read lunch poems

hunker down

changes

Life goes by

quite merrily

blue

NO HELP WANTED

Hunting For The Whale

"and if the weather plays me fair
I'm happy every day."

The white that dries clear
the heart attack
the congressional medal of honor
A house in the country

NOT ENOUGH

Conversation

	"My name
"My name	"My name
"My name	"My name
"My name	is Wesley
is Wesley	Wesley
is Wesley	Jackson,
is Wesley Jackson,	"My name is Wesley Jackson,
I am	I am
I am	I am

25 years	25 years
old,	old,
I am 25 years old,	I am 25 years old,
I am 25 years old,	and
and	my favorite
my favorite	my favorite
favorite	favorite
and my favorite	song
song	song
and my favorite	and my favorite song
and my favorite song	my favorite song
and my favorite song	is
is *Valencia.*"	*Valencia.*"
	"Isn't
"Isn't	that
"Isn't that	beautiful,"
beautiful,"	"Isn't that beautiful,"
"Isn't that beautiful,"	Frank
Frank	said.
Frank said.	

To Southampton

Go
Get in Volkswagen
Ride to the Atlantic
Step out
See
Your shadows
On fog

At the second stop
The same ocean as
At the first

Back in Volkswagen
Ron's or somebody's
Backs up
Steps on the gas

COCA COLA 20 Cents

Machine noise

Satisfaction

Home
Away from home.

Sunday Morning

FOR LOU REED

1.

It's A Fact

If you stroke a cat about 1,000,000 times, you will
generate enough electricity to light up the largest
American Flag in the world for about one minute.

2.

Turnabout

In former times people who committed adultery
got stoned;
Nowadays it's just a crashing bringdown.

3.

A Mongolian Sausage

By definition: a long stocking: you fill it full of shit,
and then you punch holes in it. Then you swing it over
your head in circles until everybody goes home.

Something Amazing Just Happened

FOR JIM CARROLL, ON HIS BIRTHDAY

A lovely body gracefully is nodding
Out of a blue Buffalo
                    Monday morning
                                        curls
softly rising color the air
                        it's yellow
above the black plane
                    beneath a red tensor

I've been dreaming. The telephone kept ringing & ringing
Clear & direct, purposeful yet pleasant, still taking pleasure
in bringing the good news, a young man in horn-rims' voice
                                                            is speaking
while I listen. Mr. Berrigan, he says, & without waiting for an answer
    goes on,
I'm happy to be able to inform you that your request for a Guggenheim
    Foundation Grant
Has been favorably received by the committee, & approved. When
    would you like to leave?

Uh, not just yet, I said, uh, what exactly did I say with regards to leaving,
    in my application . . . I'm a little hazy at the moment.
Yes. Your project, as outlined in your application for a grant for the
    purpose

of giving Jim Carroll the best possible birthday present you could get
him, through our Foundation, actually left the project, that is,
how the monies
would be spent, up to us. You indicated, wisely, I think, that we knew
more about what kind of project we would approve than you did,
so we should
make one up for you, since all you wanted was money, to buy Jim a
birthday gift.

Aha! I said. So, what's up?

We have arranged for you and Jim to spend a year in London, in a flat
off of King's Row.
You will receive 250 pounds each a month expenses, all travel expenses
paid, & a clothing allowance of 25 pounds each per month.
During the year,
At your leisure, you might send us from time to time copies of your
London works. By year's end I'm sure you each will have enough
new poems for two books,
Which we would then publish in a deluxe boxed hardcover edition, for
the rights to which we shall be prepared to pay a considerable
sum, as is your due.
We feel that this inspired project will most surely result in The first major
boxed set of works since Tom Sawyer & Huckleberry Finn!
Innocents Abroad
in reverse, so to speak! We know your poems, yours & Jim's, will tell it
like it is, & that is what we are desperate to know! So, when
would you like to leave?
Immediately, I shouted! & Jim! I called, Jim! Happy Birthday! Wake up!

Today in Ann Arbor

FOR JAYNE NODLAND

Today I woke up
bright & early

Then I went back to sleep

I had a nice dream
which left me weak
so
I woke up again
dull, but still early.

I drank some coke
& took a pill

It made me feel ill, but

optimistic. So,

I went to the Michigan Union for cigarettes.

*

I cashed a check today—
but that was later. Now
I bought cigarettes, &
The Detroit Free Press.

I decided to eat some vanilla wafers
& drink coffee
at my desk

*

There was no cream for
the coffee. & the mail
wasn't out yet.

It pissed me off.

I drank some coffee, black
& it was horrible.

*

Life is horrible, &

I am stupid.

I think . . . . NOTHING.

Then I think, more coffee . . .
upstairs!

Jackie's face
picks me up.

She says, "there's cream
upstairs"

Up more stairs via the elevator:

cream talk amiably to Bert
Hornbach

*

Come downstairs
&
the mail has
come!

Lots
of mail! I feel pretty good.

Together with my mail back in office.

Sitting.

*

Johnny Stanton says: "Ted,

you are a myth in my heart."

He is a myth in my heart!

So, we are both myths!

*

Warmed by this, & coffee,

I go on. American Express
says:

"You owe us $1,906. Please

Pay *NOW.*"

I say, *sure!*

("Now" means "later")

*

Somebody else sends a postcard (Bill).

He says,
"I am advertising your presence
at YALE, so please come!"

I say to Bill,

"Have Faith, old

brother! I'll be there
when you need me."

In fact, I say that to everyone.

That is the truth,

& so,

*

I open a beautiful letter

from you. When we are both dead,

that letter
will be Part Two
of this poem.

*

But now we are both alive

& terrific!

In the Wheel

The pregnant waitress
asks
        "Would you like
some more coffee?"
Surprised out of the question
I wait   seconds   "Yes,
I think I would!" I hand her
        my empty cup, &
"thank you!" she says. My pleasure.

Wind

Every day when the sun comes up
The angels emerge from the rivers
Drily happy & all wet. Easy going
But hard to keep my place. Easy
On the avenue underneath my face.
Difficult alone trying to get true.
Difficult inside alone with you.
The rivers' blackness flowing just sits
Orange & reds blaze up inside the sky
I sit here & I've been thinking this
Red, blue, yellow, green, & white.

Things to Do on Speed

mind clicks into gear
& fingers clatter over the keyboard
as intricate insights stream
out of your head:

this goes on for ten hours:

then, take a break: clean
all desk drawers, arrange all
pens & pencils in precise parallel patterns;
stack all books with exactitude in one pile
to coincide perfectly with the right angle
of the desk's corner.

Whistle thru ten more hours of
arcane insights:

drink a quart of ice-cold pepsi:
clean the ice-box:
past out for ten solid hours

interesting dreams.

2.

Finish papers, wax floors, lose weight, write songs, sing songs, have
conference, sculpt, wake up & think more clearly. Clear up asthma.

treat your obesity, avoid mild depression, decongest, cure your
narcolepsy,
treat your hyper-kinetic brain-damaged children. Open the
Pandora's Box of amphetamine abuse.

3.

Stretch the emotional sine curve; follow euphoric peaks with descents
into troughs

that are unbearable wells of despair & depression. Become a ravaged
scarecrow.

Cock your emaciated body in
twisted postures   grind your caved-in jaw

scratch your torn & pock-marked skin,
keep talking, endlessly.

4.

Jump off a roof on the lower East Side

or

Write a 453 page unintelligible book

5.

Dismantle 12 radios

string beads interminably

empty your purse

sit curled in a chair
& draw intricate designs
in the corner of an envelope

6.

"I felt it rush almost instantly into
my head like a short circuit. My body
began to pulsate, & grew tiny antennae
all quivering in anticipation. I began
to receive telepathic communication from
the people around me. I felt elated."

7.

get pissed off.

Feel your tongue begin to shred,
lips to crack, the inside of the mouth
become eaten out. Itch all over. See
your fingernails flake off, hair & teeth
fall out.

Buy a Rolls-Royce

Become chief of the Mafia

Consider anti-matter.

8.

Notice that tiny bugs are crawling over your whole body
around, between and over your many new pimples.

Cut away pieces of bad flesh.

Discuss mother's promiscuity

Sense the presence of danger at the movies

Reveal

get tough

turn queer

9.

In the Winter, switch to heroin, so you won't catch pneumonia.

In the Spring, go back to speed.

Television

San Gabriel
Placer, Nevada. New York:
Buffalo. 24 Huntington, just off of Main.
$12.95 takes you
                    where you want to go
quick; & quickly do you go.
$.30 will bring you back
sweating, worn out. Twice
as fast (as when you went) is
slow.

Farewell Address

TO RICHARD TAYLOR

Goodbye House, 24 Huntington, one block past Hertel
    on the downtown side of Main, second house on the left.
    Your good spirit kept me cool this summer, your ample space.
Goodbye house.

Goodbye our room, on the third floor. Your beds were much appreciated;
    We used them gratefully & well, me & Alice. & Alice's yellow blanket
    spread across to the yellow slanted ceiling to make a lovely light,
    Buffalo mornings. There we talked, O did we ever! Goodbye, our
Third floor room.

& Goodbye other room across the hall. Typewriter music filled my heart.
    Buffalo nights as I read on my bed while Alice wrote unseen. Her
    Buffalo poems were terrific, & they were even about me! Some
    had you in them, too! So,
Goodbye room.

Goodbye second floor. Your bathroom's character one could grow to
understand. I liked the sexy closed door of Chris's room, &
light showing under the master's door at night; a good omen to me,
always! Even your unused office offered us its ironing board, by
moonlight.
You were friendly. Goodbye second floor of Richard's house.

Goodbye stairs. Alice knew you well.

& Goodbye first floor. Goodbye kitchen, you were a delight; you
fed us morning, noon & night; I liked your weird yellow light, &
your wall clock was out of sight! Meals we shared with Richard
were gentle & polite; we liked them; we liked those times a lot.
Goodbye kitchen, you'll not be forgot.

& Goodbye Arboretum. (I mean TV room) Mornings, alone, I loved to sit
in you, to read the news from the world of sports, as light
poured into & through the house. Mornings were quiet pepsis.
Nights I'd talk with Richard over beers. Good manners had some
meaning here; I learned better ones with great delight. Goodbye
TV room. Thanks for your mornings and nights.

Goodbye vast dining hall, where we three & three dogs often ate
of beef & drank red wine. Your table was long, & your chandelier
a sight. Richard ate quickly, as did Alice, while I took my time,
talking beneath your light. May we dine thusly many a night, days
To come. Goodbye dining room, & dogs who ate our bones with delight.

Goodbye Thelonius. Only Allen Ginsberg, for beauty, matches you. &
Goodbye Ishmael. I liked your ghastly rough-house ways. You
were the love/hate delight of Alice's days & nights. Many a fond
lick you lolled her way, each of her trips. Goodbye Ishmael.
Goodbye Oliver. You didn't say much, but you were always there,
calling "Hey, wait for me!" like in those movies I used to like
the best. When you three ate Bobby Dylan's SELF PORTRAIT, it
put our friendship to the test. But it survived. & so,
Goodbye Ishmael, Thelonius, Oliver; friends, my brothers, dogs.

& Richard, goodbye, too, to you. You were the best of all our Buffalo
life. Sharing with you made it *be* a life. We were at home in
your house, because it's yours. It was a great pleasure, to come & go
through your doors. Nothing gets lost, in anyone's life;
I'm glad of that. We three had our summer, which will last. Poems
last (like this one has); and so do memories. They last in poems,
& in the people in them (who are us). So, although this morning
under the sky, we go, Alice & I, you'll be flying with us as we fly.
You come to visit, where we go, & we'll sometimes visit you in
Buffalo. Bring the dogs, too. & until then, our love to you, Richard.

Goodbye.

Three Sonnets and a Coda for Tom Clark

1.

In The Early Morning Rain
To my family & friends "Hello"
And money. With something inside us we float up
On this electric chair each breath nearer the last
Now is spinning
Seven thousand feet over / The American Midwest
Gus walked up under the arc light as far as the first person
the part that goes over the fence last
And down into a green forest ravine near to "her"
Winds in the stratosphere
Apologise to the malcontents
Downstairs. The black bag & the wise man may be found
in the brain-room.

what sky out there Take it away
& it's off
one foot
is expressing itself as continuum
the other, sock

2.

Tomorrow. I need to kill
Blank mind part Confusions of the cloth
White snow whirls everywhere. Across the fields
in the sky the
Soft, loose
stars swarm. Nature makes my teeth "to hurt"
shivering now on 32nd Street in my face & in my head
does Bobby Dylan ever come around here? listen
it's alive where exposed nerve jangles
& I looming over Jap's American flag
In Public, In Private The Sky Pilot In No Man's Land
The World Number 14 is tipsy as pinballs on the ocean
We are bored through . . . through . . . with our professionalism
Outside her
Windows

3.

I'm amazed to be here
A man who can do the average thing
when everybody else is
going crazy Lord I wonder just exactly what can happen
my heart is filled (filling) with light
& there's a breeze & I'm going
way over
the white skyline do what I want to
Fuck it.
Tied up wit

Tie with red roses   The war of the Roses, &
War is shit.   White man, tomorrow you die!
Tomorrow means *now.*   "You kidding me?" now.
Light up   you will be great
It's a complication.   Thanksgiving, 1970, Fall.

CODA:

Being a new day my heart
is confirmed in its pure Buddhahood
activity under the clear blue sky
The front is hiding the rear (not)
which means we have (not) "protected ourselves"
by forgetting all we were dealt
I love all the nuts I've been in bed (with)
hope to go everywhere in good time
like, Africa: it would be tremendous (or not)
to drink up rivers. Be seeing *you*
to ride the river (with)   heads riding gently
its personal place   feet doing their stuff   up in the air
Where someone (J.) dies, so that we can be rude to friends
While you find me right here coming through again.

Landscape with Figures (Southampton)

There's a strange lady in my front yard
She's wearing blue slacks & a white car-coat
& "C'mon!" she's snarling at a little boy
He isn't old enough to snarl, so he's whining
On the string as first she & then he disappear
Into (or is it behind) the Rivers' garage.

That's 11 a.m.
In the country. "Everything is really golden,"
Alice, in bed, says. I look, & out the window, see
Three shades of green; & the sky, not so high,
So blue & white. "You're right, it really is!"

What I'd Like for Christmas, 1970

Black brothers to get happy
The Puerto Ricans to say hello
The old folks to take it easy &
as it comes

The United States to get straight

Power to butt out
Money to fuck off
Business with honor

Religion
&
Art

Love
A home
A typewriter
A GUN.

Lady

Nancy, Jimmy, Larry, Frank, & Berdie
George & Bill
Dagwood Bumstead
Donna, Joe, & Phil

Making shapes this place
so rightly ours
to fill

as we wish,
& Andy's flowers too, do.

✲

I've been sitting, looking
thinking sounds of pictures
names
of you

✲

of how I smile now

&

Let It Be.

✲

& now I think to add
"steel teeth"
"sucking cigarette"
"A photograph of Bad."
Everything you are gone slightly mad.

America.

36th Birthday Afternoon

Green TIDE; behind, pink against blue
Blue CHEER; an expectorant, *Moving On*
Gun in hand, shooting down
Anyone who comes to mind

IN OLD SOUTHAMPTON, blue, shooting up
THE SCRIPTURE OF THE GOLDEN ETERNITY
A new sharpness, peel apart to open, bloody water
& Alice is putting her panties on, taking off

A flowery dress for London's purple one
It seems to be getting longer, the robot
Keeps punching, opening up
A bit at a time. Up above

Spread atop the bed a red head sees
Two hands, one writing, one holding on.

Today's News

My body heavy with poverty (starch)
It uses up my sexual energy
        constantly, &
I feel constantly crowded

On the other hand, *One*
Day In The Afternoon of
    The World
Pervaded my life with a
    heavy grace
            today

I'll never smile again

Bad Teeth

But
I'm dancing with tears in my eyes
(I can't help myself!)   Tom
writes he loves Alice's sonnets,
        takes four, I'd love

to be more attentive to her, more
        here.
The situation having become intolerable
the only alternatives are:
        Murder & Suicide.

They are too dumb! So, one
becomes a goof. Raindrops
start falling on my roof. I say
Hooray! Then I say, I'm going out

At the drugstore I say, Gimme some pills!
        Charge 'em! They say
Sure. I say See you later.

Read the paper. Talk to Alice.
She laughs to hear
    Hokusai had 947 changes of address
In his life. Ha-ha. Plus everything
    else in the world
going on here.

Wishes

Now I wish I were asleep, to see my dreams taking place
I wish I were more awake
I wish a sweet rush of tears to my eyes
Wish a nose like an eagle
I wish blue sky in the afternoon
Bigger windows, & a panorama—light, buildings & people in street air
Wish my teeth were white and sparkled
Wish my legs were not where they are—where they are
I wish the days warmly cool & clothes I like to be inside of
Wish I were walking around in Chelsea (NY) & it was 5:15 a.m., the
        sun coming up, alone, you asleep at home
I wish red rage came easier
I wish death, but not just now
I wish I were driving alone across America in a gold Cadillac
        toward California, & my best friend
I wish I were in love, & you here

Ophelia

ripped
out of her mind

a marvelous construction

thinking

no place; & you
not once properly handled

Ophelia

&

you can't handle yourself
feeling
no inclination
toward that
solitude,
love
by yourself

Ophelia

& feeling free you drift
far more beautifully
than we

As one now understands

He never did see you
you moving so while talking flashed
& failed
to let you go

Ophelia

Scorpion, Eagle & Dove (A Love Poem)

FOR PAT

November, dancing, or
Going to the store in the country,
Where green changes itself into LIFE,
MOVING ON, Jockey Shorts, Katzenmiaou
A Chesterfield King & the blue book
IN OLD SOUTHAMPTON,
you make my days special

You do Jimmy's, & Alice's,
Phoebe's, Linda's,
Lewis' & Joanne's, too . . .
& Kathy's (a friend who is new) . . .

& Gram's . . .
who loved you,
like I do
once . . .

& who surely does so since
that 4th of July last,
a Saturday,
a day that left her free
to be with & love you
(& me)
(all of us)
just purely;
clean;
& selflessly;

✲

no thoughts

✲

Just, It's true. As I would be
& as I am, to you
this
November.

Things to Do in Providence

Crash

Take Valium Sleep

Dream &,

forget it.

*

Wake up now & strange

displaced

at home.

Read The Providence Evening Bulletin

No one you knew

got married
had children
got divorced
died

got born

tho many familiar names flicker &
disappear.

*

Sit

watch TV

draw blanks

swallow

pepsi
meatballs

. . .

give yourself the needle:

"Shit! There's gotta be something
to do
here!"

*

JOURNEY TO SHILOH: Seven young men on horses, leaving Texas.
They've got to do what's right! So, after
a long trip, they'll fight for the South in the War.
No war in Texas, but they've heard about it, & they want
to fight for their country. Have some adventures & make
their folks proud! Two hours later all are dead;
one by one they died, stupidly, & they never did find out
why! There were no niggers in South Texas! Only
the leader,
with one arm shot off, survives to head back for Texas:
all his friends behind him, dead. What will happen?

*

Watching him, I cry big tears. His friends
were beautiful, with boyish American good manners,
cowboys!

*

Telephone New York: "hello!"

"Hello! I'm drunk! &
I have no clothes on!"

"My goodness," I say.

"See you tomorrow."

*

Wide awake all night reading: *The Life of Turner*
("He first saw the light in Maiden Lane")
A. C. Becker: Wholesale Jewels
Catalogue 1912
The Book of Marvels, 1934:
The year I was born.

No mention of my birth in here. Hmmm.

Saturday The Rabbi Stayed Home

(that way he got to solve the murder)

LIFE on the Moon by LIFE Magazine.

*

My mother wakes up, 4 a.m.: Someone to talk with!

Over coffee we chat, two grownups
I have two children, I'm an adult now, too.
Now we are two people talking who have known each other
a long time,
Like Edwin & Rudy. Our talk is a great pleasure: my mother
a spunky woman. Her name was Peggy Dugan when she was young.
Now, 61 years old, she blushes to tell me I was conceived
before the wedding! "I've always been embarrassed about telling you
til now," she says. "I didn't know what you might think!"
"I think it's really sweet," I say. "It means I'm really
a love child." She too was conceived before her mother's wedding,
I know. We talk, daylight comes, & the Providence Morning Journal.
My mother leaves for work. I'm still here.

✲

Put out the cat

Take in the clothes

off of the line

Take a walk,

buy cigarettes

✲

two teen-agers whistle

as I walk up

They say: "Only your hairdresser

knows for sure!"

Then they say,

"ulp!"

because I am closer to them.

They see I am not hippie kid, frail like Mick Jagger,

but some horrible 35 year old big guy!

The neighborhood I live in is mine!

"How'd you like a broken head, kid?"

I say fiercely.

(but I am laughing & they are not one bit scared.)

So, I go home.

✲ ✲ ✲ ✲

Alice Clifford waits me. Soon she'll die
at the Greenwood Nursing Home; my mother's
mother, 79 years & 7 months old.
But first, a nap, til my mother comes home
from work, with the car.

✲

The heart stops briefly when someone dies,
a quick pain as you hear the news, & someone passes
from your outside life to inside. Slowly the heart adjusts
to its new weight, & slowly everything continues, sanely.

✲

Living's a pleasure:
I'd like to take the whole trip

despite the possible indignities of growing old,
moving, to die in poverty, among strangers:
that can't be helped.

✲

So, everything, now
is just all right. I'm with you.

No more last night.

✲

Friday's great

10 o'clock morning sun is shining!

I can hear today's key sounds fading softly

& almost see opening sleep's epic novels.

* * * *

Frank O'Hara

Winter in the country, Southampton, pale horse
as the soot rises, then settles, over the pictures
The birds that were singing this morning have shut up
I thought I saw a couple, kissing, but Larry said no
It's a strange bird. He should know. & I think now
"Grandmother divided by monkey equals outer space." Ron
put me in that picture. In another picture, a good-
looking poet is thinking it over; nevertheless, he will
never speak of that it. But, his face is open, his eyes
are clear, and, leaning lightly on an elbow, fist below
his ear, he will never be less than perfectly frank,
listening, completely interested in whatever there may
be to hear. Attentive to me alone here. Between friends,
nothing would seem stranger to me than true intimacy.
What seems genuine, truly real, is thinking of you, how
that makes me feel. You are dead. And you'll never
write again about the country, that's true.
But the people in the sky really love
to have dinner & to take a walk with you.

Crystal

Be awake mornings. See light spread across the lawn
(snow) as the sky refuses to be any color, today
I like this boat-ride I'm being taken for, although
It never leaves the shore, this boat. Its fires burn
Like a pair of lovely legs. It's a garage that grew up
Sometimes I can't talk, my mouth too full of words, but
I have hands & other parts, to talk lots! Light the fire
Babble for you. I dream a green undersea man
Has been assigned to me, to keep me company, to smirk
At me when I am being foolish. A not unpleasant dream.
My secret doors open as the mail arrives. Fresh air
Pours in, around, before they close again. The winds are rushing
Up off of the ocean, up Little Plains Road. Catch the Wind
In my head, a quiet song. And, "Everything belongs to me
Because I am poor." Waiting in sexy silence, someone
Turns over in bed, & waiting is just a way of being with
Now a tiny fire flares out front the fireplace. Chesterfield
King lights up! Wood is crackling inside
Elephants' rush & roar. Refrigerator's gentle drone
Imagined footsteps moving towards my door. Sounds in dreams
In bed. You are all there is inside my head.

Clown

There's a strange lady in my front yard
A girl naked in the shower, saying
"I'm keeping my boxes dry!" A naked artist
Smoking. Bad teeth. Wooden planks: furniture. Sky
One minute ago I stopped thought: 12 years of cops
In my life. & Alice is putting her panties on

Takes off a flowery dress for London's purple one
Out of the blue, a host of words, floating
March: awaiting rescue: smoke, or don't
Strapped: deprived. Shoot yourself: stay alive.
& you can't handle yourself, love, feeling
No inclination toward that solitude.
Take it easy, & as it comes. Coffee
Suss. Feel. Whine. *Shut up*. Exercise.
Turn. Turn around. Turn. *Kill dog*.
Today woke up bright & early, no mail, life
Is horrible, & I am stupid, & I think . . . Nothing.
"Have faith, old brother. You are a myth in my heart.
We are both alive. Today we may go to India."

Chinese Nightingale

We are involved in a transpersonified state
Revolution, which is turning yourself around
I am asleep next to "The Hulk." "The Hulk" often sleeps
While I am awake & vice versa. Life is less than ideal
For a monkey in love with a nymphomaniac! God is fired!
Do I need the moon to remain free? To explode softly
In a halo of moon rays? Do I need to be
On my human feet, straight, talking, free
Will sleep cure the deaf-mute's heartbreak? Am I
In my own way, America? Rolling downhill, & away?
The door to the river is closed, my heart is breaking
Loose from sheer inertia. All I do is bumble. No
Matter. We live together in the jungle.

Wrong Train

Here comes the man! He's talking a lot
I'm sitting, by myself. I've got
A ticket to ride. Outside is, "Out to Lunch."
It's no great pleasure, being on the make.
Well, who is? Or, well everyone is, tho.
"I'm laying there, & some guy comes up
& hits me with a billyclub!" A fat guy
Says. Shut up. & like that we cross a river
Into the Afterlife. Everything goes on as before
But never does any single experience make total use
Of you. You are always slightly ahead,
Slightly behind. It merely baffles, it doesn't hurt.
It's total pain & it breaks your heart
In a less than interesting way. Every day
Is payday. Never enough pay. A déjà-vu
That lasts. It's no big thing, anyway.
A lukewarm greasy hamburger, ice-cold pepsi
                that hurts your teeth.

Buddha on the Bounty

"A little loving can solve a lot of things"
She locates two spatial equivalents in
The same time continuum. "You are lovely. I
am lame." "Now it's me." "If a man is in
Solitude, the world is translated, my world
& wings sprout from the shoulders of 'The Slave' "
Yeah. I like the fiery butterfly puzzles
Of this pilgrimage toward clarities
Of great mud intelligence & feeling.

"The Elephant is the wisest of all animals
The only one who remembers his former lives
& he remains motionless for long periods of time
Meditating thereon." I'm not here, now,
            & it is good, absence.

Scorpio

If I don't love you I
Won't let it show. But I'll
Make it clear, by
Never letting you know.

& if I love you, I will
Love you true: insofar
As Love, itself,
Will do.

& while I live, I'll be
Whatever I am, whose
Constant, impure, fire
Is outwardly only a man.

I Used to Be but Now I Am

I used to be inexorable,
But now I am elusive.

I used to be the future of America,
But now I am America.

I used to be part of the problem,
But now I am the problem.

I used to be part of the solution, if not all of it,
But now I am not that person.

I used to be intense, & useful,
But now I am heavy, & boring.

I used to be sentimental about myself, & therefore ruthless,
But now I am, I think, a sympathetic person, although
easily amused.

I used to be a believer,
But now, alas, I believe.

The Complete Prelude

FOR CLARK COOLIDGE & FOR MY MOTHER

1.

Upon the river, point me out my course
That blows from the green fields and from the clouds
And from the sky: be nothing better
Than a wandering cloud
Come fast upon me
Such as were not made for me.
I cannot miss my way. I breathe again
That burthen of my own natural self
The heavy weight of many a weary day;
Coming from a house
Shall be my harbour; promises of human life
Are mine in prospect;
Now I am free, enfranchis'd and at large.
The earth is all before me, with a heart

2.

And the result was elevating thoughts
Among new objects simplified, arranged
And out of what had been, what was, the place
"O'er the blue firmament a radiant white,"
Was thronged with impregnations, like those wilds
That into music touch the passing wind;
Had been inspired, and walk'd about in dreams,
And, in Eclipse, my meditations turn'd
And unencroached upon, now, seemed brighter far,
Though fallen from bliss, a solitary, full of caverns, rocks
And audible seclusions: here also found an element
    that pleased her
Tried her strength; made it live. Here
Neither guilt, nor vice, nor misery forced upon my sight
Could overthrow my trust in Courage, Tenderness, & Grace.
In the tender scenes I most did take my delight.

3.

Thus strangely did I war against myself
What then remained in such Eclipse? What night?
The wizard instantaneously dissolves
Through all the habitations of past years
And those to come, and hence an emptiness;
& shall continue evermore to make
& shall perform to exalt and to refine
Inspired, celestial presence ever pure
From all the sources of her former strength.
Then I said: "and these were mine,

Not a deaf echo, merely, of thought,
But living sounds. Yea, even the visible universe was scann'd
And as by the simple waving of a wand
With something of a kindred spirit, fell
Beneath the domination of a taste, its animation & its deeper sway."

Easter Monday

FOR EDWARD DORN

Chicago Morning

TO PHILIP GUSTON

Under a red face, black velvet shyness
Milking an emaciated gaffer. God lies down
Here. Rattling of a shot, heard
From the first row. The president of the United States
And the Director of the FBI stand over
a dead mule. "Yes, it is nice to hear the fountain
With the green trees around it, as well as
People who need me." Quote Lovers of speech unquote. It's
        a nice thought
& typical of a rat. And, it is far more elaborate
Than expected. And the thing is, we don't *need*
        that much money.
Sunday morning; blues, blacks, red & yellow wander
In the soup. Gray in the windows' frames. The angular
Explosion in the hips. A huge camel rests
        in a massive hand
Casts clouds a smoggish white out & up over the Loop, while
Two factories (bricks) & a fortress of an oven (kiln)
Rise, barely visible inside a grey metallic gust.
        "The Fop's Tunic."
She gets down, off of the table, breaking a few more plates.
Natives paint their insides crystal white here (rooms)
Outside is more bricks, off-white. Europe at Night.

The End

Despair farms a curse, slackness
In the sleep of animals, with mangled limbs
Dogs, frogs, game elephants, while
There's your new life, blasted with milk.
It's the last day of summer, it's the first
Day of fall: soot sits on Chicago like
A fat head's hat. The quick abounds. Turn
To the left; turn to the right. On Bear's Head
Two Malted Milk balls. "Through not taking himself
Quietly enough he strained his insides." He
Encourages criticism, but he never forgives it.
You who are the class in the sky, receive him
Into where you dwell. May he rest long and well.
God help him, he invented us, that is, a future
Open living beneath his spell. One goes not where
One came from. One sitting says, "I stand corrected."

Newtown

Sunday morning: here we live jostling & tricky
blues, blacks, reds & yellows all are gray
in each window: the urbanites have muscles
in their butts & backs; shy, rough, compassionate
& good natured, "they have sex in their pockets"
To women in love with my flesh I speak.
All the Irish major statements & half the best
Low-slung stone. Upstairs is sleep. Downstairs
is heat. She seems exceedingly thin and transparent
Two suspicious characters in my head. They park & then
Start, the same way you get out of bed. The pansy is

Grouchy. The Ideal Family awaits distribution on
The Planet. Another sensation tugged at his heart
Which he could not yet identify,
half   Rumanian   deathbed   diamond
Wildly singing in the mountains with cancer of the spine.

Method Action

FOR HANK KANABUS

Frog sees dog.   log?

See the lamp?

It is out.

"Do you think I became
a dance-hall girl
because
I was *bad*?"

It ain't gonna work.

Because by morning
it'll be gone.

The medicine I took
to change
the way I was.

*

And I'm the man who killed him.

Swinburne & Watts-Dunton

Beer in bed, &
An unused point
Beside me
On the bench.

Goodbye To All That.

No first lines in London. . . .
Tuborg lager,
Putney High Street,
S. W. 15

"A pure case of unmitigated flatulence."

Yes, but, "He is exulted.
The ice
Meant something else
To him."

White South.

Soviet Souvenir

What strikes the eye hurts, what one hears is a lie.
The river is flowing again between its banks.
Grant one more summer, O you Gods! that once I did not ask
The windows through which the bells toll are like doors

Because she is direct in her actions and in her feelings
Under the puns of the troop, there are frescoes
On the rudder, which you set against a bracelet's fire, and
Which goes toward you with each beat.

I find myself there; am I finally ill at ease with my own
Principle? Fortune be praised! Immense density, not divinely,
  bathes us
I hear walking in my legs
The savage eyes into wood look for the head they can live in

It's my window, even now, around me, full of darkness, dumb,
  so great!
My heart willingly again beginning crying out; and at the same time
  anxious, love, to contain.

Old-fashioned Air

FOR LEE CRABTREE

I'm living in Battersea, July,
1973, not sleeping, reading
Jet noise throbs building fading
Into baby talking, no, "speechifying"
"Ah wob chuk sh 'guh!" Glee.
There's a famous Power Station I can't see
Up the street. Across there is
Battersea Park
I walked across this morning toward
A truly gorgeous radiant flush;
Sun; fumes of the Battersea
Power Station; London air;
I walked down long avenues of trees
That leant not gracefully
Over the concrete walk. Wet green lawn
Opened spaciously
Out on either side of me. I saw
A great flock of geese taking their morning walk
Unhurriedly.

I didn't hurry either, Lee.
I stopped & watched them walk back up toward
& down into their lake,
Smoked a Senior Service on a bench
As they swam past me in a long dumb graceful cluttered line,
Then, taking my time, I found my way
Out of that park;
A Gate that was locked. I jumped the fence.
From there I picked up the *London Times*, came home,
Anselm awake in his bed, Alice
Sleeping in mine: I changed
A diaper, read a small poem I'd had
In mind, then thought to write this line:
"Now is Monday morning so, that's a garbage truck I hear,
        not bells"
And we are back where we started from, Lee, you
        & me, alive & well!

The Ancient Art of Wooing

A master square weaver, one's favoured medium,
That is what is behind the boom.
Brusquely hugely schemefully ignored
Free in the language of wooing, but not included

The close elaborate current square panorama
quiver   now one quivers
The aerial view of vineyards spreading out, encircling
        the house
Backlit, color coming from within, light & dark
        closely akin to skin

This slow constant weave seems badly adapted
To the grave overpowering expression of
    a decorative opulent emotion.
Oh, does it? Behind this boom one can see one is getting
After the false starts & necessary resistance,
    one's bones' worth.

On display they in the center become alive. They
    are handsome in themselves.
The possible in mural scale model in Marriage
    is formalized.

Late November

What said your light
you know, an answer refusing
I go to my store I maintain
animal inextricably between

illuminated, on the line
something lords in chair
all fixtured silvered
heart, your curtain, air

breathy air stirs white
knowing refusing running
Waitomo Cave, New Zealand
couldn't catch the day, its curve, its more

Committed robbery with the Smothers Brothers
cops pursue us infinitely

At Loma Linda

"The pressure's on, old son."
"We're going to salvage just about all you have left."
"Right. And I'm going with you."
"I'm also staying right here with you."

"It's the way you've been going about it that worries us."
"All this remote control business."
"I'm the principal stockholder and I'm moving my equities out."
"He believes if he's hard enough on a body they'll give way."

"It's funny to have lived all this time in the midlands
And not seen all these lovely things about."
"Where's the Doctor?" "I *am* the Doctor."
"Is everything ready for surgery?"

"Yes, & you don't need a sauna to get steamed up, here."
"You'll find the patient's files in these cabinets here."

L.G.T.T.H.

Queen Victoria dove headfirst into the swimming pool, which was filled
 with blue milk.
I used to be baboons, but now I am person.
I used to be secretary to an eminent brain surgeon, but now I am quite
 ordinary. Oops! I've spilled the beans!
I wish mountains could be more appealing to the eye.
I wash sometimes. Meanwhile
Two-ton Tony Galento began to rub beef gravy over his entire body.
I wish you were more here.
I used to be Millicent, but now I am Franny.
I used to be a bowl of black China tea, but now I am walking back
 to the green fields of the People's Republic.

Herman Melville is elbowing his way through the stringbeans toward us.
Oscar Levant handed the blue pill to Oscar Wilde during the fish course.
        Then he slapped him.
I used to be blue, but now I am pretty. I wish broken bad person.
I wish not to see you tonight.
I wish to exchange this chemistry set for a goldfish please.
I used to be a little fairy, but now I am President of The United States.

Peking

These are the very rich garments of the poor
Tousling gradations of rainbow, song & soothing tricks
With a crooked margin there & there is here: we
Are the waiting fragments of his sky, bouncing
        a red rubber ball in the veins.

Do you have a will? And one existing so forgets all
Desuetude desultory having to move again, take power from snow,
Evening out not more mild than beastly kind, into a symbol.
I hate that. I think the couple to be smiles over glasses, and

Questions not to find you, the which they have. O Marriage
Talking as you is like talking for a computer, needing to be
Abacus, adding machine, me. Up from the cave's belly, down
        from the airy populace
That lace my soul, a few tears from the last the sole surviving
        Texas Ranger,

Freed, freely merge with your air, dance. Blue are its snowflakes
Besprinkled blue lights on his eyes, & flakes. For her

I'd gladly let the snake wait under my back, and think, to walk,
And pass our long love's day. Landscape rushing away.

From A List of the Delusions of the Insane, What They Are Afraid Of

That they are starving.
That their blood has turned to water.
That they give off a bad smell.
Being poor.
That they are in hell.
That they are the tools of another power.
That they have stolen something.
That they have committed an unpardonable sin.
Being unfit to live.
That evil chemicals have entered the air.
Being ill with a mysterious disease.
That they will not recover.
That their children are burning.

Chicago English Afternoon

He never listened while friends talked
Less original than penetrating, very often
Illuminating   He worked steadily to the even
Current of sound   sunlit oblongs   bramble   transfer
White South   nothing is gained by assurance as
To what is insecure   beer in bed, & an unused point
Beside me on the bench   time of, major energy product
Over Bellevue Road that silence said
To mean an angel is passing overhead   my baby
Throws my shoes out the door   & one cannot go back
Except in time   "Yes, but he is exultant; the ice
Meant something else to him"   highly reduced

For the sake of maintaining scale   *Goodbye To All That*
"I have only one work, & I hardly know what it is."
It was silence that stopped him working, silence in which
        he might look up
& see terror waiting in their eyes for his attention.
"Ladies & Gentlemen, you will depart the aircraft
At the Terminal Area to your Right. Thank you for flying United."

She (Not to be confused with she, a girl)

She alters all our lives for the better, merely
By her presence in it. She is a star. She is
Radiant, & She is vibrant (integrity). She animates
And gathers this community. Half the world's population
Is under 25. She permits everybody to be themselves more often
        than not.
She is elegant. I love her.
                                        She writes poetry of an easy & graceful
Intimacy. She is brave. She is always slightly breathless, or
Almost always slightly. She is witty. She owns a proud & lovely
Dignity, & She is always willing to see it through.
She is an open circle, Her many selves at or near the center, &
She is here right now. Technically, She is impeccable, &
If She is clumsy in places, those are clumsy places. She knows
Exactly what she is doing & not before She is doing it. What
She discovers She discovered before She discovers it, and so
The fresh discovery of each new day. Her songs are joyous songs,
& they are prayers, never failing to catch the rush of hope
        (anticipation)

Despair, insanity & desperation pouring in any given moment. She
Knows more than She will ever say. She will always say
More than she knows. She is a pain. She is much less than
Too good to be true. She is plain. She is ordinary. She
        is a miracle.

Innocents Abroad

TO GORDON BROTHERSTON

Fluke Holland:	—The Tennessee Third
Stew Carnall:	He was horrifed: The Little Pill.
Coy Bacon:	A nincomparable nanimal:
Hunk Jordan:	His Ghost.
Margo Veno:	Pigtails : ink
Rugby Kissick	"Sally Bowles"
Helen Keller:	"Nuff said."
Sue Bear:	Car Crash. (Change)
Joe Don Looney:	*Rexroth's Tune*
Cream Saroyan:	"Her first is a song."
Trane DeVore:	Hands Up!
Kid Dorn:	I am dog.
Ava Smothers:	Defies calipers
St. Paul. (Bag.)	Still. *Say it ain't so.*

Sister Moon

Where do the words come from? (come in?)
Where did that silt?   How much lives?
A rock is next to the bee.
The window is never totally thought through.
So
"Silver" is used to stand for something nothing
really ever quite is. Let it stand against.
Or in other words what next?
                                        There's time enough
A lot of unalloyed nouns.   for a list to occur
                                        between the lines.
Weather, as all strata in a possible day.
Sleet against window glass. A cigarette starts sounding.
You can see how "a depth" makes "west" and "south" agree.
A philosophy: "I guess yes."
milks & honeys, stuns, salutes, flashes . . .
                                        now & again, "a glimpse"

An Orange Clock

Sash the faces of lust
Beast. And get your salutation
An Electric Train wreck in the eye
Everything good is from the Indian. A curtain.
The word reminds me of Abydos and spinach.
I am not a pygmy soothed
By light that breathes like a hand
Sober dog, O expert caresses

In the twisted chamber, for you the silent men, &
Flowers, so as to weave the inhabitants
This small immobile yellow coat persona:
And you must receive songs in its name, O
Library of rapid boons
Irrespective of merit. & now I do not know his name.
Sash the faces of lush
Beast. & Get Your Salutation.

Gainsborough

I belong for what it is worth
To the family of the Phoenix; also
Dragon blood flows in my veins;
And when the time came to assign "us" berths,
Instead of "Proletarian," it was under "Criminal"

I found my name, albeit without
Difficulty, although it took some time. Neither
Among the last nor, happily, the first. It was Alphabetical
& "By the Numbers" in those days. Plus, I got
"Innocence," with a funny dash of "Butch."

And there you have it:

Not uncommonly provided just handles enough
To open up, close down, repeat, evade, hit, slip, & turn on:
With luck you could have it both ways & better with each change.

"He wanted the quiet, the domestic & the personal . . ."

"It's really just the sense of around & around."

Easter Monday

"Antlers have grown out the top of my shaggy head."
"And his conclusions to be unaccompanied by any opinions. . . ."
"You can't have two insides having an affair."
"Why not then spiritualize one's midday food with a little liquor?"
"The question seems prosecutorial." "The house is lost
In the room." "Loyalty is hard to explain."
"Hard fight gets no reward." "A woman has a spirit of her own."
"A man's spirit is built upon experience & rage."—Max Jacob.
In the air, in the house, in the night, bear with me
"I always chat to the golden partner."
"I'm working out the structures of men that don't exist yet."
"A gladness as remote from ecstasy as it is from fear."
"To go on telling the story."
"Give not that which is holy to dog."

Four Gates to the City

Everything good is from the Indian
Sober dog, O expert caresses
By light that breathes like a hand
Small   immobile   yellow   yo-yo plumage
On the cold bomb-shelter. A cur
Is a pre-sound without a rage
Come with me the nurse ferocity
Whose clouds are really toots from the nearby—it is
A well-lit afternoon
                                        but the lights go on

& you know I'm there.

Back in those previous frames

Is a walk through a town.

It sobers you up

To dance like that. Extraordinary to dance
Like that. Ordinarily, can be seen, dancing
In the streets. Ah, well, thanks for the shoes, god
Like Goethe on his divan at Weimar, I'm wearing them
on my right feet!

In Blood

"Old gods work"

"I gather up my tics & tilts, my stutters & imaginaries
into the "up" leg
In this can-can . . ." "Are you my philosophy
If I love you which I do . . . ?" "I want to know
It sensationally like the truth;" "I see in waves
Through you past me;" "But now I stop—" "I can love
What's for wear:" "But I dredge what I've bottomlessly canned
When I can't tell you . . ." "I love natural
Coffee beautifully . . ." "I'm conjugally love
Loose & tight in the same working" "I make myself
Feature by feature" "The angel from which each thing is most itself,
from each, each,"
"I know there's a faithful anonymous performance"
"I wish never to abandon you" "I me room he" To
"Burn! this is not negligible, being poetic, & not feeble."

The Joke & The Stars

What we have here is Animal Magick: the fox
is crossing the water: he is the forest from whence
he came, and toward which he swims: he is the hawk
circling the waters in the sun; and he is also the foxfire
on each bank in Summer wind. He is also the grandfather clock
that stands in the corner of the bedroom, one eye open, both hands up.

And though I am an Irishman in my American
I have not found in me one single he or she
who would sit on a midden and dream stars: for
Although I hate it, I walk with the savage gods.

"It's because you are guilty about being another person,
isn't it?" But back at the organ
The angel was able to play a great green tree
for the opening of the new First National Bank.

And New York City is the most beautiful city in the world
And it is horrible in that sense of hell. But then
So are you. And you, and you, and you, and you, and you.
And no I don't mean any of you: I just mean you.

Incomplete Sonnet #254

FOR DOUGLAS OLIVER

the number two, &
the number three, &
they being the number one

And as I have, almost
unbelievably, passed the
number four, I wonder

Will I ever "reach", or worse,
Stop at the number Seven?

For though one of me
has a sentimental longing for number

I never have believed in
the Number, Heaven.

But in numberless hells
I never once stopped at eleven.

Where the Ceiling Light Burns

Since we had changed
The smell of snow, stinging in nostrils as the wind lifts it from
        a beach
Today a hockey player died in
the green of days: the chimneys
Morning again, nothing has to be done,
                maybe buy a piano or make fudge
Totally abashed and smiling
                                I walk in
                                sit down and
                                face the frigidaire
You say that everything is very simple and interesting
'the picturesque
common lot'   the unwarranted light
the fever & obscurity of your organisms . . .
on what grounds shall we criticize the City Manager?

So Going Around Cities

TO DOUG & JAN OLIVER

"I order you to operate. I was not made to suffer."
Probing for old wills, and friendships, for to free
to New York City, to be in History, New York City being
History at that time. "And I traded my nights
for Intensity; & I barter my right to Gold; & I'd traded
my eyes much earlier, when I was circa say seven years old
for ears to hear Who was speaking, & just exactly who
was being told . . . ." & I'm glad
                    I hear your words so clearly
                    & I would not have done it
                              differently
                    & I'm amused at such simplicity, even so,
inside each & every door. And now I'm with you, instantly,
& I'll see you tomorrow night, and I see you constantly, hopefully
though one or the other of us is often, to the body-mind's own self
more or less out of sight! Taking walks down any street, High
Street, Main Street, walk past my doors! Newtown; Nymph Rd
          (on the Mesa); Waveland
Meeting House Lane, in old Southampton; or BelleVue Road
          in England, etcetera
Other roads; Manhattan; see them there where open or shut up behind
          "I've traded sweet times for answers . . ."
"They don't serve me anymore." They still serve me on the floor.
          Or,
as now, as floor. Now we look out the windows, go in &
          out the doors. The Door.
(That front door which was but & then at that time My door).
          I closed it
On the wooing of Helen. "And so we left schools for her." For
She is not one bit fiction; & she is easy to see;
          & she leaves me small room

For contradiction. And she is not alone; & she is not one bit
lonely in the large high room, &
invention is just vanity, which is plain. She
is the heart's own body, the body's own mind in itself
self-contained.
& she talks like you; & she has created truly not single-handedly
Our tragic thing, America. And though I would be I am not afraid
of her, & you also not. You, yourself, I,
Me, myself, me. And no, we certainly have not pulled down
our vanity: but
We wear it lightly here,
here where I traded evenly,
& even gladly
health, for sanity; here
where we live day-by-day
on the same spot.
My English friends, whom I love & miss, we talk to ourselves here,
& we two
rarely fail to remember, although we write seldom, & so must seem
gone forever.
In the stained sky over this morning the clouds seem about to burst.
What is being remembering
Is how we are, together. Like you we are always bothered, except
by the worse; & we are living
as with you we also were
fired, only, mostly, by changes in the weather. For Oh dear hearts,
When precious baby blows her fuse / it's just our way
of keeping amused.
That we offer of & as excuse. Here's to you. All the very best.
What's your pleasure? Cheers.

Quarter to Three

"who is not here
causes us to drift"

wake up, throat dry,
that way, perpetually,

"and why deprived unless
you feel that you ought to be?" and

"Clarity is immobile." And, "We are hungry
for devices to keep the baby happy . . ."

She writes, "My hunger creates a food
that everybody needs."

"I can't live without you no
matter who you are." "I think."

I write this in cold blood,
        enjoy.

A Little American Feedback

Yes, it's true, strategy is fascinating
& watching its workings out of, its
successes & failures, participating even,
can be amusing at times, but

*

Lords & Ladies do express
the courtly elegance, the
rude vulgarity, only truly
in the self's own body-mind's
living daily day-to-day the living
Self-contained containing

self-abandonment as self is
eyes as they caress or
blaze with particular hate, say, at
living being thought while a particularly
self-engrossing mind-game going on is
still, & only, one pronoun temporarily
haranguing the others while
the rest of One's self waits, truly
impatiently, for blessed natural savagery to arrive,
and finally save the party, by ordering
the musicians to resume their play
& the dancing picks up once again.

Boulder

Up a hill, short
of breath, then
breathing
Up stairs, & down, & up, & down again

to

NOISE

Your warm powerful Helloes
friends
still slightly breathless

in
a three-way street
hug

Outside

& we can move
& we move

Inside

to Starbursts   of noise!

The human voice is how.

✲

Lewis's, boyish, & clear; & Allen's, which persists,

& His,   & Hers,   & all of them Thems,

& then

Anne's, once again, (and as I am)   "Ted!"

Then

O, Lady!,   O, See,   among all things which exist

O this!, this breathing, we.

Picnic

The dancer grins at the ground.
The mildest of alchemists will save him.
(Note random hill of chairs). & he will prove
useful to her
in time. The ground to be their floor.

like pennies to a three year old,
like a novel, the right novel, to a 12 year old,
like a 39 Ford to a Highschool kid
like a woman to a man, a girl
who is a woman
is her self's own soul
and her man is himself
his own
& whole.

Addenda

& I can't buy
with submission
& tho I feel often
& why not
battered
I can't be beaten.

But I have been eaten, 7 times
by myself
& I go my way, by myself, I being
by myself only when useful, as for example,
you are to me now,
to you.

Narragansett Park

Inhabiting a night with shaky normal taboo hatred and fear
and a steep diagonal body
Peculiar and beautiful language correspond to my ordinary
tension
The major planets are shifting (shivering?) but out of my
natural habit,
Self-kindness,
I play them
something Nashville something quality
and there is the too easy knell of the games chapel
The tempting scornful opposite
Cathedral virus and goof immunization:

The curves of the Spirit are not very interested in
  the conquest of matter.
Color is the idiot's delight. I'm the curves, what's
  the matter? or
I'm the matter, the curves nag:
Call it Amber, it doesn't ride nor take to rider
Amber it doesn't make me want to pray, it makes me see color
as we fail to break through our clasped hands.

Carrying a Torch

What thoughts I have of where I'll be, & when, & doing what
Belong to a ghost world, by no means my first,
And may or may not be entertaining; for example
  living in a state of innocence in Kansas.
They hardly compare to when, passing through the air,
  it thinks about the air.

Just as, now, you are standing here
Expecting me to remember something
When years of trying the opposite of something
Leave that vision unfulfilled.

Mostly I have to go on checking the windows will but don't break
  while you get on with taking your own sweet time.
It's like coming awake thirsty & hungry, mid-way in dreams
  you have to have;
It stops or changes if you don't get up
& it changes, by stopping, if you do.

You do. Because you're carrying a torch. A sudden circular bath
  of symbols
Assails the structure. Better turn on the overhead light.

A Note from Yang-Kuan

You stay in the Mental Institute of your life.
God sees dog—in the mirror. In this city
Below the river, my private life is of no interest,
Though allowed. For example, it would be nicer to kiss
    than to shoot up.
Visual indifference is a growth. Used. Was used. Useful.
A new way of appreciating has arrived?
Should be a ride at Disneyland. People
Have basically split. And the heart flutters.
Stunned, the metrics & melody of
The multiplication tables, I am a father, watching,
Tho poor, her broad thoughts, this local lifetime.
Here I shall be with it but never of it.
Being nothing in front of no-one again.

Work Postures

The rain comes and falls.
A host of assorted artillery come up out of the lake.
The man who knows everything is a fool.
In front of him is his head. Behind him, men.

Few listeners get close. And
"Love must turn to power or it die."
This is a terrible present.
"Is this any way to run a Railroad?"

Flashing back 7 years I hear, "you will never go
any place for the second time again."
It's hard to fight, when your body is not with you.
& it's equally hard not to.

There is the dread that mind & body are One.
The cruelty of fear & misery works here.

Excursion & Visitation

The rains come & Fall.
Good grief, it's Le Jongleur de Dieu!
A gun wheels out of an overcoat.
It's I will fight. But I won't rule.

So, pay, and leave. So, when the light turned green,
She went. "I've gone
to get everything."   A Voice—
"to reappear in careers?"   Un-uh.

These are the days of naming things?
Watch my feet, not my answers.
Oh, good grief, it's Le Jongleur de Dieu!
He's the godson of the ghost-dancers!

On Earth we call The Sea of Tranquility "The North Atlantic."
And a voice once locked in the ground now speaks in me.

Everybody Seemed So Laid Back in the Park

Marie in her pin-striped suit singing
"Where Have All The Flowers Gone?" in German
Not alfalfa covers the ground of Lilac Park.
"C'mere for a second!" shouts the invisible
Old lady. She crosses the park in a hat of nylon.
Marie falls down, still singing.
I see a woman with a baby running.
Two Africans in turbans wiggle their hips.
Marie cries & yawns for her audience.
Marie lights an envelope with matches.
Frisbees fly in the hot sun.
"Try it again."
A very pale orange is sitting under the baby birds.
The community lightens, five o'clock, lifting my heart
        to a place.

A Meeting at the Bridge

He was one of the last of the Western Bandits.
"A fellow like you gets into scrapes.
"Gets life. Spends most of it in jail.
"You gotta make a stand somewhere."

I guess. "You smell of disinfectant."
I guess. "Your kind
Drift from nowhere to nowhere, until
They get close. No telling

What they do then." Yeah, I guess that's just about right.
"Do you fish?" No, I just go down and look at the water.
"Pretty, ain't it?" Is it? No, it ain't.
It ain't pretty. It's

A carnival. A pig-sty. A regular
Loop-de-loop . . . (spits) *I need some shoes.*

"I Remember"

I remember painting "I HATE TED BERRIGAN" in big black letters
all over my white wall.
I remember bright orange light coming into rooms in the late
afternoon. Horizontally.
I remember when I lived in Boston reading all of Dostoyevsky's
novels one right after the other.
I remember the way a baby's hand has of folding itself around
your finger, as tho forever.
I remember a giant gold man, taller than most buildings, at
"The Tulsa Oil Show."
I remember in Boston a portrait of Isabella Gardner by Whistler.
I remember wood carvings of funny doctors.
I remember opening jars that nobody else could open.
I remember wondering why anyone would want to be a doctor. And
I still do.
I remember Christmas card wastebaskets.
I remember not understanding why Cinderella didn't just pack up and leave,
if things were all *that* bad. I remember "Korea."
I remember one brick wall and three white walls.
I remember one very hot summer day I put ice cubes in my aquarium
and all the fish died.
I remember how heavy the cornbread was. And it still is.

To Himself

Now you can rest forever
Tired heart. The final deceit is gone,
Even though I thought it eternal. It's gone.
I know all about the sweet deception,
But not only the hope, even the desire is gone.
Be still forever. You've done enough
Beating. Your movements are really
Worth nothing nor is the world
Worth a sigh. Life is bitterness
And boredom; and that's all. The world's a mudhole.
It's about time you shut up. Give it all up
For the last time. To our kind fate gives
Only that we die. It's time you showed your contempt for
Nature and that cruel force which from hiding
Dictates our universal hurt
In the ceaseless vanity of every act.

—LEOPARDI
(TRANS. BY TED BERRIGAN, GORDON BROTHERSTON, & GEORGE SCHNEEMAN)

Whitman in Black

For my sins I live in the city of New York
Whitman's city lived in in Melville's senses, urban inferno
Where love can stay for only a minute
Then has to go, to get some work done
Here the detective and the small-time criminal are one
& tho the cases get solved the machine continues to run
Big Town will wear you down
But it's only here you can turn around 360 degrees
And everything is clear from here at the center

To every point along the circle of horizon
Here you can see for miles & miles & miles
Be born again daily, die nightly for a change of style
Hear clearly here; see with affection; bleakly cultivate compassion
Whitman's walk unchanged after its fashion

Heloise

When I search the past for you
Without knowing why
You are the waiting fragments of this sky
Which encases me, and

What about the light that comes in then?
And the heavy spins and the neon buzzing of night-time?
I go on loving you like water, but,
Bouncing a red rubber ball in the veins

In wind without flesh, without bone, and inside
The drowsy melody of languish, silence:
And inside the silence, one ordained to praise
In ordinary places. And inside my head, my brain.

You have made the world so it shall grow, so,
The revolutions not done, I've tucked the earth
        between my legs, to sing.

Southwest

We think by feeling and so we ride together
The child who has fallen in love with maps & charts,
The last, the sole surviving Texas Ranger, cajoling
Scheming, scolding, the cleverest of them all. What is there to know?

Questions. The very rich garments of the poor.
The very rack & crucifix of weather, winter's wild silence
In red weather. A too resilient mind. The snake
Waiting under each back. Not to forget to mention the chief thing:

Underneath a new old sign, a far too resilient mind;
And the heavy not which you were bringing back alone,
Cycling across an Africa of green & white, but to be a part
Of the treetops & the blueness, with a bark that will not bite.

The fields breathe sweet, as one of you sleeps while the other is fuming
with rage.
Is he too ill for pills? Am I gonna ride that little black train
one year from tonight?

From the House Journal

1.

I belong here, I was born
To breathe in dust
I came to you
I cannot remember anything of then
up there among the lettuce plots

I cough a lot, so I stay awake
I cannot possibly think of you
I get a cinder in my eye because
I hate the revolutionary vision of

"I have a terrible age," & I part
I have no kindness left
I do have the lame dog with me & the cloud
I kiss your cup, but I know so much.

I must have leisure for leisure bears
I to you and you to me the endless oceans of

2.

Now it next to my flesh, & I don't mean dust
I am sober and industrious
I see you standing in clear light
I see a life of civil happiness
I see now tigers by the sea,
the withering weathers of
I stagger out of bed
I stumble over furniture I fall into a gloomy hammock
I'm having a real day of it
I'm not sure there's a cure

You are so serious, as if you are someone
Yet a tragic instance may be immanent
Yes it's sickening that yes it's true, and
Yes it's disgusting that yes if it's necessary, I'll do it.

Visits from a Small Enigma

The bunnies plug-in & elaborate
Spongy thought-streams some days
Attempting in innocence to cash in on
Fire feedback on the flaming bridge
The trailing scads of diaphanous ribbons
Whatever & all like that. Their missiles crack

Of their own sound at the Barrier Gate, as
Punk-log fog shreds the aether, and mountains
Of any consequence simply sit, comic & invisible,
On their faces. Then, golden discs sweep up
Appearing to be signals, signalling
A possible common version of whiteness; sweep up
Out of an iodine-colored Chinese Puzzle box.
White-gold light. Slightly kinky sweepings.

Revery

Up inside the walls of air listen
A sound of footsteps in the spaces out there
In the frightening purple weather
And hazy lights whose color night decomposes.

Late at night, rise up carcass and walk;
Head hanging, let somebody tell the story.
Maybe the machine under the palms will start up
For one who waits

Under the arch of clouds, with familiar face,
Heart beating all out of proportion,
Eyes barely open, ears long since awake to what's coming:
It is very possibly Autumn, returning,

Leaving no footprints, leaving danger behind.
The head being out of line has fallen. I still want
    everything that's mine.

My Tibetan Rose

A new old song continues. He worked into the plane
A slight instability, to lessen his chances
Of succumbing to drowsiness, over the green sea.
Above his head clanged. And there were no dreams in this
    lack of sleep.
Your lover will be guilty of murder & you will turn her in.
Sometimes I'd like to take off these oak leaves and feel
    like an ordinary man.
You get older the more you remember. And one lives, alone,
    for pure courtship, as
To move is to love, & the scrutiny of things is merely syllogistic.
Postmortems on old corpses are no fun.
I have so much to do I'm going to bed.
I'll live on the side of a mountain, at 14,000 feet,
In a tough black yak-hide tent, turn blue, force down
Hot arak & yak butter, & wait for this coma to subside.
Come along with me, my Tibetan Rose!

Nothing for You

TO DICK GALLUP

People of the Future

People of the future
while you are reading these poems, remember
you didn't write them,
I did.

Valentine

I have been here too many times before
you & now it's time to go
crazy again will that make you like me? I think so
often about you & all those bon aperitifs we had
wanted to have but didn't in Paris where we
never got to did we No we didn't although now
Here I am & everyone loves me so
where are you? & why don't they go
away? I didn't ask for this I asked for you
love but you said No, you didn't say
May I? true & crazy here I am
again unkempt in my passion at that May I?

Doubts

TO DAVID BEARDEN

Don't call me "Berrigan"
Or "Edmund"
If ever you touch me
Rivers of annoyance undermine the arrangements

If you would own me
Spit
The broken eggshell of morning
A proper application
Of stately rhythms
Timing
Accessible to adepts
All
May pierce this piercing wind
Penetrate this light
To hide my shadow

But the recoil
Not death but to mount the throne
Mountains of twine and
Entangling moments

Which is why I send you my signal

That is why I give you this six-gun and call you "Steve"
Have you taken the measure of the wind?
Can hands touch, and
Must we dispose of "the others"?

He

He wandered and kept on wandering. Bar-Mitzvah and Confirmation availed themselves of his myriad aimless impulses. It was no use. Days were of cheeseburgers, shoe repair, and scary. In cities

and through frenzy darkness was far away. Darkness,
you are so dark, he thought. Where oh where is a
telephone booth, and the friendliness of newsprint
on Saturday afternoons at the Stadium? He wept. Steamy

ferns made a dank obbligato to his dreams. It grew and grew.
At last he was surrounded by gaily-colored birds,
who sang to him in the key of G or E. It was
then he smiled, for always, affirmation made him happy.

Later he died of Hatred.

For Annie Rooney

My rooms were full of Ostrich feathers when
I returned from Spring, and someone had stolen
all the apricot brie! just as if they'd known
I was in training! for shame! that anyone

could be so cruel, and me with only 27 teeth!
How fortunate they never found dear
you. For surely then they would have planted
crickets, to lick the cherry glue off of all

my Princess Grace Special Delivery airmail stamps. The boors,
they'd stop at nothing. But this time their
saboteurs slipped up. I'll never let them find you,
no matter what they do, you, my secret weapon, who

assures my victories! I'm so glad we were married
in Hooversville, Ohio, in 1933!

Saturday Afternoons on the Piazza

Why have you billowed under my ancient piazza
Father? "I swan, if you don't beat everything
Anybody ever heard tell of!" Refreshment time!
Have a nonpareil? Thank you! Here we are again

In the movies and I'm holding your thigh, Mmmmmmmmmm
Feels like "a belly" to me. "Well, I declare, Feety-
Belle, ain't you ever gonna get y'rself a real . . . Shut your face
Angerbelle, you ain't doin' s'hot y'rself y'know,

my stars!" (At intermission I called her at the hotel
And she made a big thing about somebody telling her
"I'm Judy Garland's daughter.") When you're 7 or 8 or 9
You don't really care who your momma and poppa are,

Just so they really love you and have TV and all that.
Up in the blue window a white woman is reeling out her laundry.

Prayer

Rilke,
I strain to gather my absurdities
Into a symbol. I falter. These
Roisterers here assembled shatter my zest
With festivity.

Once again I turn to you, to your
Buch das Bildung. Oh Tall Tree
In the self
Flower we three into one.
May he who is you
Become me.

Hearts

At last I'm a real poet I've written a
ballade a sonnet a poem in spontaneous
prose and even a personal poem   I can use
punctuation or not and it doesn't
matter   I'm obscure when I feel like it
especially in my dream poems which I never even
call   Dream Poem   but from sheer cussedness title
Match Game Etc. (for Dick Gallup) or something like that.

For example, take this poem, I don't know how
to end it, It needs six lines to make it a sonnet, I
could just forget it and play hearts with Joe and
Pat and Dick, but lately I'm always lethargic,
and I don't even like hearts, or Pat, or Joe, or
Dick or / and especially myself, & this is no help.

Night Letter

Dear Marge, hello. It is 5:15 a.m.
Outside my room atonal sounds of rain
Drum in the pre-dawn. In my skull my brain
Aches in rhythm to that pounding morning rain.
In your letter, many questions. I read
Them over and over. And now I dread
Answering. "Deteriorating," you said.
Not a question, really, but you did
Say it. And made it hard to write. You know
Margie, tonight, and every night, in any
Season, cold images glitter brightly
In my head. Dreams of Larry Walker
In his marriage bed: of David Bearden
Paranoid: and of Martin Cochran, dead.

Jubilee

In the ear, winds dance
to drink in the house

Summer came over here today
Everyone overloads one song

Is he the handsome stranger?
I'm thinking of summoning people

I need a hoodlum in white
"kill him"

This face against its own
Endows

giggling
And forms a road upon a tract

I got so tall up there
He t-told me "you're too fallow in your footsteps"

Goodbye to burning
Brain

Heat
These feet drifting on an unangry tide

Please turn stark naked.

Some Do Not

You can make this swooped transition on your lips
Go to the sea, the lake, the tree
And the dog days come
Your head spins when the old bull rushes
Back in the aery daylight, he was not a midget

He could feel the talk sidling up into his ears and burning
His stand-in was named Herman, but came rarely
Why do you begin to yawn so soon, who seemed
So hard, feather-bitten . . . back in the aery daylight
Put away your hair. The black heart beside the 15 pieces of glass
Spins when the old bull rushes. The words say I LOVE YOU:
Go to the sea, the lake, the tree,
Glistering, bristling, cozzening whatever disguises

On the Level Everyday

I am trying very hard to be
Where you are
Where this great vision of
Our carelessness
Looks toward Namoncos
Counts on love

When feeling
Out of depth and breadth and
height
end to
Being, & ideal grace
Quiet need
Sun & candle light.

I check my engine test
My saddle-strap
My Palomino!

A love I seemed to lose
With my lost saints—

Here
Enthusiasm greets poets
Blue-back Winged Space Rainbow GRAHR!
(Hi Ma!) When the phone rings I
(no one calls!) why is it my life
? flames in the portable head

Myself with pepsi pouring
Back into your arms pill

end, a baked
You mean? Yes
Is it my turn already? Hi
It's 5:15 a.m.

A closer walk with thee
It's a little stiff.
That's the ticket! Tickets,

GRAHR! Who's
? forgot something there (mike)

At every hand, my critic — Unplugging the mike

With carelessness I sign the register — Crank does that Dwight?
The last the sole surviving Texas Ranger, — Enthusiasm greets Poets One
There's only one riot isn't there?

You

Known as "Saddik" ? — Better believe it.

Autumn's Day

AFTER RILKE

Lord, it is time. Summer was very great.
Now cast your shadow upon sundials.
Let winds remind meadows it is late.

Mellow now the last fruits on the vine.
Allow them only two more southern days.
Hasten them to fulness, and press
The last heavy sweetness through the wine.

Who has no home can not build now.
Who dwells alone must now remain alone;
Will waken, read, write long letters, and
Will wander restlessly when leaves are blowing.

String of Pearls

Lester Young! why are you playing that clarinet
you know you are Horn in my head? the middle page is
missing god damn it now how will I ever understand Nature
And New Painting? doo doot doo Where is Dick Gallup
his room is horrible it has books in it and paint peeling
a 1934 icebox living on the fifth floor it's
ridiculous

yes and it's ridiculous to be sitting here
in New York City 28 years old wife sleeping and
Lester playing the wrong sound in 1936 in Kansas City (of
all places) sounding like Benny Goodman (of all people) but
a good sound, not a surprise, a voice, & where was Billie, he
hadn't met her yet, I guess Gallup wasn't born yet neither was
my wife Just me & that icebox I hadn't read HORN by John
Clellon Holmes yet, either

What is rhythm I wonder? Which was George & which Ira
Gershwin? Why
don't I do more? wanting only to be walking in the New
York Autumn
warm from coffee I still can feel gurgling under my ribs
climbing the steps of the only major statement in New York City
(Louis Sullivan) thinking the poem I am going to write seeing
the fountains come on wishing I were he

Problems, Problems

Joy! you come winging in a hot wind on the breath
of happy sexy music, you are peeping
into my redbloodedness, and I am writing silly lines
like, "I was born, reared, and educated in Tulsa,
Oklahoma," only true of Ron Padgett and not Dan'l Boone or me

Uh-huh a sip of gritty coffee, ripping me out of
my mind, making me feel "funny" is carrying me up-
town past interesting bodegas, the interesting
bums eyeing me, my beard throws them off
tho I'm yearning for a little romance

Dontcha think it's time? thanks & your name is
walking right by my side it hurts me to see you talking
to any other guy! where is Harry Fainlight, he's on a trip
Now that's integrity! Where's Andy Warhol? Far out, but Harry
doesn't think so he prefers Vaughan Traherne Wordsworth even

Who can help but love him? it's so American of him! Lines,
you must be saying what I mean I hope I like you later. Our
Love must be sweet destiny, no other love could thrill me so
completely (unless it be going to the movies, and alone, crossing
the Mississippi for the first time, so rare

a feat for feet "born, reared and educated in Tulsa, Oklahoma"
turned blue with cold and being careful not to touch one another.)

Truth as History

1.

My rooms were full of awful features when
I was burning, dear, and you were eating goblets
of ruinous dinner! It didn't matter, tho. The
foolish wind kept blowing, and my bones were hum-
ming! That was when my eyes walked out
on to bleak piers and shrieked for you! You were standing, often,
stark-naked just as if you knew it wasn't raining
and no-one had stolen all the dazzling looks. But this
one time the saboteurs sneaked up! Hah! I didn't
let them grind you, my little Coolie-Baby, who insures
my factory. No, and it's not bad to lay buried, in Hoovers-
ville, by wires, laid on us by gentlemen, & ladies flushed
with gin. Except at night, when you are lying in the wind.

2.

I beat on the fruits of the gushy showers
burning up ginger-ale, only a pantomime mother &
father, doting on feelable widows, as my rent & these
urgent denials in my plug-ugly vision hold out! I
would take some corn to Minton's & throw it on Dizzy
Gillespie, & I mumble at babies on the bus, although
I too am reading the nickel journals, while my axles
are losing patience. Castles! my dearest, the whole town
is hiding out in six cheap hotels, sorrowful you gaping at me
as I continue to concoct ewe dreams! I would like very much
to be in your hair, in hottest blood, my Saxon Thing was nursed
on Western fiction with Doc Holliday my Christopher
Columbus to help me. But it's no use, you love Oliver Hardy, he's
the last of the old-time newsboys. I have a soggy bed.

Francis à Bientôt

The storms of Baudelaire fall on Judas' head
He send out rays of light with that river
We saw it in his hair
No use to call me again it isn't right

You string a sonnet around your fat gut
And falling on your knees you invent the shoe
For a horse   Don't cheat
The victory is not always to the sweet

That night arrives again in red
André Breton is a shit! (He sneezed on the rum
Turning it into a pun)   One must live
Even in Colorado (Take that, you horse!)

Now we are all dead
Charles, Ju, you, & Harry James
There is no time(s) past (lost?)   We
Are in The Twentieth Century (The Christian Era), and
The charms (bait) leave
Under the heels of Children.

This man was my friend.

The TV Story

1.

It is after 7 in the evening and raining cold in bed. Next day 12 noon Dick comes by we go to the Museum—with Sandy—lovely on my naked back through the open window. She has finished *Nadja*, make entry in my journal, work on my new poem, go to baby-sitting. Carol came, looking for Dick—kicks them out. Now I am—I carve a pumpkin. I read *Nadja*. 4 a.m.

—lying naked on the bed. We start talking about Marcel Duchamp. All try to figure out how pay the rent . . . 12 o'clock . . . ourselves . . . we begin touching one another in the dark, & she is reading *Prolegomena to Greek Religion*. She says she is—she takes off my clothes & we laugh. Dick & I discuss Wallace Fowlie, he gives me a copy of *Nadja*, not to keep—she says if it's ever over between us in your mind please tell me. Talk about Dada, we do, drink whiskey. He makes coffee. We let him in, he knocks again—at the door—we show him a copy of *Nadja*—he dissipates—she interprets it for him in some new way, I translate it for him, he is sleeping, Dick comes over, we discuss *Nadja* extensively, next day 12 noon we are all to go To the Museum. (TV Show).

2.

I was charging others to love me, instead
of doing so myself.

3.

The day I see my name in the papers, something
snaps, I'm finished; I sadly enjoy my fame, but
I stop writing.

4.

Now fifty years and nostalgic, I pushed open the door of a cafe and asked for a small beer. At the next table some beautiful young women were talking animatedly and my name is mentioned. "Ah," said one of them, "he may be old, he may be homely, but what difference does that make? I'd give thirty years of my life to become his wife." I looked at her with a proud, sad smile, she smiled back in surprise, I got up, I disappeared.

El Greco

A drop of boo   the wounded ham
                    might be

Saint Francis's knee
in the sombrero   of a tree.

Mouth deep
    rope   Owl hoot in spectral radiance
& fix skull

He prays.
                        his vision
    broke   his brain (lie   a hen visage
a plant among browns and grays.

        Crimson pot
                            pierces finger   gasp
Drip   fresh drips   bright   ow   fring,
Fellow, fring
                        a miniscule   wrist   limp
                    on a hollow headless
                            bone

Cento: A Note on Philosophy

FOR PAT MITCHELL

When I search the past for you
We who are the waiting fragments of his sky
"I who am about to die"
Then was the drowsy melody of languish
And staying like white water; and now of a sudden
A too resilient mind
Cajoling, scheming, scolding, the cleverest of them all
And so we ride together into the peach state!
(Remain secure from pain preserve thy hate thy heart)

Those are the very rich garments of the poor
The rack and the crucifix of winter, winter's wild
Which encases me. What about the light that comes in then?
Silence; and in between these silences
The spins and the flowing of night-time.
Praising, that's it! One ordained to praise
The wind without flesh, without bone
The morning-glory, climbing the morning long
In ordinary places.
Not to mention the chief thing

We think by feeling. What is there to know?
Bouncing a red rubber ball in the veins
Though my ship was on the way it got caught in some moorings
Melodic sighs of Arabic adventure
Darting into a tender fracas leeward and lee
The fields breathe sweet, the daisies kiss our feet
And you have made the world (and it shall grow)
The last the sole surviving Texas Ranger
The heavy not which you were bringing back alone
Abandoned, almost Dionysian

Why should I climb the look-out?
The child who has fallen in love with maps and charts
Drums in the pre-dawn. In my head my brain
But to be part of the treetops and the blueness, invisible
In red weather.
Questions, oh, I hope they do not find you
I go on loving you like water, but
I am in love with poetry. Every way I turn
I think I am bicycling across an Africa of green and white fields
Into a symbol. I hate that. I falter. These

Let the snake wait under
My back, for which act
I would not credit comment upon gracefully
How how the brig brig water the damasked roses
But helpless, as blue roses are helpless
The revolution is done. What has a bark, but cannot bite?
I've tucked the rushing earth under my legs
By those, to sing of cleanly wantonesse
To walk, and pass long love's day.

"It is such a beautiful day I had to write you a letter
On along the street. Somewhere a trolley, taking leave
Just to be leaving; hearts light as balloons
mirrored in little silver spoons."
True voyagers alone are those who leave
The falcon cannot hear the falconer
They never shrink from their fatality
Upon those under lands, the vast
And, without knowing why, say, "Let's get going! Goodbye."
& so, sauntered out that door, which was closed.

New Junket

FOR HARRY FAINLIGHT

Everywhere we went we paid the price, endurement
Of indifference, signs of regeneration: in every
Victim awaits the guest of honor, hawk-like, with
Respect to the unlocking of the dream; this hot breath
That you perfectly feel lingering. It makes you think.
You think of a faience pot, a giant eucalyptus overhung
Against the balustrade, facing assurance in the wind.
You suspect we enjoy these poses. This biggest indifference.
You were succumbing to kisses (the real purpose
Another purpose of the trip) but the trip had been
Moved up. I cared. And so we left.
Wonder changes grooves to form a Winter
Rising with Winter roses near the house. The water
Following the signal, which is following me,
Is lifting me up on the on the wings of the great machine.

Dick Gallup (Birthday)

(FOR THE *GALLUPS*)

interrupts yr privacy

25 years later

you wait between the dodge and the bush
a basket
between you and your arm: under it

INSIGHT (Vol. 1, Nr. 3)

(the condemned man is shielding a
woman, about 25, five feet
eleven inches high, hair dark, curly,
dark eyes; and though not gallant, is pure . . .

the street disappearing
into bush level
two heads above the basket

("seeking a person-
al world, where one's own
behavior has a code . . .

is no guarantee
of justice, folks.

SUNLIGHT IN
JUNGLE-LAND

. . .

that girl wreathed in blue
and that one, in yellow

corporeal

"her hair a wondrous gold"

MAIN-TRAVELED ROADS
(under the sheets)

the community
in their vicinity, is murder.
It keeps us awake.

FOLK LEGENDS do not await Verdicts.

We get on, with provisions.
It (The Dodge) continues.

Conceived in Hate

. . . Your America & mine
are lands to be discovered
and nothing
stirs us to discover
so much as the real
drama of today's newsmaking people

Blonde on Blonde

It's enough to make a girl
go out & buy a bottle
of peroxide; and many did.
But not her. She loved
Mencken, her pretty sister
whose shame & sin outshone
her dark, golden curls.

Flower Portrait

FOR SOTERE TORREGIAN & FAMILY

It's morning
                    meaning
               it
                    has arrived:

MERRY XMAS

the center of
my gray window facing life. That's
a Christmas card, from John Perreault. That's
Gary Snyder: A RANGE OF POEMS. That's
THE GERMAN GENERAL STAFF & that is

MOTHER

6.

IT'S ALL IN THE STARS
(that's a book)

CLEAR THE RANGE!

(That's a book, by me.)

Nevertheless
she
is not here,
tho it's all right here

and so are we.

* *

Birds sing in this
my world, I love you

if "you" is bacon,
toast & two eggs, over

light: we'll share a small coke & read a big boke
before we die.

* *

What am I talking about? It
's a new day! I've got
to run. Mi casa, su casa,

THE AGE OF GOLD is before me.

Selflessness

TO PETER SCHJELDAHL

This picture indicates development
You drink some coffee, you get some sleep
Everything is up in the air

especially us

who are me

Linda greets our force

forcefully

so much for that

(sing)

"I'm sittin' here thinkin'
just how sharp I am . . . ."

I ask you, can these words have issued
from M'sieur M. "The Rock" Proust,
BPOE, RSVP, ICUP?

No.

You inhabit a baby, I mean
a table . . .
the logic of that
is lost

is mixed with public opinion

and

as we get closer & closer, to it
something snaps
Music gets into this picture
of
"A Life."

& Now it's rolling . . .

& Now we are one

& it's bed-time

competitive spirits

dare we continue? we dare continue

seeking parties

full of places

we have not been at

nor ever will be at

without each other.

The Avant-Garde Literary Award

Someone something

HELP!

false start

"falling in love with religious experience"

Now you're talking!

"giving tongue
to the public consciousness"

(that's a thought)

A dope-fiend is sitting
on his dead ass,
surrounded by roaches.

"You have just won The Avant-Garde Literary Award."

From The Art of the Sonnet

1.

It is a very great thing
To call across the room
To a girl,
"Hey, I love you."

You shout very loudly.
A lot of weird freaky people
Look at you very strangely plus assorted boring square types—
The girl does not hear you.

She is puce, and yellow. You are completely ass
Because the girl you are yelling to is Whistler's Mother.
PS: You are also somewhat color-blind.
Or could it be that you are The Joker, my plum-blossomed Visionary

Friend? Those tiny broken veins on the tip of your nose are
Tres interesting. They resemble the map of Crete.

2.

Some of Denis Roche's books are missing here.
Let's go out. We can go to the park.
Dead Fingers Talk. They say, "I got some books here
That we can steal things out of.

They're all by good writers." Silence.
Orange Juice. Five dog barks then another.
Then too many to count shut up you dumb mutt.
In Korea they give puppies to GI's who fatten them up

Then they steal them back to make soup. Ack.
I think we oughtta write a great poem outta these books.
That dog is still barking. My stomach is growling: Ravi Shankar
I got all great books here to write poems from.

Maybe we could write a sonnet. Great burst of applause:
Ladies & Gentlemen, it's all about to happen, & now it's done.

3.

I've been loving you a little too long.
I can't stop now. Why should I stop now?
You don't know, do you? I think it is very nice
Of you. Incidentally, I went to the fortune teller

She looked into the crystal ball. She saw
Two New York Yankees & they were very small.
I left there in a hurry. I needed one pall mall.
I got one from a midget. It was long as he was tall.

In case you haven't figured it out, Lady of Mondrian, the lake
I made up most of the above. You see, I did it
Because I'm a nut. Yet, isn't it all right to be sort of nutty, a flak
When you are in love? Why not

Call me up sometime?
212-677-7779.

Then I'd Cry

Now twist knife all strength owing O now twist knife

And he came down tubes chosen by the waiter
Black fright
Headed down from his homely Thuggee feelings
To the babbling waiter
Whose foreign compulsion wounded his taint

In the dawn of Thuggee feelings
Then
        I tamed him

A prince sups on his head for thought
Dark grace savors him
Or tortures me

He said come forth old time wit and get me too

Air Conditioning

It's very interesting
Weighing 500 lbs
You might even say, "It's great!"
"Let's drink to that!"
I did   Dixie Cup Fanta Orange
IOWA   BACK DEATH   & now a humming
Opening it up inside
Making a fire-engine red
Desk chair bright green
A white night & amazing you!
You don't believe it.

Monolith

The right wall is BRICKS.
The left wall is FAR OUT
The front wall is PICTURES.
I CAN'T SEE the back wall.

The CEILING is High.
The Floor is QUICK.
The AIR is THIN.
The LIGHT is BRIGHT WHITE.

The CURRENT is ELECTRIC.
The POWER is ON.
The Subject is BENT.
He is POISED.

He is Listening.
This is IT.
IT is HERE.
He has been WATCHING.

He has Had To Think.
It is Done. It is
COMPETENT. It is NOT
SATISFACTORY, but

It Damn Well Will Do.

Autumn

Autumn is fun

for these kids

who love me

But comes a Voyeur

W/his champagne

to this tub

It shrinks

disappears.

The pills aren't working.

London

Messy red heart
put on black shirt
tight brown cords & slush-proof boots
stand up & look at it

Senior Service, pretty expensive
Not for me, tho, I'm an American
"There are no second acts in American life."
        cf. F. Scott Fitzgerald
& money is just a way for people to talk, anyway

For example Jim Dine talking, to me
That's one I just finished. It's a list
of names of everyone in my life
the past ten years. What a great idea,

I think. It's so simple. You just get an idea
& then you do it. Anxiety thickens the plot.

London Air

TO BOB CREELEY

1.

My heart Your heart

That's the American Way

& so,

FUCK OR WALK!

It's the American Way

* *

Messy Red Heart (American)

Put on
black shirt, tight
brown cords & bright
blue socks

Under slush-proof boots!

Is that cow-hide?

I don't know Yes it is that
It is That.

Take a *good* look, that is I
mean
have a good look

LIGHT UP (a Senior Service)

&

turning around

The turning point is turning around.

*

Now, that may seem wasteful to you
but not to me being American

That's the American bent

(sprinting with a limp)

*

It beginning having reached part 3.

Part 3.

Into the Second Act in American Life:

cf. F. Scott Fitzgerald
"There are no
Second Acts in
American Life."

I go in &
sit down
at this desk

and write

d o g   s e e s   G O D

in the mirror

c/o Jim Dine
60 Chester Square
London SW One

* *

It's 5 units sunlight, 5 units
Cincinnati

One plus Zero
equals One

That's it you

Now you're talking!

& so, let me read to you this list
of the ten greatest books of all time:

Here they are

THE TEN GREATEST BOOKS OF ALL TIME

1. Now in June by Lao-Tree

2. Sore Foot by Larry Fagin

3. Sleep & Dreams by Gay Luce & Julius Segal

4. Rape by Marcus van Heller

5. Out of The Dead City by Chip Delaney

6. Moth by James M. Cain

7. Letters for Origin (Proofs) by Charles Olson

8. Classics Revisited by Kenneth Rexroth

9. Pleasures of a Chinese Courtesan by Jonathan Payne

10. Letters to Georgian Friends by Boris Pasternak

10. Horse Under Water by Len Deighton

10. Camp Concentration by Tom Disch

&

breathing easier now

10. The Quotations of Chairman Mao.

In Bed with Joan & Alex

In the morning

Very bright the

not yellow

light

tough creamy air

it softens lightly

when you give

THE LOOK OF LOVE

having a good look
knowing / green
interesting manners
with
blackjack nuances.

Can you dig it (doing that) in the Michigan morning?
light
taking your glasses off
(clothes already off)
yellow pants
I should say gold
but gold isn't really yellow
is it?
so I don't

Joan Fagin's brown shirt's resting now
on the chair
brown
transparent, blue
buttons . . .
Some pop off
so do we all some time.
Joan, with you,
"I do."

&

Loving you

doesn't really *have* to "do"
anything
but I do.

& doing (. . . "anything" . . .) turns you on, too.
doing a few
swirls
&
spinning

moving easily
& so firm
A just plain terrific face
two eyes   opening wide
with delight
that's "doing it all" for me.

It's a little scary   it, & you, too
white & not so
blue
now a slow pink flush
across the white rhythm
& the blue . . .
Coming together
or maybe not coming at all
or coming
at leisure
"Digging one's own natural
savagery"

as the man says

is all there is

to do.

To eat ourselves

alive

& dig it.

& having looked into "that",   having *had* "it"

still having it

Now,

to look at it,

looking at it whenever

The right light appears

which is practically

anytime   & especially,

"In the morning."

2.

Looking at a cottage in the country,

Maine,

My main man's desire shines through

"that's tough!" you might say

but it's civilized.

It's terse, but fluid. (It's

a hard-nosed kike rap).

Round & round & round we go

There are trees, around

& green grass around

to stretch out
lay around
on.

Above blue sky
as clean as paint is
clear (thick & creamy
light.)

Now, that's what I call Radiance.

All of it,
& you, really here
plus, friendly
shadows
talk
"do anything you want to."

& so we did, all of it.

See that?
I'd like you to look at
& see it.

It's beautiful!   moving beautifully
in the morning

&

you can turn it on   you're here
anytime   & it's here

CODA: (to Alex Katz)

Being civilized about such things
is a great pleasure!

Wasn't it, Alex?

It's just like Real Life
(after the movies.)

You put it together
with your knife

punching it
into the sun

shining

Out of sight!

3.

Now, resting on the President's chair, the center
head inside its hair, on the grass, the white
house right over there

a Chesterfield King

& there's a light!

Clean White Smoke Wind Clear Air

me up here & you,
you up across & over there.

Between us, The United States
of Air

& Joan

still flying,

on this plane:

It's taking Joan everywhere

she feels like going

& so she does

& so do we all

& so we do,

thanks to you,

light radiance air

Alex, Joan, my friends,

you were there.

Ode to Medicine

AFTER LEWIS WARSH

Going up, slowly, I, slowly
Flashing insane (exciting) changes across each lady eye
Begin to soar. First the quiet
(trees) as Lewis and I lope none-too-gently by
Rush of light hitting walk, my
Tonight. The Pep Rally inflames the green sky
Feet crushing light, my walk lighting up
Forget them. They (I) shall return. It's cool
October's thickness (night). It needs girls
As well as well. I love these girls, & so
To cut through the dense talk growing light
I'm arriving soon. I am, & they laugh wisely
Along the diagonal: our sleep is but a birth
& a remembering, so forget all that came before.
There are girls laughing because they thought
Talk to him, he's high in New York somewhere
Sometimes, when I think about where I am
Medicine gets me high. I
Do a few spins & laugh it off. Cough

Sweet Vocations

After the first death there is plenty
Of Other but it's true
There is no other, too. One staggers
Weakly between the two. What fun is that?
It's no fun, that's what. After the first
Sniff, you notice the typewriter's been sharpened; you
Did it, so;

a, s, d, f, space . . . semi, l, k, j, space

Is it up & happy, this trip, like Merriweather Lewis
Whose California rides above the blue? or
Is it a down trip (John Keats)? I do love you:
"Down for you is up" when your head gets turned around

You look out the mirror at the self, & you preen,
You giggle because that it's so unlike you.

Here I Live

So sleeping & waking
every day

up

I live here I,

the great
mumbling

one

two three four

Laid out, voices living & dead

hovering

between

heart &

comfort.

✲ ✲

up

now

taking chances

with silence. More & more

waiting

for day . . . light

over the house.

He is counting: one two

three four

✲ ✲

When we rise

the jungle

Moves What that means

grenades come closer white
lightning

clears the range

in the morning

paper hangs on nothing

Nerve

✲ ✲

That makes some human cry

float

like sunlight

✲ ✲

But every night I sleep

going

to dawn like light.

✲ ✲

Here I live my heart

my family

assemble.

Three counts.

✲ ✲

Sun

clear

Time

my war

God

did it start.

One Two Three Four.

One

Two

Three

&

Sleep.

To Anne

I love you much
as one can
love any-
body
        baby,

                but

riding high a man is
tough as it comes,
                        It's not brutal.
                        It's a song.
                                    For Love.

                                    Of You.

Going to Chicago

FOR DON HALL

    Leaving first

        On my way,

                    "Ave Atque Valium"
                                    20 mgs.

                    & coffee

            Thanks to the Air Hostess

        dark eyes   dark hair

                    red lips
                    full

    Red Nose in the air

*

A passing thought to John Sinclair

à la bas

Right On, John

*

We see you down there

from here

up in the air

it's the same air

as one breathes in

&

one breathes out . . .

"Down to you is Up"

. . . in between

here and there

&

here.

2.

The Prison Poems of Ho Chi Minh

Lunch Poems / In Memory Of My Feelings

Meditations in An Emergency

Advertisements For Myself

The Sweet Science

The Press

An American Dream

Mollie &
Other War Stories

Joe Liebling, Frank & Norman
ride with us
here.

3.

Change is in my pocket:
A John Kennedy American
half-dollar:

heads: Philip Whalen
tails: John Ashbery

(that's an old-master story)

flip it

it's in the air

The game is underway:
"Winning is my philosophy"
"Preparedness is the
only means toward Victory"

"Not Somehow
but
Triumphantly"

(that's the motto of The Salvation Army)

"There's a new day coming"

& if it's a nice day, we win

& if it's a stormy day,

can you dig it?

flying, under the weather

dig it

Fly Over

Fly Straight through

Fly big Baby, Fly!!

To The 2nd City.

Bye-bye.

How We Live in the Jungle

I am asleep
next to The Hulk
warm behind,
inside,
all around me
Oranges,
soft purples,
greens, blue
Underneath & above
wooden planks
furniture,
Sky,
big sky,
all around the tree.
It's a house-tree.
You feel at home here
in the nut-bush.

First asleep
next going into heat
a stinging shower
& then,
cooled, with a buzz on.
The Hulk is breathing easily now
as her graceful form
moves purposefully into everyday life.
The Hulk
often sleeps
while I'm awake
& vice-versa
& vice-versa.
No matter.
We live together in the jungle.

April in the Morning, with Anne

Rain falling through the blue
across the street
near to me, & close to you; &
that's where I'll be today
walking St. Mark's Place toward Grand Central
that place
the only place we ever get together, me & you
Soot-
covered parti-colored trains come & go
out & in, the heart leaps
to its daily declarations
of love & death (poetry), beating
the ordinary day's traffic to somewhere,
beating

my heart's morning yearning for nowhere,
with windows,
upon which the early morning rain,
joining in
joins you to me, simply flowing,
now singing, now
saying, "hello!", now hoping
this trip prove true
&
now, in clean air, cleanly breathing, sounds

Train Ride

Somebody knows everything so
It doesn't make any difference,
what you do
So, do anything you want,
it's all right
You can do it. Just do it,
right?

Biddy Basketball

The guards tense, the centers jump
The fur flies! A Jickey laughs
It's sloppy going, tho, Careless Love
So to speak: can't see it; can't believe it
Can't read it even: not together

A bit busy: bemused by the weather
How it simply takes place, & had character
A clear & an open face, clearly true
To conditions as they do exist; & so
Now a day is unpleasant because no fun
Tho it does keep going on: that's how it goes
It's draggy, it's torture, it's tedious
Right from the very beginning, it loses you
And as we discover later reading *The Daily News*
When it's all over, "Both Sides Lose."

The Simple Pleasures of Buffalo

It's impossible to take a bath in this house
because I am the house-guest & the bath-room
is of the house. It's difficult not to lie, constantly
on the beds. It is not difficult to read, "The Groupie"
"Thongs", "Ball Four", "The Jocks", & "Teen-Age Sex."
It's quite difficult to jack off: God knows why. But,
It is possible to fuck a lot; lying, sitting, kneeling, standing
or simply thrashing about the beds. If you don't believe me,
just ask ______. To continue: in this house
it's a simple matter to swallow the cough syrup (codeine): to swallow
the capsules (pills) or even the spansules is even simpler:
It is not quite so simple to stick the needle into the vein.
This requires a certain amount of practice; and Witch Hazel
Can be helpful, to cover the tracks & in healing the sore arms.
Perhaps the simplest, most rewarding element this
quietly insane house affords you is time, time to be reading
for example, on your own, this terrific book,
"The Good Spirit," poems by Citizen Andrei Codrescu.

Black & White Magic

FOR ANSELM HOLLO

1.

"Who's a 'black' artist?"

*

On this plane
w/all the room in the world,

*

Dollars: 303 . . .

*

Secret Clouds
I can't get into you,
yet,
tho *Leaving Cheyenne*
was so beautiful:
it made me cry, perfectly
relaxed
a small gift I now am remembering
in Buffalo

*

2.

Breathe normally
Do not smoke

*

Awaiting rescue:
Eat, drink, sleep, or

Not . . . .

Don't.

You were stopped, & searched,
when least you expected.

What was found was *nothing*.

Don't expect it to be the same
coming back, baby.

✲

Strapped: deprived

✲

Shoot yourself: stay alive

✲

3.

Ride it out

John F. Kennedy to Heathrow (London)
which involves you in

My Life With Jackie Kennedy

✲

a human life

✲

MAYA

Where civilization is taking place.

I mean, genuine civilization: no proportionate loss

of spleen.

"The head speaks out from the heart to the head connected

to the heart."

Apologies to Val & Tom

October: half-moon rising: London sky, Piccadilly's, greyish-black
Neon makes it funky: 3 Chesterfield Kings: 5 quid a hundred dexies
City magic makes it easy for a man to be a monkey! All the geese went "honk!"
In Hyde Park where I walked today: I thought of you as I walked my way
Not that way toward where you are; that I had turned away from, from thinking
What I had meant to do yesterday. Last year's London's disappeared, broken up
The way New York City had, before & after London last year. Nevertheless I'm
here
Walking around. I wish I'd run into you both upon these grounds, Hyde Park.
I couldn't come to visit you, your home, today (& this is dumb) because
I had no place from which to come *from*. Does that make sense?
(It does.) & I miss seeing you, my friends, & talk. But Val, I liked you calling me
on the phone,
It seemed so neighbourly. & Tom, I liked reading your poems, in my room,
alone
(proofs); & the words I wrote then were truly mine, & not "to atone" . . .
I will come visit you, you two, in good time,
days to come; I'll talk a lot, show-off my loves, & sometimes rime.

One, London

In Hyde Park Gate 14 white budgie scratchings mean
What? Black orchids on a wall serve for clouds, loom
Up from an orange bed floating, a host of words; Fall; heat coming on
White breathing disappearing as it defines this room

Above a friend his mate's asleep; he's somewhere else; England
Here clucks & poetry don't mix. October 1st; half-moon rising
Soon it seems to descend. Perhaps a clock is a good idea
It tells one what to do, when

Two weeks & a day past it seemed so easy to take, NY's room
& NY's speed made it seem easy, giving; easy living
Tho NY's room was someone else's, somewhere else too
Here words take their own sweet time arriving

Here to sleep a day & a night away seems mild. Still there's plenty to do:
Birds to be looked at, pills, a warm bath, letters to be written to you.

Southampton Business

Train Ride . . .

16 coaches long!

not hardly With a song in my heart . . .

I remember my
first love, &
the last time I . . . .

✲

Here you can read

"We Arrived &
What We Did"

A girl's poem

but not now.

Now it's here.

✲

It's outside,

but you can't see

anything.

*

Now it's night here.

Take a walk

down an Elm Street

in the rain

Up

from the Train Station,

Turn, turn, turn again.

Now, you're here.

Go inside

& open up

Viva! *Fat City*

*

& the long hours pass

like buzzes

gone

down a highway.

& nothing is really happening at all

It all happens so fast,

so,

STOP

*

Get back up & go.

✲

That was life, sometimes you ran dry
Some mornings you'd wake up all wet. Today
For example, was a black day; business as usual,
However; i.e. everyone was getting the business
Our nation's leaders stared blankly straight
At us with expressions of grave concern
the sun
Came up while the rain was coming down, like
Nobody's business, so, nobody didn't see you
In the altogether period me needling business
Myself, & then,
a burst of political jabber
before you

✲

SLEEP

✲

Talk like you don't hear any more
not since the old days

✲

Love Poetry

cigarette

Huey Long, get shot

✲

& all the time

the girl in the Keane painting

awake

upstairs

sleeping

*

while the morning Times was saying
$75,000 was paid for a Roy Lichtenstein yesterday. A
James Rosenquist went for 26. Highest price ever for one
Of those. & a life-size kitchen stove complete with sagging
Pots & Pans, $46,000. The Germans took the prizes, the Americans
Got the business, the Times went on to note. By god,
That's not how it was in the old days! Oh well, I think I'd
like to have a de Kooning, for nothing, myself. Or else, to be
Perfectly frank, just go on minding my own business.

*

Keeping it up going on

& on

& on & on . . .

*

No more Monkey-business

*

I think

✲

No, I'd just as soon be where you are, asleep,
Awake, kissing your neck before we'd fuck a lot
From behind holding your breasts which are warm

✲

Nobody's business but our own

✲

Sleep, or don't: do whatever you feel like

Stay as long as you like.

THREE POEMS: GOING TO CANADA

Itinerary

Thursday & Friday:

(Southampton, New York City)

Wake up & crash land
pat the old lady
have a drink
tie shoes
take bus
change trains
go, to the doctor
score
HIGH
eat, beans &
bread pudding, get
slightly smashed on cheap red
take a walk
to clear your head
smoke hash / shoot smack
nod out / wake up with a start / take off
Go to Canada.

How to Get to Canada

borrow 50 from George
Spend 2 for *Tarantula*
  and 4 for a little Horse
  and 5 for two meals
  and 1 or 2 for King-size Chesterfields
  and 2.50 to ride the bus
  and 2 more for taxicabs
  & 1 for tips & 25 cents for 1 more
  bus . . . . buy a ticket
  for 31. Check your bag, free.
  Steal *Night Song*, & *Prison Letters*
  From A Soledad Brother. Wait . . . . . . Fly:
  15 cents is plenty to keep you in the sky.

Love

Missing you
  in Air Canada

Written on Red Roses & Yellow Light

Acid
aquamarine
squares
moving
up ashtray
Smoking
a soft white chick
head red
chic, tacky
fur ruffling over
leather
Or is that what that is?

"18"

she says,
to
the pretty, plain girl below
severe auburn
hair
her red shirt, cowboy
left pocket half-full of bosom
& on down
sleek curve of denim
thigh-meat
weird shoelets
tiny flesh-holes
Acid
green floor
waving, or
wavering
More & more
floor

shoes, black, "straight", square
out front
of monumental black
dress
above
fatty calves, no
ankles
A city lady, O, obese!

Not me!
I'm just sitting
next the other green, plush
a sofa
rich
with recent presences
now presumably inside:

Light up!
a
slow cigarette
with my
Most Valuable Player
lighter:

Now
A Head
sucking
smokey air "in"   breathing out

Waiting
in the Waiting Room
to speak of Necessities:

& Now
my turn.

"Hello, again!

Remember me, Doctor?"

"Of course! You're

the Poet. Come in,

What is it, this time?"

From "Anti-Memoirs"

FOR TONY TOWLE

Mid-Friday morn, 10 o'clock, I go to India
At the suggestion of a man I barely know: André
Malraux. Benares. The first house I enter I see
A photograph of the murderer of Ghandi on the wall.
"There are too many Reactionaries still, in India," I remember
Nehru telling André Malraux. I step closer to the picture,
Read the words printed at the bottom: *photograph by*
Rudolph Burckhardt. This is unreal! I leave India, return
On foot to Hyattsville, Maryland. 1705 Abraham Lincoln Road.
My hosts are absent still. Their children have swallowed Rat
Poison, & they are at the Hospital, caught in the puke
& ye shall be healed, that scene, fright, terror, nothing serious
In the end except it might have been. . . . The Rolling Stones fill this place
A sweet speed-freak is lost in Harlem. Mr. Chester Himes. Life
Going on quite merrily Hunting For The Whale. A wealth
Of fresh Whale-tracks considerably cheers us up.

Galaxies

Winter. You think of sex, but it's asleep
Briefly you contemplate points of revolution
A naked artist smokes. Dreaming, you wake up & you say
"Everybody is a hero, everybody makes you cry." Ah,
This morning I was footprints in the snow
Listening to the words from the burning bush all the day
We sleep & dream our lives away. You dream
I don't live here, & when you wake up, what a relief,
I do. Someone to light the fire, babble for you
I dream a 7 ft. tall Watusi in full tribal regalia
& carrying a long spear promises to send me crumbly LSD
In a New York *Times*. He does, & I am pleased, but amazed
It's 9:45 of a Saturday morning, December the 26th. Through eight
Window-panes gray white light is pouring in. No, it's leaning in
Sitting in, by the fire, a chair. "God, more money, please!" No
Coal in the bin. But there is the fire, still in sight. And there is
More wood, to light. The fire leaps up the flue. The artist's smoke
Is fixed in space. Above my head is wood. I can't see a warm bed, &
Inside it, you. But I'm beginning to see The light, not
a bit older, & less cold than last night.

In Anne's Place

It's just another April almost morning, St. Mark's Place
Harris & Alice are sleeping in beds; it's far too early
For a Scientific Massage, on St. Mark's Place, though it's
The *right* place if you feel so inclined. Later
Jim Carroll's double bums a camel from a ghost Aram Saroyan
Now, there goes Chuck, friend from out of a no longer existent past
Into the just barely existent future, wide-awake, purposeful
As Aram Saroyan's dad: a little bit more lovely writing, & then

Maybe a small bet on New York's chances this morning. It's not
Exactly love, nor is it faith, certainly it isn't hope; no
It's simply that one has a feeling, yes
You always do have a feeling & over the years it's become habit
Being moved by that; to be moved having a feeling,
So it's perfectly natural to get up & go to the telephone
To lay a little something down on your heart's choice
Calling right from where you are, in Anne's place,
As to your heart's delight, here comes sunlight.

Autobiography

FOR HENRY KANABUS

A colorful river of poetry drives forward
into what has never been named
where all women are fiery
all roses are scary
and all kisses are eternal

at its worst it leans into
soft oceans of romantic mush.

A little loving can solve a lot of things.

If a man is in solitude
the world is translated
and wings sprout from the shoulders of
The Slave.

In my solitude
I have seen things so clearly
that were not true.

For example
once I kissed a woman and nothing happened.

He is not really thinking.

His poems have too many
flaming ears
queens of daybreak
fallen stars and solar arrows

Power to the people and all like that.

He loves these things.

2.

When truth throws up
its translucent roosters
onto fountains of eggnog

He wants you to see
right through these things

Just behind them are
massive granite anguish shapes
humped over, feet on,
snout to, the earth.

If you want to see
the light show
touch that lump, you rooster!

3.

Who can like that?

I must admit I dislike
seeing human life
compared to something smaller than itself

making love
compared to a comma

death to periods.

4.

García Lorca pinched me again!

5.

I like about twenty lines
of this poem, the dust
of that mud which speaks
to sharpen silences. I like
the fiery butterfly puzzles of
this pilgrimage toward clarities
of great mud intelligence and feeling. Not
more deep, more shallow!

6.

Only the poem exists, like an
Ambassador, the American ambassador to
say, Africa. Like a vegetable, which says,
"Africa is hollow." Like an empty tourist.

And then the tourist hears
The drums of the vegetables.

Africa flies up into his own frail arms.

"I feel an absence inside, when
I hear a lovely poem . . . True, as

it is good, knowing
that glasses are to drink from."

7.

It is good, absence.

Postmarked Grand Rapids

Robert Creeley reading

Mark Twain and Mr. Clemens

STOPS

while Philip Whalen
writing
"The Epic Airplane Notebook Poem"

Pauses . . .

to discuss their drinking problem

with the Hostesses in the Sky

I'm watching
writing
drinking
waiting for my change.

Further Definitions (Waft)

(AFTER MICHAEL BROWNSTEIN)

a band of musicians: up tight

care not: like

understanding: dismissal

waiving: automatic pilot

compared to: no baloney

began to say: shut up

engraft feathers in a damaged wing: take a hike

experience to the full: kill

cultivators of land they do not own: friends

absolute: ready

pity: pull leg of

language here fails as mathematics has before it: at

is skilled in: oblivious

ended: borne

delicate constitutions: fascists

promoted: serf

one who dispenses with clothes: liar

lip to lip being the first, lip: right on

to heart, through the ear, is the second: "poof!"

graduate: push around

too clever riders are not good at horseplay: "Ma Femme"

food on a journey: chow

center of the earth: *hara*

the full moon: a friend to man

pineapples: heavy

having no wants, quite content: chatty

the power of slowly moving jaws: camp

exquisite: available night & day

critical, marking and epoch: straight

And Into Glory Peep: just for the hell of it.

Paul Blackburn

dying now, or already dead
hello. It's only Ted, interrupting
in case I hadn't said, as clearly
as I'd have it said, Paul,
I hear you, do. Crossing Park Avenue
South; 4:14 a.m.; going West at
23rd; September 1st, 1971.

Tom Clark

I take him
purely as treasure
His exquisite pain
pinpoints my evasive pleasure.

Don't think him to be
Any more than you see
& Don't be beastly
        to him. If you do
he'll let you see him
        seeing you:
& you'll wake up hating yourself
        for hating him.
You will.

Kirsten

you're so funny! I'd give you

all of my money, any-

time, just to see what you'd say!

alas, all I have is a dime.

How you talk is my heart's

delight. You are

more terrible than your step-dad,

more great than bright light.

Chicago April Morning: Snow

Anne,

A Happy Birthday, late, to you,
Never less than great to us, great
Light and air in our lives, that bus
Whose windows look always to you, so straight
so true;
love;

Ted

Brigadoon

FOR BILL BERKSON

1.

"This mushroom walks in."

2.

"And one cannot go back except in time."

3.

"Nothing is gained by assurance as to what is insecure."

4.

"I have a machine-gun trained on Scotland Yard."

5.

"The body sends out self to repel non-self."

6.

"I can get close & still stay outside."

7.

"See the why, knowing what: the clear enigma."

8.

"a fragrant flowered shrub   blush   a clean tantrum."

This Perfect Day

Six months of each other
Evoke the birth throes
This primitive magnetic expression of the heads
Above all the hypnotic presence of staring eyes that have
        a ritualistic fixity

Against the broad arcs whose force not only cuts wildly
Into a jungle of coarse energies
But whose fury is substituted for the rigorous control
        of eye & intellect
So a penchant for the grotesque is hardly absent
This perfect day.

The Green Sea

Above his head clanged
Turning
And there were no dreams
            in this sleep
Over this table.

Mi Casa, Su Casa

FOR LEWIS MACADAMS

my crib your crib
the interior burns   I read
white palm over the coffee can
in the quiet
                a manual
of gentle but determined practices
"I want human to begin with"
A small voice walks across the grey empty room.

He

He never listened while friends talked. He worked
steadily to the even current of sound; but if a note
of distress were struck he was aware of it at once.
Like a wireless operator with a novel open in front
of him, he could disregard every signal except the
ship's symbol and the S.O.S. He could even work better
when they talked than when they were silent, for so long
as his ear-drum registered those tranquil sounds—their
deep gossip, comments on the sermons preached by one
another, plots of new movies, even commentaries on and complaints
about the weather—he knew that all was well. It was
silence that stopped him working—silence in which he might
look up and see terror waiting in their eyes for
his attention.

7 Things I Do in the Hotel Chelsea

Rain or Shine:

dig it: the solitude of
someone

Call for Company Men
& Women
to become
at the very least
visible
in all of our daily lives.

Name one possible man: Jim

One possible woman: Maggie May, or
at least,
maybe

✲ ✲ ✲

Gather ye rosebuds, gimmicks,
Crystal,
Schmee,
make-up

the necessary Will

to insist on Grace
from time to time, at
your place
where light in waves
thru motes of dust
lends all your combinations
lust: this
ardor to

Believe in Now as the noun it is
when "why not"
hits this town:

"that's your given prerogative,
son"

We all do something; it goes
without saying; you
do it.
It got done.

Communism

Red Air

& I can hear the red bus

sing

Morning has broken

meticulously

labelled the East Wing is fossils

sinister habits antiques

in fact a pleasant park

a government department

bulbs

birth

severe abundance swirlings

The most
spectacular object
in it

a great
shining
prolific
automatic
electric
churchyard
map-maker

mute

flickering

imagination

bejewelled

coarse
display

the euphonious person
in hey-day
wholesomeness
taken

over-large
fuses

With a little lantern above

A sort of canopy

pitched within a room

architecture

Church

with the exception of

One steel office building

A cold violent backside to you

A little saucer dome

imp anonymity
little plateaus in various arms

Swallower of former designs

true stone fan virile shadow

functional sinews of mood & tempo of
ballcourt

COFFEE

Square bracketing vision bubble dome

Central Presences Naked in the Shroud:

Sensible in the air

bronze pedestrian tree-ape

grace-note

the dizzying staircase

non-euphonious personal

disguise.

Sandy's Sunday Best

It's made of everything, slow
stains & flash

You can see, for example,
green, past enchantment

& trees wave in passing

Even the children today are smart
& not just more people

Look!

Strolling, sassy, dashing, brilliant!

The whole world turns, to see
nods, interminably its head

Cool black cats, super white stars
will dance all night in that wake!

Of three minutes of sunlight.

Aubade

Last night
before retiring,
one of those brain-spasms
I guess all poets must have
prompted me to write
in my bedside
notebook

which, incidentally
is blue, and shaped like
a Regular Grind
MAXWELL HOUSE
Coffee can

these words:

"I advance Dagwood Bumstead as
    the pre-eminent philosopher of our time."

This morning,
I awakened to the startling
realization that
overnight I had become transformed
into the person
of that noble & decent man,

"Dr. Watson." For good.

Service at Upwey

Over Belle Vue Road that silence said
To mean an angel is passing overhead.
Anselm's round head framed peering in the garden door
Four & ½ hours before, I didn't hear
The doorbell ring—7:30 a.m. Greenwich Summer Time—
Announcing the arrival
Of the celebrated Greek-American Poet
from Chicago: John Paul! Was that
An Alice or a Mabel who let him in?
First to visit us
In Wonderful Wivenhoe, where
Once smugglers ran amok, smuggling
What? and now Alice goes out
To shoppe.

*

"I have only one work, & I hardly know what it is!"

*

My baby throws my shoes through the door.

*

Baby-talk woke up the world, today
little Anselm,
                    Alice, Mabel,
& John Paul.

*

& me writing it down here.

*

This page has ashes on it

Baltic Stanzas

Less original than
penetrating
very often
illuminating

has taken us
300 years
to recover from
the disaster of

The White Mountain
O Manhattan!
O Saturday afternoons!
you were a room

& the room cried, "love!"
I was a stove, & you
in cement were a dove

Ah, well, thanks for the shoes, god
I wear them on my right feet
since that bright winter when
rapt in your colors, O heat!

how we lay long on your orange bed
sipping iced white wine, & not thinking
the blue sky changed blues while we were drinking
Next day god said, "Hitler has to get hit on the head."

Other Contexts

I'd been
trying
to escape
that mind game

thinking that thought
itself
can possess
the world

by always & I mean
as constantly as physically
possible
lying down and

not thinking it over. Reading
for example everything I'd loved
again & again
anything new:

resisting being thought.
Exactly. Resisting
Being
Thought.

Tonight I think to do
differently, differently
to do.
I think I will.

I would
think I will. We'll have to wait
& see. I have to wait,
and see

My watch shows it to be
5:51 a.m., March the 24th
in Wivenhoe, in England.
Alice is asleep

& breathing beside me, pregnantly.
& oh yes, it's 1974. Alice
is 28 years old. Anselm is 20 months.
I'm coming up on four-oh.

A Religious Experience

I was looking at the words he
was saying . . . like . . . Okinawa . . .
bandage . . . real . . . form . . . and suddenly
I realized I had read somewhere that,
"in their language the word for 'idiot'
is also the word meaning 'to breathe through
your mouth.'" And I was simply left there,
in bed, *being looked at*.

Crossroads

The pressure's on, old son.
We're going to salvage just about all you got.
It's the way you've been going about it
that's worried us.
All this remote control business.

Where's the Doctor?
I *am* the Doctor.
You'll find the patient's files
in these cabinets.
Is everything ready for surgery?

You don't need a sauna to get heated up
here.

Isn't it funny to have lived in the midlands
all this time
& not seen all these lovely things about?

He believes if he's hard enough on somebody
they'll give way.
Well, I'm the principal shareholder,
& I'm taking my equities out!

I'm also staying right here with you.
Right. & I'm going with you.

New Personal Poem

TO MICHAEL LALLY

You had your own reasons for getting
In your own way. You didn't want to be
Clear to yourself. You knew a hell
Of a lot more than you were willing
                to let yourself know. I felt
Natural love for you on the spot. R-E-S-P-E-C-T. Right.
Beautiful. I don't use the word lightly. I
Protested with whatever love (honesty) (& frontal nudity)
A yes basically reserved Irish Catholic American Providence Rhode
                Island New Englander is able to manage. You
Are sophisticated, not uncomplicated, not

Naive, and Not simple. An Entertainer, & I am, too.
Frank O'Hara *respected* love, so do you, & so do we.
He was himself & I was me. And when we came together
Each ourselves in Iowa, all the way
That was love, & it still is, love, today. Can you see me
In what I say? Because as well I see you know
In what you have to say, I did love Frank, as I do
You, "in the right way".
That's just talk, not Logos,
            a getting down to cases:
I take it as simple particulars that
            we wear our feelings on our faces.

Elysium

FOR MARION FARRIER

It's impossible to look at it
Without the feeling as of
Being welcomed, say, to Paris
After a long boring train ride,

For women are like that:
They make one feel
he has travelled a long way
just being there.

And so well might he take
what comes, come
to what it is takes him.

Blue Targets

You see a lot
  of white when you're
looking at her eyes,
She's so quick toward
either side
    but when
you look straight
      down
  into her, it's
thru & at targets,
  reflecting, blue.

Reading Frank O'Hara

Reading Frank O'Hara you
        can't help realizing
 you know you can't feel
         any worse than he felt,
         so
       hell,
         why not be exuberant!

In the 51st State

IN THE 51ST STATE

Allen Ginsberg's "Shining City"

FOR ALICE

But that dream . . . oh, hell!
maybe, like Jack, just drink muscatel!
But that won't work. A "Pharmacia"
is where you get your pills. "Shining
City." & in its space & time one can find
a "Position inferior to Language." & occupy
beautiful, discrete, & almost ordinary
Places.—But that won't work . . .
. . . that dream . . . "oh, Hell!"

In the 51st State

FOR KATE

The life I have led
being an easy one
has made suicide
impossible, no?

Everything arrived
in fairly good time;
women, rolls, medicine
crime—poor health

like health
has been an inspiration.

When all else fails I read the magazines.

Criticism like a trombone used as a gate
satisfies some hinges, but not me.
I like artists who rub their trumpets with maps
to clean them, the trumpets or the maps.

I personally took
33 years to discover
that blowing your nose is necessary sometimes
even tho it is terrifying. (not aesthetic).

I'd still rather brindle.

I wasn't born in this town
but my son, not the one born in Chicago,
not the one born in England, not
the one born in New England, in fact, my daughter
was. She looks like her brother by another mother
and like my brother, too.

Her forehead shines like the sun
above freckles and I had mine
and I have more left.

I read only the books you find in libraries or drugstores
or at Marion's. Harris loans me Paul Pines'
to break into poetry briefly.

Au revoir.
                (I wouldn't translate that
as "Goodbye" if I were you.)

A woman rolls under the wheels in a book.
Here they are the wheels, so I hear.

Bon voyage, little ones.

Follow me down
Through the locks. There is no key.

Red Shift

Here I am at 8:08 p.m. indefinable ample rhythmic frame
The air is biting, February, fierce arabesques
        on the way to tree in winter streetscape
I drink some American poison liquid air which bubbles
        and smoke to have character and to lean
In. The streets look for Allen, Frank, or me, Allen
        is a movie, Frank disappearing in the air, it's
Heavy with that lightness, heavy on me, I heave
        through it, them, as
The Calvados is being sipped on Long Island now
        twenty years almost ago, and the man smoking
Is looking at the smilingly attentive woman, & telling.
Who would have thought that I'd be here, nothing
        wrapped up, nothing buried, everything
Love, children, hundreds of them, money, marriage-
        ethics, a politics of grace,
Up in the air, swirling, burning even or still, now
        more than ever before?
Not that practically a boy, serious in corduroy car coat
        eyes penetrating the winter twilight at 6th
& Bowery in 1961. Not that pretty girl, nineteen, who was
        going to have to go, careening into middle-age so,
To burn, & to burn more fiercely than even she could imagine
        so to go. Not that painter who from very first meeting
I would never & never will leave alone until we both vanish
        into the thin air we signed up for & so demanded
To breathe & who will never leave me, not for sex, nor politics
        nor even for stupid permanent estrangement which is
Only our human lot & means nothing. No, not him.
There's a song, "California Dreaming", but no, I won't do that.
I am 43. When will I die? I will never die, I will live
To be 110, & I will never go away, & you will never escape from me

who am always & only a ghost, despite this frame, Spirit
Who lives only to nag.
I'm only pronouns, & I am all of them, & I didn't ask for this
You did
I came into your life to change it & it did so & now nothing
will ever change
That, and that's that.
Alone & crowded, unhappy fate, nevertheless
I slip softly into the air
The world's furious song flows through my costume.

Around the Fire

What I'm trying to say is that if an experience is proposed to me—I don't have any particular interest in it—Any more than anything else. I'm interested in anything. Like I could walk out the door right now and go somewhere else. I don't have any center in that sense. If you'll look in my palm you'll see that my heart and my head line are the same and if you'll look in your palm you'll see that it's different. My heart and my head feel exactly the same. Me, I like to lay around of a Sunday and drink beer. I don't feel a necessity for being a mature person in this world. I mean all the grown-ups in this world, they're just playing house, all poets know that. How does your head feel? How I feel is what I think. I look at you today, & I expect you to look the same tomorrow. If you're having a nervous breakdown, I'm not going to be looking at you like you're going to die, because I don't think you are. If you're a woman you put yourself somewhere near the beginning and then there's this other place you put yourself in terms of everybody. "The great cosmetic strangeness of the normal deep person." Okay. Those were those people—and

I kept telling myself, I have to be here, because I don't have
a country. How tight is the string? And what is on this particular
segment of it? And the photographer, being black, and the writer,
me, being white, fell out at this point. And he didn't want to
look at it—I mean it's nothing, just some drunk Indians riding
Jersey milk cows—but I wanted to see it, I mean it was right
in front of my eyes and I wanted therefore to look at it.
And death is not any great thing, it's there or it's not. I mean
God is the progenitor of religious impetuosity in the human beast.
And Davy Crockett is right on that—I mean he's gonna shoot a bear,
but he's not gonna shoot a train, because the train is gonna run
right over him. You can't shoot the train. And I always thought
there was another way to do that. And it is necessary to do that
and we bear witness that it is necessary to do it. The only distinction
between men and women is five million shits.

Cranston Near the City Line

One clear glass slipper; a slender blue single-rose vase;
one chipped glass Scottie; an eggshell teacup & saucer, tiny,
fragile, but with sturdy handle; a gazelle? the lightest pink flowers
on the teacup, a gold circle, a line really on the saucer; gold
line curving down the handle; glass doors on the cabinet which sat
on the floor & was not too much taller than I; lace doilies? on
the shelves; me serious on the floor, no brother, shiny floor or
shining floor between the flat maroon rug & the glass doors of
the cabinet:

I never told anyone what I knew. Which was that it wasn't
for anyone else what it was for me.

The piano was black. My eyes were brown. I had rosy
cheeks, every sonofabitch in the world said. I never saw them.

My father came cutting around the corner of the A&P
& diagonally across the lot in a beeline toward our front sidewalk
& the front porch (& the downstairs door); and I could see him, his
long legs, quick steps, nervous, purposeful, coming & passing, combing
his hair, one two three quick wrist flicks that meant "worrying" &
    "quickly!"

There were lilacs in the back yard, & dandelions in the lot.
There was a fence.

Pat Dugan used to swing through that lot, on Saturdays, not too tall,
in his brown suit or blue one, white shirt, no tie, soft brown men's
slippers on his feet, & Grampa! I'd yell & run to meet him &
"Hi! Grampa," I'd say & he'd swing my arm and be singing his funny
    song:

*

"She told me that she loved me, but

    that was yesterday. She told me

that she loved me, & then

    she went away!"

*

I didn't know it must have been a sad song, for somebody!
He was so jaunty, light in his eyes and laugh lines around
them, it was his happy song, happy with me, it was 1942 or 4,
and he was 53.

An Ex-Athlete, Not Dying

TO STEVE CAREY

& so I took the whole trip
filled with breaths, heady with assurance
gained in all innocence from that self's
possession of a sure stride, a strong heart,
quick hands, & what one sport would surely describe
as that easy serenity born of seemingly having been
"a quick read." "He could read the field from before
he even knew what that was." He was so right. Long before.
It was so true. I postulated the whole thing.
It was the innocence of Second Avenue, of one
who only knew about First. I didn't win it;
I didn't buy it; I didn't bird-dog it; but I didn't dog it.
I could always hear it, not see it. But I rarely had
to listen hard to it. I sure didn't have to "bear" it.
I didn't think, "Later for that." I knew *something*,
but I didn't know that. But I didn't know,
brilliant mornings, blind in the rain's rich light,
now able always to find water, that now I would drink.

Coda : Song

When having something to do
but not yet being at it
because I'm alone, because of you
I lay down the book, & pick up the house

& move it around until it is
where it is what it is I am doing
that is the something I had to do
because I'm no longer alone, because of you.

In Anselm Hollo's Poems

The goddess stands in front of her cave.

The beetle wakes up. The frightened camper watches

The two horsemen. The walking catfish walks by.

The twins are fighting the wind let loose in the dark

To be born again the human animal young in the day's events.

The laundry-basket lid is still there.

The moving houses are very moving.

The last empress of China

Is receiving the new members of the orchestra

Through two layers of glass in The Empress Hotel.

In the wreck of the cut-rate shoe store the poet can be seen,

Drunk; a monster; the concussed consciousness in

The charge of the beautiful days. The difficulties are great.

The colors must be incredible: it all coheres:

The force of being she releases in him being

The claim of the dimensions of the world.

Postcard from the Sky

You in love with her

read my poems and wonder

what she sees in you.

Last Poem

Before I began life this time
I took a crash course in Counter-Intelligence
Once here I signed in, see name below, and added
Some words remembered from an earlier time,
"The intention of the organism is to survive."
My earliest, & happiest, memories pre-date WWII,
They involve a glass slipper & a helpless blue rose
In a slender blue single-rose vase: Mine
Was a story without a plot. The days of my years
Folded into one another, an easy fit, in which
I made money & spent it, learned to dance & forgot, gave
Blood, regained my poise, & verbalized myself a place
In Society. 101 St. Mark's Place, apt. 12A, NYC 10009
New York. Friends appeared & disappeared, or wigged out,

Or stayed; inspiring strangers sadly died; everyone
I ever knew aged tremendously, except me. I remained
Somewhere between 2 and 9 years old. But frequent
Reification of my own experiences delivered to me
Several new vocabularies, I loved that almost most of all.
I once had the honor of meeting Beckett & I dug him.
The pills kept me going, until now. Love, & work,
Were my great happinesses, that other people die the source
Of my great, terrible, & inarticulate one grief. In my time
I grew tall & huge of frame, obviously possessed
Of a disconnected head, I had a perfect heart. The end
Came quickly & completely without pain, one quiet night as I
Was sitting, writing, next to you in bed, words chosen randomly
From a tired brain, it, like them, suitable, & fitting.
Let none regret my end who called me friend.

Small Role Felicity

FOR TOM CLARK

Anselm is sleeping; Edmund is feverish, &
Chatting; Alice doing the *Times* Crossword Puzzle:
I, having bathed, am pinned, nude, to the bed
Between *Green Hills of Africa* &
The Pro Football Mystique. Steam is hissing
In the pipes, cold air blowing across my legs . . .
Tobacco smoke is rising up my nose, as Significance
Crackles & leaps about inside my nightly no-mind.
Already it's past two, of a night like any other:
O, Old Glory, atop the Empire State, a building, &
Between the Hudson & the East rivers, O, purple, & O, murky black,
If only . . . but O, finally, you, O, Leonardo, you at last arose
Bent, and racked with fit after fit of coughing, & Cursing!

Terrible curses! No Joke! What will happen? Who
be served? Whose call go unanswered? And
Who can 44 down, "Pretender to
The Crown of Georgia?" be . . .
(Boris Pasternak?)

Under the Southern Cross

FOR DICK GALLUP

Peeling rubber all the way up
SECOND AVENUE into Harlem Heights
Our yellow Triumph took us out of Manhattan tenement hells

Into the deer-ridden black earth dairylands.
Corn-fed murderers, COPS, waved us past
Low-slung Frank Lloyd Wright basements. We missed most deer.

You left me in Detroit, for money. In Freeport, Maine, our host
Shotgunned his wife into cold death, who was warm. Fuck him. Scoot
Ferried us to Portland, then leaped out of his life from atop the
UN Building.

Enplaning next to the flatlands, we rubber-stamped our own passports
And in one year changed the face of American Poetry. Hepatitis
felled you
Then on the very steps where the Peace Corps first reared its no-head.

Though it helped pass the long weekends, polygamy unsettled me
considerably
In Ann Arbor, where each day's mail meant one more lover dead.
My favorite
Elm tree died there as well. But Europe beckoned, and we went, first

Pausing to don the habits of Buffalo, in Buffalo. After that it was
weak pins
& strong needles, but travel truly does broaden. It broadened us,
And we grew fat & famous, or at least I did. You fell

For a Lady from Baltimore near the Arno. Then you fell
Into the Arno. You drowned & kept on drowning; while I, in my
Silver threads, toured the Historical Tate, & mutilated

A well-thought of Blake while England slept.
In Liverpool a Liverpudlian dropped his bottle of milk beneath a
neon light,
Smashing it to smithereens. The sidewalk white with milk made us cry.

And so we left. Back in the USA, on crutches, we acquired ourselves
a wife
For 12 goats and a matched pair of Arabian thoroughbreds picked up
on a whim
From a rug-peddler in Turkestan. God knows what we gave to him.

Now I'm living in New York City once again, gone grey, and mostly
stay in bed
While you are pacing your floor in Baltimore. But we aren't "back"
yet, not
By a long shot. Oh No! This trip doesn't end

Until we drop off our yellow Triumph somewhere still far away
From where we are now. No, this ain't it yet.
There's black coffee & glazed donuts still due us, bubba,

At a place called The Jesse James Cafe. So, hit it. Let's burn rubber.
TIMES CRITIC DESPISES CURRENT PLAY, a Post reports.
Dangling from it, in the wind, his body gently sways.

Come on, floor this Mother! Whoops! Don't hit that lonely old
grubber.

THE MORNING LINE

FOR ALICE

Sonnet: *Homage to Ron*

Back to dawn by police word
                                        to sprinkle it
Over the lotions that change
On locks

To sprinkle I say

In funny times
The large pig at which the intense cones beat
So the old fat flies toward the brain
Under the sun and the rain

So we are face to face
                                   again

Nothing in these drawers

Which is terror to the idiot
& the non-idiot alike. No?

44th Birthday Evening, at Harris's

Nine stories high Second Avenue
On the roof there's a party
All the friends are there watching
By the light of the moon the blazing sun
Go down over the side of the planet
To light up the underside of Earth
There are long bent telescopes for the friends
To watch this through. The friends are all in shadow.

I can see them from my bed inside my head.
44 years I've loved these dreams today.
17 years since I wrote for the first time a poem
On my birthday, why did I wait so long?
                                        my land a good land
its highways go to many good places where
many good people were found: a home land, whose song comes up
from the throat of a hummingbird & it ends
where the sun goes to across the skies of blue.
I live there with you.

An UnSchneeman

I appear in the kitchen
duffle-bag in left hand.
"Anybody here?" I say. You
hearing me from the front room,
"Hi. How was it?" "Any pepsi?"
I say hopefully. "No." "Well,
Central Washington was Out of the
Question!, but you are now looking
at The Complete Toast of Guam!" "You
were gone *Forever*!"

A Quiet Dream

Will the little girl outside

reading this

writing

being written

by a man

inside

Now

moving easily

eyes clear & blue courteously

gravely rise

& lightly, turn turn & turn

again

& softly, go.

Part of My History

FOR LEWIS WARSH

Will "Reclining Figure, One Arm"
Soon become or is she already Mrs.
Ted Berrigan? "Take one dexamyl
Every morning, son," my dead father
told me over the phone, and, "Be
A good boy. It's called a 'Life Style.'"
What you don't know will hurt somebody else.
Cast in 1934, 5 ft. 14 in. in height,
The figure has three fingers missing

On the left hand (as did Mordecai, "three-
fingers," Brown, which didn't keep him
Out of Cooperstown!). Body well-preserved,
Chubby, flesh-colored, sweetly
Draped. Both ends are broken here & there,
But the surface is well preserved. I took
Another puff on my Chesterfield King, and,
As she walked around in my room, saw orange
& blue raise themselves ere she walked.
They were my mind. And then, I saw cupcakes,
pink & flushed pink, floating about
in the air, aglow in their own poise.
Cold air stabbed into my heart, as, suddenly,
In serious drag, I felt my body getting
Colder & colder, & felt, rather than saw,
My fez, hovering above my head, like a typical set
of Berrigan-thoughts, imprisoned in lacquer, European-
style, tailor-made. I could see I was sitting
at a table in a Hoboken Truck-Stop. When the smoke
Cleared I saw a red telephone on the table by my
Left hand. A heart-stimulant shot into my heart
From out the immediate darkness to my right. I picked up
The telephone, & that was all that kept me alive.

Contemporary Justice

tin roof   slanting sunlight

cows

boys with sticks

a pick-up whines   dust rises,

crows hover cane stalks

a Watusi

and on his porch my grandfather

watching

À la Recherche du Temps Perdu

Somebody knows everything, so

Between friends nothing would seem stranger

to me than true intimacy, so

Pity me, Patty

or, on

the other hand

The insane brother was focussed malevolently on murder.

Which wasn't me, was it?

Amityville Times

self suspended in age time warp put out to grass
seeing through ears ask intelligent questions
behind eyes doubt use formal balance a lot
to throw something on to it
by mildly defending honor of minor character endlessly
while positively seething with absolutely no emotion
whatsoever in any way shape or form & can this be done?

To Ron

Everybody is not so clever as you. You are cleverer than I am. You are the cleverest of all. I think a great deal. That is why you speak so little. Listen, are not all your brothers going to the field? Have not all your sisters gone to the field? My friend, I keep it in order to look at it. Let us light a candle. Let us go into the field. I have read this book so often that I know it by heart. I have a word to say to you. Did you go to the Captain's Ball?

The Morning Line

Every man-jack boot-brain slack-jaw son of a chump
surely the result of fuzzy thinking
parceled in his "noise of thousands"
is a poem to shove somewhere

The man on First Avenue

with a large suitcase knows that

He's leaving town

asleep there, already back.

Velvet &

FOR STEVE CAREY

Voice of ride

Fire of sight

Value of late

taste of great

job of departure

Night Chick

sky-mate

fits

(also little aches.)

Avec la Mécanique sous les Palmes

C'est automne qui revient

Les arbres ont l'air de sourire

Le clou   est là

    Retient la tête

Les lampes sont allumées

Le vent passe en chantant

Les cheveux balayant la nuit

Il y a quelqu'un qui cherche

Une adresse perdue dans le chemin caché

La tête s'en va

Qu'on nous raconte cette histoire

C'est celle d'un malade

Il te resemble

Il fait froid   sur la lune   ma tête fume

Dreamland

FOR ELIO SCHNEEMAN

this steady twelve-tone humming inbetween my ears

weather sweeps in gentle wavelets across my features

the edges of space stacked into mostly indistinguishable images

on 3 sides: half a face, mine, clearly there

thick dark red and whitish flowers rise, & then drooping

over a purple waterfall, death, also clear

a suitcase—to stay—not to get out of here

on it, water, aspirin, glasses, a watch

above my head tones of voice, steady, clear

making lists in a life,

moving in the face of need, to be here.

"appropriately named Beauty, has just been a star
halfback on the high school football team, and also
hit by a car, scribbling in his *Diary*. Over his bed
there hung contributing sports stories from the *Lowell
Sun*. For a time resided next to a Funeral Parlor: he
was a voracious consumer of Pop culture, of whatever
could be joyously drunk in; a phosphorescent Christ
on a black lacquered cross—it glowed the Jesus in
the Dark, in the movies, in the funnies, and on the radio
over Memere's bed. I gulped for fear every time I passed it
at the moment the sun went down. Probably couldn't have stood
this 'double dose', had it not been for the arrangement of
the shadows. Above all loved The Shadow, Lamont Cranston, Dr. Sax.
Ah, shadow! Ah, Sax!"

Shelley

I saw you first in half-darkness
by candle-light two round table-tops away
sitting in perfect attention with perfect self-awareness
waiting, for the poetry to begin, in *The Blue Store;*
I accepted a drink from your companion's surprising flask,
never taking my eyes off of you, radiant nineteen-year-old,
and I thought, as I was losing my heart,
"*Jesus*, there's obviously a lot more to Bob Rosenthal
than meets the eye!" . . .

That Poem George Found

In the year 1327, at the opening of the first hour,
on the 6th of April, I entered the labyrinth.
My wandering since has been without purpose.
Here, look at it. Wanna see this? No, I want
to find out what's happening with the Indians.
What Indians, the ones that were torturing Jane Bowles
to death? No, the Algonquins & the Iroquois. Eileen
& I already finished that other book. Well,
Fuck yourself then.

DNA

FOR ALICE NOTLEY

: *Ms. Sensitive Princess:*

As furious as Ho Chih Minh
As clever as Mr. Pound
As graceful as a Ben Jonson lyric, "this mountain belly of mine"
As noisy as Bob Dylan
As crooked as Lawrence, as bent as they come
As curious as Philip Whalen, like Beckett, say, is
As pale as Creeley, as Emily Dickinson
As frantic as Jane Bowles, or, as frantic as Jack Kerouac
As awkward as George Smiley
As scarce as Samuel Johnson
As ridiculous as Tennyson, or Kenneth Koch
As loyal as Henry Miller, like Charles de Gaulle is
As permanent as Israel must seem to Chas. Dickens
At as late as 3 o'clock in the morning, or 5:15 a.m., or noon!

Run a check on that, will you Watson?

Back in the Old Place

Thinking about past times in New York by talking
about them reminds me of talking on the steps
We took to get where we are and our current moral view
which is centered around loose suspicion
that our friends for example only tolerate us because
of our mysterious lack of magic
And so actually hate us because of our power, which we do have.
So pretty soon it'll be Christmas, in about six months
& if we are lucky those friends will have been hit by trucks by then

the tea in the white cup is either half-gone or
I am, in any case, soon you will come back up from
Christmas sitting on the steps with the trucks roaring by
thinking I am not that person, so why did I act like that?
because I see one of my friends on a truck & he is talking
about his former friend, the enemy; and I see that *I* am that enemy &
I also see that the street is covered with fish because of a terrible
accident
No, I don't see that, I only see that I *am* that enemy, & I dig that
it makes me feel like the street is covered with fish . . .
& the street *is* covered with fish, & they are *my* fish, those fish—
but it doesn't matter, along comes a real truck, there's a terrible
accident, & the street is covered with fish
The name of the street is Pearl Street & it is crawling with worms
Some of my friends come over, we have funny-tasting coffee
but it is not funny to be drowning

When the yellow bird's note was almost stopped
it was then I spread a little bit of butter on my bread
& when the yellow butter covered the tiny top
I began to imagine that someone was there cooking it
It was fun to imagine that; fun standing still, & fun taking it

to be a fountain my friend said was a pile of old birds
but what my friend said was a pile of old words, yes sir,
I said to the mountain, why don't you move out
of the country of the young & back down into the big city, where
all there is is muscle butter music?

WRITTEN WITH JACK COLLOM

Blue Tilt

FOR TOM CLARK

"But & then at that time
also . . ."
I could and would
often did
dig
the aesthetics of change:
*
the mechanics made me yawn so, tho,
to see all that to-do
over a simple little
ball
& all that money
involved? Jesus Christ!
Keep your electricity,
go dotty,
I'm tipsy!

"It's simple. You've got a twisted pelvis."
Dr. Reuben Greenberg said,

proving about as useful as his brother-
in-law,
Clement.

Just give me a good well-made hand-crafted
wooden leg,
& I'll dig even my next, 45th,
Fall.

Little American Poetry Festival

FOR BILL & JOANNE

Often I try so hard with stimulants
which only graze the surface

As my voice fondly plays your name
without music

but Jim Dine's toothbrush eases two pills
for
Stupefied aborigines
who study for the first time
the sentient earlobes
that hang suspended from no ears at all

venting expletives
at the velvet moon

no more stupefied than I was
upon first being folded into
and then hopelessly knowing
this whole world's activity

under the clear blue sky; I have come
to change all that: bells, ring; daylight, fade;
fly, resting on your shoulder blades for hours

On the count of three, drums will clatter
    like rain
from the hills

& Sleep the lazy owl of Night
& Sleep will make you whole
& Sleep the bushes of the field
& Sleep will make you grow
& you will grow odd
For inside you is a delirious god

& if the drought don/t get you
then the corn worms will

if you don't sober up, kick the brunette out of bed
& go "out" to earn your pay

but I continue, I simply stay
to burn the Midnight lamp

until the restaurant closes and the streets
are empty of every passer-by

It's heavy, it's hard, but
it means out: & Sleep, the Angels
in the sky, Sleep will make you fly,

I know. After all,

I am an obelisk of Egypt; & we
    are the Beautiful People of Africa,

etcetera

Whereas the real state is called golden
    where things are exactly what they are

which is why I wish to become surface,

like Sleep, & Wake-up!

After Peire Vidal, & Myself

FOR SHELLEY

Oh you, the sprightliest & most puggish, the brightest star
Of all my lively loves, all Ladies, & to whom once I gave up
My heart entire, thenceforth yours to keep forever
Locked up in your own heart's tiniest room, my best hope, or
To throw away, carelessly, at your leisure, should that prove
Yr best pleasure, Who is that dumpy matron, decked out in worn & faded
Shabby army fatigues which pooch out both before & behind, now screeching
Out my small name in a dingy Public Library on the lower East Side? & now
Scoring me painfully in philistine Commedia dell'arte farce, low summer fare
Across a pedestrian Ferry's stretch of water in some meshugganah Snug Harbor
And once more, even, fiercely pecking at me in the cold drab Parish Hall of
Manhattan's Landmark Episcopal Church, where a once Avant-garde now Grade
School
Poetry Project continues to dwell, St. Mark's Church in-the-Bouwerie, whose
Stones hold in tight grip one wooden leg & all of Peter Stuyvesant's bones?
Who is that midget-witch who preens & prances as she flaunts her lost wares,
Otherwise hidden beneath some ancient boy's flannel-shirt, its tail out &
flapping, / & who
Is shrieking even now these mean words:

"Hey Ted!" "Hey, you Fat God!"
& calling me, "Fickle!" "Fickle!"
& she points a long boney finger
at me, & croons, gleefully.
"Limbo!" "That's where you *really* live!"

& She is claiming to be you

as she whispers, visciously,
"Alone, &
In Pain, in Limbo, is where *you* live in your little cloud-9 home Ted!
Pitiful!"

She has a small purse, & removing it from one of her shopping bags
She brings out from inside that small purse, my withered heart; & lifting it
high into the air over her head with her two hands, she turns it upside down
unzips its fasteners, & shakes it out over the plywood floor, happily. "Empty,"
she cries loudly, "just like I always knew it would be!" "Empty!" "Empty" "Empty!"

I watch her, and think,
That's not really you, up there, is it,
Rose? Rochelle? Shelley?
O, don't be sad, little Rose! It's still
Your ribbon I wear, your favor tied to the grip of my lance, when I
ride out to give battle,
these golden days.

UNCOLLECTED POEMS

Old Moon

I can't sleep walking through walls
taking pleasure in nothing of either of us
losing shape in room clock lamp air
heavy & the inverse who now may see desire

hovering over the body, lifting, diminish
down into oversize misshaper head-size, inside
thin down to the fine bright line of white light
across under distant locked door too far for human feet

although your face stays, while I can will, & perform
in the same way that this is performance
you give it body, that face, and it is your body
it is yours & makes my own return

marks my own return striped with red, eyes, and lashes
that are stretch-marks breathing against your lashes.

From the Execution Position

"Members of the brain, welcome to New York City
on a soft day weighted with rain, where
slightly ahead of time, trifoliate, but humanly low,
reading in a man's book this line, you fibrillate—

'It is easier to die than to remember.'—

You turn to the nurse, but he shakes your hand
With the fin of a fish: &
Why this self-deprivation of full human heritage?
& this does not happen all that seldom.

However, these days you do get
to do what you will, if
not always what you would wish. Tell me, is it
Ghost or Dancer straight? Substance or shadow, who is swish?"

The weight of the rain remains inside

trying to read, sorting, ordering,

doing in the waves of her walking

from coffee to cup & back to chair, sitting unseen

by the bed

where by now I am

going in the execution position.

Normal Depth Exceeds Specified Value

20th Century man strives toward the unfinished-machine exalted state.
Do not judge a man by his actions.

Birds cannot express the satisfaction I feel.
Happiness is often a rebound from hard work.

So, let us draw the patterns from the particulars—
In a pig's butt!

Americans emphasize genius over discipline
& it isn't going to work:

the temptation to remain alone in the house . . .
to live Revolution his own way on a day-to-day basis . . .

If you're not out in 5 minutes, we're going to burn the place down!
. . . Never act one-on-one with a co-actor.

The past six months every knock on the door
has been someone in anguish . . .

Winged Pessary

There I was
flat on my back at 30,000 ft.
getting my kicks
from a head
stuck in its own cloudy trousers
Your river is deep
it's muddy
My river is wide brown mud from
it seems an unacceptable tube
You puzzle me
The corn is green
Goya doesn't
Your blood is the color of baked clay
Your lines are always parallel
and short
Your orchards a chalice
Your acres one sandbox
after another
precariously balanced

tilt
you're beneath my notice
up above my head it's blue a funny thing
& I can hear a band of angels
& Joni James sing:

"it's time you knew
Old girl you're through
All you can do is count the raindrops
Falling on little girl blue."

Now passing over Oklahoma
23 minutes in a life I
guess I was just passing through

That kind of love is awful

This wheel's on fire

smoke clouds

hot wind

air-bag

Mayday.

Do You Know Rene?

One and one
leave me alone
I have to get some sleep
It's tiring always being a bore
sassy & fast but kind of crass
why am I writing now
this is the other thing to do

It's all I do
you can go home again
Philadelphia likes that
Merlin & Herman like it too
The Prisoner of Second Avenue
Hubba Hubba
Help, he's an intellectual dear dear

oh dear. The Mamas & The Papas
got old. The fat one died. I'm
practically asleep now.

        Sunset Blvd:
Peter lives there. With a Filipino gardener
& his Brooke.
It's only a mystery.

I'm positively boiling myself

It's not that I yearn for him
I just need him

In desperation I got on top

What an ugly view
looking down at you

Steve Carey

Huge collapsed Mountain Enters from Stage Right,
Deftly lowers Selfe to Floor, next to Bed,
&, Seated, Pours Forth with Basso-Profundo Eloquence
in Seemingly Limitless string (Stream),
Icebergs, fragments
of the Poem of These States,
from Backwards to 1977—
1978.

43

no strange countries

no women

no dance, no clothes

still a wild & strange tune

a song that rises in the blood

not much blood

no virgins

no velvet

no tropical laziness

more eyes though

two more

two eyes,

what do you make of that?

A Spanish Tragedy

He's literally a shambles as a person
who is in a responsible position Hanging
by a thread in one of the rooms of his
house Essentially what she is doing skitters
off into the air so slovenly that the most
fragmented shell does it to him & he does it
right back to her. This reminds me of cynical
& other good things that are totally pretentious
but sort of hold water so I absolutely won't
lift a finger why should I? to help these
Four Horsemen of the Apocalypse.

ISOLATE

Iris
petal
Custom chopper
lake

smoke
hickory logs
whinny
Austin-Healy.

cuts
insect
nest
smoke.

A rosette
A niggertoe

flower
almond

Eggs
scooters
a shed
dirt

The Atlantic fleet.

PHOSPHORUS
Old Hen
and egg
an egg.

brooch in
a wet bird
diamond rodent
A rubber hose

crinoline
BLUE   Aphid
Spore
Traps

Nucleii
Flocking
Vegetal
Belfry

Cages
Lava
Poppy
Wing

Aerial
Plankton
mirror
hutch

light

venom

hydrocarbons

premises
tubs
Eat
a pan

edible
antlers
deer
Cradle

Druid?

Hinges
Lava
Xerox

National
Eclair

MUCUS
HAY
Orchid
smoke

song
Pharmacology

piss
Church
Bourbon
Anutt

Old Mines

Turtle
Leper
smokes
a cake.

Scarlet Fever
a baton

Coda: (to I S O L A T E)

Antique
Bank
Cover
of which
is number

.FOR BRUCE ANDREWS
(FROM *FILM NOIR*).

Ronka

I'm gonna embarrass
my mother
&
I'm gonna embarrass
my brother

&

I'm gonna embarrass,

even, my wife,

but I'm not gonna embarrass my life,

O No,

I'm not gonna embarrass my life,

not ever,

I'm not gonna embarrass my life,

Not for you, or her, or anyone.

I'm never gonna embarrass my life—

except if I do . . .

& if it does,

Tough Shit.

My 5 Favorite Records

FOR DENNIS COOPER

1. Le Marteau Sans Maitre : Pierre Boulez (Odyssey 32 16 0154); McKay, alto; Gleghorn, flute; Thomas, viola; Kraft, vibraphone; Remsen, xylorimba; Norman, guitar; Goodwin, percussion; Robert Craft conducting.

2. Nonet : Ludwig Spohr (London Stereo Treasury STS–1-5074) Members of the Vienna Philharmonic.

3. Missa Caput : Guillaume Dufay (HNH 4009) Clemencic Consort.

4. Nonaah : Roscoe Mitchell (Nessa N–9/10) Mitchell, Braxton, Favours, Abrams, Lewis, Jarman, McMillan, Threadgill.

5. The Knot Garden : Sir Michael Tippit (Philips 6700 063) Minton, Barstow, Gomez, Hemsley, Carey, Tear, Herincx; Orchestra of the Royal Opera Covent House Garden, Colin Davis conducting.

(Research by Art Lange, music critic, *The Chicago Reader*, Chicago, Illinois.)

From Sketches of Amsterdam

FOR ALICE

"I wrote these songs when
I was young
but, I'm here again"
stepping out
down Oude-Zuids Voorburgwal
above the yellow moon sliding
over the canals of Amsterdam
a sojourner macrocosm
carrying
SOJOURNER MICROCOSMS
& Frank's COLLECTED POEMS along
with my own books of songs
going too quickly
but not *too* quickly
I hope
in the directions (a map)
of
De Kosmos
for to sing with my brothers & sisters

of the pleasures of living with you
that surround me now
in busy congenial gloomy evening air
where
tho I'm seething with rage
like any star
it's cool
the half-darkness
of this not unusual day's
oncoming night
because
everywhere I am you are
clear & bright & right.

Look Fred, You're a Doctor, My Problem Is Something Like This:

In the Summer between 5th & 6th grade
We moved from Cranston near the City Line
down into the heart of South Providence, or, from
an urban suburb to the White Irish working-class
inner-city. It was 1946. From that
time on, in grade-school, no, that year was
anonymous except spasmodically, but from the
next year on, Jr-High School, on into & thru
High School, at various jobs, thru one
semester at Catholic Providence College, then
3 years in the Army, Korea, and return
to College in Tulsa, Oklahoma (1957) right
up to about 1960, no matter where I
was, in what situation, with the exception of
on the football playground, in card games, and at
home, reading, I didn't
know the language and I didn't know

the rules; and naturally I didn't
know what it was I didn't know, nor,
therefore, what was it I did know, be-
cause I did know *something*. In the
army I began to learn about knowing
the rules, and so about myself and rules.
Back in College, while easing
into knowing the rules & what to do with that,
I evidently had begun *hearing* the language. In
1960, & from then on, I got hit by that special
useful sense that one could, easily, anytime or where,
pick up, & so "know" the language *and* the rules. It
all had to do with Surface, and it didn't have
to be shallow.

I took that self to New York City, into
poetry, to Art News, into Readings, thru marriage, into
teaching and then into not teaching, and in and out of
small-time crime. Now, there's a new, further
place, whose name I didn't quite catch, and, there-
fore, whose language & rules I can barely discern as
up ahead, let alone "what" they might be. It's
1979. I'm 44.

Compleynt to the Muse

AFTER PHILIP WHALEN

Lady, why will you insist on
Coming back into my life only when
It's too late, I've just this moment

Ago stepped out the backdoor
Of my body, gone ahead into Relativity,
Am looking down over 300 years

Past, Present & Future of my people,
Whom shall be known hereafter as
The White Mountain. They act like

You are with *them,* each & every
One of the big dumb-bells, & so
They drink and fuck and throw pots

And pick up the children at school
Or Write seventeen poems a week, ad-
Dressing You in the familiar, but I,

I don't mind at all, now that I'm simply
Air, a large hunk of see-through molecules,
A benevolent smile, & at night a closeness,

Cooling one hemisphere at a time, my bumps
Glittering over & above everyone are perceived
As stars, & friends drink wine far below where

I am grinning & don't care. I mean, not heavily.
But now you return, and so, I have too,
Into my ashy beard & dusty head, my pink baby's torso

And you are laughing, and I am once again
Lying in the world, and I'm holding my own, and I'm
Chuckling like Father Christmas to keep from crying.

And it's all right, my dear, I'm glad you came back. No,
Please stay. Honestly, I'm not dying. Not
For a long time, yet. I'm only just lying.

Rouge

"it" means "this".
I myself now
"know"
that. so,
"it" is true.
i.e., as a matter of course, all
knowing
being
self-evident:
(knowledge):
"it" and "that",
here & there &
vice-versa
constellate reality.
It made, all systems
"Go".
Just talk.

Coffee And

I am thinking of my old houses
369 Smith Street & 249 Potters Avenue
and the communicability
of houses—and that a house
can't be just a home, and I
tore up my oldish poem, "Hello, Goodbye"
and
another even older one, "One View / 1960"

and started on this new one, "Dogtown."
Now I'm across the street I crossed
when at last I came to it—and
        beginning
getting down to it.

Three Little Words

FOR LEWIS WARSH

I had a really sad childhood, lived mostly alone,
        like everyone else did. Adolescence
Was murder, & weird; but I could dig it.
        Manhood was *far out*—and also, during it,
I paid back one hundred times over each & every son-of-a-bitch
        male & female, dog, lizard & insect
Who'd fluffed up my lonely sad childhood with *Absolute Terror*
        or whatever it was that eventually grew up to be this blind, seething
Rage, still & always rising up from out those tiny "unforgettable moments"
        we are all all of us the cause of, tho Time
Excuses due to mitigating circumstances but
        never forgets; and guilt is always freely given,
Freely received, come rain or come shine, or
        haven't you noticed? You will, believe me.
Now old, or at least more often, I spend much
        of each day
Contriving these, my dumb born songs, my memoirs. And to no
        purpose; rather, quite simply, this is what one
Has been given. I was born in the Bronx, one hot November 9th,
        in 1944. Having reached 5 December, 1980, this cold
Saturday afternoon, I'm almost finished reading to the serious
        Manhattan hodgepodge of my current fans & friends,

The large aged husbands & the matronly sexpot wives, with
    their daughters at my feet & their sons at the breast,
While they guzzle the bourbons & beers that lighten up today.
These are my companions for life, & they love me. But you pay
    and you pay and you pay.

Round About Oscar

FOR STEVE CAREY

Reality is the totality of all things possessing Actuality
Existence, or Essence. Ergo, nowhere one goes
Will one ever be away enough
From wherever one was. The tracks lead uphill.
Power sits heavily for us on those we've grown up with.
    However,
Uphill tracks usually offer good views, after a while,
While the answer to what's new is, often, an
Indictment of an intolerable situation.
HOGS SIZE DISTURBS SYCAMORES. BRUINS
DEVOUR MAPLE LEAFS. STEEL CURTAIN FALLS ON HOUSTON.
COWBOY DUO RIDES RAMS INTO SUNSET. Quality tells.
Absolute quality tells absolutely nothing.

The By-Laws

FOR GEORGE SCHNEEMAN

I'd like to show you something. Please look at it.

I get blamed for everything that goes wrong. I'm always left holding the bag.

I'm sorry I threw away the notes I took in High School. I should have been
nicer to them.

If you're not sure about how to spell a word, how can you look it up in the
dictionary.

Please take these things off my desk. They're breaking my heart.

If there aren't enough workers at the factory, production will be fucked up.

He'll read the speech over before delivering it. He wants to enliven it with
mistakes.

He's a very successful young man. He's really getting off.

He didn't tell us the entire truth. He was afraid something smelled.

I found out he was lying by standing around in his background.

The two men wanted to fight, but their friends shouted them down.

Because of rain the game was wet for several hours.

Before the Vice-President can make a decision, he has to lock up the
President.

Before handing in your test, check it out for mistakes.

The woman disliked the hotel, so she didn't pay.

She felt tired, so she went to the doctor for a speed prescription.

She spent her money so fast that now she doesn't hold it back.

She's been in a bad mood for days. Why does she get a kick out of it.

I finally told him what I thought of him. I took charge of him.

Jesse James was a famous outlaw, who ran out of banks and trains.

Don't forget to write to us soon. Look up to us. Take us into account.

Thin Breast Doom

That's really beautiful!
'thin breast doom.' How'd
ya ever think of that?
PHILIP WHALEN

I have these great dreams, like
Sailing up on a lift, & then riding a bicycle
Down through a flaming basket. I have the dream at night
& the sailing in the dream is exactly what
I would be doing the next day. "Fuck, I'm never
Going to make my way." Right. But it's a beautiful feeling
To outdo your own misjudgements in the air.

That's what happens to people who died.

It slows things down instead of making them hectic
& frantic. "I'm not going to be careful anymore."
I can see all my people flow by so slowly. But
I'm still addicted to consciousness, tho I've probably
Only been conscious once in the last six years. But
I am conscious, that's for sure. Plus, Purity.
Purity means that you have something up
Your sleeve besides a right or a left arm. My
Arms are shot but my something is not. Because
It's something I learned when I was in a state.

I may have been in a state, but it was my state,
I even gave it a name: New York. Most people are in other
York, they aren't even in Old York yet, let alone York.

If your new light is intact, your vision is in the tunnel
& your decay has got to keep moving when it's near the abyss
(move your head). The world sucks, & everything is fucked up
But just do your best within without and you try to get along
Because in impure light things are coming apart because
You have something to move toward and you are in a state:

Don't get rich
Don't understand through the heart
Don't strain your music with verbal skill
but when you hear certain counterpoint
Don't try to fool the fist that's tightening
right beneath your heart
Don't lay back, look pretty, & strike a pose
Don't be a fool; be Showbiz naturally, &

Give everyone a chance to regroup. Use your bag of tricks.
Generosity is easy, that doesn't mean it's bad. But

Don't show up all substance & polish unless you can stop, look,
listen, & then take off
Taking at least one image away. Everyone has a right to be
judged by their best.
Be dumb enough to actually like it. Don't worry about Nuclear
War. You won't get killed.

Memories Are Made of This

Mistress isn't used much in poetry these days.
Comrade isn't used much in poetry these days.
Moxie isn't used much in poetry these days.
The Spring Monsoons isn't used much in poetry these days,
which is a shame.
Doubloons isn't used much in poetry these days.
I'm not blue, I'm just feeling a little bit lonesome for some
love again, isn't used much in poetry these days.
O Ghost Who walks, Boom-lay, Boom-lay, Boomly, Boom! isn't used
much in poetry these days.

&, I will gather stars, out of the blue, for you, isn't used much
in poetry these days.
Now, "I've got a guy" isn't used much in poetry these days
And, "Tweet-tweet!" isn't used much in poetry these days, at least
not at all in its code meaning, which was, "Eat my Birdie!"
Me & Brother Bill Went Hunting isn't used much in poetry
these days,
& Uijongbu sure isn't used much in poetry these days (sigh!).
Oh well, Mary McGinnis isn't used much in poetry these days,
just like, & I have to say it,
"Brigadoon" isn't used much in poetry these days.

Another New Old Song

FOR DOBE CAREY

My Grandfather was a Hasidic scholar,
he had his picture in LIFE Magazine, swaying
slightly from side to side, his voice with its
characteristic quaver gently raised in sing-song pitch,
engaged in high concentration in the now all but lost art
of *pilpul*. Last year
two Swiss scientists coined a new word, *punding*, now the name
for obsessive behavior due to amphetamine abuse. Hah!
The woman, now that I could see her,
was wearing a plain but expensive summer print,
no jewelry, her hair was dark & showed gray,
it was neither short nor long. She was as grand as
Stella Adler, as regal & tough as Bette Davis, a
saltier Mary Worth, all at once or each in turn.
Just what a semi-brokendown 44 year old Private Eye
really needed.

He lived in Cranston, near the city line, next-door to
The Riviera Cafe. She
used to work in Chicago, not in a Department Store. They
are survived beautifully, that unlikely pair, by
their daughter Peg,
an indomitable beauty, who has herself survived
these past 21 years
her own husband, Ed, that enigmatic man,
whose son each passing year makes more clear I am.
Crossing Western Europe on an Eastbound train
I had these half-thoughts & know well they will fade & remain.

A Certain Slant of Sunlight

FOR TOM CAREY

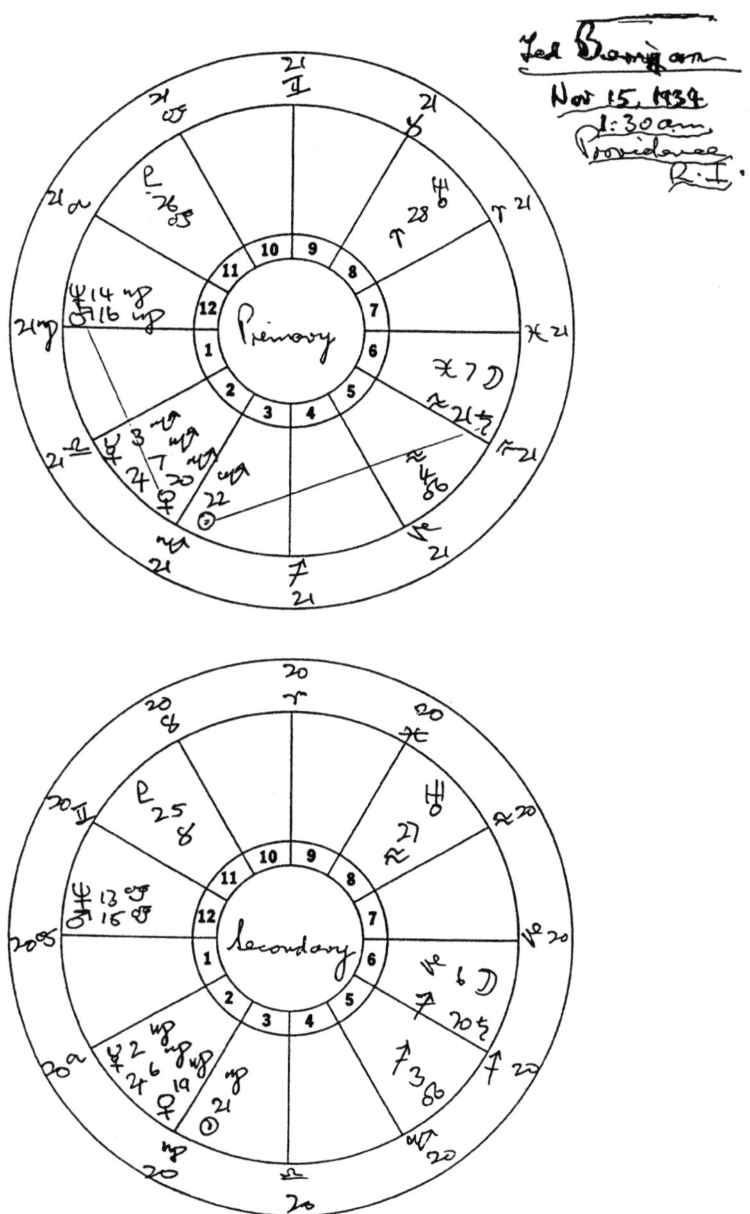
Nov 15, 1934
1:30 am
Providence, R.I.
Primary
Secondary

Poem

Yea, though I walk
through the Valley of
the Shadow of Death, I
Shall fear no evil—
for I am a lot more
insane than
This Valley.

*

You'll do good if you play it like you're
        not getting paid.
But you'll do it better if the motherfuckers pay you.

(Motto of THE WHORES
& POETS GUILD—trans.
from The Palatine Anth-
ology by Alice Notley &
Ted Berrigan. 20 Feb 82)

*

With
daring
and
strength
men
like

Pollock,
de Kooning,
Tobey,
Rothko,
Smith
and
Kline
filled
their
work
with
the
drama,
anger,
pain,
and
confusion
of
contemporary
life.

Just
like
me.

A Certain Slant of Sunlight

In Africa the wine is cheap, and it is
on St. Mark's Place too, beneath a white moon.
I'll go there tomorrow, dark bulk hooded
against what is hurled down at me in my no hat
which is weather: the tall pretty girl in the print dress
under the fur collar of her cloth coat will be standing

by the wire fence where the wild flowers grow not too tall
her eyes will be deep brown and her hair styled 1941 American
          will be too; but
I'll be shattered by then
But now I'm not and can also picture white clouds
impossibly high in blue sky over small boy heartbroken
to be dressed in black knickers, black coat, white shirt,
          buster-brown collar, flowing black bow-tie
her hand lightly fallen on his shoulder, faded sunlight falling
across the picture, mother & son, 33 & 7, First Communion Day, 1941—
I'll go out for a drink with one of my demons tonight
they are dry in Colorado 1980 spring snow.

Blue Galahad

FOR JIM CARROLL

Beauty, I wasn't born
High enough for you: Truth
I served; her knight: Love
In a Cold Climate.

Salutation

"Listen, you cheap little liar . . ."

The Einstein Intersection

This distinguished boat
Now for oblivion, at sea, a
Sweet & horrid joke in dubious taste,
That once, a Super-Ego of strength, did both haunt
Your dreams and also save you much bother, brought
You to The American Shore; Out of The Dead City carried you,
Free, Awake, in Fever and in Sleep, to the
City of A Thousand Suns where, there, in the innocent heart's
Cry & the Mechanized Roar of one's very own this, The 20th
        Century, one's
Own betrayed momentary, fragmented Beauty got
Forgotten, one Snowy Evening, Near a Woods, because
The Horse Knows the Way; because of, "The Hat on the Bed," and
Because of having "Entered the Labyrinth, finding No Exit.", is
That self-same ship, the "U.S.S. Nature" by name, that D. H. Lawrence
        wrote one of his very best poems about;
THE SHIP OF DEATH. (a/k/a THE CAT CAME BACK)!

Pinsk After Dark

Reborn a rabbi in Pinsk, reincarnated
        backward time,
I gasped thru my beard full of mushroom barley
        soup;
two rough-faced blonde Cossacks, drinking
        wine,
paid me no heed, not remembering their futures—
        Verlaine, & Rimbaud.

Reds

There isn't much to say to Marxists in Nicaragua
with .45's
afraid of the U.S. Secretary of State, eating
celery.
Back in New York, "we saw a beautiful movie,"
Allen said. "It made me cry."
"I hadda loan him my big green handkerchief, so
he could blow his nose!" Peter Orlovsky laughed.

People Who Change Their Names

Abraham & Sarah.

Naomi—("Call me not Naomi,
call me Mara; for The Almighty
hath dealt very bitterly with me.")

Simon, who shall be called Peter.

St. Paul (formerly Saul).

Joseph of Arimathea.

Cain.

Libby Notley ("when I was six I found out my
real name was Alice");

Francis Russell O'Hara; Didi Susan Dubleyew;
Ron Padgett; Dick Gallup;

STEVE CAREY:

Kenneth Koch (formerly Jay Kenneth Koch):

Jackson Pollock; "Rene" Rilke; William Carlos
Williams;
                    my mother, Peg;
                                                Guillaume Apollinaire;

"Joe" Liebling: John Kerouac: Joe Howard
Brainard: "Babe Ruth":

Tom Clark; Anselm Hollo; Clark Coolidge;

                George & Katie Schneeman.

Samuel R. "Chip" Delany.

In the Land of Pygmies & Giants

Anselm!   Edmund!
        Get me an ashtray!
No one in this house
In any way is any longer sick!
                And I am the Lord, and owner
                                of their faces.
                    They call me, Dad!

Angst

I had angst.

Caesar

Caesar,
I could care less
whether your Grandma
was black,
or white—
you'll always be a nigger to me.

GAIUS VALERIUS CATULLUS
(TRANS. TED BERRIGAN)

"Poets Tribute to Philip Guston"

I hear walking in my legs
Aborigines in the pipes
I am the man your father was
Innocence bleats at my last
Black breaths—and tho I was considered a royal
pain in the ass by
Shakespeare's father, the high alderman,
All the deadly virtuous plague my death!
I could care less?

Blue Herring

fiction appears) for I and only one per-
son's eyes. In my more iconoclastic
moments I stifle the impulse to send
such poems, which I do come across
them, back to their authors, taking

same authors to task for presuming
too much and asking them to send
their poem right on to the faceless
As if you hands were innocent
and the lobsters in your groin
And the heart of the scarecrow opens like snow
And something in the branches makes the pigeons
spread their wings
You reach into the branches and grab the red herrings—
the
Fountain of Youth is uncharted
You are its overflowing outline
You can only laugh.

Joy of Shipwrecks

FOR JEFF WRIGHT

Stoop where I sit, am crazy
in sunlight on, brown as stone,
like me, (stoned, not brown; I
am white, like writer trash), see
that stick figure, chalky, also
white, with tentative grin, walking
toward us? Feel your blood stirring?
That's Eileen, as typical as sunlight
in the morning; typical as the morning
the morning after a typical Eileen night

"Eileen" (detail)

FOR GEORGE SCHNEEMAN

When she comes, landscape listens; heavenly
Winter afternoons; shadows hold their breath;
she is the seal on despair; affection; tunes
sent us of the air.

None may teach her anything; weight;
despair; imperious death;
She is light; she is certain; she
is where the meanings are.

Going, even, she's impressive; like
internal distance; death; Myles
Where the meanings are; she sends us;
She is of and like the air; a star.

O Captain, My Commander, I Think

I like First Avenue
when the time of the fearful trip is come
& the Lady is for burning, as the day's begun
to duck
          behind the Levy-Cohen Housing Project
whose sand-pond can be seen still, through binoculars,
by the First Tyrant-Mistress of The Near West;
sky falls; & night; & me, too, yr star:
When the lilacs come I'll flip
til thrice I hear your call, darkling thrush.

Polish Haiku

The Pope's learning Welsh:
(he's an alien)
More power to him!

Ode

Spring banged me up a bit
& bruised & ruddy &
devastatingly attractive
I made
2 A. M. Phone call to Bill Brown
'How long is your foot?'
'Oh about 12 inches.'
'Well stick it up your Ass.'

*

"and Day rang from pool to hilltop
like a bell."

Sunny, Light Winds

those exhausting dreams
of angry identification, a dog
like ego, Snowflakes as kisses—the
ability to forget is a sign of a
happy mind—at least,

Philip thinks it is, & he's happy,
sometimes.
But I don't *want* no cornbread &
molasses!
Never. I don't *want* to live in the un-
tidy
moment! Forget it. I don't want no
lover
who always wants to be the boss!
Want! Want! Want!—it's all right, I'm
Just having a little fun, Mother.
unhappy love affairs,
are only for madmen

revery

What a Dump
or,
Easter

FOR KATIE SCHNEEMAN

a metal fragrant white
        Capitol of beantown
sans dome; rubber & metal pieces
        of Kentucky; chicken-bones &
Light Cavaliers; jeans; tops; balls; caps;

"Now I have to have life
        after dreams"

"& now I'm running running
        running
down the King's Highway"

"& now I am Lily, Rosemary, & the Jack
        of Hearts;
One-eyed Jill; Pietro Gigli; 2 cats:
Howard; & Katie, my heart; & mine"

"Mine is melancholy"

"Mine is ½ gristle, ½ dust"

"Mine is Luke Skywalker, & his parts:
the Wookie part; the Landro part; the Han dynasty;
C-3PO"

"Mine is this 'Squeeze-box';
the Good; the Beautiful; the True; & Bucky Dent.
He just *has to* have a chance to be in The Hall of Fame!"

All pleased rise
Cleansed
Pure
In perfect order go.

Paciorek

FOR ANSELM HOLLO

Light takes the bat, &
shoulder; who can tell us
how? (I wake to sleep, &
take my waking fast). O low-
ly worm, falling down upstairs,
& down is a lowly thing, how
fast is no longer a joy?

9:16 & 2:44, & 25 Minutes to 5

Dear Management's beautiful daughters,
sweetly
made Marion, & Alice, the Elephant—
the
trouble with you two is just happened for
the first time ever, which is once more than
I can hold my head up under ever after again—If
Anybody asks you who made up this song, just tell 'em
It was me, & I've done been here & gone.

My Life & Love

FOR PHIL WHALEN

"Do you
think I'll
ever see
him again?

"Beauty
whose action is
no stronger than a
flower?

"I think I'm about to be
surpassed again.

"Do you think we'd better go to
California?"

"Naw. Don't be silly. Send him a round
cheese or something. A can
of peaches."

Hello, Sunshine,

Take off your head; un-
loose the duck; lift up your
heart, and quack! I am the
Morning Glory, I take no
back talk. . . .

Take me twice each morning;

be funny that way.

In Morton's Grille

In Morton's Grille I
always get nostalgia for Morton's Grille
which wasn't called Morton's Grille
at all, but THE RIVIERA CAFE, way out on
Elmwood Avenue. They had a machine,
this was before TV, you put a quarter in
& a zany 3 minute movie of the Hatfields
shooting at the McCoys out a log cabin
window came on; the McCoys ran out of
bullets, so they started singing, "Pass the
Biscuits, Mirandy!" Grandma's biscuits were
so hard, terrible, but saved the day when thrown
at the real McCoys.

St. Mark's in the Bouwerie

FOR HARRIS SCHIFF

Naked
with a lion
a small lesbian
smoking a pipe
some silent young men
"Shit!" they exclaim
"Fuck all women!"
They all start singing patriotic songs

Dinner at George & Katie Schneeman's

She was pretty swacked by the time she
Put the spaghetti & meatballs into the orgy pasta
    bowl—There was mixed salt & pepper in the
"Tittie-tweak" pasta bowl—We drank some dago red
    from glazed girlie demi-tasse cups—after
which we engaged in heterosexual intercourse, mutual
    masturbation, fellatio, & cunnilingus. For
dessert we stared at a cupboard full of art critic
    friends, sgraffitoed into underglazes on vases. We did
have a very nice time.

Listen, Old Friend

"This ability, to do things well,
and to do them with precision & with
modesty, is nothing but plain & simple
                                        Vanity.
"It is Pride overfertilizes the soil
till alone the blue rose, grow—I know
Dante Alighieri told me so."

(signed:)

THE SLOTH

Dinosaur Love

FOR ANNE & REED

Anne Lesley Waldman says, No Fossil Fuels
The best of the free times are still yet to come
With all of our running & all of our coming if we
Couldn't laugh we'd both go insane—with changes
        of attitudes
At the Horse Latitudes—if we couldn't laugh, we'd
        All be insane—
but right here with you, the living seems true, &
the gods are not burning us just to keep warm.

Spell

A sparrow whispers in my loins
Geranium plus Geronimo forever
Across the wide Missouri
We drive us.

For Robt. Creeley

  "In My Green Age"
  like they say,
        much compassion,
          little dismay,
            such exuberance—
  Loving: *Caught:*   *Back:*

There's a place—
"tho are be were as now is now. . . ."

Fine Mothers

With sound Sun melts snow
Elms fill in
and wind blows green. ("When the wind
was green" . . .) This is the Spring I knew
would come.
The rosy finches row through.

day moves then, my room— light-
nights bat their yellow dust against
the windows, & I dream I am black
running, rising, to the sea:

Evenings, night heroes stop here, or,
gently pass
The trees release into sky.
Travelling by,
from grove to Mars,
SEVEN arc over.
I call them angels. O, angels,
O, common & amazing.

Pandora's Box, an Ode

. . . was 30 when we met. I was
21. & yet he gave me the impression
he was vitally interested in what I
was doing & what was inside me! One
was Tremendous Power over all friends.
Power to make them do whatever. Wed. Bed.
Dig the streets. Two is speeding and pills
to beef up on on top of speeding ills. Three,
assumptions. Four, flattery. Five, highly

articulate streets, & when he saw me I was witty.
I was good poetry. Love was all I was. As
the case is, he had or was a charm
of his own. I had the unmistakable signature
of a mean spirit. Very close to breaking in.
I was like Allen Ginsberg's face, Jack's face,
eye to eye on me. Face of Allen. Face of Kerouac.
It was all in California. Now,
all of my kingdoms are here.

To Book-Keepers

The Final Chapters
of the History
        of
Modernism are
going to be written
in blood. Yours,
you poor Immigrants!

The School Windows Song

AFTER VACHEL LINDSAY

High School windows are always broken;
Somebody's always throwing rocks,
Somebody always throws a stone,
Playing ugly playing tricks.

Jr. High windows are always broken, too:
There are plenty of other windows that never
get broken;
No one's going into Midtown & throwing rocks
At & through big, Midtown, store-windows.

Even the Grade School windows are always
Broken: where the little kids go to school.
Something is already long past terribly wrong.
End of The Public-School Windows Song.

Transition of Nothing Noted as Fascinating

The Chinese ate their roots; it
made them puke. We don't know til
we see our own. You are irre-
sistible. It makes me blush. How you
see yourself is my politics. O Turkey,
Resonance in me that didn't even want to know
what it was, still there, don't ever make jokes
about reality in Berkeley, they don't
understand either one there.
Donald Allen, Donald Keene, Wm. "Ted" deBary,
it's hard to respect oneself,
but I would like to be free.
China Night. Cry of cuckoo. Chinese moon.

Whoa Back Buck & Gee By Land!

FOR WYSTAN AUDEN, &
THELONIOUS SPHERE MONK

This night my soul, & yr soul, will be wrapped in
        the same dark shroud
While whole days go by and later their years;
Sleep, Big Baby, sleep your fill
With those daimones of Earth, the Erinyes,
Women in the night who moan yr name.
"Man, that was Leadbelly!"

Frances

Now that I
With you
Since
Leaving
Each day seems
The night
Tired with
Languisht
Suffering
While you
Nor I
With that
I feel.

Sweet Iris

Take these beads from my shoulders
There's your paintings on the walls
Turn around slow & slowly
Help me make it through the night
Then I'll take you out for breakfast
Never see you all my life

I Dreamt I See Three Ladies in a Tree

FOR DOUGLAS OLIVER, DENISE RILEY, & WENDY MULFORD

If someone doesn't help me soon I
believe I'm going to lose my mind, I
mean my tone of voice, my first clue
as to what this speaker is like. Help! (he).

is a beautiful piece of work in that it
has to spill out & still stand as
meeting own requirements: dedicated to Betty
Chapman of Coon, Minnesota: take me deeper

via from the outside, you, my unforgettables, my
best. Hand, 2 hands, wheel, & blood; O broken-hearted
Mystery that used to sing to me: now I'm too misty,
and too much in love. O lovely line that doesn't give an
        inch, but gives.

Moat Trouble

He was wounded & so
    was having
    Moat Trouble.

Hollywood

paid Lillian Gish $800,000 to
disappear so lovely so pure like milk
seems but isn't because of the fall-out
but it would have only cost me five & didn't,
so I did, but when Garbo is the temptress
doesn't it seem absolutely perfect-
ly right? just being there? nothing
costs anything that's something, does it?
like soaking at a Rosenthal / Ceravolo Poetry Reading
or blazing while "The White Snake" unfolds
itself: in the city, there one feels free, while
in the country, Peace, it's wonderful, & worrisome
I've never seen a peaceful demonstration, have you?
NO MORE NUKES

Last Poem

FOR TOM PICKARD

I am the man yr father & Mum was
When you were just a wee insolent tyke
until at 5 o'clock in the afternoon
on one of the days of infamy, & there
were many, & more to come yet, the goons
& the scabs of Management set upon us
Jarrow boys, & left us broken, confused
and alone in the ensuing brouhaha. They
outnumbered us 5 to 1; & each had club
knife or gun. Kill them, kill them, my
sons. Kill their sons.

Mutiny!

The Admirals brushed
the dandruff off their
epaulets and steamed
on the H. M. S. Hesper
toward Argentina. I
like doggies on their "little
feet", don't you, I said, but
they kept rolling over, be-
neath the tracer bullets and
the Antarctic moon, beneath the
daunting missiles and the Prince
in his helicopter, they were
steaming toward interesting places,
to meet interesting people, and
kill them. They were at sea,
and it was also beneath them.

Jo-Mama

The St. Mark's Poetry Project
is closed for the summer. But
all over the world, poets
are writing poems. Why?

Montezuma's Revenge

In order to make friends with the natives
In my home town, I let them cut off my face
By the shores of Lake Butter, on
The 7th anniversary of their arrival
In our Utopia. It was the First of May.
Nose-less, eye-less, speechless, and
With no ears, I understood their reasoning,
And will spend the rest of my days
helping them cover their asses. Free.

Turk

FOR ERJE AYDEN

"There's no place
to go
my heart,
for all your
100,000
words."

M'Sieur & Madame Butterfly

I go on loving you
Like water Yggdrasil
Where you are 100,000 flowers
bloom while across the
broken eggshell field the ink
rises from the fossils, as my
tongue drifts lightly into the Gobi Desert of yr
ear & we become a person's lungs & take to the air.

Wantonesse

Heart of my heart
Fair, & enjoyable
Harmlessly spooky
Loving her back

Creature

FOR ALICE NOTLEY

Before I was alive
I were a long, dark, continent
Lonely from the beginning of time
Behind Midnight's screen on St. Mark's Place

And my thin, black, rage
Did envelop my pale, dusty, willowy-green-
Shell in dark bricks & black concrete
'til I was a Hell that was not fire, but only hot.

Then I called you to bring me
    One more drink, & your good legs
And translucent heart brought me
    A city, which I put on, & became
Glad, & I walked toward Marion's &
    Helena's, to be seen, & found beautiful,
And was, & I came alive, & I cried Love!

XIII

(AFTER JACK KEROUAC)

O Will Hubbard in the night! A great writer today he is,
he is a shadow hovering over Western Literature, and
no great writer ever lived without that soft and
tender curiosity, verging on maternal care, about what
others say & think, (think & say), no great writer
ever packed off from this scene on earth without
amazement like the amazement he felt because
I was myself.

Providence

Lefty Cahir, loan me your football shoes again—
Clark, let me borrow the brown suit once more—
I hear a fluttering against my windows.
River, don't rise above the 3rd floor.

Paris, Frances

I tried to put the coffee back together
For I knew I would not be able to raise the fine
Lady who sits wrapped in her amber shawl
Mrs. of everything that's mine right now, an interior
Noon smokes in its streets, as useless as
Mein host's London Fog, and black umbrella, & these pills
Is it Easter? Did we go? All around the purple heather?
Go fly! my dears. Go fly! I'm in the weather.

Windshield

There is no windshield.

Stars & Stripes Forever

FOR DICK JEROME

How terrible a life is
And you're crazy all the time
Because the words don't fit
The heart isn't breakable
And it has a lot of dirt on it
The white stuff doesn't clean it & it can't
be written on
Black doesn't go anywhere
Except away & there isn't any
Just a body very wet & chemistry
which can explode like salt & snow
& does so, often.

Minnesota

If I didn't feel so
bad, I'd feel so good!

I Heard Brew Moore Say, One Day

FOR ALLEN GINSBERG

Go in Manhattan,
Suffer Death's dream Armies in battle!
Wake me up naked:
Solomon's Temple The Pyramids & Sphinx sent me here!

The tent flapped happily spacious & didn't fall down—
Mts. rising over the white lake 6 a.m.—mist drifting
between water & sky—
Middle-aged & huge of frame, Martian, dim, nevertheless I
flew from bunk
into shoe of brown & sock of blue, up into shining morning
light, by suns,

landed, & walked outside me, & the bomb'd dropped
all over the Lower East Side! What new element
Now borne in Nature?, I cried. If I had heart attack now
Am I ready to face my mother? What do? Whither go?
How choose now?, I cried. And, Go in Manhattan, Brew Moore
replied.

Postcard

THE SENDER OF THIS
POSTCARD IS SECRETLY
(STILL) UNSURE OF YOUR WORTH
AS (EITHER) A FRIEND OR A
HUMAN BEING. YOU COCKSUCKER.

Smashed Ashcan Lid

FOR GEORGE SCHNEEMAN

Oh, George—that
utter arrogance! So
that people can't tell that
you're any good—

"chases dirt", for Chrissakes!!

Okay. First. . . .

"Truth is that which,
Being so, does do its
work."
(I said That.)

July 11, 1982

Dear Alice,

The reason I love
you so much is be-
cause you're very
beautiful & kind. I
also appreciate your
intelligence, though what
"intelligence" is I'm not
sure, & your wit, which
resembles nothing I've
ever thought about.

Your loving husband,

Ted Berrigan

The Way It Was in Wheeling

(AFTER FREDDY FENDER)

I met her in The Stone Age,
        riding shotgun—I can
Still recall that neon sign she
        wore—She was
Cramlin' through the prairie near
        the off-ramp, & I
Knew that she was rotten to the core.

I screamed, in pain, I'd live off her
        forever—She
Sd to me, she'd have a ham-on-
        rye—but who'd have
Thought she'd yodel, while in labor?
        I never had a chance
To say Good-bye!

My Autobiography

For love of Megan I danced all night,
fell down, and broke my leg in two places.
I didn't want to go to the doctor.
Felt like a goddam fool, that's why.
But Megan got on the phone, called
my mother. Told her, Dick's broken
his leg, & he won't go to the doctor!
Put him on the phone, said my mother.
Dickie, she said, you get yourself
up to the doctor right this minute!
Awwww, Ma, I said. All right, Ma.
Now I've got a cast on my leg from
hip to toe, and I lie in bed all day
and think. God, how I love that girl!

Down on Mission

There is a shoulder in New York City
Lined, perfectly relaxed, quoted really, quite high
Only in the picture by virtue of getting in
to hear Allen Ginsberg read, 1961
And though the game is over it's beginning lots of
        years ago,
And all your Cities of Angels, & San Francisco's are
        going to have to fall, & burn again.

In Your Fucking Utopias

Let the heart of the young
        exile the heart of the old: Let the heart of the old
Stand exiled from the heart of the young: Let
        other people die: Let Death be inaugurated.
Let there be Plenty Money. & Let the
Darktown Strutters pay their way in
To The Gandy-Dancers Ball. But Woe unto you, O
        Ye Lawyers, because I'll be there, and
                I'll be there.

Dice Riders

Nothing stands between us
except Flying Tigers
Future Funk
The Avenue B Break Boys
    and

The Voidoids—
Sometimes,
Time gets in the way, &
sometimes, lots of sometimes,
We get in its way, so,
Love, love me, do.

The Heads of the Town

FOR HARRIS SCHIFF

They killed all the whales
now they're killing all the acorns
I'm almost the last Rhinoceros
I guess I'd better kill them.

To Be Serious

You will dream about me
All the months of your life.
You won't know whether
That means anything to me or not.
You will know that.
It's about time
You know something.

W/O Scruple

FOR BERNADETTE MAYER

The wicked will tremble, the food will rejoice
When he & I grow young again
For an hour or two on
Second Avenue, at Tenth
About 35 days from now—
    Although that will not get it;
    And that will not be that.

George's Coronation Address

With Faith we shall be able . . .
There will be peace on earth . . .
    & Capricious day . . .
maybe we'll be there, or true.
Speed the day then.

Tough Cookies

You took a wrong turn in
1938. Don't worry about it.

The sun shines brightest when
the others are sleeping.

There is a Briss in your
immediate future.

Take heart. Shakespeare was
probably an asshole too.

Your life is rare and precious
& it has no mud. Stay with it.

You have strange friends, but
they are going to be strangers.

Everything is Maya, but
you will never know it.

Your gaiety is not cowardice,
but it may be hepatitis.

Skeats and the Industrial Revolution

(DICK JEROME, 3/4 View)
ink on paper

God: perhaps, 'The being worshipped. To
whom sacrifice is offered. *Not* allied to
'good', (which is an adjective, not a
'being.' *Godwit:* a bird, or, more recently,
a 'twittering-machine'; (from the Anglo-Saxon,
God-wiht: just possibly meaning, 'worthy creature.'
Viz. Isle of Wight—Isle of Creatures. See, also,
Song, folk; Childe Ballad # 478: "I've been
a creature for a thousand years." . . . .)

Besa

(TO THE GODS)

He is guardian to the small kitten.
He looks so determined.
He has a graceful hunch.
Light swirls around his crown,
        wispy, blondish, round.
Three shades of blue surround
        him—denim,
Doorway, sky. His hands are up,
His eyes are in his head. He's
        my brother, Jack;
Kill him & I kill you.

Natchez

FOR ROSINA KUHN

I stand by the window
In the top I bought to please you

As green rain falls across Chinatown
You are blissed out, wired, & taping,
        15 blocks uptown

When I am alone in the wet & the wind
Flutes of rain hire me

Boogie-Men drop in to inspire me

In the Deer Park

FOR TOM CAREY

"I know where I'm going
"& I know where I came from
"& I know who I love
"but the Dear knows who I'll marry. . . ."

I bought that
striped polo shirt,
long-sleeves, for 75 cents,
& wore it every minute, that year

I got a sunburn
on my face & hands
I hadn't noticed it.
But when someone pointed it out
I said it felt good.

I was over
a year in that
Park. Never did
feel in a hurry.
I was "in love."

Tompkins Square Park

All my friends in the
park speak Latin: when
they see me coming, they
say, "Valium?"

Warrior

FOR JEFF WRIGHT

I watch the road: I am a line-
   man for the County. City streets
await me, under lustrous purple skies, purple
   light,
each night. Manhattan is a needle
   in the wall. While
it's true, the personal, insistent, instant-
   myth music cuts
a little close to the bone
& I have to get up early for work tomorrow, still
   there's
lots of quail in Verona, & I am
jubilant with horror
because I'm searching for pain underneath
another overload.
I hear you singing in the wires.

Space

is when you walk around a corner
& I see you see me across Second Avenue
You're dressed in identifiable white
over your jeans & I'm wearing Navy—
Jacob Riis is beams of sunlight as
I cross against the light & we inter-
cept at the Indian Candy Store. The

Family has gone off to Parkersburg, W. Virginia
The Chrysler Building is making the Empire State
stand tall, & friendly it leans your way
There's appointments for everybody
They don't have to be kept, either.

Dresses for Alice

We are the dresses for Alice.
We go on, or off, for solace.

New York Post

FOR MICHAEL BROWNSTEIN

Two cops cruise East 9th
between First and A. Talk
about schedules, they're on
the Graveyard Shift: 11 to 7
in the morning. They are definitely
not boring. As they pass, I waver,
with my pepsis, two beers, & paper:
what am I doing here?
Shouldn't I be home, or them?
But I guess I'm on this case, too. . . .

Let No Willful Fate Misunderstand

When I see Birches, I think
of my father, and I can see him.
He had a pair of black shoes & a pair of
brown shoes,
bought when he was young and prosperous.
"And he polished those shoes, too, Man!"
"Earth's the right place for Love,"
he used to say. "It's no help,
but it's better than nothing."
We are flesh of our flesh,
O, blood of my blood; and we,
We have a Night Tie all our own; & all
day & all night it is dreaming, unaware
that for all its blood, Time is the Sand-
paper; that The Rock can be broken; that
Distance is like Treason. Something
There is that doesn't love a wall: I
am that Something.

Unconditional Release at 38

FOR DICK GALLUP

like carrying a gun
like ringing a doorbell
like kidnapping Hitler
like just a little walk in the warm Italian sun . . .
like, "a piece of cake."
like a broken Magnavox
like the refrigerator on acid
like a rope bridge across the Amazon in the rain
like looking at her for a long few seconds

like going to the store for a newspaper
like a chair in a dingy waiting-room
like marriage
like bleak morning in a rented room in a pleasant, new city
like nothing else in the world now or ever

Ass-face

"This is the only language you understand, Ass-Face!"

Minuet

the bear eats honey

between the harbored sighs
inside my heart

where you were
no longer exists

blank bitch

Buenos Aires

Strings like stories shine
And past the window flakes of paper
Testimony to live valentine
A gracious start then hand to the chest
    in pain
And looking out that window.

Ms. Villonelle

What is it all about—this endless
Talking & walking a night away—
Smoking—then sleeping half the day?
Typing a résumé, you say, smilingly.

The Who's Last Tour

Who's gonna kiss your pretty little
        feet?

Who's gonna hold your hand?

Who's gonna kiss your red, ruby
        lips?

Who's gonna be your man, love,

      Who's gonna be yr

          man? Why,

I am. Don'tcha know? Why, I am.

To Sing the Song, That Is Fantastic

Christmas in July, or
Now in November in
        Montreal
Where the schools are closed,
& the cinnamon girls
       Sing in the sunshine
Just like Yellowman:

The soldiers shoot the old woman
        down
They shoot the girl-child on
        the ground: we
Steal & sell the M-16s, use
The money to buy the weed
The sky is blue & the Erie is
      Clean;
Come to us with your M-16:
Soldier, sailor, Policeman, Chief,
Your day is here & you have come
      to Grief.
Sing the songs, & smoke the weed;
The children play & the wind is green.

Interstices

"Above his head
changed"

And then one morning to waken perfect-faced
Before my life began
cold rosy dawn in New York City
call me Berrigan

Every day when the sun comes up
I live in the city of New York
Green TIDE behind; pink against blue
Here I am at 8:08 p.m. indefinable ample rhythmic frame

not asleep, I belong here, I was born, I'm amazed to be here
It is a human universe: & I interrupts yr privacy
Last night's congenial velvet sky left behind . . . kings . . . panties
My body heavy with poverty (starch) missing you mind clicks
        into gear

November. New York's lovely weather hurts my forehead
On the 15th day of November in the year of the motorcar
But, "old gods work" so   sleeping & waking   someone I
        love calls me
into the clear

Bad Timing

Somethings gotta be done! I thought.

Rusty I was?

BANG!   ("I fell right down
                         on the floor. Just like
                         Dave DeBusschere.")

Slept a few days.

I woke up; just as Red's voice
                    said, "She is
                    hurting, we
                    must DEFEND tons
    of indistinguishable tones."

            I said, "This sense

there was a way, I met in the possible

O.K.

Under my roof.

Mars. Autumn. Bills (on the Bill
                        scene).

        BILL ME.

This Guy

He eats toenails.
Is rude, vain, cruel, gloomy.
He talks with bitter cryptic wit.
Is unclean.   "Is this some
    new kind
of meatball?". . . . sitting in
    a rowboat,
waiting for a bite . . . . has
just asked—with considerable
gravitas—if he might be
    allowed
to become one of my suitors.
And I said yes.

A City Winter

My friends are crazy with grief
& sorrows—their children are born
and their morning lies broken—
& now it's afternoon.

Give Them Back, Who Never Were

I am lonesome after mine own kind—the
hussy Irish barmaid; the Yankee drunk who was once
a horsecart Dr.'s son, & who still is, for that matter;
The shining Catholic schoolboy face, in serious glasses,
with proper trim of hair, bent over a text by Peire Vidal,
& already you can see a rakish quality of intellect there;

Geraldine Weicker, who played Nurse in MY HEART'S IN
THE HIGHLANDS, on pills, & who eventually married whom? The
fat kid from Oregon, who grew up to be our only real poet;
& the jaunty Jamaica, Queens, stick-figure, ex US Navy, former
French Negro poet, to whom Frank O'Hara once wrote an Ode,
or meant to, before everything died, Fire Island, New
York, Summer, 1966.

Via Air

Honey,
        I wish you were here.
                                I wrote some poems about it.
And though it goes,
                        and it's going,
                                    it will never leave us.

Christmas Card

O little town of Bethlehem,
Merry Christmas
to Jim
& Rosemary.

Christmas Card

FOR BARRY & CARLA

Take me, third factory of life!
But don't put me in the wrong guild.
So far my heart has borne even
the things I haven't described.

Never be born, never be died.

Poem

The Nature of the Commonwealth
the whole body of the People
flexed her toes and
breathed in pine.

I'm the one that's so
radical, 'cause all I do is pine. Oh I just
can't think of anything—
No politics. No music. Nobody. Nothing but sweet

Romance. Per se. De gustibus non disputandum est.
Flutters eyelashes. Francis, my house is falling down.
Repair it. Merry Christmas.

A Certain Slant of Sunlight: Out-takes

Bardolino

Allen & Peter, heads close together, Allen
        weeps magically during "Reds":
later, drinking pepsi in my living room
they discuss with Robert Lowell Dr. Williams'
        Communist wheelbarrow—but
Peter says his own
        Wheelbarrow is blue.

Postcard 12/2/82

Feb. 11, 1982. Last night reading *Permanent War*
Economy by Sennyor Melman for 30 pages
& toward the end of the book in the
appendix Says 1F-16 Super fighter plain costing
6 or 10 million could provide Houses for 240
families—Peter Orlovsky

("Reading this note, and thinking about Thomas Wolfe:

12 Feb 82

—Ted Berrigan").

New Poets of England & America

"the taste is pleasant, and the insane
                                perfection, mild. . . ."

Get Away from Me You Little Fool

"I have always been emotional beyond belief, so
there simply must be plenty money in my life: it's
not that I *like* money, I just need not to
not have enough, ever! So, if I had to be
a leaf, why ever so many kinds would do—
they all tremble, don't they? I know that my
Redeemer liveth; there is a Lord will provide,
somewhere, for specialists! I'm not cold meat loaf,
after all, damp & wooly, dontcha know?"

"You lack charm."

4 Metaphysical Poems

"Get a job at the railroad"

"Loan me a few bucks"

"I gotta buy some pills"

"So I can understand John Ashbery."

Who Was Sylvia?

Queen   name

      ice   sign

            was all that remained

                  of her suicide note.

Anselm

it is a well-lit afternoon

across the incredible static of time-space-language

reading a book

"to be born again"

between bouts

through two layers of glass

I call your name.

In the mirror

Anselm's dreams

the dimensions of the world

the performance of the world

my beauties

smoke

writing

Wednesday Evening Services

Blindfold shores leaving sad
an audience of dancers
Frank O'Hara's dead & we are not
The General Returns
From One Place
To Another
the program was dedicated to him
but I couldn't make it

Head Lice

I have no brain.

My body is covered with vermin (a few).

People are calling me names.

I deserve these names.

My body is being transformed into glass,

with a few vermin on it.

So be it.

Little Travelogue

When seeking sky you're left with sky, then
"we kill ourselves to propagate our kinde"—We sleep
and these guys come in with hypodermics & spray us
with ice water—

Monkeys press switches & little babies freak out & cry,
"pick me!" "pick me!"—Oh, Daddy, I was a flower, &
When I listened to George Shearing, they told me, I broke

the World's Record for rapid eye movement! Then, I don't know
What I did then, but it was green, & then red, & then
blue & yellow!

Sleeping Alone

It's a previous carnation, where?
I think it lived in the shiny lapel
of my rust colored dinner jacket
slung over the closet doorknob
the night of the senior prom
at St. Xavier's High, when I was
Babe Harrington's date and she
was selected queen of the prom
& we danced the first dance alone
just the two of us, to her own
personal request "Embraceable You."
The closet was in the blue room
far away upstairs. Babe married
Joe Fogerty and gained four pounds.

*

"Another has

come to the

sky mirror . . ."

(He in the peeling silver eats my drugs)

The Pope's Nose

FOR ANNE WALDMAN

a nose, heavy, square, & massive;
large, flesh irrigated with blood;
a light grave voice; his face
a long rectangle; pink; poetry
pours out of it like kool-aid
at unofficial noon it is crumpled
like a kleenex:
here, blow.

The LADY, JUST WHEN I THINK I KNOW YOU, YOU TAKE CAPRICIOUS FORM Travelling Circus & Road Show (or, IN THE LABYRINTH)

Geranium's
another word
for

"my heart is on my
sleeve"

. . . coming from the corner,
heading for the stairs.

NOW APPEARING IN:
MANHATTAN
TODAY THRU ________

Treason of the Clerks

They set you up. Took yr stuff. Gave
    it to me.
I made a Little Monster with it.
He's the enemy of a Wookie.
He turns grass black and puts it
    on him so
You can't see certain parts of his body.
(The *Bad* parts.) I can't talk to you.

All A-Glower Went My Love Riding

Hitch on here
My little timeless
Teeth & gums, you tiny
Particles of mid-Victorian Bakery
Furniture, that Dickens, Tennyson, &
Bob Creeley saw, where fingertip & moon
Remain infinitely separate, the way
Specific chemical hatred & twizzlers
Do, or one-inch foot in Nature's
Chrysler Building, blue and gold, sí,
That is what they, we, are. And
Why not? You take a hike? I'll be
Your legazine, oh buss! &
we'll leave their golden worlds
while the band plays on, we drive us.

Climbed by Grandma We Stand on Morning's Hill

Now she guards her chalice in a temple
          of fear; once
a Hardy Boy, a philosopher, a
          blue Christmas light:
Boils secretly Biotherm . . .
       . . . the time you . . . when you . . .
In praise of %*@!!! *?@! and
          in class shouting "Dig it!"
(I told them you were left-handed).

With Eileen in Locarno

We commemorated a joyous (if
unrequited) love—because
it was in another country—
because we were each other people
—because the love that we
celebrated, did that in commem-
oration of, had been neither ours,
nor, most certainly, unrequited. We
were both so sad, we laughed & then
we cried in Locarno. We wished
our ashes to be mingled together
forever & forever & forever. Next
year, in Cho-fu-sa.

St. Mark's By-the-Pacific

Light, informal, & human
Are your seasons, danger
Waters coming, pass us by,
bye-bye—lightly warm &
humid are your tropics, high
above the footpath past the sty.
The pigs grunt no more beneath
the window, I'm glad we ate them
The goats are gone, so no one else
can get them—& the clouds' re-
flections look like a pride of lions
in your eyes. This disease isn't terminal,
so it's restful; we fuck & think over wine
here, there are eggs & cream in the fridge,
it's so divine to be here!

Three Lost Years

FOR PEGGY DECOURSEY

For a brief time Acting Chief
Didn't harmonize actively with an easy
View of life—pinball machines being played
By preposterous kid-wits on the backs
        of Flat-bed Pick-up trucks—by
Land's End in glad—or else sad-ness—But
Why should I care? Grace falls
On anyone who can walk out of Ballroom A;
And out off into the Sky-Vista! *Sure.* &
        So does Peggy.

Butchie's Tune

FOR ALEX & ADA

What's the number I request.
When the band began to play?
a fragrant flowered shrub   blush
and one cannot go back, except in time
This mushroom walks in.
"Hi, Mom! Hi, Dad!"
He is not really thinking.
Yet I take him purely as treasure.
This morning we were footprints in the
snow. And The Band Played On.
Listening to the words from the morning bush
        all the day,
We sleep & dream our lives away.   & so, a
tendency to get surprised rarely is absent,
        this perfect day.

La Bohème

I'm not difficult but there are just certain things
that this here that are not this here, & no
matter what you say, No! (no) I don't ever do that . . .
But when you think about it, it seems that
this here doing nothing could use a head if anyone
nice has one they aren't using, no?

Turkeys

FOR TOM CAREY

They have bent.
They cling.
They attack & capture.
It is a treat, a nightmare, a punch in the face.

He wanders by himself.
He lingers. He idles
In his little house.
He absorbs, and is absorbed.

He begins to bear down on what he sees:
Young faces, puzzling argot, meat, or "the postulant":
You nod and scrunch up your face and chuckle.
Let me out of here you silently shriek.

"I've got to hang up now, a man is yelling at me."

A pill always seems to be about something.

To a Young Painter*

"Ah Fitz but we are profound
chaps—we word lads."

"We ride in our round paper boats
From Ireland and Israel & Iceland without
coats. We feed our slaves
Locusts, our kids Moths & oats; and we starve
our cave-painters because they are sloths!" Love,
Mr. P. F. C. Hemingstein

* "(He had a way of wearing very casual clothes.)"

Upside Down

You don't have to be Marie Curie
or even Simone de Beauvoir already
to write your memoirs, you know? after
all, we *all* have a polymorphous perverse
first person singular, don't we? . . . .
If you don't want to see & hear, don't feel
like it, say . . . maybe wd rather worry, or
sulk. . . . Still you do have to remember, there's
no way to put blinders on one's insides, you
know . . . or do you? Sure you can.

Der Asra

Every day back & forth
The exquisite daughter of the Sultan walked
At evening by the fountain,
Where the white water splashes.

Every day the young slave
Stood at evening by the fountain,
Where the white water splashes;
Every day he grew pale, and paler.

Then, one evening, the Princess, turning
Came up to him with these words:
Thy name will I know! thy
Country! thy Kin!

And the slave spoke: I am called
Mohamet. I am from Yemen.
And my people are the Asra
who die, when they love.

HEINRICH HEINE
(TRANS. TED BERRIGAN & GORDON BROTHERSTON)

Fern

I had this dream
I was supposed
to get married
to a sensitive prince, &
together
we wd score for hash
from our maid-of-honor, Sancho Panza—

A choir of Windmills in their cassocks & surplices
were going to surround us in song for
the rest of our lives,
beautiful boy sopranos, singing with aching purity, the
only song they know: THE LITTLE DRUMMER BOY.

my whole life? I hid myself beside a burning
bush,
My verdant response
to monogamy
in Spring. And
The sea was tumbling in harness
As I sailed out to die.

San Francisco

You took me
for everything
I have

I had it

Thanks
for that
You

O, Sexual Reserve

Why don't we
call up
David
Hockney &
ask him for
a thousand?

One Day in the Afternoon of the World

FOR ERJE AYDEN

I never said I was right, or wrong.
I said I was lucky. I waved a leg
in the air. First, I'm going to eat this,
Then I'm going to eat you! Just two
High livers, stretched-out on the Elephant grass,
mouths dripping with blood, & wheezing like fire-sirens,
We passed our long love's morn:
So ends my song, like a pair of she-lions.

Two Serious Ladies

That's all
one life needs—
Two serious ladies.

Down Moon River

Talking
To Charlie on the stoop
Wearing asbestos suit
I see the really horrible fly
On top of the yellow rose—I

Can't believe it, it's so ugly
I just don't have much conversation
to give, these days, now I've sung my ABC's:
(next time won't you sing with me?): She
sang beside herself, beyond
The genius of the Sea.

At 80 Langton Street (S.F.)

FOR BILL BERKSON

I stand at the dock in judgement
literally already condemned
but also am here to be informed,
as my illustrious colleagues Anselm Hollo,
Lorenzo Thomas, and Kathy Acker
have done before me.
I am pleased and flattered
to be joined in such Noble

Company, & only wish that I too might spark
giant & seething controversies & provoke angry
exchanges & bloody fistfights; but, like Anselm Hollo
I am merely a National Treasure, so, what I am
going to do is talk, which is what I do, plus read my poems.
Bill Berkson will take care of the rest, the doing what must
be done part.
So, let us begin. I'm about to do so, I will offer you this
one word of advice, in front.
Duck.

Last Poems

Robert (Lowell)

Like the philosopher Thales
who thought all things water
and fell into a well . . . trying to
find a car key . . . ("it can't be here . . .")
We rest from all discussion,
drinking, smoking, pills . . .
                                        want nothing
but to be old, do nothing, type & think. . . .

        But in new December's air
I could not sleep, I could not write my name—
Luck, we've had it; our character's gone public—
We could have done worse. I hope we did.

Today in New York City

FOR BERNADETTE & LEWIS

Gay doormen face a severe shortage of cocaine
The White House announced today.
The crisis
Which could blow the lid off
Of Boys Town
is a result of Latest Great Depression
Brought on by
Savage game of "Go Fish"
In Congress
On the street where you live.

Citizens are being asked
To tie up their children
And to walk their clones
In groups of five
At 55 mph
Police said today.

2.

The President said
When Mars squares Saturn
With a trained squirrel
He will burn whale blubber
& is contemplating
The return of Billy,
Suicide,
3-Mile Island,
Unleashing "The Hammer"
Running naked
To breathe
Evacuate
Phone Grandma, if necessary
During "60 Minutes"
On television.

3.

At reduced temperatures
During months having an "R" in them
Wander lonely as a cloud
Crawl on all fours when it's time.

4. (Coda)

Enraged Shepherd
Tears up his EXXON card
Admits he is a droid
Has his teeth bronzed
Redesigns his novel
Dies Early
Bye-bye.

The Short Poems

FOR SUSAN CATALDO

THE SOCIETY CLUB

"I never shut my mouth, in case
I have to yawn."

Too Late

The boat has left.

ARGENTINA

Don't cry, Argentina.

TED RON
BERRIGAN & PADGETT

"Flow gently, sweet Thames,
'til I end yr song.

✲

fire-hydrant

✲

censored

12TH NIGHT

"I will go."

CITY MONEY

In God we trust because she got
something stuck in her throat
and bent their ears.

THE OLD ONE

is Ted Berrigan.

Something to Remember

Caesar's ghost must be above suspicion.

To Jacques Roubaud

I'm sorry for your trouble
Jacques.
I'm very sorry
for your trouble.

Villonnette

Oh, Mrs. Gabriele Picabia-Buffet,
why did they want so badly to be
like us, those wonderful jack-offs of yesterday?
And where have they gone? Where are they now? those jack-offs
of yesterday?

After Petrarch

Inquiry & Reply

FOR ANNE WALDMAN

Virtue, Honor, Beauty, Kind gestures
Sweet words have reached the high branches
wherein my heart is warmly entwined.

*

Then lead the person to the unmade bed.

*

1327, at daybreak,
on the 6th of April,
entered the labyrinth;
no exit have I found.

*

So, old friend, not dead, don't lead me on.

Old Armenian Proverb

"Only the guilty need money."

Ambiguity

I am ambiguity.

(FOR ED FOSTER)

Stand-up Comedy Routine

FOR: BOB HOLMAN
OR ED FRIEDMAN

Good Evening, ladies, and all you hungry children in Asia," A very funny thing happened to me on my way over here from a tough Italian Neighborhood, where I just bought this suit made out of recycled lint. Any other paisanos out there? (Gives them the finger). A bum came up and asked me to call him a Taxi, so I did my impression of Richard Nixon, which goes something like this: (Gives audience the finger). But seriously, my friends, I just arrived in your fine city after three wonderful weeks of playing Sammy Davis Senior. During that engagement I ran into an old high school classmate who set off an alarm clock so everybody can wake up and go home, so I bit him.

Speaking of that, what do you think about solitaire in the drunk tank of a southern jail, jerks? (Gives audience the finger). Believe me, when I was younger, nobody would even dream of refusing to die for his country, and I mean that sincerely. As you may know, I grew up in Anaheim, Azusa, and Cucamonga. Also in Las Vegas. And Brooklyn. Anybody out there from Brooklyn? (Gives audience the finger again). I'll never forget the first girl I dated. She was so buck-toothed that she ate corn on the cob through a picket fence! She grew up to be my close friend, Liza Minelli. She once told me a funny story about the Pope meeting Bo Derek on a train. Then she married me, so lets give her a big hand! (Gives audience the finger w/both hands). Now, as I've grown a little older, I'm just thankful for all you other women out there, and for my hotel room, which is so small the mice are all hunchbacks.

Say, here's a joke for you. A fella goes to a psychiatrist and says, "Doc, I imagine I'm a rabbit." So the psychiatrist says, "That's nothing. My wife ran off with our marriage counselor." How come nobody's laughing at this material? There are hungry children in Asia who would gladly trade places with you.

Incidentally, before I finish my act, I've been asked by several of you to add a little class to this routine by doing some gay Polish jokes. (Gives audience the finger). But what I'd really like to do is leave you with a bit of wisdom that was passed on to me by Sammy Davis, Senior. When I told him I was going into show business, he just smiled, and said, "The devil may wear many coats, but all of them need mending."

Are there any other psychotics out there? (Gives audience the finger viciously, first to the left side of the room, then to the center, and then to the right side).

I hope you'll remember that, as I have. Thank you, and God bless.

Positively Fourth Street

There's nothing new under the sun, and
There's nothing new under the rock, either.

Down on Me

It's very interesting
    but
The Buddha-minds are freaked out—

translate
Snake
into
Pea

Turn around
Look at me.

Don Quixote & Sancho Panza

It is 1934. Edmund
Wilson is going to Russia
Next year. There's a brunette
Dwarf asleep in his bed. Scarlatina.
Bedbugs. Dear Henry Allen Moe:
    Can you wire me a $100 loan, to Paris?
I have learned everything I can here.
253 lbs later, it is May, 1983.
Did Henry Allen Moe get burned?
Tomorrow I will need $50, Summer Camp
for Sonny, & supper. I can hear
my own voice on the telephone: hello, Ed?
(Edward Halsey Foster) Hi, Ed. Got any dollars?
Today I am 48 years, 5 months and 16 days old,
In perfect health. May Day.

This Will Be Her Shining Hour

✲

"This movie has Fred Astaire and Robert Ryan in it!

✲

"He got off the train!

✲

"I have a feeling this is an unknown movie."

✲

(laughs) Q: "What the hell is going on?"
A: (laughing) "Dialogue.

✲

"This movie has no plot.

✲

"Fred Astaire was on this train with a whole lot of soldiers, going to Japan. And then, he got off the train!

✲

"Robert Ryan keeps saying, 'Let's kill Japs,' & Fred Astaire keeps saying, 'Fuck that.'

✲

"He fell in love with her!

✲

Q: "Who?"
A: "Joan Leslie. She's a photographer. There keeps being a whole lot of stuff by Johnny Mercer."

✲

Q: "Joan Leslie is just my type. Is she?"
A: "Un-uh. Fred Astaire is nobody's type, either.

✲

(laughing) "He changed all the lyrics."

✲

Q: "To what?"
A: (sings)
"This will be my shining hour
drinking rum & bacardi
like the face of Mischa Auer
on the Beauty Shop marquee."

✲

(laughs)
"You have to watch it.

✲

"You have no right to get anything out of my
evening!"

✲

Q: "Give me the Book Review section, will
you?"
A: "Sure. You'll *love* it."

✲

"I haven't written anything for years. I'm going
to move away.

✲

"Oh God, she's gorgeous:
(for a little ugly person)."

✲

"I can't tell which is Waldo."

"Pretty good line, huh?

'I can't tell which is Waldo.'

✲

Q: "Did you write that down?"
A: "No."

✲

(laughs)

"You? Working?"

(laughs again)

✲

(laughs)

"This is my wife. She follows me around."

✲

Q: "Where are they?"
A: "They're in some giant building. Fred Astaire is yelling, 'Help, save me!!'

✲

"I think this movie is some Homage to Balanchine . . . . It's out of the question.

✲

"Man, instead of cracking an egg on that woman's hand, they're putting diamonds on it.

✲

"I think my life is really awful.

✲

"Oh God, write all this down.
"Oh, what a great song!"

✲

"This is my night at the canteen. . . ."

✲

"It's nice work if you can. . . ."

*

"Oh, great. . . ."

*

"She's dancing.

*

"They're in New York City!"
"Of course they are."
"Just like us.

*

"Oh God, he's so great!

*

"Oh, he just got taken down from the table.
He did a snake dance."
(It was a Johnny Mercer snake dance.)

*

It's 4 a.m.

*

(laughs)
"Wordsworth put it pretty well."

*

"He hasn't done too much in this one.
"Now he's going to do it. . . .

*

"It's all so wartime.

*

"It's so wartime no one gets to do much of anything.

*

"It's all so unfair.

*

"Are you having fun?

✲

"You are too! (sigh)

✲

"That's Robert Ryan. You should come see him. He's being in a musical.

✲

"Oh God, he looks so great!"

✲

"He looks too much like my father.

✲

"It has Averill Harriman in it."
"Doesn't everything?"

✲

"Have you ever said to her how your life would be incomplete without her?"

✲

Setting: Beekman Place. The usual Penthouse. It's almost summer.

✲

Hmmmmm.

✲

"I haven't seen a movie in ten years."

✲

"Oh God, I'm seeing double."

✲

"You're the one he'll never forget."

✲

"Will you keep it on while I get in bed?"

✲

"What?"

✲

"Will you keep it on while I get in bed?"

✲

"Sure."

✲

"Their lives are as fragile as *The Glass Menagerie*."

✲

Saturday Night on TV

✲

"Oh, she dances, Ted. . . . and it's so great!!
"She's not supposed to be able to dance!

✲

"You're making a big mistake,
writing a poem,
and not watching this."

✲

"Shut up. I'm getting the last lines."
"You are not."

Early Uncollected Poems

Sonnet to Patricia

duty is the primal curse
from which we must redeem ourselves
G. B. SHAW 1891

If by my hasty words I gave offence,
Know I would stop my tongue in recompense
Were that an answer or an end to rage:
But I am no philosopher, nor sage;
If love and friendship hasty words can kill,
I would not speak; but I must speak my will.
These days I burn: and I cannot be still:
Burn I must; and with fire must I kill
Those unmixed humours in me which bring rage
Upon those whose griefs I would most assuage.
Now then, I must myself ask recompense
For cause which causes me to give offence.
So Duty me no Duties: Be not strange:
Give me your hand, your love, and I will change.

One View/1960

Now she guards her chalice
In a temple of fear. Once
She softly held me near, til
Rain, falling lightly, flooded pain.

Alone, the pale darkness
Became too much to bear. Then
She quickly drew away, drawing
Darkness down on Summer's day.

Alone, this sudden darkness
Became too much to bear.
Then,

        Afraid to draw away,
I closed my eyes
To close of Summer's day.

In Place of Sunday Mass

My beard is a leaping staff
I love to hear it creak
it gathers moss in the morning mist
in the middle of my weakness and
when I stand and clank
it gives me shoes

My eyes scurry towards the sea
legs scuttling beneath them
shell glistening like split peas
in the sun. I have two, a right one,
and a left. In spring my eyes go deaf
and are rancid and rank with
blue

And my belly! ah, it is a shining thing
it sings at sunup on the back fence of
my buttocks, burping and belching in the sheer joy
of strumps. It clumps. I offer my belly the sumps
of my simple sorrow, which once knew
whom to name, and so it grew.

I am a bog, a ditch, a burrow beneath a
sole survivor of study. Unbowed
I am bloody with bad confetti, and I go
in a flagon of gore. Oh sweet stalactites
upon this shore,

"I ain't coming back
No more!"

What are you thinking . . .

Did you see me that night
I climbed the wallpaper tree, white
with rage, whiskey in my pocket? Fright
could never fathom my undressings, nor blight
my loneliness, which sits here at my desk, in sight
of homeless waifs, who bite
my thighs my heart for sustenance. My plight

Is insignificant but you, surely you saw my light
burning for you alone, the night I sliced the slight-
ly lengthy tail from the scraggly poet's kite?
For you I starred in the movie made on the site
of Benedict Arnold's triumph, Ticonderoga, and I indict
you to take my hand, which reaches out for yours, in spite
of the change of season, this Spring which holds me tight.

Lady Takes a Holiday

TO CAROL CLIFFORD

became in Alamogordo. Then the blast-
off into total boredom. Referred to as
a "weird-o." The sleeping sleazus of
honey love. Circumference equals piR^2.

Evergreen concatenations of airmail stamps
bringing me fearsome and rust. Wood in the dust
bowl. Howl in the woodhole. Cold manifestation
of last of the cruel and the "name" to the first.

Sundown. Manifesto. Color and cognizance.
Then to cleave to a cast-off emotion,
(clarity! clarity!) a semblance of motion, omniscience.

For Bernie

Ah, Bernie, to think of you alone, suffering
from German measles, only a part-time mother and
        father
bringing you ginger ale; and
the great speckle bird now extinct;

what frolicsome times we'd have had, eating
ants and clover in the yard, Ayax
pissing on the grass! Is it possible
great black rat packs

were running amuck amidst the murk away back east,
and you, and me, and Ayax,
giggling happy here? But it never was,
never. You were a Campfire Girl
and I was afraid.

Homage to Beaumont Bruestle

Giants in the sky; roses in streams that castle; rocks
in roll; the flower-bird drops singing smitten low; and always
waste of faces bullet it; and more than these: ground
moons! High! and seas to rot upon the tides! the
loveliness that longs for butterfly! There is no pad
against the lack of pinned: there are in the world of vast
reflected limp. And beauty piles stone. But every garden shows
have learned the secret. Dreams beauties beauty in the world,
blossoms, snatched, are thrown, and die men's foes. And
lack of soul is no to fill the youth.

Of dumbed bondage the heavy accent of.
The flames of love are horsed to pull the knee
Of downward pressing lips. The Earth of waste's
Deep hill. It is. It need not go.
Such powers weld by chain that must not know.
When cart is in of progress, down saddest the world,
Then lack to beauty tragedy are used.

And there is no.

Lines from Across the Room

(FOR ANNE KEPLER)

Futile rhapsodies resound from hotly
blind to dank venetian blinds upon
whose verdant crevices blue scary
shadows bound and bound and grow
and then grow still. Yes it is not

yet daylight, no light creeps with
hesitance across the blind, my desk
is shadow, silence lies in the room:
Sleep half sleep half silence and
with reason portends new seasons,

nor shadow, nor substance; blind
fascination reduced to contemplation.
Then, praise for this golden surge
of energy! It is time to rise in
silence, raise the blind, and turn

again to poetry, away from sleep.

Prose Keys to American Poetry

You come into my life a little yellow
Around the gills and I offer you 41
Pills of indeterminate mixture but you
Will not swallow them you are like

The Sunflower: you are waiting for a
Madman! Now you are like a madam, I
lean over and gaze intently into your
Eyeballs for 32 hours whereupon you swoon
And say, "Perceval, you're wonderful!"

"Everybody sucks nobody fucks" says John
Stanton in PROSE KEYS TO AMERICAN POETRY
Which I must admit is disconcerting in light of
My premature weaning! Because actually I was in love
With all of those Saturday Serials even if Charley Mackin

did beat me up every week for sixteen weeks
straight! I simply repressed it all!

Games

(FOR MARTIN COCHRAN)

Across the trolley tracks
deep in the cemetery
were the Jr. Marines.
                    "Let's Remember Pearl Harbor
as
  We did the Alamo"

Gregory, high
up on Porkchop hill,
sleepy, grumpy, dopey,
Oliver Hazard Perry, and
of man's first disobedience and
the forbidden fruit

This too, and love,
three
          "they'll pick us off like sittin' ducks"
his mouth tightened
He buckled on his gun, the one
Steve had left him
        "Gather ye rosebuds," he ordered.

Homage to Mayakofsky

The white poet with his book
And the ox-blood, do they agree?
With his throat which is beating,
Does he agree?
And the hands oh so plentiful,
And the architecture,
Symbols in his journals of summer?

The hands
Are words in the journal.
Wind giving presence to fragments.
In the book of his music the corners have straightened:
Torrents have faded down the bent frontier.

It Is a Big Red House

Voici la tête d'un chien
Il est à la fenêtre noire
For fire for warmth for hands for growth
So green and formal to the bone
Whose hands hold up whose head?
Wind fans the red fire and its flames burn hand bones
Is there room in the room that you room in?
Fire it, and hand me the bones, over the blue wind
That I receive fire, fire to pierce like the wind
So black, bête noire, in the burnt-by-fire plume

Canzone

A darksome tiger
dreams in "The Poems."
No one put the tiger
In "The Poems." A tiger
In a dream
Is still a tiger.

In "The Poems" where the Tiger
Is, dreams are alive.
We are alive
When a tiger
Leaves his cage
In "The Poems." "The Poems" are not a cage.

We are not a cage
Nor a tiger
In a cage
Where a cage
Keeps "The Poems"
From "The Tiger"
Although we dream
A darksome dream
Of a cage.
"The Tiger" is a dream. Alive
We are alive.

"The Poems" are alive
In a cage
Where alive
Is more a dream than alive.
Like a tiger
Is alive
In a cage, this alive
Are "The Poems."
We are "The Poems"
When we're alive
But when we dream
Then we dream.

"The Poems" are not a dream.
"The Tiger" in "The Poems"
Is a dream
When "The Poems" are a dream.
Then "The Poems" are a cage
And a cage is not a dream.
So a Tiger's not a dream
But a Tiger
Is not a Tiger
But a dream
In a cage. "The Poems"
Are not a dream of "The Poems."

We dream up "The Poems"
In a dream
And "The Poems"
Contain a Tiger. "The Poems"
Are alive.
The tiger in "The Poems"
Except in "The Poems"
Is a cage
And will cage
Up "The Poems"
Unless we are the tiger
In "The Poems" dreamed up by "The Tiger."

A darksome tiger
Dreams in his cage.
"The Poems" dream "The Poems."
We have had this dream
And we are alive.

Grace After a Meal

FOR JOHN WIENERS

Out we go to get away from today's
delicate pinpricks: awake and scheme
to pay the rent; the room is littered
with laundry, my desk turns
my stomach; in my stomach a white pill
turns to warmth; I stretch and begin
to flow; a door opens; the day
is warm, and we join hands
for a journey to courage in a loft.

        A man signs a shovel, and
so he digs. I fear to become a crank,
alone in a dreary room, grinding out
poem after poem, confused, con-
cerned, annoyed.
                But Edwin offers us
cookies, and coffee and beer and grace.
By his presence he offers us leads, and
his graciousness adds to our courage.

                                John,
we must not be afraid
to be civilised, meaning
Love.
    It is 5:23 a.m., and the sun
is coming.

Notes

These notes are not intended to be exhaustive but rather to provide assistance in reading a poetry characterized by a profound density of reference and naming. The notes would ideally offer reading clues that would transfer from poem to poem, rather than supply definitions to fit capitalized nouns. References are so layered, embedded, and characteristic of both conscious and "subconscious" levels of thought that full explanation would not only be too lengthy—and too contrary to the purposes of poetry—but also impossible. We offer a quick glossary of the proper names used most frequently in the poems, but it's useful to remember that one doesn't really need to know: the poetry, in its various ways, takes care of the reader all by itself. These notes are also intended to demonstrate the wide range of formal methods used in the poems.

The Sonnets

Both the "C" Press edition (New York, 1964) and the Grove Press edition (New York, 1967) of *The Sonnets* were composed of sixty-six sonnets. The United Artists edition of 1982 included six new sonnets, XXXIV, XXXV, LX, LXI, LXXVII, and LXXXI. The Penguin Poets edition of 2000 included seven more: XIV, XXII, XXV, XXVIII, XXIX, XXXIII, and LIX, fulfilling Ted's instructions to me in late 1982, when the latter seven were finally judged ready. This leaves the following sonnets: XX, XXIV,

LIV, LVIII, LXII, LXIII, LXIX, LXXIX, and LXXXVI. They are not strong enough to be published.

Joe Brainard was the cover artist for the "C" Press edition. A second cover illustration by him, intended for the Grove Press edition but not used by Grove, finally adorned the Penguin edition in 2000. Louise Hamlin was the artist for the front and back covers of the United Artists edition.

The Penguin edition for *The Sonnets* includes an introduction by me, as well as notes based on Ted's annotations of an early typescript of the entire sequence. This typescript will be referred to from time to time in these notes.

NAMES IN *THE SONNETS*

Names—of friends, writers, artists—appear throughout *The Sonnets* and, to a lesser degree, all Ted's work. One can almost always tell if the name refers to a "friend" or a "poet/artist" or both, or can gauge the formality/informality of the reference (a friend referred to by full name in a dedication is being treated differently from the same friend named familiarly in another poem). A name is a word like any other in poetry, and the use of names is an old literary tradition (Dante, Catullus). The reader has had her/his own friends and knows what a friend is in the mind; the reader can look up certain other names in the encyclopedia or on the Internet. Detailed annotation would be contrary to the spirit of the poems, which, though literary, is egalitarian and intimate. However, I would like to offer some examples of usage, focusing on five lines in Sonnet XXX which are particularly replete with names:

> Dear Marge, hello. It is 5:15 a.m.
> Andy Butt was drunk in the Parthenon
> Harum-scarum haze on the Pollock streets
> This excitement to be all of night, Henry
> Ah, Bernie, to think of you alone, suffering

Marge Kepler was a friend/girlfriend of Ted's: this is rather obvious, she is "Marge," she is "Dear Marge." Andy Butt is a name that works like that of a character in a novel: he is a fiction, like a man in a rather bad novel, "drunk in the Parthenon" (though "Butt" and "Parthenon" conjure up certain associations). The

"Pollock streets" suggests the lines of paint in Jackson Pollock's great paintings. The reader doesn't know for sure who "Henry" is, though one suspects him of being Henri Michaux, the French poet, who is often mentioned in these poems (see "Mess Occupations," which is also Sonnet XXXIX "*after Michaux*"). The point is less that he might be Henri Michaux than that someone named Henry is being addressed; and more, that the word "Henry" works metrically. "To be all of night, Henry!" sounds just right, as "Dear Marge, hello" works clearly on a point of sentiment. "Ah, Bernie" feels like it refers to a friend, and does; the whole line is funny, because Bernie's name—a real name—sounds antithetical to "suffering" (but all real people suffer).

By the repetition of names, a relational tension is built up over the course of the sequence, which is modeled very generally on Shakespeare's sequence, with its love plot and its pitches of exaltation and viciousness. The reader experiences this tension through the lens of the poet's mind in process, as the poet mulls over the past and present actions of himself and his friends and lovers.

A quotation from an interview by Tom Clark is clarifying ("Interview with Tom Clark," *Talking in Tranquility: Interviews with Ted Berrigan*, ed. Scalapino and Ratcliffe [Bolinas and Oakland: Avenue B and O Books, 1991]). Speaking of *The Sonnets*, Ted says, "There is no such thing as a message and media in the abstract. I mean, they're the same thing to the perfect extent. That is, surpassing McLuhan where he says the message is the media. No. When it all works right there's no message, it's only sort of the media. Which is fascinating because of just the words." That words are, materially, words, somewhat as paint is paint, applies in varying degrees to all of Ted's work.

SONNETS I–VI

I made a dating error in the Penguin edition, in regard to the dates of the inception of *The Sonnets*. I was following Ted's annotations on the typescript of the sequence, and he appears to have misremembered. The genesis of the first six sonnets in November and December of 1962, not in early 1963, is confirmed by two sources: a handmade booklet called *Rain Dance* containing the six as a gift to Pat (Mitchell) Padgett for Christmas of 1962, and an entry in Ted's journals (see *from Journals*, excerpts chosen by Larry Fagin, in *Shiny*, no. 9/10, 1999):

(1962)
20 Nov 5 5:15 a.m.
Wrote (?) (Made) five sonnets tonight, by taking one line from each of a group of poems, at random, going from first to last poem then back again until 12 lines, then making the final couplet from any 2 poems, in the group, one line at random from each. Wrote by ear, and automatically. Very interesting results.

Groups used
Sonnet #1—Six poems 1962
#2—Personal Poems
#3—Le Bateau Ivre
#4—My 14 Selected Poems
#5—My 10 Newest Poems

All this was partly inspired by reading about DADA but mostly inspired by my activities along the same line for the past 10 months (or since reading LOCUS SOLUS TWO & seeing the Assemblage Show & Working on Collages with Joe (see our Self-Portrait)

Now back to more Dada.

The sixth sonnet in *Rain Dance* is Sonnet VI, made from lines by Dick Gallup.

The above journal entry indicates the kind of compositional method used throughout *The Sonnets*, as well as the types of materials employed. Ted incorporated old and new work by himself, a translation of an Arthur Rimbaud poem, and lines by Dick Gallup into the first six sonnets. One sees that though Ted is using a method, he is also working by ear and that he is being influenced by Dada and by collage and assemblage, as practiced both by the original Dadaists and by his contemporary and friend Joe Brainard.

I Ted told me that the "he/his" in this poem is meant to be Ezra Pound, though the poem of Ted's from which the opening lines are taken is called "Homage to Mayakovsky" (see *Early Poems*).

II "How Much Longer Shall I Be Able To Inhabit The Divine": "How much longer shall I be able to inhabit the divine sepulcher" is the title and first line of a poem by John Ashbery in *The Tennis Court Oath*. *The Tennis Court Oath*, with its broken, phrasal texture, was a major influence on *The Sonnets*.

Poem in the Traditional Manner and **Poem in the Modern Manner** Not all of *The Sonnets* are sonnets, as these two sixteen-line poems prove. Here we are being shown what the two "manners" are that this sequence will mix and change. The point would also seem to be to keep the surface of the whole work various.

In "Poem in the Traditional Manner," Dick Gallup is called "Richard Gallup" in an allusion to Edward Arlington Robinson's poem "Richard Cory." *The Asiatics* (see also Sonnet XXV) was a novel by Frederick Prokosch, published in 1935.

In "Poem in the Modern Manner," Huitzilopochtli refers to the Aztec god of war. Cos is the Greek island.

From a Secret Journal Also Sonnet IX. Ted's note on the typescript says: "Made from Joe's 'Secret Journal', a prose work by method. probably made earlier—62 or not? my best." Joe is Joe Brainard. The "secret journal," which remains unpublished, is actually called "Self-Portrait on Christmas Night."

Penn Station "Gomangani," according to Ted's notes on the typescript, is "either White Ape (Tarzan) or Black Apes (The Apes) hence I forget—i.e. clarity is in the language not its precision." That is, the word is taken from the Tarzan novels of Edgar Rice Burroughs.

XIV "Blake-blues" probably refers to Blind Blake, the blues guitarist (b. early 1890s, d. 1933) as much as to William Blake.

XV This is perhaps the most famous of all the sonnets. It is obvious how this broken work can be put back together into its first version, Sonnet LIX, by reading first line, last line, second line, second-to-last line, etc. Sonnet LIX was omitted from the first two versions of the sequence and reinstated in the Penguin edition. One of the most interesting things about Sonnet XV is that it becomes stranger after you understand how to reassemble it: its disjunctive form seems to assert itself more and more strongly as the real one.

XVI According to Ted's notes on the typescript used for the Penguin edition, "'The Going Down of the Morning Land' is how Lauren Owen's father translated 'The Decline of the West' to me in 1960 in Tulsa—slow was my word." Thus "the slow going down of the morning land" refers to Oswald Spengler's book *The Decline of the West.*

XIX Mysterious Billy Smith was a welterweight boxer, whom Ted had read about in A. J. Liebling's boxing classic, *The Sweet Science.* Liebling quotes boxing manager Jack Kearns on Smith: "He was always doing something mysterious. . . . Like he would step on your foot, and when you looked down, he would bite you in the ear."

XXI A rearrangement of the lines of "Penn Station," which is also Sonnet XII.

XXIII "The 15th day of November" is Ted's birthday. "Between Oologah and Pawnee" (two towns in Oklahoma): an allusion to Apollinaire's poem "*Annie,*" which contains the phrase "*Entre Mobile et Galveston.*" According to Ron Padgett in *Ted: A Personal Memoir of Ted Berrigan* (Great Barrington, Mass: The Figures, 1993), the phrase is also a reference to Woody Guthrie.

XXXI This sonnet was influenced by Kenneth Koch's poem "You Were Wearing," which contains the line "I smelled the mould of your seaside resort hotel bedroom on your hair held in place by a John Greenleaf Whittier clip."

XXXVI and **LXXVI** These two personal poems were printed again in *Many Happy Returns.* In the course of *The Sonnets* they are fragmented and later reconstituted, as many of the poems are—they are part of its total process. In *Many Happy Returns* they are simply poems in their original forms.

Uijongbu is a town in Korea where Ted was stationed during his military service at the end of the Korean War.

XXXVIII General Benedict Arnold, famous as a traitor to the American side in the Revolutionary War, actually led the Continental Army, with Ethan Allen, to a victory at Fort Ticonderoga.

"A man signs a shovel / And so he digs": these lines refer to one of Marcel Duchamp's readymades, a snow shovel with the words "In Advance of the Broken Arm" written thereon.

XLI Ira Hayes (1923–1955): Pima Indian war hero, one of the soldiers who raised the American flag on Iwo Jima in 1945, as portrayed in a famous (staged) photograph. He later died of alcoholism and exposure on the Pima reservation.

XLVII William Bonney is the real name of the outlaw Billy the Kid.

XLVIII Francis Marion: Revolutionary War hero and specialist in guerrilla tactics, also known as the Swamp Fox.

LI Gus Cannon (1883–1979): banjoist, jug player, and songwriter. He wrote the song "Walk Right In," later quoted from in "Things to Do in Anne's Room," in *In the Early Morning Rain.*

LII "It is a human universe" refers to Charles Olson's essay "Human Universe." Richard White was a poet whom Ted knew in Tulsa and with whom he discussed Olson's work.

LXI Big Bill Broonzy (1893–1958): musician, one of the seminal figures of the Chicago blues.

LXX Ted's translation of Rimbaud's "Le Bateau Ivre," quoted from throughout the book, is finally used in its entirety here.

LXXX Louis Sullivan (1856–1924): major American architect. See also the poem "String of Pearls" in *Nothing for You.* The building referred to is probably the Bayard Building on Bleecker Street, in Manhattan.

LXXXI Huddie Ledbetter: real name of the great folksinger Leadbelly (1885–1949). Lonnie Johnson (1894–1970): blues guitarist. Hans Hofmann (1880–1960): American abstract expressionist, influential painter and teacher, originator of the theory of "push-pull."

According to Ron Padgett (in a letter to me), Ted saw Lonnie Johnson "perform at Folk City in the early 1960s and was quite bowled over by him. There was a great moment when, near the end of a long set, Victoria Spivey leaped onto the bandstand wearing a tight white dress covered with dark rubber snakes and did several stunning numbers with Johnson."

Great Stories of the Chair

THE SECRET LIFE OF FORD MADOX FORD

The manuscript source is a folder retained by Ted until his death. The sequence has never been published in a book until now.

The Secret Life of Ford Madox Ford comprises poems first published over the course of two issues of "C" *(A Journal of Poetry)*. Volume 1, no. 8 (April 1964) contains *The Secret Life of Ford Madox Ford* as three poems: "Stop Stop Six" (the first poem of the sequence as finalized), "Then I'd Cry" (omitted from the final sequence), and "Fauna Time" (the third poem of the final sequence). The same issue contains, as a separate poem, "Reeling Midnight" (the second poem of the final sequence), dedicated "to Pierre Reverdy." Volume 1, no. 9 (Summer Etc. 1964) contains *The Rest of the Secret Life of Ford Madox Ford*, composed of "On His Own" (our fourth poem), "The Dance of the Broken Bomb" (fifth poem), "Putting Away" (seventh poem), "Owe" (sixth poem), and "We Are Jungles" (eighth poem).

These poems are transliterations from Pierre Reverdy's *Quelques Poèmes*, which had previously inspired Ron Padgett's own transliterative work, *Some Bombs*. As he says in "Interview with Barry Alpert" (in *Talking in Tranquility*), Ted decided to duplicate Padgett's process himself. Ted states: "Ron's French is pretty good whereas my French is quite low, not very good at all. So when I went through and did the same thing Ron did, my poems are slower and heavier than Ron's. They have a lot more direct highly conscious meaning relating to the specific circumstances I was in—which is all obscured in the versions themselves but you can get the feeling, the feeling is very heavy. They were very negative poems; I was very angry."

In a letter to me, Padgett states that part 8, "We Are Jungles," may have been influenced by an early poem by David Shapiro called "We Are Gentle."

Padgett's *Some Bombs* also inspired the following poem of Ted's:

POEM IN HONOR OF SOME BOMBS

Ron Padgett a ton ses quelques poemes
a dix Pierre Reverdy a homage de "patsee"
et la distinction et erudition au cul de chaud
pour le "je ne sais pas" (shrug shrug). Et voila!
Ici est grotesque dans la albee de R K O tres beeg beeg
And les underwear des some jeunes filles a giant significance
pour Ronald et Edmund (je n'ai pas Doubts).

Also: fragMENT des Patsee de Christine egalite la "kill
Chrissie Beak
Making Teresa dans la nuit de bete noire et "It is a big *Red*
House." Homage a Blaise Cendrars mais no je ne read pas
Some Poems of his. So what. Vie doux la tant pis
et pix frank sur la table pour la sensible the pun
(pode bal) (see a pneu from Marchand baby whoop whoop
hobbyhorse!

Let us stay with what we know / quelle Ronald
est la fraisne toute hot and "way out west!" / that
Ted Berrigan mais jeune filles oui oui en flagrant delicto e'toil
dans la SONNETS: "mon grand reve une stabs dans mon Coeur
(blanks)."
/ That Chrissie est a Patsee est a Chris est Beatrice est Sandra est
Kenneth est Frank est John / et Ronald et Ted throwing je t'aime a
tout la monde / Out.

GREAT STORIES OF THE CHAIR

Also published as *Situations* #7, New York City, 1998.

One may speculate as to why *Great Stories of the Chair* wasn't published in a book. Perhaps it, like *The Secret Life of Ford Madox Ford*, was too "heavy" for both *Many Happy Returns* and *In the Early Morning Rain*. Ted preferred a purer air, and he may have seen "heaviness" and "anger" as a kind of sentimentality. There was a point, a few years later, when Ted deliberately cultivated sentimentality (see such poems as "Peace" and "Grey Morning" in *In the Early Morning Rain* and "Things to Do in Providence" in *Red Wagon*), but the attempt was more to formalize feeling than to be dominated by it. As Ted often said, he was a formalist.

Mother Cabrini Mother Cabrini (1850–1917), an American nun, founded the Missionary Sisters of the Sacred Heart of Jesus.

The Sunset Motel In the *Situations* chapbook, which reprints the sequence as published in *Angel Hair* 4, the fourth poem is called "The Sunset Hotel." Ted made a change from "Hotel" to "Motel" on a manuscript photocopied from *Angel Hair* 4, and we have retained the change.

Klein's, a New York City department store, was located at Union Square. The original reference—and much of the material in "The Sunset Motel"—is from the poem "For You," written in the early 60s and first published in *Many Happy Returns*.

What's the Racket "Ode to the Confederate Dead" refers to Allen Tate's poem. When young, Ted paid attention to poets such as Tate, William Empson, Richard Eberhart, Richard Wilbur, Theodore Roethke, Delmore Schwartz, and Conrad Aiken, to whom he sent a copy of *The Sonnets* (and who replied critically but at some length). Ted first came to poetry through anthologies and also recordings of poets reading their work (he did a hilariously nasal imitation of Empson reading "Missing Dates").

The Conscience of a Conservative The title refers to Senator Barry Goldwater's book by the same name, published in 1960. "Spuyten Duyvil" is a town outside New York.

Some Trips to Go On "Clear the Range" refers to Ted's novel *Clear the Range* (New York: Adventures in Poetry/Coach House South, 1977), probably in process at the time.

A Letter from Dick Gallup "Furtive Days" is the title of a collaborative novel by Ted and Ron Padgett, an excerpt from which was published in *Bean Spasms*.

A BOKE

The first book publication of this poem was in *So Going Around Cities.*

Boke is an early spelling of *book.* Joe Brainard published Ted's poem "Living with Chris" (see *Many Happy Returns*), illustrated by himself, under his imprint, Boke Press.

As stated in the introduction, though Ted dates "A Boke" as being from 1966 in *So Going Around Cities* (with the epigraph "Poetry."), it was first published in *Kulchur* in the autumn 1965 issue. This probably places its composition just previous to the period when "Tambourine Life" was written, that poem being dated "Oct. 1965–Jan. 1966." Ted referred to "Tambourine Life" as his first long poem, but "A Boke," which is thirteen pages long and a truly bizarre poem, feels like a long poem. It can be seen, on one level, as an abstract realization of the longer form. "Tambourine Life" was followed, within a few years, by long poems such as "Train Ride" and "Memorial Day" (written in collaboration with Anne Waldman), not to mention medium-length poems such as "Things to Do in Providence" and "Things to Do on Speed."

"remember the fragrance of Grandma's kitchen?": Though the balance of the poem is derived from an article by James Dickey in *The New Yorker,* this repeated line was borrowed from William Burroughs. According to Dick Gallup, in a letter to me, "We heard a recording of Burroughs saying the line in his sinister Midwestern drawl."

Many Happy Returns

Published by Ted Wilentz's Corinth Books in 1969. We present the book in its entirety. The cover for the original edition of *Many Happy Returns* was by Joe Brainard.

Some of these poems were published as broadsides; "Living with Chris," as previously noted, was published as a chapbook with illustrations by Joe Brainard (New York: Boke Press, 1968). For a description of all such publications in Ted's oeuvre, as well as all editions of full-length books up to 1998, see *Ted Berrigan: An Annotated Checklist,* ed. Aaron Fischer (New York: Granary Books, 1998).

Personal Poem #2 and **Personal Poem #9** "Personal Poem #2" is Sonnet LXXVI in *The Sonnets,* and "Personal Poem #9" is Sonnet XXXVI (*after Frank O'Hara*).

We've allowed them to be repeated since Ted is presenting a small "set" of four personal poems, and since these two poems are functional in Ted's poetic universe as both sonnets and personal poems. The personal poem (as named) was invented by Frank O'Hara, who has only one poem called "Personal Poem" but makes reference to "my 'I do this I do that' / poems" in "Getting Up Ahead of Someone (Sun)." Ted further systematized the form by adopting the phrase "personal poem" and using numbers, e.g., "Personal Poem #2."

A Personal Memoir of Tulsa, Oklahoma / 1955–60 This poem was first published in *Bean Spasms* (New York: Kulchur Press, 1967), a volume of collaborations with Ron Padgett, illustrated by Joe Brainard. See note on the book *Bean Spasms*.

TAMBOURINE LIFE

"Tambourine Life" is a major poem by any definition. Its inspiration was Ron Padgett's "Tone Arm," first published as a chapbook by Tom Clark's Once Editions in 1966 and subsequently in the collection *Great Balls of Fire* (New York: Holt, Rhinehart & Winston, 1969). "Tambourine Life" resembles "Tone Arm," first of all, in being in numbered sections. Ted also copied Padgett's device of naming different animals throughout the poem, which he referred to as "false continuity," superficial in the sense of creating a surface of design and play. Otherwise, Ted's poem feels opposite to "Tone Arm," being open where "Tone Arm" is difficult. "Tambourine Life" was at first laid out according to the flush-left columnar convention that "Tone Arm" observes. It was after Ted had fifteen or sixteen pages that he began to open up the text, placing it all over the page in an open-field fashion. In "Interview with Barry Alper," he refers to the look of the poem as being akin to that of a "graph or cardiogram." And in "Interview with Tom Clark," he refers to an influence by the painters Hans Hofmann and Joe Brainard on his open-field poetry of this period in the late 60s and early 70s: "In the open poems, I'm taking a cluster of about five words, not all on one line, and putting them up like blocks like Hans Hofmann. In fact that's what I'm influenced by, that push. Joe Brainard I got it from more or less, but it's that push-pull." The obvious poetic influences for the layout of "Tambourine Life" are Frank O'Hara's long poem "Biotherm" and the work of Paul Blackburn.

"Tambourine Life" was anthologized in *The Young American Poets,* ed. Paul Carroll, introduction by James Dickey (Chicago: Big Table Publishing Company, 1968). This was a highly influential anthology that crossed over into both mainstream and avant-garde territories, including poets like Ted, Ron Padgett, Tom Clark, and Anne Waldman, alongside poets like Mark Strand, Louise Gluck, James Tate, and Charles Simic. The publication of this twenty-eight-page poem in such a book made Ted famous, and "Tambourine Life" was his best-known poem for many years.

"(Tuli's)": Tuli Kupferberg, poet and musician, and member of the poetry-rock group The Fugs. The Fugs have maintained a continuous existence since the 60s, with some changes of personnel, but with Kupferberg and poet Ed Sanders remaining constant. At the time of the writing of "Tambourine Life," Ted's friend Lee Crabtree was also one of The Fugs. Ted wrote the lyrics for a Fugs song, called "I'm Doing All Right," with music by Lee Crabtree and Vinny Leary. The song appeared on *The Fugs' Second Album.*

"Thanks to Jack": Jack Kerouac, but also anyone, as one would call anyone "Jack" (like "Bud"). The name Dick, primarily referring to Dick Gallup, is often used similarly but with the sexual nuance.

"Mr. Pierre Loti and his nameless dog": reference to the well-known painting by Henri Rousseau of the French novelist and journalist Pierre Loti (1850–1923), dressed as a Turk, with his dog. Dick Gallup suggests (in a letter to me) that "Tambourine Life" opens with a view of Ted's desk: "a quite elaborate affair with boxes of books and various pictures tacked up here and there. I'm pretty sure he had a copy of the Pierre Loti portrait by R. on the wall."

"THE RUSSIAN REVOLUTION": probably refers to an image of Larry Rivers's enormous (thirty-two-by-fourteen-foot) work titled *The History of the Russian Revolution: From Marx to Mayakovsky* (1965). In Ted's copy of *So Going Around Cities* he has changed the date attached to these words from "circa 1967" to "circa 1965." The Rivers work consists of paintings, photos, drawings, and objects and may have been an influence on "Tambourine Life."

"The apples are red again in Chandler's valley": reference to Kenneth Patchen's poem "The Lute in the Attic." According to Ron Padgett (in a letter to me): "Ted and

I (and others in Tulsa) were infatuated with Patchen's reading of it, to music provided by the Chamber Jazz Sextet, on a record called *Kenneth Patchen*, produced by Cadence Records in the late 1950s."

"John-Cage-Animal-Cracker / Method of Composition": Ted was greatly influenced by John Cage's compositional theories and by his book *Silence*. Although chance methods aren't at play in "Tambourine Life," the poem has the feel of having been "composed" as much as "written," and its white spaces are quick silences which create rhythms that can't be anticipated. See the note on the book *Bean Spasms* for an account of Ted's "An Interview with John Cage."

"LADY BRETT": Not really Lady Brett Ashley of Hemingway's *The Sun Also Rises*, but Brett deBary (later an Asian Studies scholar), with whom Ted hitchhiked to the Berkeley Poetry Conference in 1965.

"like the three pricks / Alice gave / Joe Gould": The portraitist Alice Neel painted a nude of writer and Greenwich Village denizen Joe Gould, in which she endowed him with three penises. Ted wrote a short introduction to a portfolio, including the nude portrait of Gould and also a clothed portrait, which appeared in *Mother* no. 6 (1965). Around the same time Ted wrote an article on Neel's work for *Art News* (published in January 1966).

"Jacques-Louis David": Ted isn't really referring to the nineteenth-century French painter, but to Ted's baby son, David. The words "Jacques-Louis David" create a balance with the words "Mr. Jean-Paul Sartre."

"Dancers / Buildings and / People in the Street": *Dancers, Buildings, and People in the Street* is the title of both an essay and a collection of essays by Edwin Denby. The words function syntactically as themselves but also refer to Denby's title.

"Count Korzybski": Alfred Habdank Korzybski (1879–1950) was a Polish American linguist, whose work Ted had read in 1960. Korzybski's theories hinged on a complete separation between the word and the object it referred to. Ted believed in the theories but claimed that reading Korzybski's books turned one into a crank: "Someone says to you 'The plate fell,' and you say 'The plate didn't fall, you dropped it.' Then they hate you."

"someone I love is dead": Anne Kepler died during the composition of the poem. As described in the poem "People Who Died" in *In the Early Morning*

Rain, she was "killed by smoke-poisoning while playing the flute at the Yonkers Children's Hospital during a fire set by a 16 year old arsonist."

Bean Spasms This painterly, large-scale poem was first published in the collaborative book *Bean Spasms.* George Schneeman had given Ted a handmade book containing a few images, and Ted wrote the poem on the blank parts of the pages. In "An Interview with Barry Alpert," Ted states, "It was an attempt to write a very heavy, palimpsest-like open poem, in which things would be coming up and down at you as well as flitting by very quickly on the page. It's constantly dragging you back even though you are going forward very quickly. It goes around in a lot of circles, it's really a labyrinth, but it's not exhausting because it doesn't really put anything heavy on you, say the way Pound's *Cantos* do. It doesn't act like you're supposed to stop and go read about the Roman Empire in the sixth century, though there are a million literary references in it actually."

Ron Padgett states (in a letter to me) that he wrote short parts of "Bean Spasms."

Frank O'Hara's Question from "Writers and Issues" by John Ashbery This poem contains a misquotation from O'Hara's poem "Biotherm": O'Hara's line, which would be the last line of Ted's poem, is "I am guarding it from mess and measure," not "mess and message." In a personal copy of *Many Happy Returns* Ted changed "message" to "measure"; but he retained the word *message* in subsequent publications of the poem (it is the last section of "An Autobiography in Five Parts" in *In the Early Morning Rain* and is also reprinted in *So Going Around Cities*). Ted was interested in the fact that often when he "appropriated" a text he unconsciously changed it. He considered this tendency to be part of his creative process.

Things to Do in New York City and **10 Things I Do Every Day** These poems mark the first appearance of the things-to-do form in Ted's work. Ted was particularly interested in "10 Things I Do Every Day," a short, formalistic poem which is a condensed presentation of a list (Gary Snyder's "things to do" poems, which list things to do in various world locales, are longer and more casual in form). Ted later used the "list" as a framework for an expansive, discursive poem, opening the space between "items" into a talking, pondering space. This is the technique, for example, of "Things to Do in Providence," in *Red Wagon.*

In the Early Morning Rain

In the Early Morning Rain was published by Cape Goliard in 1970. Ted worked closely with the editor (and filmmaker) Barry Hall on this volume. The cover art and drawings were by George Schneeman.

Hello Most of the text of this poem comes from a postcard (the kind you would find in gas stations); the poem introduces immediately an important strand of the book involving found material. The book itself is a collage of old and new styles, idiosyncratic textual surfaces, translation, collaboration, and a new, transparent lyrical manner. There are a number of open-field lyrics in this volume spinning off the style of "Tambourine Life," which had created a new possibility for a shorter poem. The new style was first realized in *Many Happy Returns,* in such poems as the title poem and "Things to Do in New York (City)." Shorter poems in *In the Early Morning Rain* that further exploit the new style include "American Express," "February Air," "Grey Morning," "Things to Do in Anne's Room," and "Heroin."

80th Congress *In the Early Morning Rain* contains three poems which are explicit collaborations with other poets. The book is, on one level, "about" community, as its dedication, "To my family & friends," implies.

The Circle This is the first of several short meditative poems that appear in the book. See also "It's Important" and "Dial-A-Poem."

***5 New Sonnets:* A Poem** These sonnets are constructed of lines from *The Sonnets* but are not in any way part of the sequence. They are "new" sonnets.

Poem (Seven thousand feet over . . .) First appeared in *A Lily for My Love,* an early chapbook of Ted's. As the chapbook title indicates, this was very sentimental work, and Ted destroyed every copy he could find. He retained "Poem" however, adding the dedication to Bill Berkson because Berkson had said he liked the poem.

Ted left the dedication off in *So Going Around Cities*, but it seems to belong in *In the Early Morning Rain*, which is especially replete with dedications. "Poem" was originally printed under the title "Poem" in *The White Dove Review* 2 (edited by Ron Padgett); the title was subsequently changed to "Grief" in *A Lily for My Love* and then back to "Poem." The poem was written in 1958 under the influence of Kenneth Rexroth's theory of "natural numbers," which posits a short, syllabic line.

Ikonostasis We have inserted the poem "Ikonostasis," not originally published in *In the Early Morning Rain*, between "Presence" and "The Upper Arm." Ted had found it difficult to choose between "Ikonostasis" and "Presence," both obviously influenced by John Ashbery's *The Tennis Court Oath*, but was certain a choice was necessary. That choice doesn't seem to matter so much now. "Ikonostasis" was later published in *So Going Around Cities*.

The Upper Arm The second-to-last line originally read "bows that spell" not "boughs that spell." It is difficult for the tongue to gauge which pronunciation of "bows" to use when reading the poem aloud, so Ted changed the spelling to "boughs" for *So Going Around Cities*.

Corridors of Blood Structured somewhat similarly to "Rusty Nails," this poem employs language drawn from Simone de Beauvoir's diaries. Ted admired de Beauvoir's work—and her life lived—but was fascinated, in the case of this poem, by the flatness of the language of translation, how the diaries sounded after being translated from French to English.

Rusty Nails Ted composed this work by taking lines from various books by other authors, then assigning to them, in a completely automatic fashion, titles from a list given him by Ron Padgett. In "An Interview with Barry Alpert," he says "I meant "Rusty Nails" to be like a novel; each one of those things is a chapter."

LIFE OF A MAN

This sequence of poems, transliterated from Giuseppe Ungaretti's *Vita di un uomo*, first appeared in *Bean Spasms* in a different order and with the omission of

"Tonight" and "Joy of Shipwrecks." Two poems from the earlier version, "Long Time No See" and Que Sera Sera," were discarded from this second version.

Life Among the Woods First published in *Bean Spasms*, this prose work is a giddy mistranslation from a French grammar book for children.

In Three Parts and **In 4 Parts** These two poems, influenced by John Giorno's treatment of found materials, were first published in *Bean Spasms.*

AN AUTOBIOGRAPHY IN 5 PARTS

This work, made entirely of found materials, was first published in Bill Berkson's magazine/anthology *Best & Co.* in 1969. In that presentation, there were headings beneath the overall title corresponding to each of the five sections: "Childhood," "Army Life," "Dope Scene," "Manners," and "Poetry." Ted omitted the headings from *In the Early Morning Rain.*

March 17th, 1970 Ted had become interested in the "occasional" poem. The occasion for this poem is St. Patrick's Day; the poem addresses what that holiday might mean to an Irish American who both liked and disliked "Irish-American-ness."

Epithalamion First published in *Bean Spasms.*

Poop First published in *Bean Spasms.*

February Air The poem originally did not repeat the last line, "You'd Better Move On" (from a Rolling Stones song). The repetition was added in *So Going Around Cities*, in which this poem appears in the section called *Many Happy Returns.*

Black Power Much of this poem is incorporated into the poem "Bean Spasms."

The Ten Greatest Books of the Year (1967) This list poem, which originally did not appear in *In the Early Morning Rain*, has been inserted before "The Ten

Greatest Books of the Year, 1968." The poem was first published in *So Going Around Cities.*

interstices and **bent** These are the first one-word poems published by Ted. The avowed influence is Aram Saroyan, whose book of minimal poems, *Aram Saroyan,* had been published in 1968.

The Great Genius This poem originally read as follows: "The Great Genius is / A man who can do the / Average thing when everybody / Else is going crazy." Ted rewrote the poem in his personal copy of the book, and we have used the rewritten version.

Poem for Philip Whalen Ted made a handful of punctuational changes in this poem, in his personal copy of the book, all of which we have incorporated.

Anti-War Poem This is one of Ted's few overtly political poems. The "anti-war poem" seemed a necessary form in the late 60s. Ted's version refers to a personal war ("I thought a lot about dying / But I said *Fuck it*") as well as to the American war in Vietnam. In "An Interview with Ralph Hawkins" *(Talking in Tranquility),* Ted states: "I think that every single poem I've ever written is a political act. They were all written in the face of a complete desire of the state in the platonic sense to exclude me as a poet, the entire possibility that there is of being a poet. I don't believe the state as the body politic can exist in a healthy manner without poetry and without poems. Every poem I write is a political act and I have written some specific political poems, but generally the subject matter of politics is not interesting to write about. I'm totally interested in it as take-in, as material."

Dial-A-Poem Around 1969 John Giorno ran a telephone service called Dial-A-Poem, which one could call in order to listen to a poet reading a poem. In this poem, the telephone dial becomes the wheel of life: one's sexuality is an aspect of the poem one dials "this time around."

Hall of Mirrors The title refers to Robert Stone's novel *A Hall of Mirrors.*

Ann Arbor Song As Ted took to writing shorter poems as seriously as he had composed his longer works, he also began to consolidate a public-reading style and to consider more how to bring pleasure to a live audience. *The Sonnets* and "Tambourine Life," while they read well aloud, were unwieldy for public readings. In *In the Early Morning Rain* there are a handful of works which remained among his public-reading favorites, "Ann Arbor Song" being one. He also liked, for reading aloud, the poems "Heroin" and "People Who Died."

People Who Died Ted considered that with this work he had invented a form which anyone might use to write a poem. That is, every person has a list of "people who died." Jim Carroll took Ted at his word and wrote and recorded a song called "People Who Died," which is his own list of dead friends.

Telegram This poem is based on Marcel Duchamp's 1953 telegram to Francis Picabia as Picabia was dying: "Francis à Bientôt." "Francis, see you soon."

Train Ride

Train Ride was first published by Annabel Levitt's Vehicle Editions in 1978, although the book itself bears only the 1971 date (of composition): the copyright page reads "copyright Ted Berrigan 1971." *Train Ride* had cover art by Joe Brainard.

Ted had some difficulty converting the handwritten notebook into a correspondingly presented typewritten poem; Ted and Annabel Levitt worked hard at layout for the edition. Open-field poems always posed publication problems, and Ted was finicky. The pleasurable exigencies of these kinds of translations, from handwriting to typescript and from typescript to print, seem to have disappeared with the advent of the computer. Ted was a poet of the notebook and typewriter; the medium he wrote in always permeated the poem. It is arguable that what I call, in the introduction, Ted's "graven-ness"—that quality by which each word seems etched into the page, cannot be easily obtained if one composes on the computer.

The writing of *Train Ride* was occasioned by the circumstance that Ted had an empty notebook and was sitting on a train from New York to Providence, but also by the circumstance that he was reading a gay pornographic novel that Joe Brainard had given him back in New York. The poem is thus "about" the fact of the train—passengers and how they look and talk, what's out the window, etc.; the fact of the notebook—Ted actually leaves blank pages for Brainard (to whom the poem is addressed) to fill in words if he wishes; and sex—the pornographic novel provokes a long meditation on "fucking," a word that is repeated many times. Sex eventually segues into love, and Ted expresses his love for his friend Joe; but there is another subject in the poem, as immediate as sex/love, the notebook, the train, which is money. Ted has hardly any money in his pocket: he will get off the train with four dollars and spend most of it on a cab. *Train Ride* is a poem written exactly in the now moment, about who is there, both materially and in mind, and what is urgent. By the early 70s Ted had become quite adept at this kind of in-the-instant work.

Memorial Day

Memorial Day was published twice as a chapbook, once in 1971 by the Poetry Project, in mimeo format, and once in 1974 by Aloes Books, London (editors Jim Pennington, Allen Fisher, and Dick Miller). For the Poetry Project edition, Anne Waldman and Ted ran off copies for the occasion of the May 1971 reading mentioned in the introduction. Donna Dennis did the original cover art, which was reproduced in facsimile in the Aloes Books edition. *Memorial Day* was reprinted in *So Going Around Cities*.

"I dreamed you brought home a baby": One of Ted's and Anne Waldman's intentions in *Memorial Day* was to include other voices. This sonnet by me, designated by the number "22" and beginning with the line "I dreamed you brought home a baby" is number 22 of a sonnet sequence called *165 Meeting House Lane* (New York: "C" Press, 1971).

"having met the man at the Met": In this convoluted passage written by Ted, the "man" is Frank O'Hara, "Joe" is Frank's partner Joe LeSueur, and Vincent is Frank's lover, Vincent Warren.

"It is night. You are asleep. & beautiful tears": This is Sonnet XXXVII from *The Sonnets*.

"I doan wanna hear any more about that . . . I tried my best to do my father's will": One of the rules for the performance was that Ted and Anne Waldman would each have to sing one of their sections. Waldman sang the passage beginning "I doan wanna hear anymore about/that"; and Ted sang the passage beginning "I tried my best to do my father's will," which was modeled on the song "Talking Casey" by Mississippi John Hurt.

During the time that Ted was co-writing *Memorial Day*, he was listening obsessively to two record albums, Mississippi John Hurt's *Today!* (which contained "Talking Casey") and an album by the Byrds. His composition process involved being interactive with the music, as if there were something about "voice" he wanted to get from actual singing. And the finished poem is for alternating voices, Waldman's arrangement of the text alternating sections by the two of them.

"The windows are closed": The final litany, written by Ted, was read by the two poets in voices alternating for each phrase ending with "is closed." After the reading at the Poetry Project, Ted obtained a copy of the tape and listened to it as obsessively as he had to the John Hurt and Byrds albums. He continued to learn from this collaboration for many years and in the early 80s occasionally asked me to read the final litany with him, as a separate piece, at poetry readings.

Short Poems

IN A BLUE RIVER

As explained in the introduction, this chapbook was first published by Susan Cataldo's Little Light Books in 1981. The majority of the poems were written in the late 60s and early 70s. The dedication is to Kenneth Koch, whom Ted credited for having first interested him in the short poem as a form. The cover art for the original edition was by Susan Cataldo.

Four poems have been omitted here and kept elsewhere. "After Breakfast," which originally appeared in *In a Blue River* after "Chair," has already been printed in the *Life of a Man* section in *In the Early Morning Rain*. "The Green Sea" and "Angst," which originally appeared one right after the other after "Connecticut," have also been omitted. "The Green Sea" is placed instead in *Nothing for You*, and "Angst" in *A Certain Slant of Sunlight*, where the editors feel that each is more necessary in "making a book." "People of the Future," which originally appeared after "Paris Review," has been retained as the italicized introductory poem to *Nothing for You*, where it obviously serves an indispensable function.

Salut! This poem was composed spontaneously, on the tongue, for the birthday of novelist C. D. B. Bryan, at a party in Iowa City in 1969. Ted recited it to me at the party, and I instantly memorized it. Later when Ted was working on the manuscript of *In a Blue River* in 1981, I reminded him of the poem by reciting it to him. I'm not sure he had written it down before or given it a title.

Man Alone "Man Alone" was originally the back cover copy for Ted's novel *Clear the Range*. The poem is indicative of the texture and manner of Ted's novel.

bear with me Ted had considered calling the chapbook *Bear With Me* but decided against it, keeping this untitled poem.

Category / MOONDOG The late, eccentric composer called Moondog was well-known to New Yorkers in the 60s and 70s. Tall, long-braided, wearing a Viking hat and lederhosen, he stood in the Times Square area publicizing and selling his compositions, which were all strict canons. In the later part of his life his work actually began to be performed and recorded in Europe and America.

Buddhist Text Ted strongly identified with the elephant as a totemic animal.

Setback This poem, originally written in England in 1974, had for a title "Setback: Che." The third line read, "Che was wounded in the foot" instead of "He was wounded in the foot."

Kinks In the 70s, Ted was asked to write a poem about the British rock group the Kinks for a special "Kinks" issue of the *Milk Quarterly*, edited by Peter Kostakis. This poem was Ted's contribution.

Near the Ocean The poem obviously refers to Robert Lowell's book by the same name and is about reading Lowell's book in bed, though it might also refer to being in bed with a crabby partner. This is one of several references to Lowell in Ted's poetry. Though Ted could not help having a smart mouth, he respected and admired Lowell and his work.

(Untitled) It's Morning! *In a Blue River* contains an untitled (undemarcated) sequence of poems, written in 1979, composed of "Untitled (It's Morning!)," "Air," "Untitled*(Keep my . . .)," "Amsterdam," "A True Story," "On St. Mark's Place," "Just Friends," and "For Rosina." Ted participated in the One World poetry festival in Amsterdam in 1978 and during the same trip collaborated with the Swiss artist Rosina Kühn on a set of poems / paintings. These poems are his texts from that collaboration.

UNCOLLECTED SHORT POEMS

Laments, Winter, Think of Anything, Out the Second-Floor Window, and **Life in the Future** These five poems were first printed in *So Going Around Cities*. The remaining poems in this section have never been printed in books and were kept in manuscript folders. Most of the poems date from between 1968 and 1972.

Think of Anything In this collaboration with Robert Creeley, the "Rose of Sharon" refers to a woman named Sharon DeVries, and "Grand Valley" is Grand Valley, Michigan, where Ted and Creeley were participating in a poetry festival.

Poem (to Tom Clark) Ted's poetry tended to have a communal focus, even be a communal activity (the collaborations, the dedications and personal references). The short epigrammatic poem is traditionally amenable to this focus. The short poem may also "speak to" a particular person, on the grounds that that person will understand it. "Poem (to Tom Clark)," which is a list of titles by Evelyn Waugh, is dedicated to Clark because he would "get it," but also because Tom Clark's name contributes another name to a texture of title and name.

Untitled (Orange Black / BACK DEATH) This little poem refers to a collaborative collage by Ted and Joe Brainard, dominated by the colors orange and black and the words BACK DEATH. Ted was the possessor of the collage for many years, before passing it on to the late Michael Scholnick. A number of his poems are, or contain, considerations, descriptions, meditations on the artwork hanging on the walls surrounding him as he wrote. His art collection provided both environment (points of concrete reference) and iconic presences, and he was very deliberate about exploiting it in his poetry.

Congratulations Lee Lally, poet Michael Lally's wife, had just given birth to their son, Miles.

Neal Cassady Talk An imitation of the speech of Neal Cassady, on whom the character Dean Moriarty, in Kerouac's *On the Road*, was modeled. In the 60s Ted had briefly spent time with Cassady. The poem was written in the late 70s for the mimeo rag *Caveman*, a scandalous erratic publication with a complicated history, which satirized Lower East Side and Poetry Project activities and figures.

Inflation The manuscript copy is dated "Apr 74."

Flying United This poem is used in its entirety as the last two lines of the poem "Chicago English Afternoon" in *Easter Monday*. In the latter the words are run together to make long lines, and part of their effect is to provide an "exit" from a complexly textured eighteen-line poem. This short, gracefully spaced poem uses the same words, taken from the bland language of public spaces, to create a spooky moment.

The D.A. The manuscript copy of the poem is dated "5 Mar 82." *The Digger's Game* is a novel by George V. Higgins.

Song The opening quotation is from Lew Welch's "Chicago Poem" (*Ring of Bone: Collected Poems 1950–1971* [Bolinas, Calif.: Grey Fox Press, 1979]). One recognizes the line "bear with me" again in this poem.

Red Wagon

Red Wagon was published in Chicago by the Yellow Press, whose editors included Richard Friedman, Darlene Pearlstein, Art Lange, and Peter Kostaskis. The cover was by Rochelle Kraut.

She A translation/adaptation from the French poet Paul Eluard.

3 Pages This is a transcription of Ted's words from a set of three black-and-white silkscreen collaborations with George Schneeman.

Conversation "Conversation" is actually a collaboration by Ted and me and first appeared under my name in my book *Phoebe Light* (Bolinas, Calif.: Big Sky, 1973). It was part of an unfinished project of imitations that would each be attributed to the imitated poet, in this case John Giorno. Ted's contribution to the collaboration consisted of selecting and offering to me the two sentences to be Giorno-ized: Giorno had recently added an intense, formal repetition to his style. The sentences were remembered from a conversation Ted had once had with Frank O'Hara, in which O'Hara spoke admiringly of the first sentence of William Saroyan's *The Adventures of Wesley Jackson* but misquoted the sentence. The actual "conversation" of the poem is between the two sentences (between O'Hara and Saroyan), though there is an implied conversation between O'Hara and Ted (and between Ted and me, as well as between us and John Giorno). The layout and line arrangement are entirely by me, and I unconsciously scored the poem for my voice.

Sunday Morning This poem, referring by title to the lovely song by the Velvet Underground, is completely antithetical to that song's spirit, being constructed out of rather vulgar language from postcards.

Something Amazing Just Happened The long-lined exuberant style of this poem, and of "Farewell Address," was never really repeated in Ted's work.

In the Wheel The Wheel was a coffee shop in Ann Arbor, Michigan. The poem plays on the Buddhist notion of the wheel of death and rebirth.

Wind "Wind" was inspired by a small painting by Larry Rivers that hung on the wall of Bill Berkson's East Tenth Street apartment in New York, circa 1970. The painting was abstract, with bright colors against a black background. Thus "the angels" which "emerge from the rivers" are the colors listed; and "rivers" refers both to the dark ground of the painting and to Larry Rivers himself.

Things to Do on Speed This poem was constructed out of an article about speed and speed freaks that appeared in the *New York Times* Sunday magazine in the summer of 1970. Ted and I were supposedly speed freaks, and he was struck by the chasm that lay between journalistic language and our—anyone's—reality. He doctored, simplified, idiomized, and generally played with the text, converting it into his new favorite form, the longer "things to do" poem. His version is infinitely better than the magazine article, funnier and more condensed, humanizing, and pleasing to the ear.

Farewell Address The poem was inspired by Ron Padgett's "Homage to Max Jacob" in *Great Balls of Fire.*

Three Sonnets and a Coda for Tom Clark This work is constructed out of lines and phrases from *In the Early Morning Rain* and was written at the time of that book's publication in 1970. It is both a homage to the book and a meditation on the time and experience it covers.

Wishes "Wishes," as well as "I Used to Be but Now I Am," are the first of a number of poems that Ted wrote following forms devised by Kenneth Koch for teaching poetry writing to children, students, old people, people in nursing homes, hospitals, etc. The source for these two list forms was Koch's *Wishes, Lies, and Dreams.*

Scorpion, Eagle & Dove (A Love Poem) The symbolism in the title, which is associated with the astrological sign Scorpio (the natal sign of all the people listed in the poem), is based on a reading of John Jocelyn's *Meditations on the Signs of the Zodiac.* See also the poem "Scorpio" in this section, and the prefatory note to *A Certain Slant of Sunlight.* Astrology was famously a 60s preoccupation, but had also been important in French Surrealist circles. Ted had translated the "Scorpion" section of *Miroir d'astrologie* by Max Jacob and Claude Valence.

Things to Do in Providence One of Ted's most well-known poems, "Things to Do in Providence" was written in a notebook in 1970. Ted studied it for several months before typing it up, being in a slight quandary as to whether or not it was a poem, in that form. The "situation" in the poem is a visit to Providence, Rhode

Island, where Ted's mother, Peggy (Dugan) Berrigan, lived and where his grandmother, Alice Clifford, was dying in a nursing home. This poem is probably the apex of Ted's experiments with open sentiment; sentiment later became more embedded, layered in. The poem is not "sentimental," being formalistic (the "things to do" grid) and is infused with different kinds of language, quotidian event, and tones of voice. Lines from the poem toward the end, after "The heart stops briefly when someone dies," are often quoted by both poets and non-poets.

Frank O'Hara The six poems from "Frank O'Hara" through "Buddha on the Bounty" are best considered as belonging together, though they aren't marked as a sequence in *Red Wagon*. Originally part of a disbanded sequence called *Southampton Winter* (along with the poem "Galaxies," in *Nothing for You*), they tend to be more discursive than sonnets (though "Chinese Nightingale" and "Buddha on the Bounty" are each fourteen lines long). The source of material was largely Ted's own words: poems by him and also lines and phrases drawn from a handmade book, which he had filled with as much writing as possible in order to cull lines from later. The poem "Frank O'Hara" contains lines from Ted's translation of Jean Cocteau's poem "*La Mort de Guillaume Apollinaire*."

I Used To Be but Now I Am A number of poems have been omitted from *Red Wagon* so that they could be included in *Easter Monday*. They consist of the following titles, which, in the order given, originally appeared after the poem "I Used To Be but Now I Am": "Old-Fashioned Air," "Chicago Morning," "Newtown," "The End," "Chicago English Afternoon," "From a List of Delusions of the Insane, What They Are Afraid Of," "Late November," "Quarter to Three," "She (Not to be confused with she, a girl)," "Sister Moon," "Four Gates to the City," "L.G.T.T.H.," "In Blood," "Peking," "Soviet Souvenir," "So Going Around Cities," and "Picnic."

There was a set of five of *The Sonnets* originally included in *Red Wagon*, after the poem "Picnic." They were XXXIV, LXXXI, LXVII, LXV, LVI, and LXXVII, XXXIV and LXXVII being published then for the first time.

The Complete Prelude The version which originally appeared in *Red Wagon* was titled "THE COMPLETE PRELUDE: Title Not Yet Fixed Upon." The dedication in the earlier version read "for Clark," and there were stanzas instead of numbered sections. The later version in *So Going Around Cities* had the dedication "for Clark Coolidge," which we have retained with the addition of a further dedication, "& for my mother," which he had added in his own copy of *So Going Around Cities.* Ted's mother was conceived of as the woman in the lines in the third part "& shall continue evermore to make / & shall perform to exalt and to refine / Inspired, celestial presence ever pure / From all the sources of her former strength."

Easter Monday

As explained in the introduction, the manuscript source is a folder which Ted worked with until shortly before his death. Though he had largely finished writing the individual poems in 1977, he didn't achieve the final sequence until 1983.

The first four poems originated in Chicago between 1972 and 1973. The subsequent twenty-one poems were written in England between 1973 and 1974. "So Going Around Cities" dates from Chicago, summer 1975. Most of the others were written in New York, except for "Boulder" and "Picnic," which were originally written in Boulder, Colorado, in 1975, when Ted was a guest teacher at the Naropa Institute. The final four poems date from 1977.

According to a notebook kept in England, Ted had originally considered including the following poems in the sequence: the "Southampton Winter" series of poems (see note on "Frank O'Hara" in *Red Wagon*); "The Complete Prelude" (in *Red Wagon*); "Brigadoon," "New Personal Poem," "Baltic Stanzas," "Other Contexts," "Communism," "The Green Sea," and "Service at Upwey" (in *Nothing for You*). There are other titles listed, but those poems seem to have disappeared.

Chicago Morning Dedicated to the painter Philip Guston, the poem invokes the industrial density of Chicago, and also the political feeling of the early 70s: "The president of the United States / And the Director of the FBI stand over / A dead mule." From the sentence beginning "A huge camel" through " 'The Fop's Tunic' " the poem more or less describes two drawings by Guston, which were printed in *CHICAGO*, a magazine I edited. Guston had by now made his celebrated style change, and his work was replete with Ku Klux Klan–like figures ("The Fop's Tunic"). The manuscript copy of the poem is dated "Jan 1972 Chi."

The End From the line "He / Encourages criticism" through "beneath his spell" the reference is to Ezra Pound, who had recently died. These lines also contain material from Ted's translation of Cocteau's "*La Mort de Guillaume Apollinaire.*"

Newtown "Wildly singing in the mountains with cancer of the spine" refers to Arthur Waley, the translator and Sinologist.

Method Action The poem is atypically textured for the sequence, being like "Boulder" and "Picnic" in an open-field arrangement. It was written in Chicago and appeared in *CHICAGO* 5, no. 1 (Nov. 1972).

Swinburne & Watts-Dunton This is the first of the poems in the sequence written in England, in this case in Putney, London. The title refers to Algernon Swinburne and Theodore Watts-Dunton, British poets and literary figures. Watts-Dunton took care of Swinburne when his health was poor (due to both epilepsy and excess) and restored him; the poet here seems to become both men.

Old-fashioned Air Written in Battersea, London, and dedicated to the musician Lee Crabtree, "Old-Fashioned Air" is unique in the sequence in being in Ted's personal, speaking voice. What the poem never says is that Lee Crabtree has just committed suicide in New York (summer of 1973). The poem is, rather, an address to a friend's living presence.

The Ancient Art of Wooing Written in Wivehoe, Essex, where the remainder of the British portion of the sequence was composed.

At Loma Linda This poem is composed largely of language taken from British daytime television. However, Loma Linda is the hospital in California where my father, Albert Notley, had a medical checkup in 1973 or 1974 (he died in 1975). See "Crossroads," in *Nothing for You*, for a different version of the poem.

L. G. T. T. H. These letters stand for "Let's Go to the Hop" (title of a popular song from the 50s) and refer to the Frank O'Hara poem "At the Old Place," which contains, almost but not quite, the same set of initials: "Button's buddy lips frame L G T TH O P?"—the letters in that case standing for "Let's go to the Old Place."

From A List of the Delusions of the Insane, What They Are Afraid Of This sonnet is composed of lines from David Antin's longer work, *A List of the Delusions of the Insane What They Are Afraid of.*

She (Not to be confused with she, a girl) The poem is made from Ted's much longer jacket copy written for Anne Waldman's book *Baby Breakdown.*

Innocents Abroad This is a notably obscure work, and many of the references are simply private. One sees that the word "(Change)" comes at the end of the eighth line, a point of change in the traditional sonnet. The poem is operating on a level of abstraction and reflection in which the sonnet form and personal experience become highly compressed together. There are no sentences, and few signals. The poem is dedicated to the British translator and scholar Gordon Brotherston.

Sister Moon and **An Orange Clock** As Ted's friends grew further away geographically, he talked to them by reading their poems and writing responses such as these. "Sister Moon" is an engagement with the work of Clark Coolidge, as the poem that follows it, "An Orange Clock," is an engagement with the work of Tom Clark.

Gainsborough *Easter Monday* is sometimes under the influence of the music of Bob Dylan. This is more a matter of tone and diction than of specific reference. You can hear it in poems like "Gainsborough" (and also in "The Joke & the Stars," "Excursion & Visitation," and "So Going Around Cities").

Four Gates to the City This poem is dated "1974" on the manuscript. It contains lines by Tom Clark, Ron Padgett, Martha and the Vandellas, and the French poet Théophile Gautier (1811–1872). Ted and Gordon Brotherston had translated two of Gautier's poems, "*L'Art*" and "*Préface,*" from *Emaux et camées* (Enamels and Cameos). The reference to Goethe's "divan at Weimar" is from "*L'Art.*"

In Blood The poem is composed largely of words from my poems, notably a sonnet sequence entitled *Great Interiors, Wines & Spirits of the World.* The closing line, however, is from Frank O'Hara's poem "Cambridge"; in O'Hara's poem the line refers to Boris Pasternak.

So Going Around Cities This, the longest poem of the sequence, signals a return to the United States. It was written in Chicago, circa 1974–1975 and is dedicated, and addressed, to "Doug & Jan Oliver." Douglas Oliver, the late British poet, was a student at the University of Essex where Ted taught from 1973 to 1974. He is one of the three dedicatees of the book *So Going Around Cities.* The title phrase (of both the poem and the book) is from the poem "Rivers and Mountains" by John Ashbery. The refrain of lines beginning with the words "I traded" owes a debt to the song "City Singer" by musician / songwriter Larry Estridge.

Narragansett Park From this poem onward all the poems in the sequence were written in New York City at 101 St. Mark's Place.

A Note from Yang-Kuan We have made a handful of changes from texts as presented in *So Going Around Cities,* based on Ted's final manuscript of the sequence. In "A Note from Yang-Kuan," in the eighth line, a comma has been removed after the word "And." In the same poem, in the twelfth line, the phrase "The poor" has been amended to "Tho poor." "Yang-Kuan" is a place-name in a poem by the Chinese poet Wang Wei and also occurs in my poem "After Wang Wei."

Everybody Seemed So Laid Back in the Park Constructed from prose sentences by Bernadette Mayer.

A Meeting at the Bridge We have made punctuation changes from the version in *So Going Around Cities,* consistent with Ted's final manuscript copy. The changes are too complicated to describe, but they occur in the third stanza and last couplet.

"I Remember" A sonnet composed of lines from Joe Brainard's opus *I Remember.*

To Himself After Giacomo Leopardi's "A *se stesso,*" "To Himself" is the result of a lengthy process of translation involving several people. In the *Easter Monday* folder Ted has appended the following notes to the poem: "trans by Ted Berrigan from prose version by George Schneeman & poem version worked at by Berrigan & Engl. trans, poet, & Latin American specialist Gordon Brotherston."

Whitman in Black One of Ted's most widely anthologized poems, this sonnet, inspired by the crime novelist Ross MacDonald, turns the, or a, poet into both a criminal and a detective, invoking Whitman for corroboration. The MacDonald source is *On Crime Writing* (Santa Barbara, Calif.: Capra Press, 1973).

Heloise Dated "27 Aug 77" in the final manuscript. Ted wrote "Heloise" after reading Helen Waddell's novel *Abelard.*

From the House Journal Dated "30 Aug 77" in the final manuscript, this poem is composed of lines beginning with the pronoun "I," taken from the index of first lines and titles in *The Collected Poems of Frank O'Hara.*

Visits from a Small Enigma Written using Jim Brodey's words, this poem is dated "31 Aug 77" in the final manuscript.

Revery Reverdy. That is, this poem uses language translated from the poetry of Pierre Reverdy.

My Tibetan Rose This final poem in the sequence is dated "1 Sept. 77." It was written after Ted read Lionel Davidson's thriller *The Rose of Tibet.*

Nothing for You

Published by United Artists (Lewis Warsh and Bernadette Mayer, editors) in 1977. The original front and back cover art for *Nothing for You* was by George Schneeman.

Several poems that originally appeared in the book *Nothing for You* have been omitted from this section and appear elsewhere in this volume. "Poem" ("of morning, Iowa City, blue . . ."), which originally appeared after "Monolith," has been omitted by the editors, since it appears previously in the section *In the Early Morning Rain.* "Method Action," which originally appeared after "*Mi Casa, Su Casa,*" "A Little American Feedback," which originally appeared after "New Personal Poem," and "A Note from Yang Kuan," which originally appeared after "Blue Targets," have been omitted since they were finally included in *Easter Monday.*

A number of the poems in *Nothing for You* were later reprinted in *So Going Around Cities,* with small changes. We have invariably honored the later changes.

Valentine The opening sixteen pages of *Nothing for You* consist of poems written in the early 60s. Ted had continued to tinker with them over the years and was particularly obsessed with "Valentine," "Hearts," and "String of Pearls." "Valentine," as presented here, seems finally perfect, the result of almost twenty years of consideration of twelve lines. In "Valentine" an ellipsis that appeared in the last line in the United Artists publication of *Nothing for You* was removed for publication in *So Going Around Cities* (and here).

Doubts In "Doubts" and in "He," "For Annie Rooney," "Saturday Afternoons on the Piazza," "Prayer," "Night Letter," "Some Do Not," "Autumn's Day," "Truth as History," "Francis à Bientôt," and "New Junket" may be found material that was used in *The Sonnets.* These poems, along with those in *Early Poems,* are source works for that sequence.

Prayer, Night Letter, and **The TV Story** These three early poems printed in *So Going Around Cities* have been added to this "early poems" part of *Nothing for You.* To accommodate these additions more gracefully we have moved the poem "Saturday Afternoons on the Piazza," originally appearing after "Francis à Bientôt," to a position immediately after "For Annie Rooney."

Some Do Not *Some Do Not* is the title of the first volume of Ford Madox Ford's tetrology, *Parade's End.* ("Ford Madox Ford is not a dream" is a recurring line in *The Sonnets.*)

On the Level Everyday This poem originally appeared, in a different version, in *Bean Spasms,* under the title "The Level of Everyday." The second version, rewritten for *Nothing for You,* seems superior to the first. It should be noted that Ted could not help playing with his poems, especially older, less famous ones whose identities were not yet frozen for his audience.

Autumn's Day Rather than being designated *"after Rilke,"* this translation/adaptation was originally attributed to "Rilke (trans. Ted Berrigan)," at the bottom of the poem, in *Nothing for You.*

String of Pearls For its presentation in *So Going Around Cities* Ted removed some in-line spaces from the version originally appearing in *Nothing for You.*

Francis à Bientôt See the note for "Telegram" in *In the Early Morning Rain.*

Cento: A Note on Philosophy This poem did not include the dedication "for Pat Mitchell" in *Nothing for You* but did in *So Going Around Cities.* We have thus kept the dedication.

New Junket *"for Harry Fainlight"*: In a moving obituary for Fainlight written for the Poetry Project *Newsletter* in 1982, Ted states, in regard to meeting Fainlight in 1963: "Harry & I met like two boys in a John Buchan novel; a Yank, with no connotations other than friend on that word, and a Brit, one who as it turned out had American citizenship by birth, but had grown up entirely in England and was Oxford London to the core. . . . We liked one another from the first, like they say, and spent long hours and nights in Ratner's, comparing maps of the worlds of poetry."

***From* The Art of the Sonnet** *The Art of the Sonnet* is a six-part collaborative work written with Tom Clark in New York in 1967. This version consists of numbers 1, 3, and 6; Ted has made changes in parts 3 and 6 in the manuscript copy we retain.

Air Conditioning and **Monolith** These poems were both written in Iowa City circa 1968–1969. They are about Ted's being in his office at the Writers' Workshop, University of Iowa.

London and **London Air** These poems were both written during Ted's first trip to England in the summer of 1969. "London Air" is dedicated to Robert Creeley, who was also in London at the time. This poem, and Creeley's "In London," mark the beginning of their friendship and cross-influence. In "London Air," "My heart Your heart" is a quotation from Frank O'Hara's "Poem" (to Donald M. Allen), transformed in the addition of the capital M and the capital Y. From the beginning of this poem Ted is playing with punctuation, emphasis, pronouns, and linguistic exactitude, in a manner reminiscent of Creeley's but also of poems of his own like "Tambourine Life."

In Bed with Joan & Alex This was, like "London Air," an important poem for Ted at the time of its writing, in this case the fall of 1969 in Ann Arbor, Michigan. As in many of the poems of this period, Ted is alone in his room, and the subject is solitude and what's "around." Though this poem is built on sexual innuendo, it is founded on a room washed with light and color, containing two objects which remind the poet of two people who aren't there. The first object is a shirt, resting on a chair, sewn for Ted by Joan Fagin, a designer and seamstress, at the time married to Larry Fagin; Joan and Larry Fagin had recently visited Ted in Ann Arbor (see "Ann Arbor Song," *In the Early Morning Rain*). The second object is a painting of a Maine cottage by Alex Katz, a small study for a larger work. Ted's poem takes the two objects/presences and sets them into motion in a sort of waltz: "Round & round & round we go," in the words of a Neil Young song that was popular then.

Sweet Vocations In the last line, "its" (in the version in *Nothing for You*) has been changed to "it's" (as in the version in *So Going Around Cities*).

Going to Chicago Like "Black & White Magic," "Going to Chicago" was written on an airplane. When Ted salutes the poet John Sinclair, Sinclair is presumably below in Detroit as the plane passes overhead. Ted had read with Sinclair at the Berkeley Poetry Conference of 1965. At the time of "Going to Chicago" (1969) Sinclair, a political activist, had just been sentenced to ten years in prison for possession of a joint of marijuana. The dedication to "Going to Chicago" originally read "for Donald Hall" in *Nothing for You* and was changed to "for Don Hall" in *So Going Around Cities*. Also the titles in part 2 were not italicized in *Nothing for You*.

How We Live in the Jungle Stanza breaks which originally appeared in *Nothing for You*, after the line ending with "furniture" and the line ending with "a buzz on," were removed for *So Going Around Cities*.

Black & White Magic "*Secret Clouds* / I can't get into you": in these and the following lines Ted is embedding book titles into syntax, creating a new kind of metaphor. "Secret Clouds" is a story/poem by Harris Schiff, and *Leaving Cheyenne* is a novel by Larry McMurtry. The poem ends with an excerpt from Ted's back cover copy for Anselm Hollo's book *Maya*, published by Golliard/Grossman in 1970. Ted's comment contains the following sentences: "By 'civilized' I mean genuinely civilized, that is, with no proportionate loss of spleen. The hits in the poems take place in your head when you read them, but the poems are not a head trip. The head speaks out of the heart to the head connected to the heart."

Three Poems: Going to Canada Originally, in *Nothing for You*, "Three Poems: Going to Canada" was called "Three Poems," with the poems laid out on separate pages. In the first of those poems, "Itinerary," a stanza break before the line "Go to Canada" was eliminated for *So Going Around Cities*.

Galaxies The poem "Galaxies" was originally part of the disbanded *Southampton Winter* sequence.

Postmarked Grand Rapids The word *pauses* was not italicized in *Nothing for You* but was italicized in *So Going Around Cities*.

Further Definitions (Waft) Ted is in dialogue with Michael Brownstein's poem "Definitions," which, laid out similarly to this one, defined certain words. Ted has taken Brownstein's definitions of those words and defined *them*. Thus Brownstein's definitions are on the left, and Ted's definitions of the definitions are on the right.

Kirsten Kirsten is Kirsten Creeley. "How you talk" was originally, in *Nothing for You*, "How she talks," and "You are" was originally "She is." These particularly crucial changes, again, were made for *So Going Around Cities*.

He "He" contains material that was incorporated into "Chicago English Afternoon" in *Easter Monday.*

Communism This poem was constructed from a failed poem of mine during the *Easter Monday* period. In "An Interview with Ralph Hawkins" (in *Talking in Tranquility*), Ted, referring to the poems "Peking" and "Soviet Souvenir," both in *Easter Monday,* states, "Marriage is like communism—ideally speaking—much more than it is capitalism or even socialism. I think it's like communism, from whatever sense I have of communism. From each according to his means, to each according to his needs at best."

Crossroads See the poem "At Loma Linda" in *Easter Monday.*

Elysium The dedication *"for Marion Farrier"* was added for *So Going Around Cities.* "Elysium" is heaven in classical mythology, but the reference here is from Shakespeare: "And what should I do in Illyria? / My brother he is in Elysium" (*Twelfth Night, Or What You Will,* act 1, scene 2).

In the 51st State

IN THE 51ST STATE

The poems in this section, all written in the late 70s, were first published in *So Going Around Cities.*

In the 51st State In the seventh stanza there is the question of the word *brindle,* which is not considered a verb in the dictionary. "I'd still rather brindle" might mean that the speaker would still rather evince streaks or spots, as the word would imply, according to its usage as a noun ("brindle") or an adjective ("brindled"). Perhaps Ted used the word in order not quite to make sense; this is a strange poem, opaque and clear, depressed and loving all at once (brindled?). The line "A woman rolls under the wheels in a book" refers to Tolstoy's *Anna Karenina.*

Red Shift This important "personal" poem was written according to method. "Red Shift" essentially follows an outline for a fill-in-the-blanks "New York School poem," as printed in a one-shot mimeo magazine *The Poets' Home Companion*, edited by Carol Gallup. The form itself was devised by Linda O'Brien (Schjeldahl). The magazine was published in the late 60s, but Ted rediscovered it in the 70s and within it the parodic procedure for writing a poem such as one of his own personal poems. By following the parody, he rejuvenated the original form and created a brilliant, passionate work.

Around the Fire The poem contains language from three different sources, as if there were three people speaking "around the fire." The sources of words are interviews, poems, and speculations by Ed Dorn, me, and Ted. That is, Dorn's and my words were already written down. Ted was more likely to draw on text than to "overhear," though he sometimes did that too. The feminist last line of the poem is pure Berrigan.

Cranston Near the City Line This poem was written using ideas derived from Kenneth Koch's *I Never Told Anybody*, a book of suggestions for teaching poetry writing in nursing homes. Ted decided to combine several ideas for poems into a single poem, including the retrieval of an early memory using exact description, the telling of something that one had "never told anybody," and the naming of colors of objects. When Ted performed the poem at readings, he sang the "She told me that she loved me" section.

Coda : Song This poem was published under the title "Song" in *Clown War* 16 (1977), ed. Bob Heman.

In Anselm Hollo's Poems Another of Ted's delvings into the poetry / language of a friend and colleague.

Last Poem Ted conceived of the "last poem" as a form: a poem that any poet might want to write. (See the note on "People Who Died," *In the Early Morning Rain.*) The poem was written more than four years before his death, but people have a tendency to treat it as virtually Ted's last poem and testament. It is far from his last poem; and it is quite funny, among its other qualities. Besides the words essentially from Creeley, from "frequent / Reification" through "and I dug him," one hears language echoing trashy spy novels, a poem from *Easter Monday*, the poem "Cranston Near the City Line," and the initial voice-over for the soap opera *The Days of Our Lives*. "Last Poem" was originally published in the magazine *Inc.* #3, edited by John Daley, in which it is dated "13 Jan 79 / nyc."

THE MORNING LINE

Published by Richard Aaron's Am Here Books/Immediate Editions in 1982. The cover art was by Tom Clark.

Sonnet: *Homage to Ron* This poem is made up entirely of lines from Ron Padgett's poetry, except for the last word, "No?" "A la Recherche du Temps Perdu" uses a similar method, with the same poet's material.

44th Birthday Evening, at Harris's Written in November of 1978.

An UnSchneeman In an interview I conducted with George Schneeman (published in *Waltzing Matilda* [New York: Kulchur, 1981]), George described his painting technique as the "unhandling" of paint. See also *Train Ride*, where Schneeman is referred to by Ted as "the bad painter," in the "Let's bitch our friends" passage. Schneeman was stating, in the interview, that his intention was not to compete with previous generations of perhaps obsessively virtuoso painters.

Part of My History Ted lived for years without a telephone, until 1980 when his mother fell ill with cancer and the "red telephone" was installed. This is an "autobiographical" poem in which there are few facts and nothing's transparent. The poet gradually finds himself stuck in a self and poem he knows too well—"a typical set / of Berrigan-thoughts," until finally he thinks to make a phone call. The poem might be termed "anti-autobiographical." The dedicatee, Lewis Warsh, is the author of a book called *Part of My History*.

The Morning Line The first line is, more or less, by Steve Carey, also the dedicatee of the subsequent poem, "Velvet &." Carey, who lived in the neighborhood, often came over to recite a new line of poetry he'd thought up and was trying to extend into a whole poem. "Every man-jack boot-brain slack-jaw son of a chump" was that kind of line, the "morning line."

Avec la Mécanique sous les Palmes This is made up of lines by Pierre Reverdy.

Kerouac (continued) "Kerouac" was made from an article about Jack Kerouac in the *New York Times* Sunday magazine.

That Poem George Found The opening lines refer to a sonnet by Petrarch and will now recur in Ted's poems; see, for example, "The Einstein Intersection" in *A Certain Slant of Sunlight.*

DNA A sonnet enclosed between two extra lines (*": Ms. Sensitive Princess:"* and "Run a check on that, will you Watson?"), this poem is reminiscent of the more cryptic poems in *Easter Monday*, such as "Innocents Abroad" and "Incomplete Sonnet #254." It is an analysis of the DNA of a poet.

Little American Poetry Festival Written during the One World Poetry Festival in Amsterdam, in 1978, this poem intercuts work by Ted, Joanne Kyger, Anne Waldman, and Lorenzo Thomas, that is, it's supposed to *sound like* the festival.

After Peire Vidal, & Myself See the introduction.

UNCOLLECTED POEMS

These poems, never before published in books, date roughly from between 1976 and 1981 and are reproduced from manuscript copies.

Normal Depth Exceeds Specified Value A variant of the poem was published in *Clown War 16* under the title "In a Loud Restaurant." The poem is dated "24 Sept 77" in our manuscript.

Winged Pessary and **Do You Know Rene?** These two poems in a similar style date from around 1978. The "Rene" in the title of the second poem is poet, critic, and artist Rene Ricard; the poem is written as if spoken by him.

43 Dated "22 June 78 / nyc."

A Spanish Tragedy This poem was written in a notebook while someone else was speaking, presumably Larry Fagin. Ted may have asked Fagin to talk while he wrote. A dedication to Fagin, after the title, has been crossed out in the manuscript. The poem is dated "20 July 78 / Boulder."

Ronka The word "Ronka" refers to the folksinger Dave Van Ronk, recording artist and well-known Greenwich Village figure. A "ronka" would be a song such as Dave Van Ronk would sing. Although "Ronka" appears as one of the postcards shown in facsimile in the O Books edition of *A Certain Slant of Sunlight*, it was never intended to be part of that series and was always kept in a folder with the other poems in this section of uncollected work. Ted had five hundred blank postcards to fill for the postcards project proper, as distinct from the book he was writing, and he often used poems from other books and folders for it. In manuscript "Ronka" is first dated "June 1978 . nyc."

My 5 Favorite Records See the introduction.

Look Fred, You're a Doctor, My Problem Is Something Like This: The "Fred" in the title is Fred Yackulic, a psychiatrist; husband of my sister Margaret Notley, the musicologist. This poem was included in "An Interview with Tom Savage" *(Talking in Tranquility)*, which was conducted for the Columbia Oral History Archives. It belongs with the other autobiographical poems from the late 70s and early 80s, but is more literal than, for example, "Last Poem," "Part of My History," and "Another New Old Song."

Compleynt to the Muse This poem is dated "Nov 79/Nov 80" on our manuscript.

Coffee And "One View/1960" is contained in the *Early Poems* section of the present volume, so Ted didn't really tear it up. "Dogtown" is a reference to Olson's *Maximus Poems* and to all that the word implies. The title itself is from Frank O'Hara's poem "Poem Read at Joan Mitchell's": "and the Sagamore's terrific 'coffee and, Andy,'" meaning "with a cheese Danish."

Three Little Words Another "autobiographical" poem, this is written from the point of view of Lewis Warsh. It is dated 3/11/80 on the manuscript copy.

Round About Oscar This is dated "17.IX.80."

The By-Laws This poem was made from a set of booklets written by George Schneeman as an aid to teaching English to foreigners. The "By-Laws" were those adopted by the Advisory Board of the Poetry Project in the late 70s.

Thin Breast Doom Dated "2/80" in manuscript. The allusion is to "A Round of English" by Lew Welch, one of Ted's favorite poems. In Welch's poem there is the line *"Carved my initials on her thin breast bone,"* followed by the lines "Thin brass dome, beautiful! / How'd you ever think of a thin brass dome?" Those latter lines had been spoken, in real life, by Philip Whalen, mishearing Welch when he recited the initial line. Ted's title, and dedication, with the change to "thin breast doom," is thus a further "mishearing."

Another New Old Song This poem, dated "3/81" in manuscript, begins as fictional autobiography and gradually invokes Ted's parents, particularly his mother.

A Certain Slant of Sunlight

This book was published by Leslie Scalapino's O Books in 1988. The cover design of the original O Books edition, using facsimile postcards, was by Leslie Scalapino. The front cover incorporated the postcard "Windshield," with its drawing by George Schneeman. The introduction was written by me.

See the introduction for an account of the postcards project. Poets who contributed phrases or lines to these poems (taking into account the poems in the *Out-takes* as well) included Allen Ginsberg, Peter Orlovsky, Steve Carey, Greg Masters, Joanne Kyger, Steve Levine, Tom Pickard, Jeff Wright, Eileen Myles, Anne Waldman, Harris Schiff, Bernadette Mayer, James Schuyler, Tom Carey, Ada Katz, and myself. Artists who provided images for the original five hundred postcards included George Schneeman, Dick Jerome, Rosemary Mayer, Shelley Kraut, Steve Levine, and myself. There were undoubtedly others.

Facsimile of Horoscope Ted wanted the horoscope included as part of the book when published, but it was somehow overlooked in the publication of the O Books edition. It is printed here for the first time. One might view it as symbolic of fate, or as another kind of poet "DNA." The "Secondary" chart was done according to Arab astrology. Ted was not precisely a believer, but he was interested in the symbolism of the zodiac, and at one time had thought a lot about his natal sign, Scorpio. See also the note to "Scorpion, Eagle, & Dove (A Love Poem)," in *Red Wagon*.

*** (You'll do good if you play it like you're not getting paid . . .)** The first sentence in the untitled second poem is an old show-biz saying found in one of George Burns's autobiographies.

*** (With / daring / and / strength . . .)** The untitled third poem of the sequence is the last part of the poem "In Three Parts" in *In the Early Morning Rain*, with the addition, at the end, of the lines "Just / like / me."

A Certain Slant of Sunlight Most of the sequence dates from 1982 and is arranged chronologically. However, the title poem was written in the spring of 1980, in Boulder, Colorado, using a word list I'd drawn up. The procedure with such a list was to employ one word per line in the order given, with the result being a poem of as many lines as there were words in the list (usually twelve). Ted took the list into a class he was teaching at Naropa and then did the assignment along with the class, employing the words as it occurred to him rather than according to grid.

Salutation One should imagine each poem as if printed on a postcard. That is, imagine receiving a postcard with the poem "Salutation" on the "picture" side: "Listen, you cheap little liar . . ."

The Einstein Intersection The title is that of a book by science fiction writer Samuel R. Delany. Two others of Delany's titles are included in the body of the poem: *Out of the Dead City* and *City of a Thousand Suns*. The poem fetishizes titles, using capital letters to turn phrases familiar from literature or *somewhere*, into titlelike entities.

Pinsk After Dark and **Reds** There are, throughout the sequence, small clusters of poems that involve initiating phrases by the same person. Both "Pinsk After Dark" and "Reds" contain some words by Allen Ginsberg and are "about" Ginsberg and Peter Orlovsky. Other sets of poems, occurring sequentially in twos and threes, have to do with words (or images) by Eileen Myles, Joanne Kyger, Tom Pickard, George Schneeman, Jeff Wright, Greg Masters, Dick Jerome. However, not all the poems involving words or lines by a particular person are kept in sets—that would have been too rigid a procedure. Also, people came back and put words on further postcards: Ted's friends became rather addicted to being part of this project.

People Who Change Their Names This poem may be read as a sonnet, with the words STEVE CAREY: occurring at the ninth line, the point of change in a sonnet. The idea for the poem came from an autobiographical prose work of my own, titled *Tell Me Again* (Santa Barbara, Calif.: Am Here Books, Immediate Editions, 1981). In it I refer to a favorite category of mine from the Bible, "people who changed their names"—thus the title and first four lines of Ted's poem.

Caesar This is an extremely free translation of Catullus's "*Nil nimium studeo, Caesar,*" which alludes to the persistent rumor, in ancient Rome, that Julius Caesar's grandmother had been black.

"Poets Tribute to Philip Guston" A memorial evening had been held for Guston, after his death in 1980, at the St. Mark's Poetry Project. For his part of the evening, Ted staged a scandalous abstract expressionist–like event, in which he kept talking on and on way past his "allotted time," goading the audience into booing him, and then finally reading a couple of poems—that is, doing what he was "supposed to." Afterward no one was sure of whether or not he had been deliberately excessive: he had.

Blue Herring The line "As if you hands were innocent" is correct; "you hands" is not a typo.

St. Mark's in the Bouwerie This poem is section 10, "Henry IV," of "Corridors of Blood," in *In the Early Morning Rain.*

Dinner at George & Katie Schneeman's In the 70s and 80s George Schneeman made ceramic dishware and vases decorated with chains of naked figures, engaged in sexual acts in a void: the second circle of Dante's *Inferno.*

Pandora's Box: An Ode This poem is both synthetic and personal. The opening source is a text which presents a magnetic, magnanimous "he." "I"—the speaker—is self-critical, idol-worshipping, loving, desperate, on the verge of becoming like the unnamed figure at the poem's beginning who changed him into something like a Beat poet, when Pandora's Box was opened.

The School Windows Song Based on Vachel Lindsay's poem "The Factory Windows Song." Ted discusses his poem, in relation to Lindsay's, in "Workshops at the Jack Kerouac Conference" (*On the Level, Everyday: Selected Talks on Poetry and the Art of Living*, ed. Joel Lewis [Jersey City, N.J.: Talisman House, 1997]). "I thought I could make, perhaps, something that was accurate and also was something more accurate—was as accurate now as his was then. Also it gave me a great take on how his was very accurate then."

Transition of Nothing Noted as Fascinating "Donald Allen, Donald Keene, Wm. 'Ted' deBary" had all been stationed together in Japan after World War II. Don Allen, distinguished editor and publisher, was Ted's editor for the Grove Press edition of *The Sonnets.* Keene and deBary are well-known scholars of Japanese literature. This is, then, a sort of "orientalist" poem. DeBary's daughter, Brett deBary, is the "Lady Brett" of "Tambourine Life."

Whoa Back Buck & Gee By Land! The title is a rendering from memory of a Leadbelly line, "Who, back, Buck, an' gee, by de Lamb!" As sung on recordings, Leadbelly's lyrics can be hard to make out, and Ted knew he'd never heard the line correctly. The poem is a little elegy for Thelonius Monk, who had recently died, but also for Auden and Leadbelly. The second line, "While whole days go by and later their years" is a re-rendering into the present tense of the first line of O'Hara's poem "River." "Sleep, Big Baby, sleep your fill" is from one of Auden's last poems, "A Lullaby." The Erinyes are the Fates in Greek mythology. And "Women in the night who moan yr name" is from John Wieners's "Act #2" in *Ace of Pentacles:* "He's gone and taken / my morphine with him / *Oh Johnny.* Women in / the night moan yr. name."

Frances The "Frances" of this poem and of "Paris, Frances" is Anne Waldman's mother, Frances Waldman, who became gravely ill and then died in 1982.

I Dreamt I See Three Ladies in a Tree The three dedicatees of the poem, as well as Tom Pickard (see "Last Poem" and "Mutiny!")—all British poets—were in New York in the spring of 1982 for a festival of British poetry.

Last Poem (for Tom Pickard) Another version of a "last poem," but as if spoken by one of the "Jarrow boys," who marched from Jarrow to London in the English hunger marches of the 1930s. The poet Tom Pickard is the co-author, with Joanna Voit, of a history called *Jarrow March.*

Mutiny! This poem concerns the British war in the Falkland Islands in the spring of 1982.

Wantonesse The poem was written in conjunction with a photo of upstairs neighbor, Megan Williams. She was at that time a dress designer; the photo was of her back, showing off a deep V in a dress she'd made. Thus the last line of the poem, "Loving her back." This is one example of the way Ted's mind worked in relation to the images on the cards.

Creature "Creature" is made of materials from my poems, especially the poem "When I Was Alive."

Providence This poem records the death of Ted's mother in July 1982. Clark Coolidge's "brown suit" was one Ted had previously borrowed for ceremonial occasions: Coolidge too was from Providence, and the suit was kept at his mother's house. In "On Poems from '500 American Postcards'" (from *On the Level Everyday*), Ted comments, "Providence. There, your whole downtown part of the city is built across a bay, and about every fifteen years there's . . . There are water marks all over town saying how high the water came at such and such time."

I Heard Brew Moore Say, One Day Brew Moore (1924–1973) was a jazz saxophonist influenced by Lester Young (see "String of Pearls," in *Nothing for You*). His name is very suggestive. For stylistic clues to the poem, see Allen Ginsberg's "Manhattan May Day Midnight," first published in *Plutonian Ode*.

Untitled (July 11, 1982) The untitled poem dated "July 11, 1982" and beginning "Dear Alice" was written entirely by me.

The Way It Was in Wheeling A "Country Western" song, "The Way It Was in Wheeling" was written following a *Mad-Libs* form.

My Autobiography This poem, again, concerns Megan Williams, whose partner, the artist Dick Jerome, had broken his leg. Megan told Ted the story outlined in the poem, which he transformed into a narrative from Dick's point of view.

Down on Mission From "On Poems from '500 American Postcards'": "This is one of those poems where it might be difficult to sort out the references, and what each line means in reference to the story, if you were trying to do that, but if you are just interested in hearing it, it's clear enough I think. . . . It's a kind of doomsaying poem, but it's also about . . . oh, cycles of personal growth, you, all your own sense of the legends you found yourself on, all crumble periodically."

In Your Fucking Utopias The poem begins with a line from Whitman's poem "Respondez!" which is famous as Whitman's "only" angry poem. Whitman's line is very angry, and this is an angry poem too: one could only follow such a line in kind. "The Gandy-Dancers Ball," not nearly as famous a song as "The Darktown Strutters Ball," was a Frankie Laine hit in the 50s. The poem is about all exclusion as a kind of racism and money as the great American excluder.

Tough Cookies These "Chinese fortunes" are inspired by Frank O'Hara's poem "Lines for the Fortune Cookies."

Skeats and the Industrial Revolution The poem takes off from the etymology of the word *god* in Skeat's *Etymological Dictionary.*

Let No Willful Fate Misunderstand As Ted says in "On Poems from '500 American Postcards,'" the poem is "sprinkled with lines from Robert Frost." However, "Night Tie" is the title of a collage made by Aram Saroyan and given to Ted, and this poem "sounds like" Saroyan in places, as if Ted's father and Aram's father (the writer William Saroyan) merge.

To Sing the Song, That Is Fantastic Section 9 of O'Hara's "Second Avenue" opens with the lines "Now in November, by Josephine Johnson. The Heroes, / by John Ashbery. Topper's Roumanian Broilings. The Swimmer." Ted performed this quite political poem in a reggae-chant manner, in imitation of the singer Yellowman.

This Guy One of two poems written in the last year of Ted's life (the other being "Robert (Lowell)" in the *Last Poems* section) that concern Ted's literary relationship to Lowell. Though Lowell isn't referred to by name, in this poem, he is "This Guy."

Give Them Back, Who Never Were A beautiful instance of the technique of identity merge, which Ted seems to have perfected in the book. It is as if every poet or person is the same one, and each one is and isn't her/himself. For example, toward the end of this poem, "the fat kid from Oregon" would be Phil Whalen, who was really from Washington; "who grew up to be our only real poet" refers to something once said about John Ashbery; the "jaunty Jamaica, Queens stick-figure" is Lorenzo Thomas, who though "Negro" is not a "French Negro poet" (see Frank O'Hara's "Ode to the French Negro Poets") but translated some poems of the French Negro poets many years after O'Hara's death.

Christmas Card (for Barry and Carla) The dedicatees are poet Barrett Watten and experimental prose writer Carla Harryman. *Third Factory* (1926) is a book by the Russian Formalist Viktor Shklovsky, highly influential in Language Poetry circles.

A Certain Slant of Sunlight: Out-takes

Ted kept two folders for the postcard project: a folder of poems to be included in the final book, and another folder of poems either not first-rate enough, or unfinished, or in some way repetitive. These out-takes are mostly a selection from the second folder. A number of the poems are dated in the manuscript, but as dates were not included in *A Certain Slant of Sunlight*, and Ted most often omitted dates in his books, we haven't included them as part of the poems.

Bardolino and Postcard 12/2/82 "Bardolino," which is dated "2/82" in our manuscript, and "Postcard 12/2/82" fall within the same set and moment as "Pinsk After Dark" and "Reds" in *A Certain Slant of Sunlight.*

New Poets of England & America Dated "17 Feb" in the manuscript. *New Poets of England and America* was a poetry anthology edited by Donald Hall, Robert Pack, and Louis Simpson, with an introduction by Robert Frost (Cleveland and New York: Meridian Books, 1957).

Get Away From Me You Little Fool An obvious interaction with the poetry of James Schuyler.

4 Metaphysical Poems and **Who Was Sylvia?** Both poems involved the participation of Steve Carey. The former poem is dated "17 Feb 82" and the latter "20 Feb."

Anselm Though the poem called "Anselm" contains language by Anselm Hollo, it also refers to Anselm Berrigan. Ted invoked the two of them simultaneously more than once, the other notable instance being in the dedications to *So Going Around Cities.*

Wednesday Evening Services Dated "20 Mar 82."

Head Lice Dated "24 Feb 82."

Little Travelogue Dated "6 Mar 82."

Sleeping Alone This poem was lost after Ted's death, at least as text. He considered it integral to the sequence, and it should have appeared in *A Certain Slant of Sunlight.* We present a version reconstituted by us from a taped reading. For a slightly different reconstitution by an anonymous tape transcriber, see "Workshops at the Jack Kerouac Conference," in *On the Level Everyday.*

*** (Another has . . .)** The poem was never typed up by Ted, existing only as a postcard—a gift to me—until this publication. The postcard, entirely of Ted's design, has a baseball sticker affixed to it, with a photo of one of the Minnesota Twins of 1982: that is, a twin self to the poet. "Another" has arrived. Ron Padgett states (in a letter to me) that the initial lines of the poem are a "variant on the first line of a 1959 poem by David Bearden: 'Another has come to the silver mirror.'" Bearden's poem was published in *The White Dove Review* 5 (summer 1960).

The Pope's Nose This poem plays with Anne Waldman's poem "Paul Eluard."

The LADY, JUST WHEN I THINK I KNOW . . . Dated "21 Mar 82."

Treason of the Clerks The poem is based on an explanation by Edmund Berrigan, then seven years old, of a drawing he'd made, probably on the postcard on which the poem was written. *Treason of the Clerks* is a book by the French writer Julien Benda: *The Treason of the Intellectuals* (*La Trahison des Clerks,* 1927), trans. Richard Aldington (New York: William Morrow, 1928). By its title, this poem would probably belong near "To Book-Keepers" in the main volume. It is dated "29 Mar" on the manuscript.

All A-Glower Went My Love Riding Dated "10 Apr 82." Along with "Fern," it involved the participation of Bernadette Mayer.

With Eileen in Locarno Dated "Easter.1982 . nyc."

Three Lost Years Grace Murphy ("Grace falls . . .") and Peggy DeCoursey were friends of each other and Ted. The poem was written in Boulder in 1980.

Butchie's Tune, La Bohème, To a Young Painter, and **Upside Down** These four poems were all written in conjunction with Ada Katz. One of Alex Katz's paintings is called "Upsidedown Ada." "Butchie's Tune" is dated "Mid Apr 82," "To a Young Painter" is dated "5/3/82," and "Upside Down" is dated "7 May 82."

Der Asra Ted and Gordon Brotherston's translation of Heinrich Heine's "Der Asra" was done during the *Easter Monday* period, in England. Ted loved this translation, which he sometimes included in poetry readings, and kept trying to find a place for it in his books; but it never seemed to belong alongside his other work.

Fern Dated "18 May 82." See the note for "All A-Glower Went My Love Riding."

O, Sexual Reserve Dated "6/15/82."

One Day in the Afternoon of the World Dated "18 Aug 82."

Two Serious Ladies Dated "1 Sep 82." The reference is to Jane Bowles's great novel *Two Serious Ladies.*

Down Moon River Dated "12 Oct 82 . nyc." "Charlie" is the late Charlie McGrath, a neighbor at 101 St. Mark's Place.

At 80 Langton Street (S.F.) Dated "1 Dec 83 NYC," this poem was also one that Ted never typed up but left to exist only on a postcard. It was transcribed by Bill Berkson, to whom the Mikolowskis finally sent the card. The poem refers to a four-day residency by Ted, at the San Francisco arts center, 80 Langton Street, in 1981, where Hollo, Thomas, and Acker had held previous residencies. There was a clash between Ted and the Language Poets, thus the final word "Duck." Bill Berkson chaired a panel during the residency.

Last Poems

The fourteen poems in Ted's final folder of poems date from between December 7, 1982, and May 15, 1983. Ted had been a sporadic dater of poems, but each of these has a date affixed, or in the case of "Don Quixote & Sancho Panza," contained in the poem. One cannot help but have the feeling he is counting down to his final moments. Ted died on July 4, 1983. The poems were first published together, under the title *Last Poems*, in *Arshile* No. 6, 1996.

Robert (Lowell) See "This Guy" in *A Certain Slant of Sunlight.* Ted was reading a biography of Lowell at the time of the composition of these two poems, and much of the language comes from material quoted from Lowell and others. The "we" in this poem is significant, including both Ted and Lowell, especially in the last line, which seems to sum up a lifetime. The last sentence is definitely Ted's words.

Today in New York City As with "The Way It Was in Wheeling," both "Today in New York City" and "Stand-up Comedy Routine" were made using *Mad-Libs* forms. "Today in New York City" involves a set of forms, probably in multiple-choice format, for writing newspaper articles. The forms disappear into the text, which is laid out like a poem and embellishes considerably on the *Mad-Libs* diagram. In places where one would have been meant to make a single choice, Ted included several: e.g., "& is contemplating / The return of Billy, / Suicide, / 3-Mile Island, / Unleashing 'The Hammer'," etc. "The Hammer" refers to Sonnet VI in *The Sonnets.* The poem is dated "7 Dec 82."

The Short Poems Dated "23 Feb 83."

Something to Remember Dated "2 Mar 83."

To Jacques Roubaud Dated "11 Mar 83," this poem is a note of condolence on the death of Roubaud's wife. Ted had met French poet Roubaud at a poetry festival in Italy, in 1979, and they had become friendly.

Villonnette Dated "29 Mar 83."

After Petrarch This poem, once again using Petrarch's "labyrinth" lines, is dated "1 Apr. 83."

Old Armenian Proverb Dated "4/83."

Ambiguity Dated "7 Apr 83."

Stand-up Comedy Routine Dated "21 Apr. 83." The *Mad-Libs* form is considerably embellished and drawn out. The show-biz names used in this poem were probably all contained in the form, except for that of "Sammy Davis, Senior," which Ted changed from Sammy Davis Jr. Sammy Davis Jr.'s father was also an entertainer, and Ted remembered him quite clearly. The dedicatees, poets Bob Holman and Ed Friedman, were both heavily involved in performance; the dedication implies that either one of them might perform the poem. Ted once read a book composed of Lenny Bruce's routines and had thought about the form of the "comedy routine" outside of the *Mad-Libs* format.

Positively Fourth Street Dated "11 May 83." The title is that of a Bob Dylan song.

Down on Me Dated "13 May 83." This title is from a song sung by Janis Joplin.

Don Quixote & Sancho Panza This, Ted's last sonnet, contains the date—"May, 1983"—in the body of the poem.

This Will Be Her Shining Hour Dated "15 May 83," Ted's real "last poem" was written over the course of a couple of hours, late on a Saturday night. I was in one room watching the Fred Astaire movie, and Ted was in the other room listening to my voice and his own, and to the voices of the actors.

Early Uncollected Poems

Each of the fifteen poems in this section contains lines (or in the case of "Prose Keys to American Poetry," the single word "Perceval") that reappeared in *The Sonnets*. Along with some of the poems in *Nothing for You*, these are the earliest usages of these materials.

What are you thinking . . . Dated "May 16th, 1962, Denver."

Lady Takes a Holiday Dated "8 June 62."

For Bernie There is another version of this poem with the same text but a different title, "The Awful Responsibility of History."

Homage to Beaumont Bruestle Bruestle was one of Ted's professors at the University of Tulsa.

Lines from Across the Room Dated "March 23, 1962."

Homage to Mayakofsky The poem leads straight into the world of *The Sonnets*. These lines referring to Mayakofsky became in Sonnet I a reference to Ezra Pound.

Other Books of Poetry

NOTE ON *BEAN SPASMS*

Bean Spasms was published by Lita Hornick's Kulchur Press in 1967. The title page qualifies the volume as "Collaborations by Ted Berrigan & Ron Padgett / Illustrated & Drawings by Joe Brainard." Brainard was also the subject, in the volume, of an interview by Ron and Pat Padgett.

Much of the work in *Bean Spasms* consists of literal collaborations between Ted and Ron Padgett, in the form of poems, an exchange of letters ("Big Travel Dialogues"), an excerpt from the collaborative novel *Furtive Days*. However, the book also contains important poems by each poet as sole author. Authorship of all work in the volume is unattributed, left up in the air; when reading the book it is impossible to know without knowing already, e.g., that Ted is the author of the poem "Bean Spasms," that Ted and Ron Padgett are the co-authors of the excerpt from *Furtive Days*, that Ron Padgett is the author of the poems "December" and "A Man Saw a Ball of Gold."

One of the more notorious pieces in the volume is "An Interview with John Cage," which purports to be an interview with Cage but is completely fabricated by Ted, out of real interviews in contemporary journals with Bob Dylan, Andy Warhol, and the French playwright Fernando Arrabal. The interview was first published in Peter Schjeldahl's and Lewis Macadams's magazine *Mother*. The interview was subsequently selected for inclusion in *The National Literary Anthology* as best interview of the year (1966), as judged by a panel including such figures as Susan Sontag and Robert Brustein. The interview had been taken at face value as an interview with Cage. After Ted's informing George Plimpton, who was somehow involved in the awards, of the interview's fabrication, Plimpton had to notify Cage. Cage asked if Ted were "for me or against me"; Plimpton assured Cage that Ted was for him, the interview having been made using methods of composition learned from Cage himself. Cage then declined his supposed share of the thousand-dollar award, on the grounds that he hadn't been involved in the interview at all, not having spoken or written a word of it.

As indicated in the introduction, Ted incorporated the poems by himself in *Bean Spasms* into subsequent books of his (as did Padgett).

NOTE ON *SO GOING AROUND CITIES*

So Going Around Cities: New and Selected Poems, 1958–1979, first published by George Mattingly's Blue Wind Press in 1980, is a unique volume, which feels less like a "selected poems" than a new book constructed by Ted. The cover art is by Donna Dennis; but the book, which is quite large, makes generous use of drawings by George Schneeman in a manner reminiscent of *In the Early Morning*

Rain. In this case there is a drawing for each section of the book, appearing after the section title.

The sections in *So Going Around Cities* present poems in groups that have overlapping chronologies: for example, the section called *Many Happy Returns* (which does not strictly correspond to the Corinth Books edition) dated 1961–1968, is followed by *A Boke,* dated 1966, which is followed by a section called *Waterloo Sunset,* which is dated 1964–1968. With the exception of the section titled *from The Sonnets,* the *Many Happy Returns* section, and *Memorial Day,* the sections do not employ titles of previously published books. Ted was, in general, honoring chronology of composition rather than chronology of publication. He was also asserting the individual identities of the previously published books: they were too unique to be excerpted from in a systematic way; and so it was necessary was to construct a whole new entity. Each section of the book bears an epigraph on its title page, as the title page of the section called *Not Dying* has the epigraph "No joke!"

Note on *Selected Poems*

Aram Saroyan edited *Selected Poems* by Ted Berrigan, for the Penguin Poets Series (New York: Penguin Books, 1994). The only one of Ted's books of poetry (until now) that Ted had no living or posthumous hand in, it covers gracefully and classically, within the limited space of a traditional "selected poems," all of Ted's major publications through *A Certain Slant of Sunlight.* It contains no previously unpublished work. There is an introduction by me.

Glossary of Names

Where no dates appear, the editor has not been able to locate the information.

Donald Allen (1912–2004) Editor, anthologist, publisher; Ted's editor at Grove Press for *The Sonnets*.

Bruce Andrews (1948–) Poet, critic; associated with Language Poetry movement.

John Ashbery (1927–) New York School poet, art critic, prose writer.

Erje Ayden Turkish-born American novelist, memoirist.

David Bearden Poet, friend of Ted's in Tulsa.

Bill Berkson (1939–) Poet, art critic.

Anselm Berrigan (1972–) Son of Ted Berrigan and Alice Notley.

David Berrigan ("Jacques-Louis David") (1963–) Son of Ted and Sandy Berrigan.

Edmund Berrigan (1974–) Son of Ted Berrigan and Alice Notley.

Kate Berrigan (1965–1987) Daughter of Ted and Sandy Berrigan.

Sandy Berrigan (1942–) Formerly Sandra Alper. Ted's first wife. Poet.

Paul Blackburn (1926–1971) Poet, translator, archivist, founder of Le Metro reading series.

Joe Brainard (1942–1994) Painter, cover artist and illustrator, collagist, assemblagist, writer. Collaborator with Ted on visual / literary works.

Jim Brodey (1942–1993) Poet, music critic.

Gordon Brotherston (1939–) British translator, author, poet, Latin American scholar.

Michael Brownstein (1943–) Poet, novelist.

Rudy Burckhardt (1914–1999) Swiss-born American filmmaker, photographer, painter.

Reed Bye (1948–) Poet, American Buddhist.

Steve Carey (1945–1989) Poet, novelist. Brother of Tom Carey.

Tom Carey (1951–) Poet, novelist, musician, Franciscan (Episcopalian) brother and priest.

Jim Carroll (1950–) Poet, novelist, musician, songwriter.

Joe Ceravolo (1934–1988) Poet.

Tom Clark (1941–) Poet, novelist, biographer, sports writer, editor.

Martin Cochran Poet, friend of Ted's in Tulsa.

Andrei Codrescu (1946–) Romanian-born American poet, novelist, essayist, radio commentator.

Jack Collom (1931–) Poet, teacher, essayist, environmentalist.

Clark Coolidge (1939–) Poet, musician, editor.

Lee Crabtree (1942–1973) Musician, member of the rock band The Fugs.

Robert Creeley (1926–2005) Poet, prose writer, teacher, associated with the Black Mountain poets.

Peggy DeCoursey (1944–) Close friend of Ted's in New York in the later period. Communications worker in advertising.

Samuel R. "Chip" Delany (1942–) Science fiction writer.

Edwin Denby (1903–1983) Poet, dance critic, essayist.

Donna Dennis (1942–) Sculptor and painter.

Ed Dorn (1929–1999) Poet, fiction writer, teacher.

Kenward Elmslie (1929–) Poet, performer, librettist.

Joan Fagin (1948–) Dress designer; former wife of Larry Fagin.

Larry Fagin (1937–) Poet, editor, publisher.

Harry Fainlight (d.1982) British poet.

Marion Farrier (1951–) Friend of Ted's at the University of Essex, England, and in New York. Publications manager. Wife of Steve Carey.

Ed Foster (1944–) Poet, critic, editor, publisher, teacher.

Jane Freilicher (1924–) Painter. Friend of New York School poets.

Ed Friedman (1950–) Poet, playwright, performer, arts administrator.

Carol Gallup (Carol Clifford) (1942–) A close friend of Ted's in New York. Former wife of Dick Gallup. Poet.

Dick Gallup (Richard Gallup) (1941–) Poet, playwright.

Merrill Gilfillan (1945–) Poet, essayist.

Allen Ginsberg (1926–1997) Poet, prose writer, political activist, musician, teacher.

John Giorno (1935–) Poet, community activist.

Lorenz Gude (1942–) With his wife, Ellen Gude, published "C" *(A Journal of Poetry)* and "C" Books in the 60s. He also took early photographs of the Tulsa group and of Joe Brainard's work.

Ellen Gude (1942–) Wife of Lorenz Gude and co-publisher of "C" *(A Journal of Poetry)* in the 60s. She provided the essential funding for "C," having a good job in an employment agency.

Barry Hall Printer, publisher, filmmaker.

Jacky Hall First wife of Barry Hall.

Donald Hall (1928–) Poet, essayist, anthologist, teacher.

David Henderson (ca. 1942–) Poet, lyricist, biographer, a founder of the Umbra workshop.

Anselm Hollo (1934–) Finnish and American poet, translator (from Finnish, German, Swedish, Russian, and French), person of letters.

Bob Holman (1948–) Poet, playwright, director, actor, community animator.

Helena Hughes (1951–) Friend of Ted's at the University of Essex and in New York. Poet. Caretaker, for some years, for James Schuyler.

Dick Jerome Artist, upstairs neighbor of Ted's in New York during the late 70s and early 80s.

Henry (Hank) Kanabus (1949–) Poet from Chicago, former student of Ed Dorn and Ted at Northeastern Illinois University.

Ada Katz (1928–) Wife of Alex Katz. She figures in many of his paintings.

Alex Katz (1927–) New York painter and visual artist (set designer, cover artist, printmaker, collaborator with poets, etc.).

Anne Kepler Marge Kepler's cousin, a flutist who came to New York around the same time as Ted, Joe Brainard, Dick Gallup, Pat Mitchell, and Ron Padgett. Her death in 1965 is recorded both in "Tambourine Life" and in "People Who Died."

Marge Kepler (Margie) Friend, girlfriend, of Ted's in Tulsa, who, according to his journals, changed his life dramatically.

Jack Kerouac (1922–1969) Beat novelist and poet. Interviewed by Ted for the *Paris Review* in 1968.

Kenneth Koch (Jay Kenneth Koch) (1925–2002) New York School poet, playwright, fiction and prose writer, teacher.

Rochelle Kraut (1952–) Poet, artist, singer. Married to Bob Rosenthal.

Rosina Kühn (1940–) Swiss painter.

Tuli Kupferberg (1923–) Poet, musician, songwriter, author, member of The Fugs.

Joanne Kyger (1934–) Poet, teacher.

Michael Lally (1945–) Poet, actor.

Lewis MacAdams (1944–) Poet, environmental activist.

Bernadette Mayer (1945–) Experimental poet and prose writer, editor, teacher of poets.

Bernie Mitchell (1945–2003) Sister of Pat Padgett.

Christine Murphy (Chris) The muselike "Chris" of *The Sonnets*, one of Ted's students in 1958–1959 when he taught eighth grade at Madalene School in Tulsa. Not the "Chris" in the poem "Living with Chris," who is Christina Gallup, the (then) baby daughter of Dick and Carol Gallup.

Eileen Myles (1949–) Poet and fiction writer.

Jayne Nodland (1943–) Photographer, artist, musician.

Alice Notley (1945–) Poet, editor, essayist; Ted's second wife.

Frank O'Hara (Francis Russell O'Hara) (1926–1966) New York School poet, art critic, Museum of Modern Art (New York) administrator and curator. Ted's most avowed poetry hero.

Douglas Oliver (1937–2000) British poet, novelist, editor, linguistic researcher.

Peter Orlovsky (1933–) Poet, companion of Allen Ginsberg.

Lauren Owen (1941–) Friend of Ted's in Tulsa and New York.

Pat Padgett (Patricia Mitchell) (1937–) Lifelong friend of Ted's in Tulsa and New York. Wife of Ron Padgett.

Ron Padgett (1942–) Poet, prose writer, memoirist, biographer, translator, editor. Frequent collaborator with Ted on poems and prose works. Co-author with Ted of the book *Bean Spasms*.

Tom Pickard (1946–) British poet and prose writer.

Fairfield Porter (1907–1975) Painter and art critic.

Tony Powers Friend of Ted's in Tulsa.

Tom Raworth (1938–) British poet.

Val Raworth (1936–) Wife of Tom Raworth.

Bob Rosenthal (1950–) Poet, prose writer, secretary to Allen Ginsberg.

Ed Sanders (1939–) Poet, musician, journalist, novelist. Member of The Fugs.

Aram Saroyan (1943–) Poet, prose writer.

Harris Schiff (1944–) Poet. Collaborator with Ted on writing projects.

Linda Schjeldahl (Linda O'Brien) (1942–) Editor, writer; at one time married to Peter Schjeldahl.

Peter Schjeldahl (1942–) Poet, art critic.

Elio Schneeman (1961–1997) Poet, son of George and Katie Schneeman.

George Schneeman (1934–) Painter, collagist, ceramicist, cover artist, illustrator, frequent collaborator with Ted on visual and literary projects.

Katie Schneeman (1938–) Close friend of Ted's in New York. Married to George Schneeman; mother of Elio, Emilio, and Paul.

James Schuyler (1923–1991) New York School poet, prose writer, art critic.

Johnny Stanton (1943–) Fiction writer.

Lorenzo Thomas (1944–) Panamanian-born African American poet, critic, essayist, teacher.

Sotere Torregian (1941–) Poet.

Tony Towle (1939–) Poet.

Tom Veitch (1941–) Novelist, poet, comic book writer.

Anne Waldman (1945–) Poet, editor, anthologist, teacher, performer, New York and Boulder poetry community figure.

Larry Walker Fiction writer, friend of Ted's in Tulsa.

Lewis Warsh (1944–) Poet, novelist, memoirist, editor, publisher, teacher.

Philip Whalen (1923–2002) Poet, novelist, Zen abbot.

Megan Williams Upstairs neighbor of Ted's in New York in the late 70s and early 80s. Dress designer.

Jeff Wright (1951–) Poet, editor, publisher.

Credits

The text of *The Sonnets* is reproduced with the permission of Penguin Group (USA), Inc. (New York: Penguin Books, 2001). *Memorial Day* is reproduced with the permission of its co-author, Anne Waldman. *A Certain Slant of Sunlight* is reproduced with the permission of Leslie Scalapino and O Books (Oakland, Calif.: O Books, 1988). All other poems are used with the permission of Alice Notley, executor of the estate of Ted Berrigan. The photograph of Ted Berrigan is reproduced with the permission of the photographer, Lorenz Gude. The cover art by George Schneeman is reproduced with the permission of the artist.

Index of Titles and First Lines

Titles appear in roman type. First lines appear in italics.

* *(Another has)*, 623
* *(Ezra Pound: A Witness)*, 317
* *(Keep my)*, 333
* *(Peter Rabbit came in)*, 330
* *(With)*, 568
* *(You'll do good if you play it like you're)*, 568

1. Le Marteau Sans Maitre : Pierre Boulez (Odyssey 32 16, 552
(2) photographs of Anne, 222
3 Pages, 351
4 Metaphysical Poems, 620
5 New Sonnets: A Poem, 169
7 Things I Do in the Hotel Chelsea, 498
9:16 & 2:44 & 25 Minutes to 5, 581
10 Things I Do Every Day, 164
10 Things I do Every Day, 351
10 years of boot, 203
XIII, 595
20th Century man strives toward the unfinished-machine exalted state, 543
30 *(The fucking enemy shows up)*, 216
36th Birthday Afternoon, 371
43 *(no strange countries)*, 547
44th Birthday Evening, at Harris's, 525
80th Congress, 167

a band of musicians: up tight, 492
A Boke, 98
A Certain Slant of Sunlight, 569
A colorful river of poetry drives forward, 489
A City Winter, 614
A darksome tiger, 660
A Dream, 150
A drop of boo the wounded ham, 442
a faint smile appears, 178
A few rape men or kill coons so I bat them, 50
À la Recherche du Temps Perdu, 529
A Letter, 200
A Letter from Dick Gallup, 97
A Little American Feedback, 411
"A little loving can solve a lot of things," 384
A lovely body gracefully is nodding, 355
A master square weaver, one's favoured medium, 396

A Meeting at the Bridge, 418
a metal fragrant white, 580
A *natural bent, no doubt*, 324
A New Old Song, 237
A *new old song continues. He worked into the plane*, 425
a nose, heavy, square, & massive, 624
A Note from Yang-Kuan, 416
A *person can lie around on an uncrowded beach*, 196
A Personal Memoir of Tulsa, Oklahoma / 1955–60, 119
A Quiet Dream, 527
A Religious Experience, 507
A Reply to the Fragile, 189
A Spanish Tragedy, 548
A *sparrow whispers in my loins*, 585
A True Story, 334
A *woman's love*, 328
(About Emily Dickinson), 221
Above his head clanged, 497
Abraham & Sarah, 572
According, 193
Acid, 341
Acid, 485
Across the trolley tracks, 659
After Breakfast, 189
After Peire Vidal, & Myself, 540
After Petrarch, 641
After the first death there is plenty, 465
Ah, Bernie, to think of you alone, suffering, 656
"Ah Fitz but we are profound, 629
Air, 332
Air Conditioning, 453
All A-Glower Went My Love Riding, 625
All my friends in the, 606
"All things considered, it's a gentle & undemanding, 347
Allen & Peter, heads close together, Allen, 619
Allen Ginsberg's "Shining City," 513
Ambiguity, 641
American Express, 207
Amityville Times, 529
Amsterdam, 333
An Autobiography in 5 Parts, 199
An Ex-Athlete, Not Dying, 519
An Observation, 329
An Orange Clock, 403
An UnSchneeman, 526
and I am lost in the ringing elevator, 173
& so I took the whole trip, 519
"And the nights shall be filled with music, 323
And then one morning to waken perfect-faced (Interstices), 612
And then one morning to waken perfect-faced (Sonnet XXXI), 45
Andy Butt was drunk in the Parthenon, 43
Angst, 573
Ann Arbor Elegy, 226
Ann Arbor Song, 235
Anne, 495
Anne Lesley Waldman says, No Fossil Fuels, 585
Anne reads her Troubadour poem, 331
"Another has, 623
Another New Old Song, 563
Anselm, 621
Anselm! Edmund!, 573
Anselm Hollo, 340
Anselm is sleeping; Edmund is feverish, &, 522
Anti-War Poem, 223
"Antlers have grown out the top of my shaggy head," 405
Apollinaire Oeuvres Poetiques, 212
Apologies to Val & Tom, 477
"appropriately named Beauty, has just been a star, 533
April in the Morning, with Anne, 472

Around the Fire, 516
As Usual, 187
Ass-Face, 610
At a quarter past six he sat & said "where's your brother? pull, 92
At 80 Langton Street (S.F.), 633
At last I'm a real poet I've written a, 433
At Loma Linda, 398
Aubade, 503
Autobiography, 341
Autobiography, 489
Autumn, 454
Autumn is fun, 454
Autumn's Day, 436
Avec la Mécanique sous les Palmes, 531

Babe Rainbow, 225
Baby sighs prepositions put the books back nights. As usual I, 89
Back in the Old Place, 536
Back to dawn by police word, 525
Bad Teeth, 338
Bad Timing, 613
banging around in a cigarette she isn't "in love" (Sonnet XLI), 51
banging around in a cigarette she isn't "in love" (Sonnet LVI), 59
Baltic Stanzas, 505
Bardolino, 619
Be awake mornings. See light spread across the lawn, 382
Bean Spasms, 152
bear with me, 321
bear with me, 321
Beautiful girl, 328
Beautiful Poem, 323
Beauty, I wasn't born, 570
became in Alamogordo. Then the blast-, 656
Beer in bed, &, 394
Before I began life this time, 521
Before I was alive, 594
Beginning with a memory of childhood New York's lovely weather, 91
bent, 218
bent, 218
Besa, 605
Beware of Benjamin Franklin, he is totally lacking in grace, 75
Biddy Basketball, 473
Black & White Magic, 475
Black brothers to get happy, 369
Black Power, 210
blank mind part, 203
Blindfold shores leaving sad, 621
Blue, 324
Blue Galahad, 570
Blue Herring, 574
Blue Targets, 510
Blue Tilt, 537
Bolinas, 343
borrow 50 from George, 484
Boulder, 412
Brigadoon, 496
Brother and sister departed, 189
Buddha on the Bounty, 384
Buddhist Text, 322
Buenos Aires, 610
"But & then at that time, 537
But that dream . . . oh, hell, 513
Butchie's Tune, 628
By Now, 336
Bye-Bye Jack, 237

Caesar, 574
Caesar's ghost must be above suspicion, 640
Can't cut it (night), 209
Canzone, 660
Carrying a Torch, 415
Category, 322
Cento: A Note on Philosophy, 443
C'est automne qui revient, 531
Chair, 324

Che Guevara's Cigars, 201
Chicago April Morning: Snow, 495
Chicago English Afternoon, 400
Chicago Morning, 391
Childe of the House, 334
Chinese Nightingale, 383
Christmas Card (for Barry & Carla), 616
Christmas Card (O little town of Bethlehem), 615
Christmas in July, or, 611
(clarity! clarity!) a semblance of motion, omniscience, 64
Climbed by Grandma We Stand on Morning's Hill, 626
Clown, 382
Coda : Song, 520
Coffee And, 557
Cold rosy dawn in New York City, 207
Come to Chicago, 340
Communism, 500
Compleynt to the Muse, 555
Conceived in Hate, 447
Congratulations, 343
Connecticut, 328
Contemporary Justice, 528
Conversation, 352
Corporal Pellegrini, 191
Corridors of Blood, 178
Cowboy Song, 328
Cranston Near the City Line, 517
Crash, 376
Craze Man Wiliiker, 199
Creature, 594
Crossroads, 507
Crystal, 382

DNA, 535
"Dear Chris, 70
Dear Management's beautiful daughters, 581
Dear Marge, hello. It is 5:15 a.m. (Night Letter), 433
Dear Marge, hello. It is 5:15 a.m. (Sonnet XVIII), 39
Dear Margie, hello. It is 5:15 a.m. (Sonnet II), 29
Dear Ron: Keats was a baiter of bears etc., 67
Dear Ron: hello. Your name is now a household name, 73
December, 189
Déjà Vu, 343
Der Asra, 630
Despair farms a curse, slackness, 392
Dial-A-Poem, 225
Dice Riders, 601
Dick Gallup (Birthday), 445
Did you see me that night, 655
Dinner at George & Katie Schneeman's, 584
Dinosaur Love, 585
Discussing Max Beerbohm, 343
"Do you, 582
Do You Know Rene?, 545
Don Quixote & Sancho Panza, 644
Don't call me "Berrigan," 429
Don't Forget Anger, 91
Doubts, 429
Down Moon River, 633
Down on Me, 644
Down on Mission, 601
Dreamland, 532
Dreams, aspirations of presence! Innocence gleaned, 63
Dreamy-eyed is how you get, 150
Dresses for Alice, 608
dying now, or already dead, 494

Each tree stands alone in stillness, 38
Easter Monday, 405
Easy Living, 230
"Eileen" (detail), 576
El Greco, 442
Elysium, 509

Entrance, 203
Epithalamion, 205
Erasable Picabia, 228
Evelyn Waugh's Prayer, 317
Evensong, 327
Every day back & forth, 630
Every day when the sun comes up, 360
Every man-jack boot-brain slack-jaw son of a chump, 530
Everybody is not so clever as you. You are cleverer than I, 530
Everybody Seemed So Laid Back in the Park, 418
Everything good is from the Indian, 405
Everywhere we went we paid the price, endurement, 445
Excursion & Visitation, 417
Ezra Pound: A Witness, 317

Farewell Address, 364
Fauna Time. *See* The Secret Life of Ford Madox Ford
Feb. 11, 1982. Last night reading Permanent War, 619
February Air, 209
Fern, 631
fiction appears) for I and only one per-, 574
Fine Mothers, 586
Flame & Fury, 189
Flower Portrait, 447
Fluke Holland: —The Tennessee Third, 402
Flying United, 346
For a brief time Acting Chief, 627
For Annie Rooney, 431
For Bernie, 656
For love of Megan I danced all night, 600
For my sins I live in the city of New York, 420
For Robt. Creeley, 585
For Rosina, 336
For You, 119
Found Picasso, 331
Four Gates to the City, 405
Fragment, 168
Frances, 589
Francis à Bientôt, 440
Francis Marion nudges himself gently into the big blue sky, 55
Frank O'Hara, 381
Frank O'Hara's Question from "Writers and Issues" by John Ashbery (An Autobiography in 5 Parts), 202
Frank O'Hara's Question from "Writers and Issues" by John Ashbery (Many Happy Returns), 159
Frog sees dog. log?, 393
From "Anti-Memoirs," 487
From A List of the Delusions of the Insane, What They Are Afraid Of, 400
From a Secret Journal, 33
from Memoirs, 200
From Sketches of Amsterdam, 553
From The Art of the Sonnet, 451
From the Execution Position, 542
From the House Journal, 422
Fuck Communism, 121
Further Definitions (Waft), 492
Futile rhapsodies resound from hotly, 657

Gainsborough, 404
Galaxies, 488
Games, 659
Gay doormen face a severe shortage of cocaine, 637
George's Coronation Address, 603
Geranium's, 624
get, in the complexity of our present, 343
"Get a job at the railroad," 620
Get Away from Me You Little Fool, 620
Get your ass in gear, 341
Giants in the sky; roses in streams that castle; rocks, 657
Give Them Back, Who Never Were, 614
Go, 353

Go in Manhattan, 597
Go fly a kite he writes, 40
God: perhaps, "The being worshipped. To, 604
Going to Chicago, 468
Going up, slowly, I, slowly, 464
Good Evening, ladies, and all you hungry children, 642
Goodbye House, 24 Huntington, one block past Hertel, 364
Grace After a Meal, 663
Grace to be born and live as variously as possible, 59
Great Stories of the Chair, 88
gray his head goes his feet green, 54
Green (grass), 226
Green Tide; behind, pink against blue, 371
Grey Morning, 219
Guevara had noticed me smoking, and remarked that of course I would, 201
Gus, 172

Hall of Mirrors, 234
Harum-scarum haze on the Pollock streets (Sonnet XIX), 39
Harum-scarum haze on the Pollock streets (Sonnet XLVI), 54
He, 430
He, 498
He called his Mama, 187
He eats of the fruits of the great Speckle, 34
He eats toenails, 614
He is guardian to the small kitten, 605
He made coffee, 189
He never listened while friends talked, 400
He never listened while friends talked. He worked, 498
He wandered and kept on wandering. Bar-Mitzvah, 430
He was one of the last of the Western Bandits, 418
He was ugly, 191
He was wounded & so, 590
Head Lice, 622
Head of lettuce, glass of chocolate milk, 237
Heart of my heart, 594
Hearts, 433
"Hello," 167
Hello, 167
Hello, Sunshine, 582
Heloise, 421
Here, 325
Here comes the Man, 243
Here comes the man! He's talking a lot, 384
Here I am again, 317
Here I am at 8:08 p.m. indefinable ample rhythmic frame, 515
Here I Live, 465
Heroin, 222
He's literally a shambles as a person, 548
High School windows are always broken, 587
His piercing pince-nez. Some dim frieze (5 New Sonnets: A Poem), 169
His piercing pince-nez. Some dim frieze (Sonnet I), 29
Hitch on here, 625
Hollywood, 591
Homage to Beaumont Bruestle, 657
Homage to Mayakofsky, 659
Homecoming, 205
Honey, 615
How strange to be gone in a minute, 71
How strange to be gone in a minute! A man, 75
How sweet the downward sweep of your prickly thighs, 62
How terrible a life is, 596
How to Get to Canada. *See* Three Poems: Going to Canada
How We Live in the Jungle, 471
Huge collapsed Mountain Enters from Stage Right, 547

I am ambiguity, 641
I am asleep, 471
I am closing my window. Tears silence the wind, 65
I am in bed, 328
I am kinks, 325
I am lonesome after mine own kind—the, 614
I am the man yr father & Mum was, 591
I am thinking of my old houses, 557
I am trying very hard to be Here, 435
I appear in the kitchen, 526
I belong for what it is worth, 404
I belong here, I was born, 422
I cannot reach it, 327
I can't sleep walking through walls, 542
I Dreamt I See Three Ladies in a Tree, 590
"I gather up my tics & tilts, my stutters & imaginaries, 406
I go in &, 325
I go on loving you, 594
I had a really sad childhood, lived mostly alone, 558
I had angst, 573
I had this dream, 631
"I have always been emotional beyond belief, so, 620
I have been here too many times before, 429
I have no brain, 622
I have these great dreams, like, 561
I hear walking in my legs, 574
I Heard Brew Moore Say, One Day, 597
I hope to go, 230
"I know what evening means, and doves, and I have seen, 66
"I know where I'm going, 606
I like First Avenue, 576
I like to beat people up, 56
I love all the girls, 230
I love you much, 468
I met her in The Stone Age, 599
I never said I was right, or wrong, 632
"I order you to operate. I was not made to suffer," 409
"I Remember," 419
I remember painting "I Hate Ted Berrigan" in big black letters, 419
I saw you first in half-darkness, 534
I sit on fat, 205
I stand at the dock in judgement, 633
I stand by the window, 605
I take him, 494
I tried to put the coffee back together, 596
I Used to Be but Now I Am, 385
I used to be inexorable, 385
I wake up back aching from soft bed Pat, 69
I wake up 11:30 back aching from soft bed Pat, 116
I was looking at the words he, 507
I watch the road: I am a line-, 607
I won't be at this boring poetry reading, 235
"I wrote these songs when, 553
I'd been, 506
I'd like to show you something. Please look at it, 560
If by my hasty words I gave offence, 653
If he bites you he's friendly, 189
If I didn't feel so, 597
If I don't love you I, 385
If someone doesn't help me soon I, 590
Ikonostasis, 176
I'll yell at these men who pass, 84
I'm a hero form of an eyelid act like you hate it, 87
I'm a piece of local architecture, 336
I'm gonna embarrass, 551
I'm living in Battersea, July, 395
I'm lying in bed, 324
I'm No Prick, 342
I'm not difficult but there are just certain things, 628
I'm not saying, 82
I'm sorry for your trouble, 640

"I'm standing toe-to-toe with you, see, looking you right in the eye, 343
Impasses come, dear beasts, 80
In 4 Parts, 196
In Africa the wine is cheap, and it is, 569
In Anne's Place, 488
In Anselm Hollo's Poems, 520
In Bed, 230
In Bed with Joan & Alex, 458
In Blood, 406
In front of him was, 320
In Hyde Park Gate 14 white budgie scratchings mean, 477
In Joe Brainard's collage its white arrow (Sonnet XV), 37
In Joe Brainard's collage its white arrow (Sonnet LIX), 60
In Morton's Grille, 583
In Morton's Grille I, 583
"In My Green Age," 585
in my paintings for they are present, 52
In My Room, 226
In Place of Sunday Mass, 654
In order to make friends with the natives, 593
In the 51st State, 513
In the Deer Park, 606
In the ear, winds dance, 434
In The Early Morning Rain, 366
In the first stage of the revolution, 323
In the House, 345
In the Land of Pygmies & Giants, 573
In the morning, 458
In the Summer between 5th & 6th grade, 554
In the Wheel, 360
In the year 1327, at the opening of the first hour, 534
In Three Parts, 193
"In Three Parts," 204
In Your Fucking Utopias, 601
Incomplete Sonnet #254, 407
Inflation, 345
Inhabiting a night with shaky normal taboo hatred and fear, 414
Innocents Abroad, 402
Inside, 225
insouciant, 318
insouciant, 318
interrupts yr privacy, 445
interstices, 217
interstices, 217
Interstices, 612
Into the closed air of the slow (Sonnet XVI), 37
Into the closed air of the slow (Sonnet XXX), 44
Iris, 548
Is there room in the room that you room in?, 62
is when you walk around a corner, 607
ISOLATE, 548
It is 7:53 Friday morning in the Universe, 117
It is 1934. Edmund, 644
It Is a Big Red House, 660
It is a human universe: & I, 57
It is a very great thing, 451
it is a well-lit afternoon, 621
It is after 7 in the evening and raining cold in bed. Next day, 440
It is important to keep old hat, 351
It is night. You are asleep. And beautiful tears, 49
"it" means "this," 557
it was summer. We were there. And There Was No, 63
Itinerary. *See* Three Poems: Going to Canada
It's 2 a.m. at Anne & Lewis's which is where it's at, 167
It's 5:03 a.m. on the 11th of July this morning, 117

It's 8:54 a.m. in Brooklyn it's the 26th of July, 118
It's 8:54 a.m. in Brooklyn it's the 28th of July and, 48
It's a cute tune possibly by Camus, 83
It's A Fact, 354
It's a great pleasure to, 160
It's a previous carnation, where?, 623
It's difficult, 345
It's Important, 225
It's important not, 225
It's impossible to look at it, 509
It's impossible to take a bath in this house, 474
It's just another April almost morning, St. Mark's Place, 488
It's made of everything, slow, 502
It's Morning, 332
It's morning, 447
It's New Year's Eve, of 1968, & a time, 223
It's not exciting to have a bar of soap, 151
It's ritzy Thrift, 210
It's very interesting (Air Conditioning), 453
It's very interesting (Down on Me), 644

Jim Dine's toothbrush eases two pills, 228
Joan, 232
Jo-Mama, 592
Joy of Shipwrecks (Life of a Man), 188
Joy of Shipwrecks (A Certain Slant of Sunlight), 575
Joy! you come winging in a hot wind on the breath, 438
Joyful ants nest on the roof of my tree, 55
Jubilee, 434
July, 93
July 11, 1982, 599
Just Friends, 335

Keep my, 333
Kerouac (continued), 533
Kings . . . panties, 176
Kinks, 325
Kirsten, 495
Kissed Maggie soundly; and the Doctor, 345

L.G.T.T.H., 398
La Bohème, 628
Ladies & Gentlemen, 346
Lady, 370
Lady, she has been my friend for some years sketches, I haven't explained, 93
Lady, why will you insist on, 555
Lady Takes a Holiday, 656
Laments, 337
Landscape with Figures (Southampton), 368
Larceny, 342
Last night, 503
Last night's congenial velvet sky, 226
Last Poem, 521
Last Poem (for Tom Pickard), 591
Late November, 397
Leaving first, 468
Left behind in New York City, & oof, 168
Lefty Cahir, loan me your football shoes again, 595
Less original than, 505
Lester Young! why are you playing that clarinet, 437
Let No Willful Fate Misunderstand, 609
Let the heart of the young, 601
Life Among the Woods, 192
Life in the Future, 340
Life of a Man, 187
Light, 327
Light takes the bat, &, 581
Light up, 225
Light, informal, & human, 627
like carrying a gun, 609
Like Poem, 232
Like the philosopher Thales, 637

Lines from Across the Room, 657
Liquor troops in deshabille from blondes a lonely song, 81
Listen, Old Friend, 584
"Listen, you cheap little liar . . . ," 570
Little American Poetry Festival, 538
Little Travelogue, 622
Livid sweet undies drawl, 79
Living with Chris, 151
L'oeil, 329
London, 455
London Air, 455
Look Fred, You're a Doctor, My Problem Is Something like This, 554
Lord, it is time. Summer was very great (Autumn's Day), 436
Lord, it is time. Summer was very great (Sonnet IV), 30
Love. *See* Three Poems: Going to Canada

Man Alone, 320
Many Happy Returns, 160
March 17th, 1970, 203
Marie in her pin-striped suit singing, 418
Matinee, 187
"Members of the brain, welcome to New York City, 542
Memorial Day, 287
Memories Are Made of This, 562
Mess Occupations, 50
Messy red heart, 455
Method Action, 393
Mi Casa, Su Casa, 497
Mid-Friday morn, 10 o'clock, I go to India, 487
mind clicks into gear, 361
Minnesota, 597
Minuet, 610
Missing you, 484
Mistress isn't used much in poetry these days, 562
Moat Trouble, 590
Monolith, 453
Montezuma's Revenge, 593
Moondog, 322
Morning, 187
Morning flushes its gray light across where I collect a face, rimmed, 88
Mother Cabrini, 89
Mountains of twine and, 36
: Ms. Sensitive Princess, 535
Ms. Villonelle, 611
M'Sieur & Madame Butterfly, 594
Mud on the first day (night, rather, 41
Musick strides through these poems, 71
Mutiny, 592
My 5 Favorite Records, 552
My Autobiography, 600
My babies parade waving their innocent flags, 33
My beard is a leaping staff, 654
My body heavy with poverty (starch), 371
my crib your crib, 497
My dream a drink with Lonnie Johnson we discuss the code of the west, 72
My friends are crazy with grief, 614
My Grandfather was a Hasidic scholar, 563
My heart is confirmed in its pure Buddhahood, 227
My heart Your heart, 455
My Life & Love, 582
"My name, 352
My rooms were full of awful features when, 439
My rooms were full of Ostrich feathers when, 431
My Tibetan Rose, 425

Naked, 583
Nancy, Jimmy, Larry, Frank, & Berdie, 370

Narragansett Park, 414
Natchez, 605
Nature makes my teeth "to hurt," 206
Neal Cassady Talk, 343
Near Paris, there is a boat. Near this boat live the beautiful Woods, 192
Near the Ocean, 328
Never hits us the day it's lovely gathers us up in its name who, 91
Never will I forget that trip. The dead were so thick in spots we tumbled over, 200
New Junket, 445
New Personal Poem, 508
New Poets of England & America, 619
New York Post, 608
New York's lovely weather, 152
New York's lovely weather hurts my forehead, 119
Newtown, 392
Night Letter, 433
Nine stories high Second Avenue, 525
no strange countries, 547
Normal Depth Exceeds Specified Value, 543
. . . *Not far from here he was inside his head there were some sands. Of these 50,* 172
Nothing stands between us, 601
November, dancing, or, 374
Now I wish I were asleep, to see my dreams taking place, 373
Now my mother's apron unfolds again in my life pills black backs, 93
Now she guards her chalice, 653
Now she guards her chalice in a temple, 626
Now she guards her chalice in a temple of fear, 44
Now that I, 589
Now twist knife all strength owing O now twist knife, 452
Now you can rest forever, 420
O, Sexual Reserve, 632
O Captain, My Commander, I Think, 576
O little town of Bethlehem, 615
O Love, 339
O love, 339
O Rose, 335
O Will Hubbard in the night! A great writer today he is, 595
October: half-moon rising: London sky, Piccadilly's, greyish-black, 477
Ode, 577
Ode to Medicine, 464
of morning, Iowa City, blue, 238
Often I try so hard with stimulants, 538
Oh, George—that, 598
Oh, Mrs. Gabriele Picabia-Buffet, 640
Oh you, the sprightliest & most puggish, the brightest star, 540
Okay. First. . . . , 598
Old Armenian Proverb, 641
Old-Fashioned Air, 395
Old Moon, 542
old prophets Help me to believe, 61
On His Own. *See* The Secret Life of Ford Madox Ford
On St. Mark's Place, 334
On St. Mark's Place (Out the Second-floor Window), 339
On the 15th day of November in the year of the motorcar, 41
On the green a white boy goes (Penn Station), 35
On the green a white boy goes (Sonnet XXI), 40
On the Level Everyday, 435
On the Road Again, 187
Once there was a rich man named craze man Wiliiker. This man was always very, 199
One and one, 545
one can only are, 319

one can only are, 319
One clear glass slipper; a slender blue single-rose vase, 517
One Day in the Afternoon of the World, 632
One View/1960, 653
One, London, 477
"Only the guilty need money," 641
Ophelia, 373
Orange Black, 342
Orange Black, 342
Other Contexts, 506
Où sont les neiges des neiges?, 46
Out the Second-Floor Window, 339
Out we go to get away from today's, 663
Over Belle Vue Road that silence said, 504
Owe. *See* The Secret Life of Ford Madox Ford

Paciorek, 581
paid Lillian Gish $800,000 to, 591
Pandora's Box, an Ode, 586
Paris, Frances, 596
Paris Review, 331
Part of My History, 527
Pat Dugan... my grandfather... throat cancer... 1947, 236
Patsy awakens in heat and ready to squabble, 60
Paul Blackburn, 494
Peace, 232
Peeling rubber all the way up, 523
Peking, 399
Penn Station, 35
People of the future, 429
People of the Future, 429
People Who Change Their Names, 572
People Who Died, 236
Personal Poem, 117
Personal Poem #2, 116
Personal Poem #7, 117
Personal Poem #9, 118
Peter Rabbit came in, 330
Picasso would be very, 329
Picnic, 413
Pills Epithalamium black backs of books I can't stand Snow Movie, 95
Pinsk After Dark, 571
poem, 330
Poem (for Larry Fagin), 329
Poem (I'm lying in bed), 324
Poem (of morning, Iowa City, blue), 238
Poem *(Seven thousand feet over),* 172
Poem (The Nature of the Commonwealth), 616
Poem (to Tom Clark), 341
Poem *(Yea, though I walk),* 568
Poem for Philip Whalen, 221
Poem in the Modern Manner, 33
Poem in the Traditional Manner, 32
Poem Made after Re-Reading the Wonderful Book of Poetry, "Air", by Tom Clark, Seven Years since He First Sent It to Me, 330
"Poets Tribute to Philip Guston," 574
Polish Haiku, 577
Poop, 206
Positively Fourth Street, 643
Postcard, 598
Postcard 12/2/82, 619
Postcard from the Sky, 521
Postmarked Grand Rapids, 492
Prayer, 432
Presence, 173
Problems, Problems, 437
Prose Keys to American Poetry, 658
Providence, 595
Pussy put her paw into the pail of paint, 205
Put the books back the brown hair pierced the shower 40 below the, 90
Putting Away. *See* The Secret Life of Ford Madox Ford

Quarter to Three, 411
Queen name, 620
Queen Victoria dove headfirst into the swimming pool, which was filled, 398

Rain, 219
Rain falling through the blue, 472
Rain or Shine, 498
Reading Frank O'Hara, 510
Reading Frank O'Hara you, 510
Real Life, 34
Reality is the totality of all things possessing Actuality, 559
Reborn a rabbi in Pinsk, reincarnated, 571
Red Air, 500
Red Shift, 515
Reds, 572
Reeling Midnight. *See* The Secret Life of Ford Madox Ford
Remembered Poem, 351
Resolution, 164
Revery, 424
revery, 579
revery, 579
Richard Gallup at 30, 95
Rilke, 432
ripped, 373
Robert (Lowell), 637
Robert Creeley reading, 492
Ronka, 551
Rouge, 557
Round About Oscar, 559
Rusty Nails, 183

Salut, 320
Salutation, 570
San Francisco, 632
San Gabriel, 364
Sandy's Sunday Best, 502
Sash the faces of lust, 403
Saturday Afternoons on the Piazza, 432
Scene of Life at the Capitol, 331
Scorpio, 385
Scorpion, Eagle & Dove (A Love Poem), 374
self suspended in age time warp put out to grass, 529
Selflessness, 449
Seriousness, 324
Service at Upwey, 504
Setback, 323
Seurat and Juan Gris combine this season, 68
Seven thousand feet over, 172
Shaking Hands, 327
She, 351
She (Not to be confused with she, a girl), 401
She alters all our lives for the better, merely, 401
She comes as in a dream with west wind eggs, 33
She is always two blue eyes, 351
She murmurs of signs to her fingers, 52
She was pretty swacked by the time she, 584
Shelley, 534
Since we had changed, 408
Sister Moon, 403
Six months of each other, 496
Skeats and the Industrial Revolution, 604
slack, 326
slack, 326
Sleep half sleep half silence and with reasons, 49
Sleeping Alone, 623
Small Role Felicity, 522
Smashed Ashcan Lid, 598
Smiling with grace the mother, the spouse, leaned, 183
So Going Around Cities, 409
So long, Jimi, 337
So sleeping & waking, 465
Some Do Not, 434
Some Trips to Go On, 94

Somebody knows everything, so, 529
Somebody knows everything so, 473
Someone something, 450
Someone who loves me calls me, 203
Something Amazing Just Happened, 355
Somethings gotta be done! I thought, 613
Sometimes it is quiet throughout the night, 345
Something to Remember, 640
Song, 347
Song: Prose & Poetry, 227
Sonnet I, 29
Sonnet II, 29
Sonnet III, 30
Sonnet IV, 30
Sonnet V, 31
Sonnet VI, 31
Sonnet XIII, 36
Sonnet XIV, 36
Sonnet XV, 37
Sonnet XVI, 37
Sonnet XVII, 38
Sonnet XVIII, 39
Sonnet XIX, 39
Sonnet XXI, 40
Sonnet XXII, 40
Sonnet XXIII, 41
Sonnet XXV, 41
Sonnet XXVI, 42
Sonnet XXVII, 43
Sonnet XXVIII, 43
Sonnet XXIX, 44
Sonnet XXX, 44
Sonnet XXXI, 45
Sonnet XXXII, 46
Sonnet XXXIII, 46
Sonnet XXXIV, 47
Sonnet XXXV, 47
Sonnet XXXVI, 48
Sonnet XXXVII, 49
Sonnet XXXVIII, 49
Sonnet XL, 51
Sonnet XLI, 51
Sonnet XLII, 52
Sonnet XLIII, 52
Sonnet XLIV, 53
Sonnet XLV, 53
Sonnet XLVI, 54
Sonnet XLVII, 54
Sonnet XLVIII, 55
Sonnet XLIX, 55
Sonnet L, 56
Sonnet LI, 57
Sonnet LII, 57
Sonnet LIII, 58
Sonnet LV, 59
Sonnet LVI, 59
Sonnet LVII, 60
Sonnet LIX, 60
Sonnet LX, 61
Sonnet LXI, 62
Sonnet LXIV, 62
Sonnet LXV, 63
Sonnet LXVI, 63
Sonnet LXVII, 64
Sonnet LXVIII, 65
Sonnet LXX, 65
Sonnet LXXI, 66
Sonnet LXXII, 66
Sonnet LXXIII, 67
Sonnet LXXIV, 68
Sonnet LXXV, 68
Sonnet LXXVI, 69
Sonnet LXXVII, 70
Sonnet LXXVIII, 70
Sonnet LXXX, 71
Sonnet LXXXI, 71
Sonnet LXXXII, 72
Sonnet LXXXIII, 73
Sonnet LXXXIV, 73
Sonnet LXXXV, 74
Sonnet LXXXVII, 75
Sonnet LXXXVIII, 75
Sonnet: Homage to Ron, 525

Sonnet to Patricia, 653
Southampton Business, 478
Southwest, 422
Soviet Souvenir, 394
Space, 607
Spell, 585
Spring banged me up a bit, 577
Squawking a gala occasion, forgetting, and, 31
St. Mark's By-the-Pacific, 627
St. Mark's in the Bouwerie, 583
Stand-Up Comedy Routine, 642
Stars & Stripes Forever, 596
Steve Carey, 547
Stoop where I sit, am crazy, 575
Stop Stop Six. *See* The Secret Life of Ford Madox Ford
Strategy, 342
Strategy is what you do how, 342
String of Pearls, 437
Strings like stories shine, 610
Strong coffee in, 332
Stronger than alcohol, more great than song, 30
Summer so histrionic, marvelous dirty days, 57
Sunday Morning, 354
Sunday morning: here we live jostling & tricky, 392
Sunlit, 337
Sunny, Light Winds, 577
surface, 344
surface, 344
Sweet Iris, 590
Sweet Vocations, 465
Sweeter than sour apples flesh to boys, 65
Swinburne & Watts-Dunton, 394

Take me, third factory of life, 616
Take off your hat & coat & give me all your money, 187
Take off your head; un-, 582
Take one hymn out west and back in step, step and punch how well, 94
Take these beads from my shoulders, 590
Talking, 633
Tambourine Life, 121
Telegram, 237
Television, 364
Tell It Like It Is, 338
Ten Things to Do in the Closet, 341
That Poem George Found, 534
That they are starving, 400
That's all, 633
The (Buddhist Text), 322
The (Larceny), 342
The academy of the future is opening its doors, 68
The Admirals brushed, 592
The Ancient Art of Wooing, 396
The Avant-Garde Literary Award, 450
the bear eats honey, 610
The best way of, 342
The blue day! In the air winds dance, 46
The bulbs burn phosphorescent, white, 31
The bunnies plug-in & elaborate, 423
The By-Laws, 560
The Chinese ate their roots; it, 588
The Circle, 169
The Collected Earlier Poems by William Carlos Williams, 213
The Complete Prelude, 386
The Conscience of a Conservative, 93
The D.A., 346
The Dance of the Broken Bomb. *See* The Secret Life of Ford Madox Ford
The dancer grins at the ground, 413
The Einstein Intersection, 571
The End, 392
The Final Chapters, 587
The front is hiding the rear, 228
The fucking enemy shows up, 216
The goddess stands in front of her cave, 520
The Great Genius, 220

The Great Genius is, 220
The Green Sea, 497
The ground is white with snow, 164
The guards tense, the centers jump, 473
The Heads of the Town, 602
The Joke & the Stars, 407
The Lady, Just When I Think I Know You, You Take Capricious Form Travelling Circus & Road Show (or, In the Labyrinth), 624
The life I have led, 513
The Light, 327
The logic of grammar is not genuine it shines forth, 66
The Moon is Yellow, 337
The Morning Line, 530
The Nature of the Commonwealth, 616
the number two, &, 407
The poem upon the page is as massive as, 58
The Pope's learning Welsh, 577
The Pope's Nose, 624
The pregnant waitress, 360
The pressure's on, old son, 507
"The pressure's on, old son," 398
The rain comes and falls, 416
The rains come & Fall, 417
The right wall is bricks, 453
The Rose of Sharon, 338
The School Windows Song, 587
The Secret Life of Ford Madox Ford: Fauna Time, 81; On His Own, 82; Owe, 84; Putting Away, 85; Reeling Midnight, 80; Stop Stop Six, 79; The Dance of the Broken Bomb, 83; We Are Jungles, 87
The Sender of This, 598
The Short Poems, 639
The Simple Pleasures of Buffalo, 474
The Society Club, 639
The St. Mark's Poetry Project, 592
The storms of Baudelaire fall on Judas' head, 440
The Sunset Motel, 91
"the taste is pleasant, and the insane, 619
The Ten Greatest Books of the Year (1967), 212
The Ten Greatest Books of the Year, 1968, 213
The torpedo was friendly, 188
The TV Story, 440
The Upper Arm, 177
The Way It Was in Wheeling, 599
The white poet with his book, 659
The Who's Last Tour, 611
The wicked will tremble, the food will rejoice, 603
The withered leaves fly higher than dolls can see, 53
Then I'd Cry, 452
there, 336
There I was, 544
There is a shoulder in New York City, 601
There is no transition from a gesture to a cry or a sound. (same thing), 96
There is no windshield, 596
There isn't much to say to Marxists in Nicaragua, 572
There we were, on fire with being there, then, 119
There's a strange lady in my front yard (Clown), 382
There's a strange lady in my front yard (Landscape with Figures [Southampton]), 368
"There's no place, 593
There's nothing new under the sun, and, 643
These are the very rich garments of the poor, 399
They basted his caption on top of the fat sheriff, "The Pig," 74
They have bent, 629
They killed all the whales, 602
They set you up. Took yr stuff. Gave, 625

Thin Breast Doom, 561
Things to Do in Anne's Room, 219
Things to Do in New York City, 163
Things to Do in Providence, 376
Things to Do on Speed, 361
Think of Anything, 338
Thinking about past times in New York by talking, 536
This, 338
"This ability, to do things well, 584
This city night, 327
This distinguished boat, 571
This excitement to be all of night, Henry, 42
This Guy, 614
"This is the only language you understand, Ass-Face," 610
"This movie has Fred Astaire and Robert Ryan in it, 645
"This mushroom walks in," 496
This night my soul, & yr soul, will be wrapped in, 589
This Perfect Day, 496
This picture indicates development, 449
this steady twelve-tone humming inbetween my ears, 532
This Will Be Her Shining Hour, 645
those exhausting dreams, 577
Three Little Words, 558
Three Lost Years, 627
Three Poems: Going to Canada: Itinerary, 483; How to Get to Canada, 484; Love, 484
Three Sonnets and a Coda for Tom Clark, 366
Thursday & Friday, 483
Time flies by like a great whale, 47
tin roof slanting sunlight, 528
To, 343
To a Young Painter*, 629
To an Eggbeater, 330
To Anne, 468
To Be Serious, 602
To Book-Keepers, 587
To England's very great relief, 329
to gentle, pleasant strains, 43
To Himself, 420
To Jacques Roubaud, 640
To Ron, 530
To Sing the Song, That Is Fantastic, 611
To Southampton, 353
Tobacco, 189
Today, 289
Today Chicago, 337
Today I had planned to fribble away, 346
Today I woke up, 357
Today in Ann Arbor, 357
Today in New York City, 637
Today is Courty Bryan's birthday, 320
Today's News, 371
Tom Clark, 494
Tompkins Square Park, 606
Tonight, 188
Too many fucking mosquitoes under the blazing sun, 70
Tooting My Horn on Duty, 190
Tooting my horn on duty in the infantry, 190
Tough Brown Coat, 224
Tough brown coat, 224
Tough Cookies, 603
Train Ride, 473
Train Ride . . . , 478
Transition of Nothing Noted as Fascinating, 588
Treason of the Clerks, 625
Truth as History, 439
"Truth is that which, 598
Tulsa Rose Gardens, 90
Turk, 593
Turkeys, 629
Turn around, 341
Two cops cruise East 9th, 608
Two Serious Ladies, 633

Unconditional Release at 38, 609
Under a red face, black velvet shyness, 391
Under the Southern Cross, 523
Untitled *(It's Morning!)*, 332
Untitled *(July 11, 1982)*, 599
Untitled *(Orange Black)*, 342
Untitled *(Want)*, 346
Up a hill, short, 412
Up inside the walls of air listen, 424
Up is waiting, 169
Upon the river, point me out my course, 386
Upon this field the physical energies of, 177
Upside Down, 330

Valentine, 429
Velvet &, 531
Via Air, 615
Vignette, 345
Villonnette, 640
Virtue, Honor, Beauty, Kind gestures, 641
Visits from a Small Enigma, 423
Voice of ride, 531
Voici la tête d'un chien, 660

Wake Up, 228
wake up, 164
Wake up high up, 163
Walk right in, 219
Wan as pale thighs making apple belly strides, 51
Want, 346
Wantonesse, 594
Warrior, 607
. . . was 30 when we met. I was, 586
Waterloo Sunset, 214
We, 334
We are involved in a transpersonified state, 383
We Are Jungles. *See* The Secret Life of Ford Madox Ford
We are the dresses for Alice, 608
We ate lunch, remember? and I paid the check, 214
We commemorated a joyous (if, 626
We miss something now, 234
We remove a hand . . . , 36
We think by feeling and so we ride together, 422
Wednesday Evening Services, 621
We'll mash your leman, plunk, 85
What a Dump or, Easter, 580
What are you thinking . . . , 655
What I'd Like for Christmas, 1970, 369
What I'm trying to say is that if an experience is, 516
What is it all about—this endless, 611
What said your light, 397
what sky (An Autobiography in 5 Parts: Frank O'Hara's Question . . .), 202
what sky (Many Happy Returns: Frank O'Hara's Question . . .), 159
What strikes the eye hurts, what one hears is a lie, 394
What thoughts I have of where I'll be, & when, & doing what, 415
What thwarts this fear I love, 53
What to do, 232
What we have here is Animal Magick: the fox, 407
What's the number I request, 628
What's the Racket, 92
When having something to do, 520
When I search the past for you (Cento: A Note on Philosophy), 443
When I search the past for you (Heloise), 421
When I see Birches, I think, 609
When seeking sky you're left with sky, then, 622
When she comes, landscape listens; heavenly, 576

When Wyn & Sally and the twins went to Minnesota to visit Wyn's father last, 200
Whenever Richard Gallup is dissevered, 32
Where, 338
Where do the words come from? (come in?), 403
Where the Ceiling Light Burns, 408
White powder, 340
Whitman in Black, 420
Who I Am and What I Think, 96
"who is not here, 411
Who Was Sylvia?, 620
Whoa Back Buck & Gee By Land, 589
"Who's a 'black' artist?," 475
Who's gonna kiss your pretty little, 611
Why don't we, 632
Why have you billowed under my ancient piazza, 432
Will "Reclining Figure, One Arm," 527
Will the little girl outside, 527
Wind, 360
Winds in the stratosphere, 188
Windshield, 596
Winged Pessary, 544
Winter, 337
Winter. You think of sex, but it's asleep, 488
Winter crisp and the brittleness of snow, 115
Winter in the country, Southampton, pale horse, 381
Wishes, 373
With, 568
With Eileen in Locarno, 626
With faith we shall be able . . . , 603
With sound Sun melts snow, 586
W/O Scruple, 603
Woke up this morning you were other people in absentia lovely fashions, 97
Woman is singing the song and summer, 73
Words for Love, 115
Work Postures, 416
Written on Red Roses & Yellow Light, 485
Wrong Train, 384

Yea, though I walk, 568
Yes, it's true, strategy is fascinating, 411
You are lovely, 329
You are very interesting, 330
You can make this swooped transition on your lips (Some Do Not), 434
You can make this swooped transition on your lips (Sonnet XXXV), 47
You come into my life a little yellow, 658
You don't have to be Marie Curie, 630
You had gone for a drive in the, 333
You had your own reasons for getting, 508
You in love with her, 521
You see a lot, 510
You stay in the Mental Institute of your life, 416
You took a wrong turn in, 603
You took me, 632
You will dream about me, 602
You'll do good if you play it like you're, 568
. . . Your America & mine, 447
You're listening to a man who in 1964 un-, 98
You're so funny! I'd give you, 495